Java and Object Orientation: An Intr

Springer
London
Berlin
Heidelberg
New York
Barcelona
Hong Kong
Milan
Paris
Singapore
Tokyo

John Hunt

Java and Object Orientation: An Introduction

Second Edition

 Springer

John Hunt
JayDee Technology Ltd., Minerva House,
Lower Bristol Road, Bath BA2 9ER, UK

British Library Cataloguing in Publication Data
Hunt, John, 1964-
    Java and object orientation : an introduction. - 2nd ed.
    1.Java (Computer program language) 2. Object-oriented
    programming (Computer science)
    I.Title
    005.7'12'62
    ISBN 1852335696

Library of Congress Cataloging-in-Publication Data
A catalog record for this book is available from the Library of Congress

ISBN 1-85233-569-6 2nd edition Springer-Verlag London Berlin Heidelberg
ISBN 3-540-76201-9 1st edition Springer-Verlag Berlin Heidelberg New York
A member of BertelsmannSpringer Science+Business Media GmbH
http://www.springer.co.uk
© Springer-Verlag London Limited 2002
Printed in Great Britain

First published 1998
Second edition 2002

Typeset by Ian Kingston Editorial Services, Nottingham, UK
Printed and bound at TJ International, Padstow, Cornwall, UK
34/3830-543210 Printed on acid-free paper SPIN 10856974

This book is dedicated to Phoebe and Adam

Preface

This book was originally written to support an introductory course in Object Orientation through the medium of Java (using Sun's JDK and later the Java 2 SDK) for those with experience of a procedural programming language such as C or Pascal. However, it can be used as a book to teach the reader Java, or to introduce object orientation, as well as to present object oriented design and analysis.

It takes as its basic premise that most computer scientists and software engineers learn best by doing, rather than by reading theoretical discussions. The chapters therefore attempt to introduce concepts by getting you, the reader, to do things, rather than by extensive theoretical discussion. This means that the chapters take a hands-on approach to the subject and assume that you have a suitable Java environment available.

The chapters are listed below and are divided into nine parts. You are advised to work through Parts 1 and 3 thoroughly in order to gain a detailed understanding of object orientation. Parts 2 and 4 introduce the Java language. You may then dip into other chapters as required. For example, if you wish to hone your Java skills then the chapters in Part 6 will be useful, whereas if you wish to gain an overview of object-oriented design then you may prefer to read Part 7. However, if you wish to discover the delights of graphical user interfaces in Java, then you should read Part 5 next.

Content Summary

Part 1: Introduction to Object Orientation

Chapter 1: Introduction to Object Orientation

This chapter introduces the range of concepts and ideas that make up object technology. It presents the background that led to the acceptance of object orientation as a mainstream technology and discusses the pedigree of the Java language.

Chapter 2: Elements of Object Orientation

This chapter provides a more formal definition of the terminology introduced in Chapter 1. It also considers the advantages and disadvantages of an object-oriented approach compared with more traditional procedural approaches.

Chapter 3: Constructing an Object-Oriented System

A typical problem for many people when being introduced to a new approach is that they understand the terminology and the concepts but not how to use them. This chapter aims to alleviate this problem by presenting a detailed worked example of the way in which an object-oriented system may be designed and constructed. It does so without reference to any particular language, so that language issues do not confuse the discussion.

Part 2: Introduction to the Java Language

Chapter 4: A Brief History of Time, the Universe and Java

This chapter provides some background on the history of Java and the development environments which are available to support it (such as the Sun Java Development Kit). It also considers some of the tools that you will encounter.

Chapter 5: A Little Java

This chapter introduces the Java syntax and examines the structure of a basic Java application.

Chapter 6: Java Building Blocks

This chapter considers classes, instances, methods and variables, as well as interface specifications in Java. These are the basic building blocks of any object-oriented program and in particular of a Java program.

Chapter 7: Java Constructs

This chapter presents further details of the Java language, including numbers, operators, variables and message passing. This chapter also looks at the `String`, `Integer` and `Character` classes.

Chapter 8: An Example Java Class

This chapter presents you with a detailed worked example of software development in Java. This example presents a very simple class definition which uses only those concepts that have been introduced at this stage. The intention is to illustrate how the constructs and language elements can be combined in a real (if simple) application.

Part 3: Java and Object Orientation

Chapter 9: Classes, Inheritance and Abstraction

This chapter considers how you should use inheritance, abstraction and classes in Java. It considers the role of classes and when to create subclasses and define abstract classes.

Chapter 10: Encapsulation and Polymorphism

This chapter considers how to achieve encapsulation in Java. It considers how the visibility of methods and variables can be modified. It presents packages and how they are defined and used. It also discusses issues associated with the polymorphic appearance of Java.

Chapter 11: Inner Classes and Reflection

Inner classes were introduced back in JDK 1.1. This chapter explains what inner classes are and how to use them. It also briefly introduces reflection.

Chapter 12: Data Structures

This chapter discusses the Java classes that are used to construct data structures. These classes include Array, Vector and Hashtable. It also includes a discussion of automatic memory management and garbage collection.

Chapter 13: The Collections API

Java now contains a set of classes that build on the original data structure classes. These classes are called the Collection classes. They provide a standardised framework for building data structure such as maps, sets and lists as well as support for converting these structures into other forms. This chapter provides a comprehensive description of the collection class framework.

Part 4: Further Java

Chapter 14: Control and Iteration

This chapter introduces control and iteration in Java.

Chapter 15: An Object-Oriented Organizer

This chapter presents a detailed example application constructed using the Vector class. The application is an electronic personal organizer that contains an address book, a diary (or appointments section) and a section for notes. The remainder of this chapter describes one way of implementing such an organizer. At the end of this chapter is a programming exercise.

Chapter 16: Streams and Files

This chapter discusses the other most common class hierarchies in Java, the Stream classes. The Stream classes are used (among other things) for accessing files.

Chapter 17: Serialization

This chapter explains how objects can be stored to file and restored from file using serialization. This provides a very basic persistent object system for Java.

Chapter 18: Observers and Observables

The Observer interface and Observable class are used to implement the Java dependency mechanism. This mechanism allows one or more objects to be informed about changes in the state of an object, without that object knowing anything about the first set of objects. It is particularly important in the construction of reusable, object-oriented, graphical user interfaces.

Part 5: Graphical Interfaces and Applets

Chapter 19: Graphic Programming Using the Abstract Window Toolkit

The Abstract Window Toolkit (AWT) is a platform-independent set of classes for constructing graphical interfaces. This chapter looks at how to construct windows and generate graphics.

Chapter 20: User Interface Programming

This chapter considers the Java Delegation Event Model and the range of GUI construction classes in the AWT.

Chapter 21: Managing Component Layout

This chapter introduces the layout managers provided with the AWT. These objects control how components are laid out within an interface in a portable and useful manner.

Chapter 22: Putting the Swing into Java

This chapter introduces the Swing set of components defined in the standard language extension javax.swing. It provides an enhanced set of graphical components that allow the construction of much more sophisticated rich graphical applications than would be possible using the basic AWT classes.

Chapter 23: A GUI Case Study

This chapter describes a detailed worked example of how to construct a user interface for a simple bank account using the Swing graphical components.

Chapter 24: The Lowdown on Layouts, Borders and Containers

This chapter builds on the discussion of layouts presented in Chapter 21 adding in the layouts defined by the swing component set. It also introduces the containers defined in Swing and the use of borders in Swing.

Chapter 25: Combining Graphics and GUI Components

This chapter aims to bring together the graphic elements described earlier in the book with the user interface components (such as buttons and layout managers) from the last few chapters. It presents a case study of a drawing tool akin to tools such as Visio, xfig and MacDraw.

Chapter 26: Swing Data Model Case Study

This chapter presents an example of a Swing component that uses a complex data model. In this case the JTree Swing component is chosen.

Chapter 27: Java: Speaking in Tongues

This chapter introduces the concept of localization within Java. That is localizing an application to a particular language or region.

Chapter 28: The CUTting edge

Operations such as drag and drop and cut and paste are now commonplace in most graphical user interfaces. This chapter describes the support provided in Java for these operations.

Part 6: Internet Working

Chapter 29: Sockets in Java

This chapter introduces TCP/IP sockets and their implementation in Java.

Chapter 30: Applets and the Internet

This chapter examines the facilities in Java for programming for the Internet. It introduces applets and URLs.

Chapter 31: Servlets: Serving Java up on the Web

Servlets are a server side extension to Java. They play a similar role to applets except that they live on a Web server rather than on a Web browser. They are thus under the full control of the host server environment and are now being widely used.

Chapter 32: Java Server Pages

An extension to servlets are Java Server Pages (JSPs). The aim of JSPs is to divorce the presentation aspect of servlets from the logic aspects of servlets.

Chapter 33: Java Database Connectivity

This chapter presents the `java.sql` package and the JDBC API for accessing relational databases.

Part 7: Java Development

Chapter 34: Java Style Guidelines

This chapter aims to promote readable, understandable, concise and efficient Java code.

Chapter 35: Exception Handling

In Java, exceptions are objects (just like almost everything else). Thus, to throw an exception you must first make an instance of an exception class. This chapter considers exceptions and how to create, throw and handle them. It also discusses defining new exceptions by creating subclasses.

Chapter 36: Concurrency

This chapter describes the concurrency mechanism of Java. That is, it describes the way in which Java implements lightweight threads.

Part 8: Object-Oriented Design

Chapter 37: Object-Oriented Analysis and Design

This chapter introduces the concepts of object-oriented analysis and design. It reviews a number of the more popular techniques such as OOA, OMT, Objectory and Booch. It also briefly considers the unification of the OMT and Booch notations.

Chapter 38: The Unified Modeling Language

The Unified Modeling Language (UML) is a third generation object-oriented modeling language which adapts and extends the published notations used in the Booch, OMT and Objectory methods. UML is intended to form a single, common, widely used modeling language for a range of object-oriented design methods (including Booch, Objectory and OMT). It should also be applicable to a wide range of applications and domains. This chapter summarizes the UML notation.

Chapter 39: The Unified Process

This chapter discusses the influential design method referred to as the Unified Process. It summarizes the main phases of the Unified Process using the UML notation.

Part 9: The Future

Chapter 40: Areas of Java and Object Technology not Covered

Java has many features that are not suitable for an introductory book. This chapter attempts to make you aware of what has not been covered, without going into any detail. It includes discussion of the current developments within the Java world. In particular, it introduces the JavaBeans (component) model, and discusses the RMI (Remote Method invocation) and Enterprise JavaBeans (EJBs). It also discusses object-oriented databases and CORBA.

Obtaining Source Code Examples

The source code for the examples in this book is available on the Web at `http://www.java-and-oo.net/)`. Each chapter has its own directory within which the class files are listed individually. The source code has all been tested using the Java Development Kit 1.1, and Java 2 up to SDK 1.4 releases. As new versions of Java are released all examples will be tested against them. Any changes necessitated by a new release will be noted at the above Web site.

Throughout the book, you are asked to develop a financial manager application. The model answers for this application are also available on the Web, in a subdirectory called finance in the appropriate chapter's source code directory. For example, in the source code directory for Chapter 15 (chap15), you will find the examples for Chapter 15 and a subdirectory called finance. In here, you will find the model answer for the financial manager project.

Typographical Conventions

In this book, the standard typeface is Minion; however source code is set in Letter Gothic (for example, a = 2 + 3;). A **bold** font indicates Java keywords, for example:

```
public class Address extends Object {. . .}
```

Trademarks

HotJava, HotJava Views, JavaChips, picoJava, microJava, UltraJava, JavaOS, JDBC, Java, Java Development Kit, Solaris, SPARC, SunOS and Sunsoft are trademarks of Sun Microsystems, Inc. VisualBasic, Visual C++, DOS, MS-DOS, MS-Windows and Windows 95, 2000, NT and XP are registered trademarks of Microsoft Corporation. Apple is a registered trademark of Apple Computer, Inc. Cafe and VisualCafe are trademarks of Symantec Corporation. Unix is a registered trademark of AT&T. The X Window System is a trademark of the Massachusetts Institute of Technology. All other brand names are trademarks of their respective holders.

Acknowledgements

I have had input from many people regarding the contents of this book. In particular, I would like to thank all those who helped me in producing the first edition of this book at the University of Wales, Aberystwyth. I would also like to thank those people who have attended courses based on this book for the many suggestions they have made.

I would also like to thank Rebecca Mowat, of Springer-Verlag, for her patience and thoroughness during the preparation of this book.

Finally, my greatest debt of gratitude is, as always, to my wife, Denise Cooke, for her constant support, encouragement and patience. Thank you.

John Hunt

Contents

Part 3   Java and Object Orientation

Part 4   Further Java

Part 5   Graphical Interfaces and Applets

Part 7   Java Development

Part 8   Object-Oriented Design

Part **1**

Introduction to Object Orientation

Chapter 1

Introduction to Object Orientation

1.1 Introduction

This book is intended as an introduction to object orientation for computer science students or those actively involved in the software industry. It assumes familiarity with standard computing concepts such as stacks and memory allocation, and with a procedural language, such as C. From this background, it provides a practical introduction to object technology using Java, one of the newest and best pure object-oriented languages available.

This book introduces a variety of concepts through practical experience with an object-oriented language. It also tries to take you beyond the level of the language syntax to the philosophy and practice of object-oriented development.

In the remainder of this chapter, we will consider the various programming paradigms which have preceded object orientation. We will then examine the primary concepts of object orientation and consider how they enable object orientation to be achieved.

1.2 Programming Paradigms

Software construction is still more of an art than a science. Despite the best efforts of many software engineers, software systems are still delivered late, over budget and not up to the requirements of the user. This situation has been with us for many years. Indeed, the first conference to raise awareness of this problem was the NATO Software Engineering Conference of 1968, which coined the term *software crisis*. Since then a variety of programming paradigms have been developed explicitly to deal with this issue or have been applied to it.

A programming paradigm embodies a particular philosophy. These philosophies usually represent an insight which sets a new type of best practice. For a programming language to support a particular paradigm, it must not just allow adoption of the paradigm (you can use object-oriented programming techniques in Assembler, but would you want to?), it must actively support implementations based on the paradigm. This usually means that the language must support constructs which make development using that paradigm straightforward.

The major programming paradigms which have appeared in computer science can be summarized as follows:

- *Functional* Lisp is the classic example of a functional language, although by no means the only one (ML is a very widely used functional language). These languages place emphasis on applying a function (often recursively) to a set of one or more data items. The function then returns a value – the result of evaluating the function. If the function changes data items, this is a side effect. There is limited support for algorithmic solutions which rely on repetition via iteration. The functional approach turned out to be an extremely useful way of implementing complex systems for early AI researchers.

- *Procedural* Pascal and C exemplify procedural languages which attempt to move to a higher level than the earlier assembler languages. The emphasis is on algorithmic solutions and procedures which operate on data items. They are extremely effective, but software developers still encounter difficulties. This is partly due to the increased complexity of the systems being developed. It is also because, although high-level procedural languages remove the possibility of certain types of error and increase productivity, developers can still cause problems for themselves. For example, the interfaces between different parts of the system may be incompatible and this may not become obvious until integration or system testing.

- *Modular* In languages such as Modula-2 and Ada, a module hides its data from users. The users of the module can only access the data through defined interfaces. These interfaces are "published" so that users know the definitions of the available interfaces and can check that they are using the correct versions.

- *Object-oriented* This is the most recent "commercial" programming paradigm. The object-oriented approach can be seen as taking modularization a step further. Not only do you have explicit modules (in this case, objects), but these objects can inherit features from one another. We can of course ask "why another programming paradigm?". The answer to this lies partly in the failure of many software development projects to keep to budget, remain within time-scales and give the users what they want. Of course, it should not be assumed that object orientation is the answer to all these problems; it is just another tool available to software developers.

This book attempts to introduce the object-oriented programming paradigm through the medium of an object-oriented programming language. It assumes that the majority of readers have a background in at least one procedural language (preferably a C-like language) and compares and contrasts the facilities provided by an object-oriented language with a procedural language.

Object orientation, even though it is quite different in many ways from the procedural approach, has developed from it. You should therefore not throw away all that you have learnt using other approaches. Many of the good practices in other languages are still good practices in an object-oriented language. However, there are new practices to learn, as well as new syntax. It is much more than a process of learning a new syntax – you have a new philosophy to learn.

1.3 Revolution Versus Evolution

In almost every area of scientific endeavour there are periods of evolution followed by periods of revolution and then evolution again. That is, some idea or theory is held to be "accepted" (not necessarily true, but at least accepted). The theory is refined by successive experiments, discoveries etc. Then the theory is challenged by a new theory. This new theory is typically held by a small set of extremely fervent believers. It is often derided by those who are staunch supporters of the existing theory. As time continues, either this new theory is proved wrong and disappears, or more and more people are drawn to the new theory until the old theory has very few supporters.

There are many examples of this phenomenon in science: for example, the Copernican theory of the Earth orbiting the Sun, Einstein's theory of relativity and Darwin's theory of evolution. Men such as Darwin and those who led him to his discoveries were revolutionaries: they went against the current belief of the times and introduced a new set of theories. These theories were initially derided but have since become generally accepted. Indeed, Darwin's theories are now being refined further. For example, Darwin believed in a mechanism of fertilization of an egg derived from an old Greek theory (pangenesis). Every organ and tissue was assumed to produce granules which combined to make up the sex cells. Of course, we now believe this to be wrong and it was Darwin's own cousin, Francis Galton, who helped to disprove the pangenesis theory. It is unlikely that we will enter a new revolutionary phase which will overturn the theory of evolution; however, Einstein's theory of relativity is already being challenged.

Programming paradigms provide another example of this cycle. The move from low-level to high-level programming was a revolution (and you can still find people who will insist that low-level machine code programming is best). Object orientation is another revolution, which is still happening. Over the past ten years, object orientation has become much more widely accepted and you will find many organizations, both suppliers and users of software, giving it lip service. However, you will also find many in the computer industry who are far from convinced. A senior colleague of mine recently told me that he believed that object orientation was severely over-hyped (which it may be) and that he really could not see the benefits it offered. I hope that this book will convince him (and others) that object orientation has a great deal to offer.

It is likely that something will come along to challenge object-oriented programming, just as it challenges procedural programming, as the appropriate software development approach. It is also likely that a difficult and painful battle will ensue, with software suppliers entering and leaving the market. Many suppliers will argue that their system always supported approach X anyway, while others will attempt to graft the concepts of approach X onto their system. When this will happen or what the new approach will be is difficult to predict, but it will happen. Until then, object orientation will be a significant force within the computer industry.

1.4 Why Learn a New Programming Paradigm?

The transition from a procedural viewpoint to an object-oriented viewpoint is not always an easy one. This prompts the question "Why bother?". As you are reading this book you must at least be partly convinced that it is a good idea. This could be because you have noticed the number of job advertisements offering employment for those with object-oriented skills. However, that aside, why should you bother learning a new programming paradigm?

I hope that some of the reasons will become clear during your reading of this book. It is worth considering at least some of the issues at this point.

1.4.1 Software Industry Blues

There is still no silver bullet for the problems in the software industry. Object-oriented technology does not remove the problems of constructing complex software systems, it just makes some of the pitfalls harder to fall into and simplifies traditionally difficult problems. However, difficulties in software development are almost inevitable; many of them arise due to the inescapable intangibility of software and not necessarily all by accident or poor development methods.

We should not, however, just throw up our hands and say "well if that's the case, it's not my fault". Many of the problems which beset our industry relate to some deficiency in how programmers build software today. For example, if a software development project runs late, then adding more people to it is likely to make matters worse rather than get the project back on time.

Object technology is not the first attempt at addressing these issues. However, past attempts have met with mixed success for a number of reasons, some of which we consider below.

Modularity of Code

Traditional procedural systems typically relied on the fact that not only would the data they were using not change, for example, its type, but the way in which they obtained that data would not alter. Invariably, the function (or functions) that used the data also obtained the data. This meant that if the way in which data was accessed had to change, all the functions which used that data had to be rewritten. If you have attended any sort of software engineering course, you will say that what was required was a function to obtain the data. This function could then be used in many different places. However, such application-specific functions tend not to get used in "real world" systems for several reasons:

- *Small subroutines are too much effort.* Although many people talk about reusable code, they often mean relatively large code units. Small functions of one, two or three lines tend to be defined by a single programmer and are rarely shared among a development team, let alone several development teams.
- *Too many subroutines leads to too little reuse.* The larger the number of subroutines available, the less likely that they are reused. It is very difficult to search through a code library of small subroutines trying to find one which does what you want. It is often much quicker to write it yourself!
- *It may not be obvious that a function is reusable.* If you are a programmer working on one part of a system, it may not be obvious that the function you are writing is of generic use. If a function is small then it is not identified by the designer as being a useful reusable component.

Ability to Package Software

Another issue is the way in which programming languages package up software for reuse. Many systems assume that the software should be partitioned into modules which are then integrated at compile time. Such fixed compile-time integration can be good for some types of problem, but in many cases it is too inflexible. For example, while this approach can ensure that the modules being reused are compatible, developers may not know until run-time which modules they wish to use, and therefore some form of run-time binding is necessary.

Unix pipes and filters are examples of software systems which can be bound at run time. They act as "glue", allowing the developer to link two or more programs in sequence together. However, in this case there is absolutely no error protection. It is quite possible to link two incompatible systems together.

What would be really useful would be a combination of these features: that is, the ability to specify either compile-time or run-time binding. In either case, there should be some form of error checking to ensure that you are integrating compatible modules. An important criterion is to avoid the need for extensive recompilation when, for example, just one line is altered. Finally, such a system should, by definition, enforce encapsulation and make packaging of the software effortless.

Flexibility of Code

In early procedural languages, for example C or Pascal, there was little or no flexibility. More recent procedural languages have introduced some flexibility but need extensive specification to achieve it. The result is internal flexibility at the cost of interface overheads, for example in Ada. Object technology allows code flexibility (and data flexibility) with little overhead.

1.4.2 The Advantages Claimed for Object Orientation

There are a range of benefits which can be identified for object-oriented programming languages. Not all of these are unique to object-oriented technology, but that does not matter; we are talking about the good things about object orientation here:

- *Increased code reuse* Languages such as Java encourage reuse. Every time you specify that one class inherits from another (which you do all the time in Java), you are involved in reuse. In time, most developers actively look to see where they can restructure classes to improve the potential for reuse. As long as this is not taken too far, it is an extremely healthy thing to do.
- *Data protection for little effort* The encapsulation facilities provided as part of the language protect your data from unscrupulous users. Unlike languages such as Ada, you do not have to write reams of specification in order to achieve this protection.
- *Easier integration with encapsulation* As users of an object cannot access the internals of the object, they must go via specified interfaces. As these interfaces can be published in advance of the object being implemented, others can develop to those interfaces knowing that they will be available when the object is implemented.
- *Easier maintenance with encapsulation* This point is really a variation on the last one. As users of an object must use the specified interfaces, as long as the external behaviour of these objects remains the same, the internals of the object can be completely changed. For example, an object can store an item of data in a flat file, read it from a sensor or obtain it from a database; external users of the object need never know.
- *Simplified code with polymorphism* With polymorphism, you do not need to worry about exactly what type of object is available at run-time, as long as it responds to the message (request for a method to be executed) you send it. This means that it is a great deal easier to write reusable, compact code than in many other languages.
- *More intuitive programming* It has been argued that object orientation is a more intuitive programming paradigm than other approaches, such as procedural programming. This is because we tend to perceive the world in terms of objects. We see dials, windows, switches, fuel pumps, and automated teller machines (ATMs). These objects respond to our use in specific ways when we interact with them. For example, an ATM requires a card, a PIN etc., in a particular sequence. Of course, those of us who have programmed before bring with us a lot of baggage, including preconceptions of what a program should be like and how you develop it. I hope that this book is about to turn all that on its head for a while, before putting everything back together again.

1.4.3 What Are the Problems and Pitfalls of Object Orientation?

No programming language is without its own set of problems and pitfalls. Indeed, part of the skill in becoming fluent in a new programming language is learning what the problems are and how to avoid them. In this section, we concentrate on the criticisms usually levelled at object orientation.

Lots of Confusing Terminology

This is a fair comment. Object orientation is littered with new terms and definitions for what appears to have been defined quite acceptably in other languages. Back in the early 1970s, when Smalltalk, one of the very first object-oriented programming languages, was being researched, many of the terms we now take for granted were already quite well established. It would be

Table 1.1 Approximate equivalent terms.

Procedural term	Object-oriented term
Procedure	Method
Procedure call	Message
Non-temporary data	Instance variable
Records and procedures	Objects

reasonable to assume that even if the inventors of the language liked their own terminology, early users would have tried to get it changed.

One possible answer is that in the past (that is, during the early and mid-1980s), object-oriented languages, such as Smalltalk, tended to be the preserve of academic and research institutions. (Indeed, I was introduced to my first object-oriented language while working on a research project at a British university during 1986–87.) It is often the case that academics enjoy the mystique that a language with terminology all of its own can create. By now, it is so well established in the object-oriented culture that newcomers just have to adapt.

The important point to remember is that the concepts are actually very simple, although the practice can be harder. To illustrate this, consider the Table 1.1, which attempts to illustrate the parallels between object-oriented terminology and procedural terminology.

These approximations should not be taken too literally, as they are intended only to help you visualize what each of the terms means. I hope that, by the end of the book, you gain your own understanding of their meaning.

Yet Another Programming Paradigm to Master

In general, people tend to like the things they are used to. This is why many people buy the same make of car again and again (even when it gives them trouble). It is also why computer scientists refuse to move to a new word processor, editor, operating system or hardware. Over the years, I have had many "discussions" with people over the use of LaTeX versus Word versus WordPerfect, the merits of Emacs and vi, of Unix versus Mac, or of Windows and DOS. In most cases, the issues raised and points made indicate that those involved in the discussions (including me) are biased, have their own "hobby horse" to promote and do not understand fully the other approach.

Object orientation both benefits and suffers from this phenomenon. There are those who hold it up almost like a religion and those who cast it aside because it is so different from what they are used to. Many justify this latter approach by pointing out that procedural programming has been around for quite a while now and many systems are successfully developed using it. This is a reasonable statement and one which promotes the status quo. However, the fact that object orientation is a new software paradigm, quite different from the procedural paradigm, should not be a reason for rejecting it.

Object orientation explicitly encourages encapsulation (information hiding), promotes code reuse and enables polymorphism. Most procedural languages have attempted to present these advantages as well; however, they have failed to do so in such a coherent and concise manner. Ada, for example, is not only a large cumbersome language, it requires an extensive specification to be written to enable two packages to work together. Any error in these specifications and the system does not compile (even if there are no errors or incompatibilities in the code). Ada95 has introduced the concept of objects and classes, although, for most object technology practitioners, the way in which it has done this is both counterintuitive and unwieldy.

Many Object-Oriented Environments Are Inefficient

Historically, object-oriented development environments have been inefficient, processor-intensive and memory hungry. Such environments tended to be designed for use on powerful workstations or minicomputers. Examples of such environments include Lisp Flavors (which even required specialist hardware, e.g. the Symbolics Lisp machine), Self and Smalltalk-80 (the forerunner of VisualWorks, a commercial Smalltalk development environment). These machines were expensive, sometimes non-standard and aimed at the research community.

With the advent of the PC, attempts were made to rectify this situation. For example, Smalltalk/V was designed specifically to run on the PC and the first version of Smalltalk that I used was on a 286 PC. The current versions of Java products, such as Symantec's VisualCafé and Borland's JBuilder, are now extremely efficient and optimized for use on PC platforms. Indeed, Sun's Java Development Kit (JDK) is available on Unix, Solaris, Windows 95/98/NT/2000/XP and Mac OS.

Although 32 Mbyte of RAM is advisable on many of these systems, any Pentium III machine or above provides ample performance. The issue of additional RAM is not large; RAM can be purchased at reasonable rates and many industry pundits predict that 256 Mbyte (and more) will soon become standard. Indeed, systems are now emerging which assume that a user has access to larger amounts of memory; for example, Borland's JBuilder requires a minimum of 64 Mbyte to run the debugger.

C++ and object-oriented versions of Pascal (such as Delphi) are no more memory- or processor-intensive than any non-object-oriented language. However, it is worth noting that these languages do not offer the same level of support for the programmer as, for example, Java and Smalltalk. In particular, they do not provide automatic memory management and garbage collection.

Java Environments Are Not Suitable for Serious Development

Many object-oriented languages are interpreted: for example, Eiffel, Smalltalk, Objective-C and Java. If you intend to construct large applications in such languages you want to be sure that the performance of the resulting application is acceptable. In addition, for real-world applications, you also wish to know that the facilities provided by the language, and any support environments, are up to the task.

We shall first consider the issue of compilation time. At present, most Java compilers produce an intermediate representation called byte codes, rather than a machine executable form. These byte codes are then interpreted by the Java Virtual Machine. The original compiler available with Sun's JDK was relatively slow (and certainly slower than compiling comparable programs with Delphi or Visual Basic). However, vendors such as Sun themselves, Symantec and IBM have developed Java compilers which are much faster. In addition some vendors such as TowerJ have produced native Java compilers that are well suited to server-side systems.

The next issue is performance. The Java interpreter provided with the JDK is not particularly fast and is certainly a lot slower than a comparable C++ program. For applications of any size, this is a serious problem. What are really required are native code compilers for Java. However, companies such as Symantec and IBM, as well as Sun, have produced Just In Time (JIT) compilers which compile a piece of code once and then cache it. This means that any code which is executed repeatedly is converted into native machine code only once, resulting in a significant improvement in performance. Although there is still a run-time overhead, it is almost certainly faster than the standard Java interpreter, and some estimates suggest up to a 20-fold improvement. Sun has introduced a variation on the JIT theme called HotSpot that interprets infrequently used code and compiles those areas that are frequently used (the hotspots) aiming to gain the benefits of both approaches.

The next issue is the application development facilities provided by the language. These can greatly affect the development time and the reliability and maintainability of a system. For example, Smalltalk is a dynamically typed language, which has significant implications for large software development. However, the designers of the Java language took into account many of the problems which programmers have to deal with when developing large applications. In particular, they considered the problems associated with C++ programs (such as memory leaks), which can be extremely difficult to identify and debug. They added features to Java to remove the potential for introducing such bugs (for example, dynamic memory allocation and garbage collection). The Java language developers also considered the compilation of source code and dependencies between source code files. They provide an automatic compilation facility (achieving the same goal as a manually defined make file) to simplify application construction.

Finally, in the real world consideration must be given to issues such as portability (both to current hardware and to future hardware), distribution (as the move towards network computing grows, the network is the computer!) and evolution of the language (as new features are required). Once again, the Java language designers have considered these issues, and Java is "architecture-neutral". It assumes nothing about the hardware on which it executes. The designers also made significant attempts to specify rigorously parts of the Java language which might be affected by different platforms. Thus the size of an integer in bytes is explicitly defined and the language explicitly incorporates facilities for dealing with TCP/IP protocols, URLs etc., allowing it to be seamlessly integrated with the Web. The aim of Java is to be "write once, run anywhere".

Packages and objects also allow new facilities to be added without significantly affecting existing ones.

1.5 Pedigree of Object-Oriented Languages

In the horse or dog breeding world, the pedigree of an animal can be determined by considering its ancestry. Whilst you cannot determine how good a language is by looking at its predecessors, you can certainly get a feel for the influences which have led to the features it possesses. The current set of commercial object-oriented languages have all been influenced to a greater or lesser extent by existing languages. Figure 1.1 illustrates some of the relationships between the various languages.

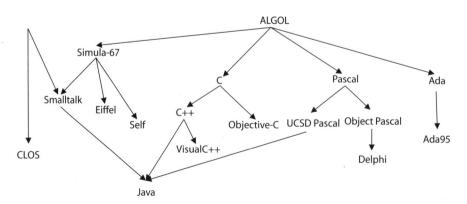

Fig. 1.1 Partial Java family tree.

Figure 1.1 only partially illustrates the family relationships as, for example, Ada95 should have a link from Smalltalk (or possibly C++). However, it attempts to illustrate the most direct influences evident in the various languages. The diagram is also ordered in roughly chronological order. That is, the further down the diagram a language appears, the more recent it is. This means, for example, that Smalltalk predates C++, and that Java is the most recent object-oriented language. Notice that Lisp, ALGOL, C, Pascal and Ada are not object-oriented, and that Simula is, at most, object-based.

The extent to which a language can be considered to be a *pure* object-oriented language (i.e. one which adheres to object-oriented concepts consistently) as opposed to a *hybrid* object-oriented language (i.e. one in which object-oriented concepts lie alongside traditional programming approaches) tends to depend on its background.

A pure object-oriented language supports only the concept of objects. Any program is made up solely of interacting objects which exchange information with each other and request operations or data from each other. This approach tends to be followed by those languages which most directly inherit features from Simula (C++ is a notable exception). Simula was designed as a language for discrete event simulation. However, it was influenced by many of the features from ALGOL 60 and was effectively the first language to use the concepts which we now describe as object-oriented. For example, it introduced the concepts of class, inheritance and polymorphism.

The language which inherits most directly from Simula is Smalltalk. This means that its ALGOL heritage is there for all to see in the form of structured programming constructs (although the syntax may, at first, seem a little bizarre). It is a pure object-oriented language in that the only concepts supported by the language are object-oriented. It also inherits from Lisp (if not syntax, then certainly the philosophy). This means that not only does it not include strong typing, it also provides dynamic memory management and automatic garbage collection. This has both benefits and drawbacks, which we will discuss at a later stage. In contrast, Eiffel, another pure object-oriented language, attempts to introduce best software engineering practice, rather than the far less formal approach of Lisp. Self is a recent, pure object-oriented language which is still at the research stage.

Many language designers have taken the *hybrid* approach. That is, object-oriented constructs have either been grafted onto, or intermixed with, the existing language (for example, C++). In some cases, the idea has been to enable a developer to take advantage of object orientation when it appears appropriate. In other situations, it has eased the transition from one approach to another. The result has often been less than satisfactory. Not only does it mean that many software developers have moved to their new object-oriented language believing that it is just a matter of learning the new syntax (which it is not), they have written procedural programs in which objects are limited to holding data, believing that this is sufficient (which it is not). It is really only safe to move to a hybrid language once you have learnt about object technology using a pure object-oriented language.

1.6 Fundamentals of Object Orientation

The object-oriented programmer's view of traditional procedural programming is of procedures wildly attacking data which is defenceless and has no control over what the procedures do to it (the rape and pillage style of programming). In contrast, object-oriented programming is viewed as polite and well-behaved data objects passing messages to one another, each data object deciding for itself whether to accept the message and how to interpret what it means.

The basic idea is that an object-oriented system is a set of interacting objects which are organized into classes. Figure 1.2 illustrates a simplified cruise control system from a car. It shows

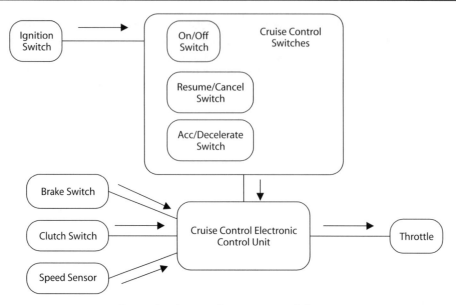

Fig. 1.2 A cruise control system as a set of objects.

the objects in the system, the links between the objects and the direction in which information flows along these links. The object-oriented implementation of this system would mirror this diagram exactly. That is, there would be an object representing each box; between the boxes, there would be links allowing one object to request a service from, or provide information to, another. For example, the cruise control electronic control unit (ECU) might request the current speed from the speed sensor. It would then use this information when asking the throttle to adjust its position. Notice that we do not talk about functions or procedures which access information from data structures and then call other functions and procedures. There is no concept such as the ECU data structure and the ECU main program. This can be a difficult change of emphasis for some people and we shall try to illustrate it further below.

The aim of object-oriented programming is to shift the focus of attention from *procedures that do things to data* to *data which is asked to do things*. The task is not to define the procedures which manipulate data but to define data objects and their attributes, and the way in which they may be examined or changed. Data objects (and procedures) can communicate with other data objects only through narrow, well-defined channels.

1.7 The Basic Principles of Object Orientation

- *Encapsulation or data hiding* Encapsulation is the process of hiding all the details of an object that do not contribute to its essential characteristics. Essentially, it means that what is inside the class is hidden; only the external interfaces can be seen by other objects. The user of an object should never need to look inside the box!
- *Inheritance* Objects may have similar (but not identical) properties. One way of managing (classifying) such properties is to have a hierarchy of classes. A class inherits from its immediate parent class and from classes above the parent (see the hierarchy in Figure 1.4). The inheritance mechanism permits common characteristics of an object to be defined once but used in many places. Any change is thus localized.

If we define a concept *animal* and a concept *dog*, we do not have to specify all the things which a dog has in common with other animals. Instead, we inherit them by saying that *dog* is a **subclass** of *animal*. This feature is unique to object-oriented languages; it promotes (and achieves) huge amounts of reuse.

- *Abstraction* An abstraction denotes the essential characteristics of an object that distinguish it from all other kinds of object and thus provides crisply defined conceptual boundaries, relative to the perspective of the viewer. That is, it states how a particular object differs from all others.

- *Polymorphism* This is the ability to send the same message to different instances which appear to perform the same function. However, the way in which the message is handled depends on the class of which the instance is an example.

An interesting question to ask is: "How do languages such as Ada, C and Lisp relate to the four concepts above?". An obvious issue is related to inheritance. That is, if we define a concept *animal* and we then define a concept *dog*, we do not have to specify all the things that a dog has in common with other animals. Instead, we inherit them by saying that a dog is a **subclass** of animal. This feature is unique to object-oriented languages; it promotes (and achieves) huge amounts of reuse. The next four sections expand on each of these basic principles in more detail

1.8 Encapsulation

Encapsulation or data hiding has been a major feature of a number of programming languages; Modula-2 and Ada both provide extensive encapsulation features. But what exactly is encapsulation? Essentially, it is the concept of hiding the data behind a software "wall". Those outside the wall cannot get direct access to the data. Instead, they must ask intermediaries (usually the owner of the data) to provide them with the data.

The advantage of encapsulation is that the user of the data does not need to know how, where, or in what form the owner of the data stores that data. This means that if the owner changes the way in which the data is stored, the user of the data need not be affected. The user still asks the owner for the data; it is the data owner that changes how the request is fulfilled.

Different programming languages implement encapsulation in different ways. For example, Ada enables encapsulation using packages which possess both data and procedures. It also specifies a set of interfaces which publish those operations the package wishes to make available to users of the package. These interfaces may implement some operations or provide access to data held within the package.

Object-oriented languages provide encapsulation facilities which present the user of an object with a set of external interfaces. These interfaces specify the requests to which the object will respond (or, in the terminology of object orientation, the requests which the object will understand). These interfaces not only avoid the need for the caller to understand the internal details of the implementation, they actually prevent the user from obtaining that information. Users of an object cannot directly access the data held by an object, as it is not visible to them. In other words, a program that calls this facility can treat it as a black box; the program knows what the facility's external interfaces guarantee to do, and that is all it needs to know.

It is worth pointing out a difference between the object-oriented approach and the package approach used in Ada. In general, a package is a large unit of code providing a wide range of facilities with a large number of data structures (for example, the TextIO package). In an object-oriented language, the encapsulation is provided at the object level. While objects may

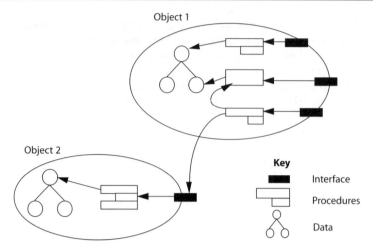

Fig. 1.3 Object structure and interaction.

well be as large and as complex as the typical Ada package, they are often much smaller. In languages such as Smalltalk and Java, where everything is an object, the smallest data and code units also naturally benefit from encapsulation. You can attempt to introduce the same level of encapsulation in Ada, but it is not natural to the language.

Figure 1.3 illustrates the way in which encapsulation works within an object-oriented language. It shows that anything outside the object can only gain access to the data the object holds through specific interfaces (the black squares). In turn, these interfaces trigger procedures which are internal to the object. These procedures may then access the data directly, use a second procedure as an intermediary or call an interface to another object.

1.9 Inheritance

A class is an example of a particular type of thing (for example, *mammal* is a class of *animal*). In the object-oriented world, a class is a definition of the characteristics of that thing. Thus, in the case of mammals, we might define that they have fur, are warm-blooded and produce live young. Animals such as dogs and cats are then instances of the class mammal. This is all quite obvious and should not present a conceptual problem for anyone. However, in most object-oriented languages (Self is an exception) the concept of the class is tightly linked to the concept of inheritance.

Inheritance allows us to state that one class is similar to another class but with a specified set of differences. Another way of putting it is that we can define all the things that are common about a class of things, and then define what is special about each sub-grouping within a subclass.

For example, if we have a class defining all the common traits of mammals, we can define how particular categories of mammals differ. The duck-billed platypus is a quite extraordinary mammal that differs from other mammals in a number of important ways. However, we do not want to define all the things that it has in common with other mammals. Not only is this extra work, but we then have two places in which we have to maintain this information. We can therefore state that a duck-billed platypus is a class of mammal that does not produce live young. Classes allow us to do this.

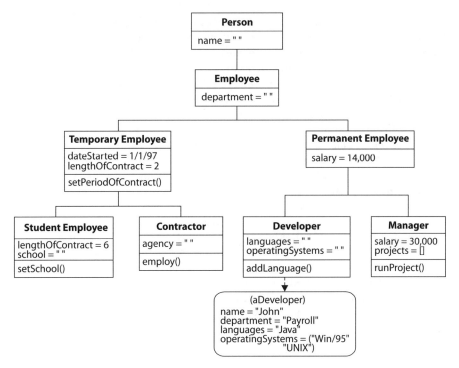

Fig. 1.4 An example of inheritance.

An example which is rather closer to home for most computer scientists is illustrated in Figure 1.4. For this example, we assume that we have been given the job of designing and implementing an administration system for a small software house that produces payroll, pensions and other financial systems. This system needs to record both permanent and temporary employees of the company. For temporary employees, we need to record their department, the length of their contract, when they started, and additional information which differs depending on whether they are contractors or students on an industrial placement. For permanent employees, we need to record their department, their salary, the languages and operating systems with which they are familiar and whether they are a manager. In the case of managers, we might also want to record the projects that they run.

Figure 1.4 illustrates a class hierarchy diagram for this application. It shows the classes we have defined and from where they inherit their information.

- *Inheritance versus instantiation* Stating that one class is a specialized version of a more generic class is different from saying that something is an example of a class of things. In the first case, we might say that *developer* is one category of employee and *manager* is another. Neither of these categories can be used to identify an individual. They are, in effect, templates for examples of those categories. In the second case, we say that "John" is an example of a developer (just as "Chris", "Myra" and "Denise" may also be examples of developers). "John" is therefore an instance of a particular class (or category) of things known as developers. It is important to get the concept of specializing a class with a subclass clear in your mind. It is all too easy to confuse an instance of a class with a subclass.
- *Inheritance of common information* We place common concepts together in a single class. For example, all people have a name and all employees have a nominated department (whether they are permanent or temporary). All temporary employees have a start

date, whether they are contractors or students. In turn, all classes below Employee inherit the concept of a department. This means that not only do all Managers and Developers have a department, but "John" has a department, which in this case is "Payroll".

- *Abstract classes* Figure 1.4 defines a number of classes of which we have no intention of making an example: Employee, Permanent Employee and Temporary Employee. These are termed abstract classes and are intended as placeholders for common features rather than as templates for a particular category of things. This is quite acceptable and is common practice in most object-oriented programs.

- *Inheritance of defaults* Just because we have stated that Permanent Employees earn a default salary of £14,000 a year does not mean that all types of employee have that default. In the diagram, Managers have a default of £30,000, illustrating that a class can overwrite the defaults defined in one of its parents.

- *Single and multiple inheritance* In Figure 1.4, we have only illustrated single inheritance. That is, a class inherits from only one other class. This is the case in many object-oriented programming languages, such as Java and Smalltalk. However, other languages such as C++ and Eiffel allow multiple inheritance. In multiple inheritance, you can bring together the characteristics of two classes to define a third class. For example, you may have two classes, Toy and Car, which can be used to create a third class Toy-Car. Multiple inheritance is a controversial subject which is still being debated. Those who think it is useful fail to see why other languages do not include it and vice versa. Java does not include multiple inheritance.

1.10 Abstraction

Abstraction is much more than just the ability to define categories of things which can hold common features of other categories of things (for example, Temporary Employee is an abstract class of Contractor and Student Employee). It is a way of specifying what is particular about a group of classes of things. Often this means defining the interface for an object, the data that such an object holds and part of the functionality of that object.

For example, we might define a class DataBuffer which is the abstract class for things that hold data and return them on request. It may define how the data is held and that operators such as put() and get() are provided to add data to, and remove it from, the DataBuffer. The implementation of these operators may be left to those implementing a subclass of DataBuffer.

The class DataBuffer might be used to implement a stack or a queue. Stack could implement get() as *return the most recent data item added*, while Queue could implement it as *return the oldest data item held*. In either case, a user of the class knows that put() and get() are available and work in the appropriate manner.

In some languages, abstraction is related to protection. For example, in C++ and and Java, you can state whether a subclass can overwrite data or procedures (and indeed whether it has to overwrite them). In Smalltalk, the developer cannot state that a procedure cannot be overwritten, but can state that a procedure (or method) is a subclass responsibility (that is, a subclass which implements the procedure in order to provide a functioning class).

Abstraction is also associated with the ability to define abstract data types (ADTs). In object-oriented terms these are classes (or groups of classes) which provide behaviour that acts as the infrastructure for a particular class of data type (for example, DataBuffer provides a stack or a queue). However, it is worth pointing out that ADTs are more commonly associated with procedural languages such as Ada. This is because the concepts in object orientation essentially supersede ADTs. That is, not only do they encompass all the elements of ADTs, they extend them by introducing inheritance.

1.11 Polymorphism

Polymorphism is a strange sounding word, derived from Greek,[1] for a relatively simple concept. It is essentially the ability to request that the same operation be performed by a wide range of different types of things. How the request is processed depends on the thing that receives the request. The programmer need not worry about how the request is handled, only that it is. This is illustrated in Figure 1.5.

Fig. 1.5 An example of polymorphism.

In this example, the variable MotorVehicle can hold an instance of a MotorVehicle and any subclass of the class MotorVehicle (such as car, MotorBike or Sports). As the class MotorVehicle defines a method drive(), they will all respond to that method. However, if each subclass defines its own version of drive they will each do their own thing. For example, driving a family car might be quite different from driving a motorbike or a sports car. However, developers do not need to worry about these details; they just need to know that they will all support the drive() method (which they will, as they are subclasses of MotorVehicle).

Effectively, this means that you can ask many different things to perform the same action. For example, you might ask a range of objects to provide a printable string describing themselves. If you ask an instance of the Manager class, a compiler object or a database object to return such a string, you use the same interface call (toString in Java).

The name "polymorphism" is unfortunate and often leads to confusion. It makes the whole process sound rather grander than it actually is. There are two types of polymorphism used in programming languages: overloading and overriding. The difference in name relates to the mechanism that resolves what code to execute.

1.11.1 Overloading Operators

Overloading occurs when procedures have the same name but apply to different data types. The compiler can determine which operator to use at compile time and can use the correct version.

Ada uses exactly this type of overloading. For example, you can define a new version of the + operator for a new data type. When a programmer uses +, the compiler uses the types associated with the operator to determine which version of + to use.

---

1 *Polymorphos* means "having many forms".

In C, although the same function, printf, is used to print any type of value, it is not a poly-morphic function. The user must specify the correct format options to ensure that a value is printed correctly.

1.11.2 Overriding Operators

Overriding occurs when a procedure is defined in a class (for example, Temporary Employee) and also in one of its subclasses (for example, Student Employee). It means that instances of Temporary Employee and Student Employee can each respond to requests for this procedure (assuming it has not been made private to the class). For example, let us assume that we define the procedure toString in these classes. The pseudocode definition of this in Temporary Employee might be:

```
toString(){
    return "I am a temporary employee"
}
```

In Student Employee, it might be defined as:

```
toString(){
    return "I am a student employee"
}
```

The procedure in Student Employee replaces the version in Temporary Employee for all instances of Student Employee. If we ask an instance of Student Employee for the result of toString, we get the string 'I am a student employee'. If you are confused, think of it this way:

> If you ask an object to perform some operation, then, to determine which version of the procedure is run, look in the class used to create the instance. If the procedure is not defined there, look in the class's parent. Keep doing this until you find a procedure which implements the operation requested. This is the version which is used.

In languages such as Java the choice of which version of the procedure to execute is not determined at compile time, because the compiler would have to be able to determine the type of object and then find the appropriate version of the procedure. Instead, the procedure is chosen at run time. The technical term for this process of identifying the procedure at run time rather than compile time is called "late binding".

1.12 Summary

In this chapter you have been introduced to the background and history of object orientation. You have explored the main concepts which underpin object orientation and have encountered some of the (sometimes arcane) terminology used. There is a great deal of new information in this chapter which can, at times, appear to make obsolete all that you already know.

The object-oriented view of the world can be daunting for a programmer who is used to a more procedural view of the world. To adjust to this new view of the world is hard (and some never do). Others fail to see the difference between an object-oriented programming language and a language such as Ada (we refer here to the pre-Ada95 version). However, object orienta-tion will become second nature to many once they have worked with object-oriented systems for a while. The key thing is to try things out as you go along and, if possible, have someone around who understands a bit about object orientation – they can often illuminate and simplify an otherwise gloomy network of tunnels.

1.13 Further Reading

There are a great many books available on object orientation. Some of the best known include Booch (1994), Budd (1991), Wirfs-Brock *et al.* (1990) and Cox and Novobilski (1991). An excellent book aimed at managers and senior programmers who want to learn how to apply object-oriented technology successfully to their projects is Booch (1996). Another good book in a similar style is Yourdon (1994).

Other books which may be of interest to those attempting to convince themselves or others that object technology can actually work are Harmon and Taylor (1993), Love (1993) and Meyer and Nerson (1993).

Other places to find useful references are the *Journal of Object-Oriented Programming* (SIGS Publications, ISSN 0896-8438) and the OOPSLA conferences. The OOPSLA conferences are annual worldwide conferences on Object-Oriented Programming: Systems, Languages and Applications. References for the proceedings of some recent conferences are listed at the back of this book. There are also references for the proceedings of the European Conference on Object-oriented Programming (ECOOP).

For further reading on the software crisis and approaches aimed at solving it see Brooks (1987) and Cox (1990). For a discussion of the nature of scientific discovery, refinement and revolution see Kuhn (1962).

Chapter *2*

Elements of Object Orientation

2.1 Introduction

This chapter is intended to reinforce what you have already learnt. It concisely defines the terminology introduced in the last chapter and attempts to clarify issues associated with hierarchies. It also discusses some of the perceived strengths and weaknesses of the object-oriented approach. It then offers some guidance on the approach to take in learning about objects.

2.2 Terminology

- *Class* A class defines a combination of data and procedures that operate on that data. Instances of other classes can only access that data or those procedures through specified interfaces. A class acts as a template when creating new instances. A class does not hold any data, but it specifies the data that is held in the instance. The relationship between a class, its superclass and any subclasses is illustrated in Figure 2.1.
- *Subclass* A subclass is a class that inherits from another class. For example, in the last chapter, Student Employee is a subclass of Temporary Employee. Subclasses are, of course, classes in their own right. Any class can have any number of subclasses.
- *Superclass* A superclass is the parent of a class. It is the class from which the current class inherits. For example, in the last chapter, Temporary Employee is the superclass of Student Employee. In Java, a class can have only one superclass.
- *Instance or object* An instance is an example of a class. All instances of a class possess the same data variables but contain their own data. Each instance of a class responds to the same set of requests.
- *Instance variable* This is the special name given to the data which is held by an object. The "state" of an object at any particular moment relates to the current values held by its instance variables. (In Java, there are also class-side variables, referred to as static variables, but these will be discussed later). Figure 2.2 illustrates a definition for a class in pseudocode. It includes some instance variable definitions: fuel, mileage and name.
- *Method* A method is a procedure defined within an object. In early versions of Smalltalk, a method was used to get an object to do something or return something. It has since become more widely used; languages such as CLOS and Java also use the term. Two methods are defined in Figure 2.2: one calculates the miles per gallon, while the other sets the name of the car object.

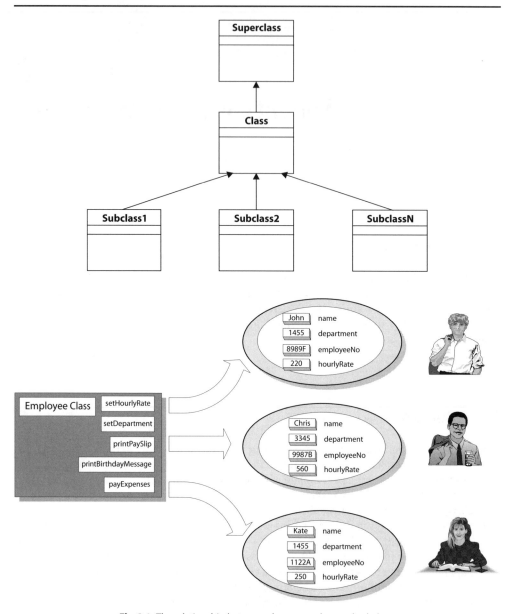

Fig. 2.1 The relationship between class, superclass and subclass.

- *Message* One object sends a message to another object requesting some operation or data. The idea is that objects are polite, well-behaved entities which carry out functions by sending messages to each other. A message may be considered akin to a procedure call in other languages.
- *This* The special (pseudo) variable, **this**, is a reference to the object within which a method is executing (see Figure 2.2). It enables messages to "this" (the current) object.
- *Single or multiple inheritance* Single and multiple inheritance refer to the number of superclasses from which a class can inherit. Java is a single inheritance system, in which a class can only inherit from one class. C++ is a multiple inheritance system in which a class can inherit from one or more classes.

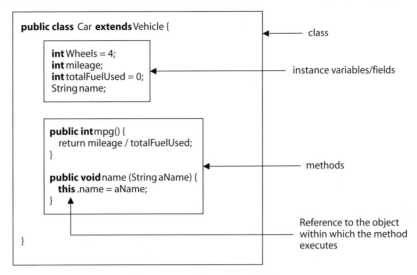

Fig. 2.2 A partial Java class definition.

2.3 Types of Hierarchy

In most object-oriented systems there are two types of hierarchy; one refers to inheritance (whether single or multiple) and the other refers to instantiation. The inheritance hierarchy (or *extends* hierarchy) has already been described. It is the way in which an object inherits features from a superclass.

The instantiation hierarchy relates to instances rather than classes and is important during the execution of the object. There are two types of instance hierarchy: one indicates a *part-of* relationship, while the other relates to a using relationship (it is referred to as an *is-a* relationship).

The difference between an *is-a* relationship and a *part-of* relationship is often confusing for new programmers (and sometimes for those who are experienced in one language but are new to object-oriented programming languages, such as Java). Figure 2.3 illustrates that a student *is-a* type of person whereas an engine is *part-of* a car. It does not make sense to say that a student is *part-of* a person or that an engine *is-a* type of car!

In Java, *extends* relationships are generally implemented by the subclassing mechanism. It is possible to build up large and complex class hierarchies which express these *extends* relationships. These classes express the concept of inheritance, allowing one class to inherit features from another. The total set of features is then used to create an instance of a class. In contrast, *part-of* relationships tend to be implemented using instance variables in Java.

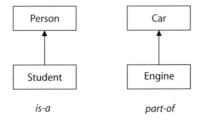

Fig. 2.3 *is-a* does not equal *part-of*.

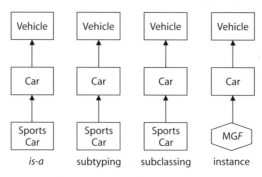

Fig. 2.4 Satisfying four relationships.

However, *is-a* relationships and classes are not exactly the same thing. For example, if you wish to construct a semantic network consisting of explicit *is-a* relationships between instances you will have to construct such a network manually. The aim of such a structure is to represent knowledge and the relationships between elements of that knowledge, and not to construct instances. The construction of such a network is outside the scope of the subclassing mechanism and would therefore be inappropriate.

If John is an instance of a class Person, it would be perfectly (semantically) correct to say that John *is-a* Person. However, here we are obviously talking about the relationship between an instance and a class rather than a subclass and its parent class.

A further confusion can occur for those encountering Java after becoming familiar with a strongly typed language. These people might at first assume that a subclass and a subtype are essentially the same. However, they are not the same, although they are very similar. The problem with classes, types and *is-a* relationships is that on the surface they appear to capture the same sorts of concept. In Figure 2.4, the diagrams all capture some aspect of the use of the phrase *is-a*. However, they are all intended to capture a different relationship.

The confusion is due to the fact that in modern English we tend to overuse the term *is-a*. We can distinguish between the different types of relationship by being more precise about our definitions in terms of a programming language, such as Java. Table 2.1 defines the relationships illustrated in Figure 2.4.

To illustrate this point, consider Figure 2.5, which illustrates the differences between the first three categories.

The first diagram illustrates the potential relationships between a set of classes that define the behaviour of different categories of vehicle. The second diagram presents the subtype relationships between the categories. The third diagram illustrates a straight specialization set of relationships. Notice that although *estate car* is a specialization of *car with hatch*, its implementation (the subclassing hierarchy) indicates that it does not share any of its implementation with the *car with hatch* class. It is worth noting that type relationships are specifications, while classes (and subclasses) are implementations of behaviour.

Table 2.1 Types of *is-a* relationship.

Specialization	One thing is a special case of another
Type	One type can be used interchangeably with another type (substitutability relationship)
Subclassing or inheritance	An implementation mechanism for sharing code and representations
Instantiation	One thing is an example of a particular category (class) of things

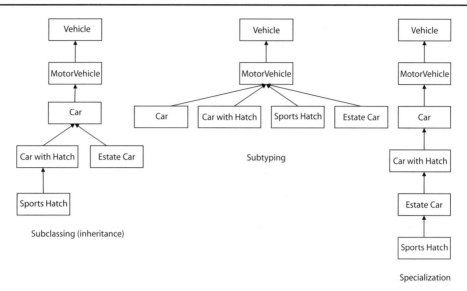

Fig. 2.5 Distinguishing between relationships.

2.4 The Move to Object Technology

At present you are still acclimatizing to object orientation. It is extremely important that from now on you do your utmost to immerse yourself in object orientation, object technology and Java. This is because when you first encounter a new language or paradigm, it is all too easy to say that it is not good because you cannot do what you could in some other language or paradigm. We are all subject to the "better the devil you know than the devil you don't" syndrome. If you embrace object orientation, warts and all, at least for the present, you will gain most.

In addition, it is a fact of life that most of us tend to fit in learning something new around our existing schedules. This may mean for example, that you are trying to read this book and do the exercises while still working in C, Visual Basic, Ada etc. From personal experience, and from teaching others about Java, I can say that you will gain most by putting aside a significant amount of time and concentrating on the subject matter involved. This is not only because object orientation is so different, but also because you need to get familiar not only with the concepts but also with Java and its development environment.

So have a go, take a "leap of faith" and stick with it until the end. If, at the end, you still cannot see the point, then fair enough, but until then accept it.

2.5 Summary

In this chapter, we reviewed some of the terminology introduced in the previous chapter. We also considered the types of hierarchy which occur in object-oriented systems and which can at first be confusing. We then considered the pros and cons of object-oriented programming. You should now be ready to start to think in terms of objects. As has already been stated, this will at first seem a strange way to develop a software system, but in time it will become second nature. In the next chapter we examine how an object-oriented system might be developed and structured. This is done without reference to any source code as the intention is to familiarize you with objects rather than with Java. It is all too easy to get through a book on Smalltalk, C++, Java etc. and understand the text but still have no idea how to start developing an object-oriented system.

2.6 Exercises

1.   Research what other authors have said about single and multiple inheritance. Why do languages such as Smalltalk and Java not include multiple inheritance?

2.   Look for terms such as class, method, member, member function, instance variable and constructor in the books listed in the further reading section. When you have found them, read their explanation of these terms and write down your understanding of their meaning.

2.7 Further Reading

Suggested further reading for this chapter includes Coad and Yourdon (1991), Winston and Narasimhan (2001) and Meyer (1988). In addition all the books mentioned in the previous chapter are still relevant.

Chapter **3**

Constructing an Object-Oriented System

3.1 Introduction

This chapter takes you through the design of a simple object-oriented system without considering implementation issues or the details of any particular language. Instead, this chapter illustrates how to use object orientation concepts to construct a software system. We first describe the application and then consider where to start looking for objects, what the objects should do and how they should do it. We conclude by discussing issues such as class inheritance, and answer questions such as "where is the structure of the program?".

3.2 The Application: Windscreen Wipe Simulation

This system aims to provide a diagnosis tutor for the equipment illustrated in Figure 3.1. Rather than use the wash–wipe system from a real car, students on a car mechanics diagnosis course use this software simulation. The software system mimics the actual system, so the behaviour of the pump depends on information provided by the relay and the water bottle.

    The operation of the wash–wipe system is controlled by a switch which can be in one of five positions: off, intermittent, slow, fast and wash. Each of these settings places the system into a different state (Table 3.1).

    For the pump and the wiper motor to work correctly, the relay must function correctly. In turn, the relay must be supplied with an electrical circuit. This electrical circuit is negatively fused and thus the fuse must be intact for the circuit to be made. Cars are negatively switched as this reduces the chances of short circuits leading to unintentional switching of circuits.

Table 3.1 System states.

Switch setting	System state
Off	The system is inactive.
Intermittent	The blades wipe the windscreen every few seconds.
Slow	The wiper blades wipe the windscreen continuously.
Fast	The wiper blades wipe the windscreen continuously and quickly.
Wash	The pump draws water from the water bottle and sprays it onto the windscreen.

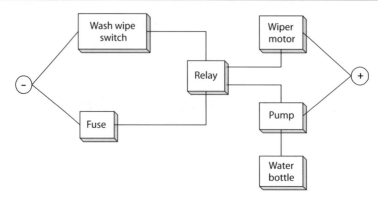

Fig. 3.1 The windscreen wash–wipe system.

3.3 Where Do We Start?

This is often a very difficult point for those new to object-oriented systems. That is, they have read the basics and understand simple diagrams, but do not know where to start. It is the old chestnut, "I understand the example but don't know how to apply the concepts myself". This is not unusual and, in the case of object orientation, is probably normal.

The answer to the question "where do I start?" may at first seem somewhat obscure; you should start with the data. Remember that objects are things which exchange messages with each other. The things possess the data which is held by the system and the messages request actions that relate to the data. Thus, an object-oriented system is fundamentally concerned with data items.

Before we go on to consider the object-oriented view of the system, let us stop and think for a while. Ask yourself "where would I start if I was going to develop such a system in C or Pascal or even Ada?". In most cases, the answer is "with some form of functional decomposition". That is, you might think about the main functions of the system and break them down into sub-functions and so on. As a natural part of this exercise, you would identify the data required to support the desired functionality. Notice that the emphasis would be on the system functionality.

Let us take this further and consider the functions we might identify for the example presented above (Table 3.2). We would then identify important system variables and sub-functions to support the above functions.

Now let us go back to the object-oriented view of the world. In this view, we place a great deal more emphasis on the data items involved and consider the operations associated with them (effectively, the reverse of the functional decomposition view). This means that we start by attempting to identify the primary data items in the system; next, we look to see what operations are applied to, or performed on, the data items; finally, we group the data items and operations together to form objects. In identifying the operations, we may well have to consider additional data items, which may be separate objects or attributes of the current object. Identifying them is mostly a matter of skill and experience.

Table 3.2 System functions.

Function	Description
Wash	Pump water from the water bottle to the windscreen.
Wipe	Move the windscreen wipers across the windscreen.

The object-oriented design approach considers the operations far less important than the data and their relationships. In the next section we examine the objects that might exist in our simulation system.

3.4 Identifying the Objects

We look at the system as a whole and ask what indicates the state of the system. We might say that the position of the switch or the status of the pump is significant. This results in the data items shown in Table 3.3.

Table 3.3 Data items and their associated state information.

Data item	States
switch setting	Is the switch set to off, intermittent, wipe, fast wipe or wash?
wiper motor	Is the motor working or not?
pump state	Is the pump working or not?
fuse condition	Has the fuse blown or not?
water bottle level	The current water level
relay status	Is current flowing or not?

The identification of the data items is considered in greater detail in Part 7. At this point, merely notice that we have not yet mentioned the functionality of the system or how it might fit together, we have only mentioned the significant items. As this is such a simple system, we can assume that each of these elements is an object and illustrate it in a simple object diagram (Figure 3.2).[1]

Notice that I have named each object after the element associated with the data item (e.g. the element associated with the fuse condition is the fuse itself) and that the actual data item (e.g.

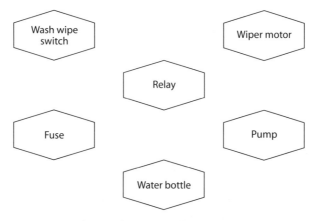

Fig. 3.2 Objects in simulation system.

1   The hexagonal shape representing instances is based on the structured cloud used in the original Unified Modeling Language version 0.8.

the condition of the fuse) is an instance variable of the object. This is a very common way of naming objects and their instance variables. We now have the basic objects required for our application.

3.5 Identifying the Services Or Methods

At the moment, we have a set of objects each of which can hold some data. For example, the water bottle can hold an integer indicating the current water level. Although object-oriented systems are structured around the data, we still need some procedural content to change the state of an object or to make the system achieve some goal. Therefore, we also need to consider the operations a user of each object might require. Notice that the emphasis here is on the **users of the object** and what they **require of the object** rather than what operations are performed on the data.

Let us start with the switch object. The switch state can take a number of values. As we do not want other objects to have direct access to this variable, we must identify the services which the switch should offer. As a user of a switch we want to be able to move it between its various settings. As these settings are essentially an enumerated type, we can have the concept of incrementing or decrementing the switch position. A switch must therefore provide a moveUp and a moveDown interface. Exactly how this is done depends on the programming language; for now, we concentrate on specifying the required facilities.

If we examine each object in our system and identify the required services, we may end up with Table 3.4.

Table 3.4 Object services.

Object	Service	Description
switch	moveUp	Increment switch value
	moveDown	Decrement switch value
	state?	Return a value indicating the current switch state
fuse	working?	Indicate whether the fuse has blown or not
wiper motor	working?	Indicate whether the wipers are working or not
relay	working?	Indicate whether the relay is active or not
pump	working?	Indicate whether the pump is active or not
water bottle	fill	Fill the water bottle with water
	extract	Remove some water from the water bottle
	empty	Empty the water bottle

We generated this table by examining each of the objects in isolation to identify the services which might reasonably be required. We may well identify further services when we attempt to put it all together.

Each of these services should relate to a method within the object. For example, the moveUp and moveDown services should relate to methods which change the state instance variable within the object. Using generic pseudocode, the moveUp method within the switch object might contain the following code:

```
define method moveUp()
  if state == "off" then
```

```
        state = "wash"
    elseif state == "wash" then
        state = "wipe"
    endif
end define method
```

This method changes the value of the `state` variable in `switch`. The new value of the instance variable depends on its previous value. You can define `moveDown` in a similar manner. Notice that the reference to the instance variable illustrates that it is global to the object. The `moveUp` method requires no parameters. In object-oriented systems, it is common for few parameters to be passed between methods (particularly of the same object), as it is the object which holds the data.

3.6 Refining the Objects

If we look back to Table 3.2, we can see that fuse, wiper motor, relay and pump all possess a service called `working?`. This is a hint that these objects may have something in common. Each of them presents the same interface to the outside world. If we then consider their attributes, they all possess a common instance variable. At this point, it is too early to say whether fuse, wiper motor, relay and pump are all instances of the same class of object (e.g. a `Component` class) or whether they are all instances of classes which inherit from some common superclass (see Figure 3.3). However, this is something we must bear in mind later.

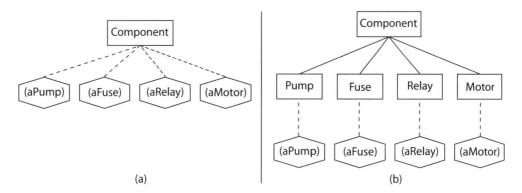

Fig. 3.3 Possible classes for components in the simulation.

3.7 Bringing it All Together

So far we have identified the primary objects in our system and the basic set of services they should present. These services were based solely on the data the objects hold. We must now consider how to make our system function. To do this, we need to consider how it might be used. The system is part of a very simple diagnosis tutor; a student uses the system to learn about the effects of various faults on the operation of a real wiper system, without the need for expensive electronics. We therefore wish to allow a user of the system to carry out the following operations:

- change the state of a component device
- ask the motor what its new state is

The moveUp and moveDown operations on the switch change the switch's state. Similar operations can be provided for the fuse, the water bottle and the relay. For the fuse and the relay, we might provide a changeState interface using the following algorithm:

```
define method changeState()
  if state == "working" then
    state = "notWorking"
  else
    state = "working"
  endif
end define method
```

Discovering the state of the motor is more complicated. We have encountered a situation where one object's state (the value of its instance variable) is dependent on information provided by other objects. If we write down procedurally how the value of other objects affect the status of the pump, we might get the following pseudocode:

```
if fuse is working then
  if switch is not off then
    if relay is working then
      pump status = "working"
    endif
  endif
endif
```

This algorithm says that the pump status depends on the relay status, the switch setting and the fuse status. This is the sort of algorithm you might expect to find in a main() program. It links the sub-functions together and processes the data.

In an object-oriented language (such as Java), we do not have a main program in the same way that a C program has. Instead the main() method in Java is an initiating point for an object-oriented system. As it is on the class-side, it can trigger the creation of instances, but it is not itself part of those instances. This can be confusing at first, however if you think of the main() method in Java as initiating a program that is outside the scope of the main() method, you are fairly close.

In an object-oriented system, well-mannered objects pass messages to one another. How then do we achieve the same effect as the above algorithm? The answer is that we must get the objects to pass messages requesting the appropriate information. One way to do that is to define a method in the pump object which gets the required information from the other objects and determines the motor's state. However, this requires the pump to have links to all the other objects so that it can send them messages. This is a little contrived and loses the structure of the underlying system. It also loses any modularity in the system. That is, if we want to add new components then we have to change the pump object, even if the new components only affect the switch. This approach also indicates that the developer is thinking too procedurally and not really in terms of objects.

In an object-oriented view of the system, the pump object only needs to know the state of the relay. It should therefore request this information from the relay. In turn, the relay must request information from the switches and the fuse.

Figure 3.4 illustrates the chain of messages initiated by the pump object:

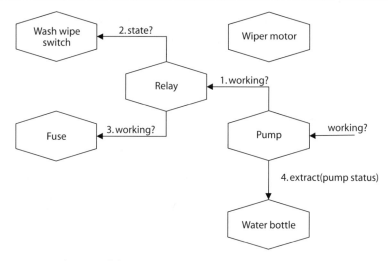

Fig. 3.4 Collaborations between the objects for wash operation.

1. pump sends a working? message to the relay
2. relay sends a state? message to the switch
   the switch replies to the relay
3. relay sends a second working? message to the fuse
   the fuse replies to the relay
   the relay replies to the motor
   If the pump is working, then the pump object sends the final message to the water bottle
4. pump sends a message extract to the water bottle

In Step 4, a parameter is passed with the message because, unlike the previous messages which merely requested state information, this message requests a change in state. The parameter indicates the rate at which the pump draws water from the water bottle.

The water bottle should not record the value of the pump's status as it does not own this value. If it needs the motor's status in the future, it should request it from the pump rather than using the (potentially obsolete) value passed to it previously.

In Figure 3.4, we assumed that the pump provided the service working?, which allows the process to start. For completeness, the pseudocode of working? for the pump object is:

```
define method working?()
  begin
    this.status = relay.working().
    if this.status == "working" then
      water_bottle.extract(this.status)
    endif
  end
end define method
```

This method is a lot simpler than the procedural program presented earlier. At no point do we change the value of any variables which are not part of the pump, although they may have been changed as a result of the messages being sent. Also, it only shows us the part of the story that is directly relevant to the pump. This means that it can be much more difficult to deduce the operation of an object-oriented system merely by reading the source code. Some Java environments (such as JBuilder and Forté for Java) alleviate this problem, to some extent, through the use of sophisticated browsers.

3.8 Where Is the Structure?

People new to object orientation may be confused because they have lost one of the key elements that they use to help them understand and structure a software system: the main program body. This is because the objects and the interactions between them are the cornerstone of the system. In many ways, Figure 3.4 shows the object-oriented equivalent of a main program. This also highlights an important feature of most object-oriented approaches: graphical illustrations. Many aspects of object technology, for example object structure, class inheritance and message chains, are most easily explained graphically.

Let us now consider the structure of our object-oriented system. It is dictated by the messages which are sent between objects. That is, an object must possess a reference to another object in order to send it a message. The resulting system structure is illustrated in Figure 3.5.

In Java, this structure is achieved by making instance variables reference the appropriate objects. This is the structure which exists between the instances in the system and does not relate to the classes, which act as templates for the instances.

We now consider the classes that create the instances. We could assume that each object is an

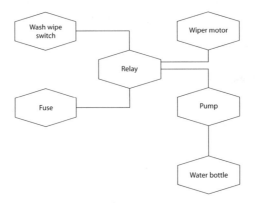

Fig. 3.5 Wash–wipe system structure.

instance of an equivalent class (see Figure 3.6(a)). However, as has already been noted, some of the classes bear a very strong resemblance. In particular, the fuse, the relay, the motor and the pump share a number of common features. Table 3.5 compares the features (instance variables and services) of these objects.

From this table, the objects differ only in name. This suggests that they are all instances of a common class such as Component (see Figure 3.6(b)). This class would possess an additional instance variable, to simplify object identification.

If they are all instances of a common class, they must all behave in exactly the same way. However, we want the pump to start the analysis process when it receives the message working?, so it must possess a different definition of working? from fuse and relay. In other ways it is very similar to fuse and relay, so they can be instances of a class (say Component) and pump and motor can be instances of classes which inherit from Component (but redefine working?). This is illustrated in Figure 3.6(c). The full class diagram is presented in Figure 3.7.

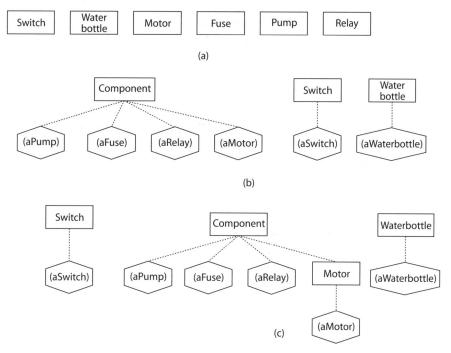

Fig. 3.6 Possible class inheritance relationships.

Table 3.5 Comparison of components.

	fuse	relay	motor	pump
Instance variable	state	state	state	state
Services	working?	working?	working?	working?

3.9 Summary

In this chapter, you have seen how a very simple system can be broken down into objects. These objects combine to provide the overall functionality of the system. You have seen how the data to be represented determines the objects used and that the interactions between objects determine the structure of the system. You should also have noted that objects and their classes, methods and instance variables are identified by more of an evolutionary process than in languages that are not object-oriented.

3.10 Exercise

1. Take a system with which you are familiar and try to break it down into objects. Carry out a similar set of steps to those described above. Do not worry about how to implement the objects or the classes. Use whatever representation best fits your way of working to de-

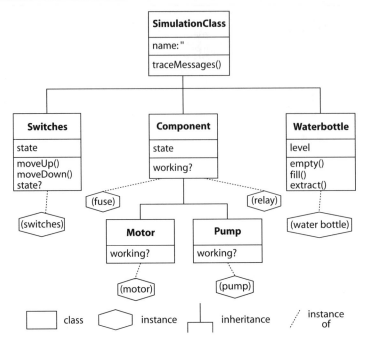

Fig. 3.7 The final class hierarchy and instance diagram.

scribe what the methods do (pseudocode or a programming language, such as C or Pascal, if you prefer). You can even use a flow chart if you are most comfortable with that. It is very important that you try to do this, as it is a useful exercise in learning to think in terms of objects.

3.11 Further Reading

A good place to start further reading on building object-oriented systems is with the first few chapters of Rumbaugh *et al* (1991). In addition, Wirfs-Brock *et al* (1990) is an excellent, non-language-specific introduction to structuring object-oriented systems. It uses a rather simplistic approach, which is ideal for learning about object-oriented system design but is not generally applicable. This is not a problem, as what you want to do at the moment is to get the background rather than specific techniques. Another good reference for further reading is Yourdon (1994).

Part **2**

Introduction to the Java Language

Chapter 4

A Brief History of Time, the Universe and Java

4.1 Introduction

I first encountered the Java language in April 1995. I was attending a conference in Amsterdam and, over breakfast with a number of American academics, was discussing suitable first programming languages. They mentioned a new language, called Java, that was quite similar to C++ but had many of the "dirty" parts of that language removed and some of the nice parts of languages such as Smalltalk added. I obtained and read the Java white paper. I thought that it looked like a nice language but that, like other object-oriented languages before it, it would not take off. After all, many people thought that Smalltalk was nicer than C++, but C++ still dominated, and languages such as Eiffel and Self were hardly being taken up at all. However, I had reckoned without the Internet and the Worldwide Web. Since its launch in 1995, Java has become a force to be taken seriously.

In this chapter we encounter Java, the Sun Java Development Kit (JDK) and the Java environment. We also learn a little about the history of Java.

4.2 What Is Java?

Java can be viewed from a number of perspectives; in this it differs from many other programming languages, which can only be viewed as a programming language and nothing else. However, Java is more than just a programming language. Below we consider some of the ways to classify Java:

- *An object-oriented programming language* Java certainly provides the syntax and semantics of an object-oriented language. It is supported by a number of compilers which take programs written in Java and produce executable code. As you will see later, they tend to produce a byte code form which is then run on a virtual machine. As for the Java language itself, it is rather compact, unlike languages such as Ada , which are very large.
- *A programming environment* I refer here to the presence of the system-provided objects rather than any particular development environment. Unlike many languages (including C++), Java has associated with it a large (and fairly standard) set of classes. These classes make Java very powerful and promote a standard development style. You spend most of your time extending the "system" rather than programming from scratch. In a number of cases, these classes provide facilities which are considered part of the language in Ada, C and Pascal. The result is that Java is anything but a small programming system.

- *An operating environment* The operating environment is the Java Virtual Machine in which all Java programs execute. This is Java's own personal machine which has been ported to a variety of platforms and operating systems. Thus, Java can run (without re-compilation) on a host of different systems.
- *The language of the Web* Java has received huge hype as the language which will bring the Web alive. However, in many ways Java is just an object-oriented language. There is no particular reason why Java should be any better as a Web language than Smalltalk or any other interpreted object-oriented language, such as Objective-C or Eiffel. However, Java got there first and has the backing of both Netscape and Sun. It is therefore likely to remain the Web language.

Thus, it is quite possible to say that Java is a programming language, a set of extensible classes, an operating environment or even a Web development tool. It is, in fact, all of these.

4.3 Objects in Java

Almost everything in Java is an object; for example, strings, arrays, windows and even integers can be objects. Objects, in turn, are examples of classes of things; for example, the string "John Hunt" is an object of the class `String`. Thus, to program in Java, you define classes, create instances and apply operations to classes and objects.

However, unlike languages such as Smalltalk, which are considered pure object-oriented languages, Java also has standard types (such as integer) and procedural programming statements. This hybrid approach can make the transition to object orientation simpler. In some languages, such as C++, this can be a disadvantage, as the developer can avoid the object-oriented nature of the language. However, Java has no concept of a procedural program; instead, everything is held within an object (even the procedural elements).

4.4 History

Java's beginnings were not particularly auspicious. Like C before it, it rose phoenix-like from the ashes of a dropped project. The original project, codenamed Green, was intended to develop "smart" consumer electronic devices (such as TV-top control boxes). It needed software to drive these small, potentially low performance, but varied devices. The Green team did not want to use C or C++ due to technical difficulties with those languages (not least, problems associated with portability). They therefore decided to develop their own language and, by August 1991, a new object-oriented language was born. This language was called Oak. One rumour is that it was named after the tree outside the team leader's office; another is that Oak stands for "Object Application Kernel". However, at that time it was just another programming language which had some nice features and was good for client–server computing.

By 1993, the Green project had been renamed "First Person Inc.". It spent much of that year, and the start of the next, attempting to sell the hardware and software technology. However, the market was not there and Sun decided to drop the project and disband the team.

In mid-1993, the first Mosaic browser was released and interest in the Internet, and, in particular, the World Wide Web, was growing. A number of the original project felt that although the hardware element of the Green project might not be useful, the software language they had developed might well be perfect for the Web. They managed to convince Sun that it would be worth funding the software part of the project for a further year, and Sun pumped $5 million into the software development during 1994.

In January 1995, Oak was renamed Java. This was, apparently, because Oak was already the name of a programming language; however, it may also be because Oak was not a particularly exciting name, whereas Java conjures up the right images.

In mid-1994, Java was used to build a new Web browser, called HotJava ,which illustrated the potential of the Java language by allowing animated (rather than static) Web pages. This was the catalyst which really started things for the language. As Java was designed to be portable, secure and small, and to operate in real time, it is ideally suited to the sort of environment that the Web imposes. However, it is worth noting that it is also an excellent object-oriented programming language in its own right and may well prove far more influential as a language for building standalone applications than merely as a language for animating the Web! Indeed, I have used it for constructing large commercial multi-tier applications that happen to use IP protocol-based communications!

Since its launch in 1995, Java has caught the imagination of not only the computing community, but also the populace in general. This is because of what it might do, rather than any marketing push provided by Sun: in his book *Just Java*, Peter van der Linden (2001) notes that, after Java's launch, Sun doubled the size of its Java marketing department – from one person to two.

The wheel appears to have come full circle, as Sun is now talking of releasing small handheld control devices for consumer products which contain a Java chip running Java programs. Thus Java will become a language for controlling consumer electronics (as it was originally intended to be).

4.5 Commercial Versions of Java

There are a number of commercial development environments for Java. These include IBM's VisualAge for Java, Sun's Forte for Java, Borland's JBuilder (Figure 4.1) and VisualCafé. Some of them are available for no cost (for example, Forte and JBuilder both have free versions). These tools provide an integrated development environment for Java. Compared to the very basic facilities of Sun's JDK and Java SDK, these tools are very sophisticated. Typically, they provide user interface building tools, graphical class hierarchy browsers, dedicated class editors etc. One interesting point to note is that some of these tools are also written in Java. For example, both Forte and JBuilder are pure Java enabling them to work on any platform for which a Java Virtual Machine is available (see below for an explanation of the role of the JVM in the Java environment).

4.6 The Java Environment

Java is different from other development environments you may have used in that, when you write Java code, it does not execute on your host machine, even when it is compiled. Instead, it executes in a virtual machine, which in turn executes on your host computer.[1] In fact, this is part of the secret behind Java's portability – you can write code on one hardware platform and, without re-compilation, run it on another hardware platform with a completely different

---

1   Java is compiled into a byte code format rather than a machine executable format. These byte codes are then executed by the virtual machine.

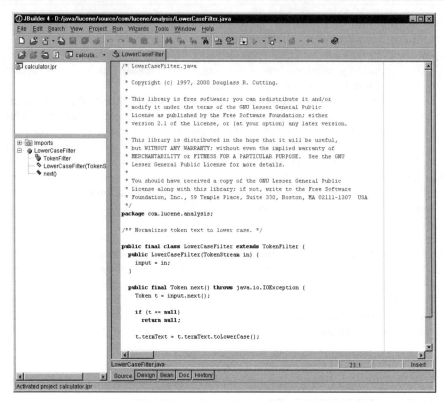

Fig. 4.1 JBuilder 4: an integrated development environment for Java written in Java.

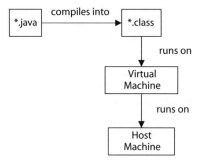

Fig. 4.2 Java environment.

windowing system. In effect, your Java code always runs on the same machine: the Java Virtual Machine. There is, therefore, no concept of an "executable" in Java terms.

Instead of an executable file, you build up "class" files that hold the byte code form of the Java source. Figure 4.2 shows that a Java source file (with a `.java` extension) is compiled into a byte-encoded file (with a `.class` extension). The byte encoded form then runs on the virtual machine, which runs on the host machine.

4.6.1 What Is in a Name?

Originally Sun provided a public domain Java development environment which was known as the Java Development Kit (JDK). The first release of the JDK was version 1.0, in early 1996. Later in 1996, version 1.0.2 was made available and version 1.1 appeared in early 1997 (rapidly followed by the nearly identical versions 1.1.1, 1.1.2 up to version 1.1.8).

Version 1.0.2 provided an improved set of graphic building classes, while version 1.1 implemented a new event-handling mechanism and revised the way in which native code is called from Java.

Following on from this in late 1998 the JDK 1.2 Beta version was released. This was a significant advance on what had gone before. In particular, it included the swing set of graphical components which allowed developers to create far more sophisticated applications.

In early December 1998 JDK 1.2 was released. However a few days later it was rebranded as the Java 2 Platform SDK, Standard Edition (v 1.2). Here SDK stands for Software Development Kit and the whole thing was referred to as the Java 2 platform. This was followed by two sub releases (v 1.2.1 and v 1.2.2). In 2000 the Java 2 SDK, Standard Edition (v 1.3) was released with v 1.3.1 released in 2001. This was followed by the v 1.4 of the Java 2 SDK, Standard Edition.

This change of name has caused a great deal of confusion and is really a marketing initiative. You will find that people still refer to the Java 2 platform as the JDK and to the version as the JDK 1.4 etc. Indeed, when you install Java you will find that it installs by default into a directory called jdk1.3 or jdk1.4 etc. (at least at the time of writing the versions available all do!).

In addition, note the reference to the Standard Edition; this is because there is also an Enterprise Edition (which effectively adds a set of server-side APIs to the standard Java APIs such as Enterprise JavaBeans) and a Micro Edition for embedded systems.

You can obtain the appropriate version of java from Sun's Java Web site (see http://java.sun.com/). Versions of the JDK or Java 2 platform can be downloaded for Solaris 2.x (both Sparc and x86), Solaris 8, for Linux and for Windows 95, 2000 and NT, and for Mac OS System 7 and above (although the Mac version tends to lag behind the versions for the other platforms).

The source code described in this book has been tested on versions 1.1 and the Java 2 platform. The only source code which requires version Java 2 is the section dealing with graphical user interfaces (as it uses the new Swing set of components).

The JDK or Java platform provides a number of tools including a compiler, the virtual machine, a debugger and a documentation tool:

- **javac** is the Java language compiler. It is often read as "javack" rather than "java see", as the latter can cause confusion (i.e. it implies a Java to C converter!). It produces .class files containing the byte codes.
- **java** is the Java Virtual Machine also known as the Java language runtime. It is a byte code interpreter which is implemented in two parts. The lower part is reimplemented for different platforms.
- **jdb** is the Java debugger. It is not as sophisticated as some debuggers, but can be very useful. However, if you have a tool such as JBuilder available you are better off using the debugger in that!
- **jar** is the Java archive tool. It can be used to combine (and compress) multiple files (in particular, class, image and sound files) into a single archive file. It enables you to deliver a Java application in a single file. This is particularly useful for applets, which can be delivered by a single HTTP transaction, rather than in a series of transactions.
- **javah** creates C header files and C stub files for a Java class. It allows code written in Java and C to work together. This book does not cover this issue.
- **javap** is the Java byte code disassembler.
- **javadoc** takes a Java source file and converts the class name, the methods and the variables into HTML documentation. It also searches for comments starting with /** and uses them to provide additional documentation.

There is also a range of tools to support remote method invocation; they are not covered in this book.

4.6.2 What Is JavaScript?

A rather confusing issue is that there is a "programming" language that can be used within HTML pages called JavaScript. This language is **not** Java and has no direct relationship with Java, other than a similarity with some of its syntax. However, the one big omission that separates Java and JavaScript is that you cannot define classes in JavaScript and thus you lose the potential power of object-oriented programming.

4.6.3 Applications and Applets

You can write three types of program in Java: applications, servlets and applets. The difference between them is essentially how they are run and what they can do:

- **Applications** are standalone programs, which have the same access rights as any other standalone program.
- **Applets** are special Java programs which can only execute within a Java enabled browser or the appletviewer. They cannot access the local file store and must inherit from the applet class.
- **Servlets** are Java programs that can only run within a Java-enabled server (such as a Web server like Apache with the TomCat extensions). They cannot be run directly and do not run within the applet sandbox.

We will look at applets and servlets in more detail later in this book. However, we concentrate on the construction of applications. Of course, an applet may act as a client for a server application or a servlet in which case it could be a substantial piece of code in its own right. The issues that are discussed for applications are true for such an applet.

4.6.4 Applications in Java

A number of large (and high-profile) applications have now been developed in Java (Table 4.1). One of the very first, of course, was HotJava, the Web browser implemented by Sun to show Java's potential. Another is Sun's StarOffice office application suite. This is a very powerful set of tools for word processing, presentations, managing your time, producing spreadsheets etc. It is now being adopted by more and more organisations. It runs on any Java-enabled platform. Of course, JBuilder, as has been mentioned, is also a Java application and illustrates the power of

Table 4.1 Java application URLs.

Application	URL
HotJava	http://java.sun.com/
StarOffice	http://www.sun.com/staroffice/
JBuilder	http://www.borland.com/
Together Control Center	http://www.together.com/

such tools. A final tool is Together Control Centre – a sophisticated design, modelling, deployment and run-time environment for enterprise scale applications.

4.7 Further Reading

There are a number of Java books produced by people from the Sun Java team, including Arnold and Gosling (2000), Gosling *et al.* (1996) and van der Linden (2001). Other authors include Flanagan (1996) and Cornell and Horstmann (1997).

4.8 Where to Get More Information

There are numerous placed on the Web that can provide useful information for the Java developer. Some of these are:

- The Java Home Page: `http://java.sun.com/`
- `http://softwaredev.earthweb.com/java`
- `http://www.javalobby.org/`
- `http://www.jars.com/`
- `http://www.javareport.com/`
- `http://www.appdevadvisor.com/`
- `http://www.sys-con.com/java/`
- `http://www.planetjava.co.uk/`

Chapter 5

A Little Java

5.1 Introduction

In the last chapter, you learned a little about the history of Java and the Java development environment. In this chapter, you encounter the Java language, the compiler, the debugger, the Java Virtual Machine and the javadoc utility.

Just to get you started, we will add two numbers together. First we do it in a procedural language, such as Pascal:

```
int a, b, c;
a := 1;
b := 2;
c := a + b;
```

This says something like, "create three variables to hold integer values (call them a, b and c). Store the value 1 into variable a and 2 into variable b. Add the two numbers together and save the result into the third variable, c". Now we look at how we could write the same thing in Java:[1]

```
Integer a b c;
a = new Integer(1);
b = new Integer(2);
c = new Integer(a + b);
```

As you can see, this looks basically the same (apart from the use of = rather than := and the need to state we are going to use a new integer instance for each value). However, although the effect is the same, and the look similar, the meaning is dramatically different. In Java, the code says:

> Define three temporary variables a, b and c. These variables will hold an object which is an instance of Integer or one of its subclasses. Create a new object of the class Integer and assign the value 1 to it. The object is then assigned to variable a. Create a new object of the class Integer and assign the value 2 to it. The object is then assigned to variable b. Take the value of the object in a, which is 1, and add that to the value of the object in b, which is 2. The result is then saved into a newly created instance of the class Integer. Then save this object into the variable c.

The concepts of messages, classes, objects etc. are explained in more detail elsewhere. I hope that, by the end of this book, you can read the above definition and say "of course".

---

1   This is slightly contrived, as we could just as easily have used the built-in integer type. However, many situations require the Integer object, so it is a useful example.

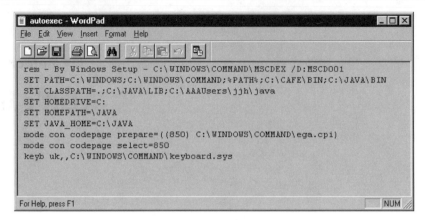

Fig. 5.1 Setting up the autoexec.bat file for Java.

5.2 Setting up the Development Environment

As was discussed in the last chapter, the JDK comes with a number of tools including a Java compiler (javac), a Java Virtual Machine (java), a tool for viewing applets (appletViewer), a rudimentary debugger (jdb) and a documentation tool (javadoc). You use these tools to create, debug, document and use Java programs. Depending on your environment and your platform, the actual details of how you install the JDK (or any set of Java tools) differ and you should follow the guidelines provided.

Whatever your platform, you should be aware of the CLASSPATH environment variable. This variable tells Java where to look for class definitions, so it should at least point to the run-time library and the current directory. It may also point to other directories in which you have defined classes. In Windows 95, you may change CLASSPATH in the autoexec.bat file (Figure 5.1 shows my personal autoexec.bat) by adding the following declaration:

    SET CLASSPATH=.;c:\java\lib\classes.zip

For Solaris 2.3, define CLASSPATH in your .cshrc file:

    setenv CLASSPATH .:/usr/local/misc/Java/lib/classes.zip

You should also add the Java bin directory to your path. You should now be ready to use the Java tools.

5.3 Compiling and Executing Java

```java
public class Hello {
  public static void main (String argv[]) {
        System.out.println("Hello World");
  }
}
```

Type in the program above very carefully to ensure that the syntax is correct. At this point, do not worry about what it means, we are only trying to get to grips with the tools provided by the JDK. Once you have typed in the text, save it to a file called:

`Hello.java`

Ensure that you use exactly the same capitalization as above. Next, bring up a command line prompt. How you do this depends on the environment you are using. For example, in a Unix box, it may involve opening an XTERM; on Windows 95 or NT you may need to bring up the DOS prompt; on a Windows 2000 machine this is called a command prompt. You can then compile your Java program using the `javac` command:

`> javac Hello.java`

If it compiles successfully, it generates a `Hello.class` file that contains the byte codes. For example, on a Windows machine, the directory listing looks like this:

```
HELLO~1  JAV   344   22/01/97   14:20   Hello.java
HELLO~1  CLA   461   20/01/97   14:24   Hello.class
```

You can then run the generated byte codes on the Java Virtual Machine, using the `java` program:

`> java Hello`

Notice that we do not provide an extension for the program, only the main part of the filename. You should then see the phrase "Hello World" appear in the window (see Figure 5.2).

Congratulations! You have now written, compiled and run your first Java application.

So what has happened here? We have not created any form of executable; rather, we have created a set of class files. The effects of compiling your Java code are illustrated in Figure 5.3.

As can be seen from this figure, the compiler compiles the `.java` files into `.class` files. These in turn run on the Java Virtual Machine (this is what runs when you type in `java` to the command prompt). The Java Virtual Machine (JVM) reads the class files and then runs them.

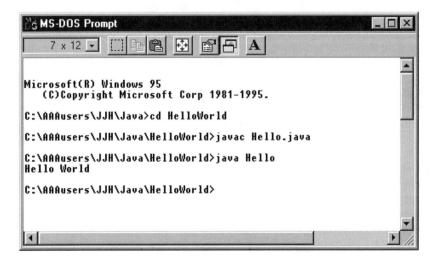

Fig. 5.2 Compiling and running a Java program.

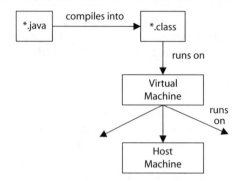

Fig. 5.3 The results of the Java compiler and Java Virtual Machine.

This may involve interpreting the class files, compiling the class files to native code or a combination of the two, depending upon the JVM being used. If we take the original approach the JVM interprets the class files. Thus the class files run on the JVM.

The JVM can be viewed as a virtual computer (that is one that exists only in software). Thus Java runs on a software computer. This software computer must then execute on the underlying host machine. This means that in effect the JVM has two aspects to it: the part that interprets Java programs and a back end that must be ported to different platforms as required. Thus, although the Java programs you write are indeed "write once, run anywhere", the JVMs they run on need to be ported to each platform on which Java will execute.

Although your Java programs do not need to be rewritten to run on Unix, NT, Linux etc. the JVM does. This means that different JVMs on different platforms can (and do) have different bugs in them. Thus it is essential to test your Java programs on all platforms that they are to be used on. Therefore, in reality Java is actually "write once, run anywhere, test everywhere" that you will use your Java programs. Note that one area which is particularly prone to platform problems is the GUI (as supported by the AWT and Swing – see later in this book).

5.4 Using the Java Documentation Tool

Now that we have written our simple program, we wish to document it. This process can be simplified by using the javadoc utility, which processes our Java class to produce a set of Web pages which document its definition, interface and variables. You run the .java file through the javadoc program:

```
> javadoc Test.java
```

While it runs, you can see the following output:

```
C:\AAAusers\JJH\Java>javadoc Test
Loading source files for Test
Generating packages.html
Generating index
Generating tree
C:\AAAusers\JJH\Java>
```

This utility generates four .html files, which contain information about the packages available, the classes in the current package, an index of all variables and methods, and the class hierarchy involving the current class:

```
PACKAG~1 HTM 505  14/02/97  14:58 packages.html
PACKAG~2 HTM 341  14/02/97  14:58 Package-Test.html
ALLNAM~1 HTM 989  14/02/97  14:58 AllNames.html
TREE~1   HTM 378  14/02/97  14:58 tree.html
```

You can read these files using any Web browser. The Test class is very basic and therefore these .html files are essentially empty.

5.5 Summary

You have now used a number of Java tools and written some Java code. You have also used some of the tools available to help you debug your code. You are now ready for the Java language itself!

5.6 Further Reading

If you are going to do any serious development in Java, then you should consider obtaining at least Volume 1 of *The Java Application Programming Interface* (Gosling and Yellin, 2000), which concentrates on programming facilities. Volume 2 concentrates on the Abstract Window Toolkit graphical facilities.

Chapter **6**

Java Building Blocks

6.1 Introduction

This chapter presents an introduction to the Java programming language. As such, it is not intended to be a comprehensive guide. It introduces the basic elements of the Java language, discusses the concept of classes and instances and how they are defined, presents methods and method definitions, and considers interface specifications.

6.2 The Basics of the Language

All Java programmers make extensive use of the existing classes even when they write relatively trivial code. For example, the following version of the "Hello World" program reuses existing classes rather than just using the language (do not worry too much about the syntax of the definition or the parameters to the main method – we will return to them later):

```java
public class HelloWorld {
  public static void main (String argv []) {
    String myName = "John Hunt";
    if (myName.endsWith("Hunt")) {
      System.out.println("Hello " + myName);}
    else {
      System.out.println("Hello World");}
  }
}
```

In this example, I have reused the String class to represent the string "John Hunt" and to find a substring in it using the message endsWith(). Some of you may say that there is nothing unusual in this and that many languages have string-handling extensions. However, in this case, it is the string contained within myName which decides how to handle the endsWith message and thus whether it contains the substring "Hunt". That is, the data itself handles the processing of the string! What is printed to standard output thus depends on which object receives the message. These features illustrate the extent to which existing classes are reused: you cannot help but reuse existing code in Java; you do so by the very act of programming.

As well as possessing objects and classes, Java also possesses an inheritance mechanism. This feature separates Java from object-based languages, such as Ada, which does not possess inheritance. For example, in the simple program above, I reuse the class `Object` (the root of all classes in Java) and the class `HelloWorld` automatically inherits all the features of `Object`.

Inheritance is very important in Java. It promotes the reuse of classes and enables the explicit representation of abstract concepts (such as the class `Dictionary`) which can then be turned into concrete concepts (such as the class `HashTable`). It is also one of the primary reasons why Java is so successful as a rapid application development tool – you inherit much of what you want and only define the ways in which your application differs from what is already available.

6.2.1 Some Terminology

We now recap some of the terminology introduced in Part 1 of this book, explaining it with reference to Java.

In Java programs, actions or operations are performed by passing *messages* to and from objects. An object (the *sender* of the message) uses a message to request that a procedure (referred to in Java as a *method*) be performed by another object (the *receiver* of the message). Just as procedure calls can contain parameters, so can messages.

Java is a typed language; however, the typing relates to the class of an object (or the interface a class implements – we will return to this later) rather than its specific type. Thus, by saying that a method can take a parameter of a particular class, you actually mean that any instance of that class (or one of its subclasses) can be passed into that method.

6.2.2 The Message-Passing Mechanism

The Java message-passing mechanism is somewhat like a procedure call in a conventional language:

- The point of control moves to the receiver; the object sending a message is suspended until it receives a response.
- The receiver of a message is not determined when the code is created (at *compile time*); it is identified when the message is sent (at *run time*).

This *dynamic* (or *late*) binding mechanism is the feature which gives Java its polymorphic capabilities (see Chapter 1 for a discussion of polymorphism).

6.2.3 The Statement Terminator

In Java, the majority of statements terminate with a semi-colon (`;`):

```
System.out.println("Hello World");
```

Note that this is a statement terminator, not a statement separator.

6.3 Classes

A class is the basic building block in Java. Classes act as *templates* which are used to construct instances. Classes allow programmers to specify the *structure* of an object (i.e. its instance variables etc.) and the function of an object (i.e. its methods) separately from the object itself. This is important, as it would be extremely time-consuming (as well as inefficient) for programmers to define each object individually. Instead, they define classes and create *instances* of the classes.

6.3.1 Class Definitions

In Java, a class definition has the following format:

```
scopeOfClass class NameOfClass extends SuperClass {
   scope static type classVariable;
   scope type instanceVariable;
}
```

You need not remember this format precisely, as the meaning of the various parts of the class definition are explained later in the book. Indeed, the above is far from complete, but it illustrates the basic features. The following code is an example of a class definition:

```
public class Person extends Object {
   private int age = 0;
   public String name = "Bob";
}
```

This code defines a new class, Person, which is a subclass of the Object class (all classes extend Object by default; it is stated here only as an illustration). The new class possesses two *instance variables* called name and age. It has no class variable and no methods.

Notice that the age instance variable contains a value of type int (this is a basic data type), while the instance variable name possesses an object of the class String. Both variables are initialized: age to zero and name to the string "Bob".

Classes are not just used as templates. They have three further responsibilities: holding methods, providing facilities for inheritance and creating instances.

6.3.2 Classes and Messages

When a message is sent to an object, it is not the object which possesses the method but the class. This is for efficiency reasons: if each object possessed a copy of all the methods defined for the class then there would be a great deal of duplication. Instead, only the class possesses the method definitions. Thus, when an object receives a message, it searches its class for a method with the name in the message. If its own class does not possess a method with the appropriate name, it goes to the superclass and searches again. This search process continues up the class hierarchy until either an appropriate method is found or the class hierarchy terminates (with the class Object). If the hierarchy terminates, an error is raised.

If an appropriate method is found, then it executes *within the context of the object*, although the definition of the method resides in the class. Thus, different objects can execute the same method at the same time without conflict.

Do not confuse methods with instance variables. Each instance possesses its own copy of the instance variables (as each instance possesses its own state). Figure 6.1 illustrates this idea more clearly.

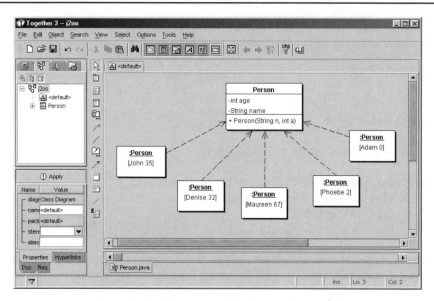

Fig. 6.1 Multiple instance variables but a single method.

6.3.3 Instances and Instance Variables

In Java, an *object* is an *instance* of a *class*. All instances of a class share the same responses to messages (methods), but they contain different data (i.e. they possess a different "state"). For example, the instances of class Point all respond in the same way to messages inquiring about the value of the *x*-coordinate, but they may provide different values.

The class definition consists of variable declarations and method definitions. The state of each instance is maintained in one or more instance variables (also known as fields).

Figure 6.1 contains five instances of the class Person. Each instance contains copies of the instance variable definitions for name and age, thus enabling them to have their own values for these instance variables. In contrast, each instance references the single definition for the method birthday, which is held by the class.

6.3.4 Classes and Inheritance

It is through classes that an object inherits facilities from other types of object. That is, a subclass inherits properties from its superclass. For example, the Person definition above is a subclass of Object. Therefore, Person inherits all the methods and instance variables that were defined in Object (except those that were overwritten in Person).

Subclasses are used to refine the behaviour and data structures of a superclass. It should be noted that Java supports single inheritance, while some object-oriented languages (most notably C++) support multiple inheritance. Multiple inheritance is where a subclass can inherit from more than one superclass. However, difficulties can arise when attempting to determine where methods are executed. Java introduces the concept of *interfaces* to overcome one of the most significant problems with single inheritance. However, the discussion of Java interfaces comes later in this chapter.

An Example of Inheritance

To illustrate how single inheritance works, consider Figure 6.2. There are three classes: Class1 is a subclass of Object, Class2 is a subclass of Class1 and Class3 is a subclass of Class2.

When an instance of Class3 is created, it contains all the instance variables defined in classes 1 to 3 and class Object. If any instance variable has the same name as an instance variable in a higher class, then the Class3 instance uses the instance variable definition from the nearest class. That is, Class3 definitions take priority over Class2 and Class2 definitions take priority over Class1, etc.

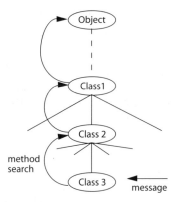

Fig. 6.2 Class inheritance in Java.

We can send an instance of Class3 a message requesting that a particular method is executed. Remember that methods are held by classes and not by instances. This means that the system first finds the class of the instance (in this case Class3) and searches it for the required method. If the method is found, then the search stops and the method is executed. However, if the method is not found, then the system searches the superclass for Class3, in this case Class2. This process is repeated until the method is found. Eventually, the search through the superclasses may reach the class Object (which is the root class in the Java system). If the required method is not found here, then the search process terminates and the Java Virtual Machine raises an exception stating that the message sent to the original instance is not understood.

This search process is repeated every time a message is sent to the instance of Class3. Thus, if the method which matches the original message sends a message to itself (i.e. the instance of Class3), then the search for that method starts again in Class3 (even if it was found in Class1).

The Yo-Yo Problem

The process described above can pose a problem for a programmer trying to follow the execution of the system by tracing methods and method execution. This problem is known as the Yo-Yo problem (see Figure 6.3) because, every time you encounter a message which is sent to "this" (the current object), you must start searching from your own class. This may result in jumping up and down the class hierarchy.

The problem occurs because you know that the execution search starts in the current instance's class, even if the method which sends the message is defined in a superclass of the current class. In Figure 6.3, the programmer starts the search in Class3, but finds the method definition in Class1; however this method sends a message to "this", which means that the

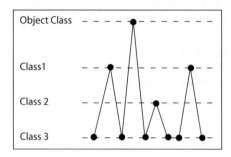

Fig. 6.3 The Yo-Yo problem.

programmer must restart the search for this method in Class3. This time, the method definition is found in the class Object, etc. Even with the browsing tools provided by today's IDEs,
this can still be a tedious and confusing process (particularly for those new to Java).

6.3.5 Instance Creation

A class creates an instance in response to a request, which is handled by a constructor. It may be
confusing, but classes can possess class-specific methods and class instance variables. These
are often referred to as class-side (or static) methods and variables, and they can respond to a
message as an instance would.

A programmer requests a new instance of a class using the following construct:

new ClassName();

Any parameters which need to be passed to the class can be placed between the parentheses.
They are then passed on to an appropriate constructor. Constructors possess the same name as
the class and are used to initialize a new instance of the class in an appropriate manner (you do
not need to know the details of the process). The whole of this process is referred to as
instantiation. An example of instantiating the class Person is presented below:

new Person("John Hunt", 37);

The class Person receives the message **new** which causes the JVM (Java Virtual Machine) to
generate a new instance of the class, with its own copy of the instance variables age and name
(see Figure 6.4). The name of the instance is "John Hunt" and the age is set to 37.

The issue of classes having methods, some of which are intended for an instance of the class
and some of which are intended for the class, is not as complicated as it may at first seem, not
least because the language syntax used with Java tends to keep the two *sides* of classes pretty
well distinct. To aid this, when developing, most programmers define the class side before

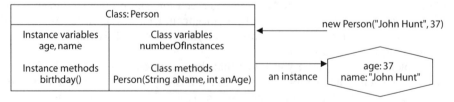

Fig. 6.4 Instance creation.

defining the instance side of the class. Some of the tools now available for Java also make this separation distinct and simplify the whole development process.

In an attempt to make it clearer, here are some definitions:

- *Instance variables* are defined in the class, but a copy is maintained in each instance, which has its own value.
- *Class (or static) variables* are defined in the class, with a single copy maintained in the class.
- *Instance methods* are defined in the class, with a single copy maintained in the class, but they are executed within the context of an object.
- *Class (or static) methods* are defined in the class, with a single copy maintained in the class, and executed within the context of the class.

The accessibility of these variables and methods depends on whether the programmer has made them public, private, default or protected. Some of these concepts are considered in greater detail later.

6.3.6 Constructors

A constructor is not a method but a special operator which is executed when a new instance of a class is created. Depending on the arguments passed to the class when the instance is generated, a different constructor can be called. For example, a class may need to have three fields initialized when it is instantiated. However, the programmer may allow the user of the class to provide one, two or three values. This can be done by defining constructors which take one, two or three parameters.

The syntax for a constructor is:

```
scopeofclass class classname {
    scopeofconstructor classname ( ... parameters ...) {
    ... statements ...
    }
}
```

By default, every class has a single default constructor with no parameters. However, as soon as you define a constructor, the default constructor is no longer available. Note that constructors, unlike methods, are not inherited.

6.3.7 Static Initialization Blocks

A class can also possess a static initialization block, which initializes the values to be held in class variables. This is useful if the initial values are not straightforward literals, but are related to some function (which may depend on other values held within the system).

```
class className {
    class variable definitions ....
    static {
        ... initialization statements ....
    }
}
```

Initialization blocks cannot call methods which may throw an exception back to the message sender (in this case, the initialization block) unless they explicitly handle the exception.

Static initialization blocks are only run when the class is loaded into the system. They are therefore only run once, and this is not under the control of the programmer.

The compiler cannot catch cycles between classes caused by static initialization blocks. Thus the result can be unpredictable and depends on the point at which the cycle occurred and the class variables which were set. For example, assume that class A's initialization block calls a class method in class B. Class B is then loaded into the system; however, its initialization block calls a class method in class A. At this point, class A's initialization block has not completed and the correct functioning of its class methods may depend on class variables which have yet to be initialized.

6.3.8 Finalize Methods

In Java, memory is managed automatically for you by the Java Virtual Machine (JVM). You do not therefore have to destroy objects or reclaim the memory they use. However, there is a Java facility which allows you to execute a special method (referred to as a finalize method) when the JVM reclaims (or collects as garbage) an object. These methods are typically used for application-specific housekeeping and are not intended as destructor methods (which you may have seen in other languages).

You define a finalize method in the following way:

```
protected void finalize() throws Throwable {
  super.finalize();
  ...
}
```

Notice that the method is **protected**. This special modifier keyword limits the visibility of the method (we look at this further in Chapter 10). The **throws** Throwable element is an exception which may be raised by the finalize method defined in the superclass (again, we return to exceptions later in the book). Finally, the first statement in the method is a call to:

```
super.finalize();
```

This is a request to run the finalize method inherited by this class before running this version of the finalize method. This allows the finalize method to be extended rather than replaced.

6.3.9 Supplied Classes

There are very many classes in any Java system. For example, JDK 1.0 provided 139 and releases 1.0.2 and 1.1 both added classes, bringing the numbers up to 211 and 503 respectively. With Java 2 and various releases of the SDK (1.2, 1.2.2, SDK 1.3 and 1.4) more and more classes were added. The number of classes now exceeds 2000 in the core SDK! However, you only need to become familiar with a very few of them. The remaining classes provide facilities that you often use without even realizing it.

6.4 Method Definitions

Methods provide a way of defining the behaviour of an object, i.e. what the object does. For example, a method may change the state of the object or it may retrieve some information. A method is the equivalent of a procedure in most other languages. A method can only be defined within the scope of an object. It has a specific structure:

```
access-control-modifier returnType methodName (args) {
    /* comments */
    local variable definitions
    statements
}
```

The *access control modifier* is one of the keywords which indicate the visibility of the method. The returnType is the type of the object returned, for example String or int. **methodName** represents the name of the method and args represents the types and names of the arguments. These arguments are accessible within the method.

6.4.1 The Comments Section

The /* comments */ section describes the operation performed by the method and any other useful information. Comments cannot be nested in Java, which can be awkward if you wish to comment out some code for later. For example, consider the following piece of Java:

```
/*
x = 12 * 4;
/* Now calculate y */
y = x * 23;
*/
```

The Java compiler reads this as a comment, followed by the code y = x * 23;, followed by the end of another comment. This causes an error. However, Java has two other types of comment. You can instruct the Java compiler to ignore everything until the end of the line by using the // indicator:

```
x = 12 * 4;
// Now calculate y
y = x * 23;
```

The final type of comment, the documentation comment, starts with /** and ends with */. Note the two asterisks at the beginning of this statement. They are picked up and processed by the documentation utility (javadoc), which generates HTML pages that can be viewed in a Web browser.

6.4.2 The Local Variables Section

In the local variable definition section, you define variables which are local to the method. These variables are typed and can appear anywhere in the method definition.

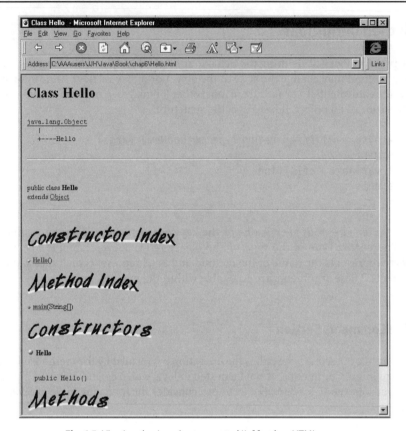

Fig. 6.5 Viewing the javadoc-generated Hello class HTML page.

```
birthday()
   int newAge = 0;
   ...
```

6.4.3 The Statements Section

The statements section represents any legal set of Java statements that implement the behaviour of the method.

One of the uses of methods is to provide an interface between an object's internal data and the outside world. Such a method, often termed an accessor method, retrieves the value of an instance variable and makes it available to other objects. For example, the class Person has two instance variables: age and name. The method getAge returns the age of an employee. Thus in response to the message getAge(), this method is executed and the value of the person's age is returned to the object sending the message.

In this situation the person's age is held explicitly. An equally valid internal representation for a Person would be to have an instance variable, dateOfBirth. The method getAge would need to calculate the age as the difference between the date of birth and the current date.

Notice that this would change the implementation of Person, but there would be no change as far as any other object in the system is concerned. This illustrates the encapsulation possible with Java (and other object-oriented programming languages).

6.4.4 The Return Operator

Once a method has executed, an answer can be returned to the sender of the message. The value returned (whether an object, a basic type or an instance of a subclass) must match the return type specified in the method definition. The return expression in Java is the last expression executed in a method, although it need not be the last expression in the method.

The Java keyword to return a value is **return** (just as in C):

```
if (x == y)
    return x;
else
    return y;
```

In this case, the value of x or y is returned, depending upon whether x and y are equal or not.

6.4.5 An Example Method

Let us examine a simple method definition in Java. We wish to define a procedure to take in a number, add 10 to it and return the result.

```
public int addTen (int aNumber) {
    int result;
    result = aNumber + 10;
    return result;
}
```

Although the format may be slightly different from code that you have been used to, it is relatively straightforward. If you have C or C++ experience you might think that it is exactly the same as what you have seen before. Be careful with that idea – things are not always what they seem!

Let us look at some of the constituent parts of the method definition. The method name is addTen. Notice that every method name is followed by () whether it takes parameters or not. If it does, then the parameters are placed within the parentheses. In this case, the method has one parameter, called aNumber, of the basic type int. Just as in any other language, the parameter variable is limited to the scope of this method. The method also defines a temporary variable, result, also of the basic type int and limited to the scope of this method.

Variable names are identifiers that contain only letters and numbers and must start with a letter (the underscore, _, and the dollar sign, $, count as letters). Some examples are:

```
anObject    MyCar    totalNumber    $total
```

A capitalization convention is used consistently throughout Java, and most Java programmers adhere to this standard:

- *Private variables and methods* (i.e. instance or temporary variables and almost all methods) start with a lower-case letter.
- *Shared variables* (e.g. class-side variables) start with an upper-case letter.
- *Shared constants* are all in upper case (e.g. TT_EOF).
- *Constructors and classes* always start with an upper-case letter.

Another convention is that if a variable or method name combines two or more words, then you should capitalize the first letter of each word, from the second word onwards, e.g. displayTotalPay, returnStudentName.

6.5 Interface Definitions

The Java interface construct is essentially a skeleton which specifies the protocol that a class must provide if it implements that interface. That is, it indicates the methods which must be available from any class which implements that interface. The interface itself does not define any functionality. The format for an interface is:

```
access-modifier interface interface-name {
    static variable definitions
    method headers ...
}
```

The following interface specifies that any class implementing the OrganizerIO interface must provide add, get and remove methods. In addition it specifies that the get method should return a string and that the remove method should return a boolean. The interface also specifies the parameters for the methods:

```
public interface OrganizerIO {
    public abstract void add(String string, Date date);
    public abstract String get(Date date);
    public abstract boolean remove(String string);
}
```

It is not necessary to define these methods as being abstract because they are abstract by default. Notice that you cannot define a class-side (static) method in an interface, as they cannot be abstract.

It may appear at this point that an interface is the same as an abstract class; however, they differ in a number of ways:

- An interface cannot, by definition, provide any functionality. An abstract class can provide default functionality.
- Any class can implement one (or more) interfaces. A class can inherit from only one parent class.
- Interfaces are a compile-time feature; they influence the static analysis of the program being compiled. Abstract classes involve run-time issues associated with method selection, execution etc.
- An abstract class can inherit from an existing class. An interface abstracts a class from which it inherits.
- An interface can extend one or more interfaces by adding new protocols. A class cannot extend an interface (it can only implement it, or "fill it out").

In addition to acting as a contract with a class which specifies what that class (and its subclasses) must provide, an interface can also be used as a type specifier. This means that you can specify an interface and then use it to specify the type of object which a variable can hold. Thus, you can define an interface which is implemented by classes in completely different hierarchies. A method parameter, for example, can take instances of both those class hierarchies and only instances of those class hierarchies:

```
public class Bozo {
  ...
  public void add (OrganizerIO temp) {
    ...
  }
}
```

This means that the method add can take an instance of any class which implements the OrganizerIO interface.

Interfaces can also inherit from other interfaces. Thus, for example, in the following the interface Records inherits from Workers, Employers and Clonable:

```
public interface Records extends Workers, Employers, Clonable {
  ...
}
```

As interfaces only provide specifications for method signatures, the issues associated with multiple inheritance are removed. That is, as no behaviour is inherited, the end result in the interface Record is the union of all the method signatures defined in that interface and those from which it inherits. If a method signature is present in more than one interface this does not matter, as only one implementation (in the implementing class) can meet the requirement to implement that method in all the interfaces.

Chapter **7**

Java Constructs

7.1 Introduction

This chapter presents more of the Java language. It considers the representation and use of numbers, strings and characters. It also discusses assignments, literals and variables. Finally, it considers messages, message types and their precedence.

7.2 Numbers and Numeric Operators

7.2.1 Numeric Values

Numbers in Java can be examples of basic types, such as `int`, or objects in their own right (e.g. instances of the class `Integer`). The availability of both approaches is necessary because some data structure objects can only hold objects. Thus they can only hold a basic type (such as 3) when it is wrapped within an integer object:

```
Integer x = new Integer(3);
```

Classes such as `Integer` can be referred to as wrappers, as this is what they do - they wrap an object around the `int` value.

A number of classes provide for the types of numbers normally used, for example `Integer`, `Float`, `Double` and `Long`. These are all considered in greater detail later in the book. For the moment, we consider what numbers look like in Java. Note that the class versions *always* start with a capital letter.

Just as in most programming languages, a numeric value in Java is a series of numbers which may or may not have a preceding sign and may contain a decimal point:

```
25    -10    1996    12.45    0.13451345    -3.14
```

Unusually for a programming language, Java explicitly specifies the number of bytes which must be used for data types such as `short`, `int`, `long`, `float` and `double` (Table 7.1).

The Java language designers' purpose in specifying the number of bytes to use for each data type was to enhance the portability of Java implementations. In C, the number of bytes used for `int` and `long` is at the discretion of the compiler writers. The only constraint placed upon them is that `int` cannot be bigger than long. This means that a program that compiles successfully on one machine may prove unreliable and have errors when recompiled on another machine. This

Table 7.1 Standard numbers of bytes for numeric data types.

Type	Bytes	Stores
byte	1	integers
short	2	integers
int	4	integers
long	8	integers
float	4	floating point numbers
double	8	floating point numbers

can make porting a program from one system to another extremely frustrating (ask anyone who has ever had to port a sizeable C system!).

7.2.2 Arithmetic Operators

In general, the arithmetic operators available in Java are the same as in any other language. There are also comparison functions and truncation functions (see Table 7.2). Numbers can also be represented by objects which are instances of classes such as Integer, Float etc. These classes are all subclasses of the class Number and provide different facilities. However, some of the methods are fairly common (Table 7.3).

Table 7.2 Basic numeric operators.

+	addition	==	equality
-	subtraction	<	less than
*	multiplication	>	greater than
/	division	!=	inequality
%	remainder	<=	less than or equal to

Table 7.3 Methods provided by numeric classes.

equals()	equality
doubleValue()	conversion
toHexString()	conversion
valueOf(aString)	conversion (class-side)
toBinaryString()	conversion
toOctalString()	conversion

A number of the numeric classes also provide class variables, such as MAX_VALUE and MIN_VALUE (i.e. in Integer, Long, Double, Float etc.), and numbers such as NEGATIVE_INFINITY and POSITIVE_INFINITY (i.e. in Double and Float).

In addition, Java provides a class called Math. This class, which is a subclass of Object, provides the usual range of mathematical operations (see Table 7.4). All these methods are class (or static) methods available from the class Math. You do not have to create an instance of the class to use them.

It is also interesting to notice that, to enhance the portability of Java, the language designers have stated that the definitions of many of the numeric methods must produce the same results as a set of published algorithms.

Table 7.4 Mathematical functions provided by `Math`.

max	maximum		min	minimum
ceil	round up		floor	round down
round	round to nearest		sqrt	square root
abs	absolute value		exp	exponential
pow	raises one number to the power of the other		random	random number generator

7.3 Characters and Strings

7.3.1 Characters

Just like numbers, characters in Java can be either basic types (such as `char`) or wrapped within the `Character` class:

```
Character aCharObject = new Character('J');
```

We consider this class and the operations it provides in greater detail later. For the moment, we consider what characters look like. In Java, a single character is defined by surrounding it with single quotes:

```
'J' 'a' '@' '1' '$'
```

7.3.2 Strings

Strings in Java are direct subclasses of the `Object` class. As such, they are made up of individual elements, similar to strings in C. However, this is the only similarity between strings in C and Java. A Java string is not terminated by a null character and should not be treated as an array of characters. It should be treated as an object which responds to an appropriate range of messages (e.g. for manipulating or extracting substrings; Table 7.5).

A string is defined by one or more characters placed between double quotes (rather than the single quotes used for characters):

```
"John Hunt"    "Tuesday"    "dog"
```

Table 7.5 Methods provided by the class `String`.

`charAt(int index)`	returns the character at position index
`compareTo (String aString)`	compares two strings lexicographically
`equals(String aString)`	compares two strings
`equalsIgnoreCase (String aString)`	compares two strings, ignoring the case of the characters
`indexOf (char aCharacter)`	returns the first index of the character in the receiving string
`substring (int start, int stop)`	creates substring from start to stop (in the receiving string)
`toLowerCase()`	returns the receiver in lower case letters
`toUpperCase()`	returns the receiver in upper case letters

You cannot create a string by generating an array of characters. This can be the source of much confusion and frustration when an apparently correct piece of code does not work. A string containing a single character is not equivalent to that single character:

```
'a' != "a"
```

The string "a" and the character 'a' are, at best, instances of different classes and, at worst, one may be an instance and one a basic type. The fact that the string contains only one character is just a coincidence.

To denote that a variable should take an instance of String, define it as being of type String:

```
String aVariable;
aVariable = "John";
```

7.4 Assignments

A variable name can refer to different objects at different times. You can make *assignments* to a variable name, using the = operator. It is often read as "becomes equal to" (even though it is not preceded by a colon as in languages such as Ada).

Some examples of assignment statements follow:

```
currentEmployeeIndex = 1;
newIndex = oldIndex;
myName = "John Hunt";
```

Like all Java operators, the assignment operator returns a value. The result of an assignment is the value of that assignment (thus the value of the expression x = 2 + 2; is 4). This means that several assignments can be made in the same statement:

```
nextObject = newObject = oldObject;
```

The above example also illustrates a feature of Java style – variable names that indicate their contents. This technique is often used where a more meaningful name (such as currentEmployeeIndex) is not available (temp might be used in other languages).

Although variables in Java are strongly typed, this typing is perhaps not as strong as in languages such as Pascal and Ada. You can state that a variable is of type Object. As Object is a class, such a variable can possess instances of the class Object or *one of its subclasses*! This means that a variable which holds a string may then be assigned a character or a vector (a type of data structure). This is quite legitimate:

```
Object temp;
temp = "John";
temp = new Character('a');
temp = new Vector();
```

An important point to note is that assignment is by reference when dealing with objects. This means that, in the following example, nextObject, newObject and oldObject all refer to the *same* object (as illustrated in Figure 7.1):

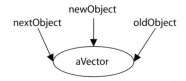

Fig. 7.1 The result of a multiple assignment.

```
newObject = oldObject = new Vector();
nextObject = newObject;
```

As all three variables point to an instance of a container class (in this case Vector), if an update is made to the contents of any one of the variables, it is made for all three!

7.5 Variables

7.5.1 Temporary Variables

These variables exist only for the duration of some activity (e.g. the execution of a method). They can be defined anywhere within a method (as long as they are defined before they are used). The definition takes the form of the type (or class) of the variable and the variable name followed by any initialization required:

```
char aChar;
char anotherChar = 'a';
Object anObject;
String myName = "John Hunt";
```

The scope of a temporary variable depends on the context in which it is defined. For example, variables declared at the top level of a method, are in scope from the point at which they are declared. However, block variables only have scope for the block within which they are defined (including nested blocks). Loop variables only have scope for the loop within which they are defined. Thus the scope of each of the following variables is different:

```
public int add (int a, int b) {          
    int result = 0;                       r
    for (int i = 0; i < 5, i++) {        ir
        if (a < i) {                     ir
            int total = b;              tir
            total = total + c * i;      tir
        }                                ir
    }                                    r
}
```

In the right-hand column, r indicates that result is in scope, i indicates the scope of the loop variable and t indicates the scope of the inner block variable, total.

7.5.2 Pseudo Variables

A pseudo variable is a special variable whose value is changed by the system, but which cannot be changed by the programmer. The value of a pseudo variable is determined by the current context and can be referenced within a method.

this is a pseudo variable which refers to the receiver of a message itself. The search for the corresponding method starts in the class of the receiver. To ensure that your source code does not become cluttered, Java assumes you mean this object if you just issue a reference to a method. The following statements have the same effect:

```
this.myName();
myName();
```

You can use this to pass a reference to the current object to another object:

```
otherObject.addLink(this);
```

super also refers to the message receiver, but the method search starts in the superclass of the receiver. It is often used if the functionality of a method is to be extended rather than overwritten:

```
public class StrangeExample {
  public void test() {
    System.out.println("In test");
  }
}

public class ExtendedStrangeExample extends StrangeExample {
  public static void main (String argv []) {
    ExtendedStrangeExample s;
  s = newExtendedStrangeExample();
    s.test();
  }

  public void test() {
    System.out.println("Hi");
    super.test();
    System.out.println("John");
  }
}
```

The result of compiling and running these two classes is:

```
Hi
In test
John
```

Do not worry about the syntax or the meaning of the above example too much at the moment, just make sure you get the idea of things. If you decide to type in the above example, you must put each class in a separate file as they are both public.

7.5.3 Variable Scope

Temporary variables are only available within the method in which they are defined. However, both class variables and instance variables are in scope (or are visible) at a number of levels. An instance variable can be defined to be visible (available) outside the class or the package, only within the package, within subclasses or only within the current class. The scope is specified by modifiers which precede the variable definition, for example `public` below:

```
public String myName = "John Hunt";
```

7.5.4 Special Values – `True`, `False` and `Null`

The **null** value is an object that represents nothing or no object. It is not of any type; nor it is an instance of any class (including `Object`). It should not be confused with the null pointer in languages such as C. It really does means *nothing* or *no value*.

The other two special values are boolean literals, `true` and `false`, representing truth and falsehood. You can wrap them in an instance of class `Boolean`, which provides a range of operations including the following methods:

- `equals(Object object)`
- `booleanValue()`
- `toString`

7.6 Messages and Message Selectors

7.6.1 Invoking Methods

Invoking a method is often referred to as *sending a message* to the object that owns the method. The expression which invokes a method is composed of a receiving object (the receiver), the method name and zero or more parameters. The combination of method name and parameters is often called the message and it indicates, to the class of the receiving object, which method to execute. Figure 7.2 illustrates the main components of a message expression.

The value of an expression is determined by the definition of the method it invokes. Some methods are defined as returning no value (e.g. `void`) while others may return a basic type or object. In the following code, the result returned by the method `marries` is saved into the variable `newStatus`:

```
newStatus = thisPerson.marries(thatPerson);
```

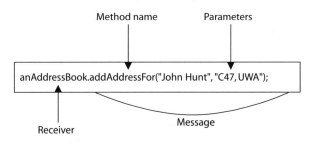

Fig. 7.2 The components of a message expression.

7.6.2 Precedence

The rules governing precedence in Java are similar to those in other languages. Precedence refers to the order in which operators are evaluated in an expression. Many languages, such as C, explicitly specify the order of evaluation of expressions such as the following:

```
2 + 5 * 3 - 4 / 2;
```

Java is no exception. The rules regarding precedence are summarized in Table 7.6. The above expression would be evaluated as:

```
(2 + (5 * 3)) - (4 / 2);
```

Notice that if operators with the same precedence are encountered they are evaluated strictly from left to right.

Table 7.6 Operator precedence.

Operation	Meaning	Precedence
++x --x	prefix increment/decrement	16
x++ x--	postfix increment/decrement	15
- ! ~	arithmetic negation/logical not/flip	14
(typename)	cast (type conversion)	13
* / %	multiplication/division/remainder	12
+ -	addition/subtraction	11
<< >> >>>	left and right bitwise operators	10
< > <= >=	relational operators	9
== !=	equality operators	8
&	bitwise and	7
^	bitwise exclusive or	6
|	bitwise or	5
&&	conditional and	4
||	conditional or	3
? :	conditional operators	2
=	assignment operator	1

7.7 Summary

In this chapter and the previous, you have learnt about classes in Java, how they are defined, how instance variables are specified and how methods are constructed. You have also encountered many of the basic Java language structures.

7.8 Further Reading

A good book to have a look at now, if you have not already done so, is Winston and Narasimhan (2001). It does not teach you very much about object orientation but it has some very nice (and simple) Java examples. It also introduces the Java language in easy stages.

Chapter **8**

An Example Java Class

8.1 Introduction

You should now be ready to write some Java code, so this chapter takes you through a worked example. It is a very simple example, in which you create a new class, define some instance variables and write a couple of methods. Therefore, although it is very simple it has all the elements of much more complex classes.

8.2 Defining a Class

The Person class is to provide a very basic set of features. It must record a person's name and their age. It must also allow the person to have a birthday (and thus increment their age).

The first thing you need to do is define a Java class in a file with the same name as the class. Note that this is important: an error is generated if the class name and the file name are not the same. Java is case-sensitive (even if your host operating system is not), so person and Person are not the same.

8.2.1 Creating the Class

1. Create an empty file called Person.java using your favourite editor. If you have a tool such as JBuilder or Forté for Java, you can use it instead (indeed, it will probably make your life much easier).
2. In the file, define a new class by typing in the following Java code:

    ```
    public class Person {
      private int age = 0;
      private String name = "";
    }
    ```

    The above code defines the class Person (by default, it is a subclass of Object) and gives it two instance variables, name and age, which are only accessible from within the class.
3. Compile the class by issuing the following command in a command window, DOS prompt or XTerm etc.:

    ```
    > javac Person.java
    ```

8.2.2 Defining a Class Comment

Normally I would also define a comment to go with this class to explain what it is intended to do. I would use the /** ... */ format of comment so that the javadoc utility can pick it up. Figure 8.1 illustrates the result of adding this comment using a Java-aware editor.

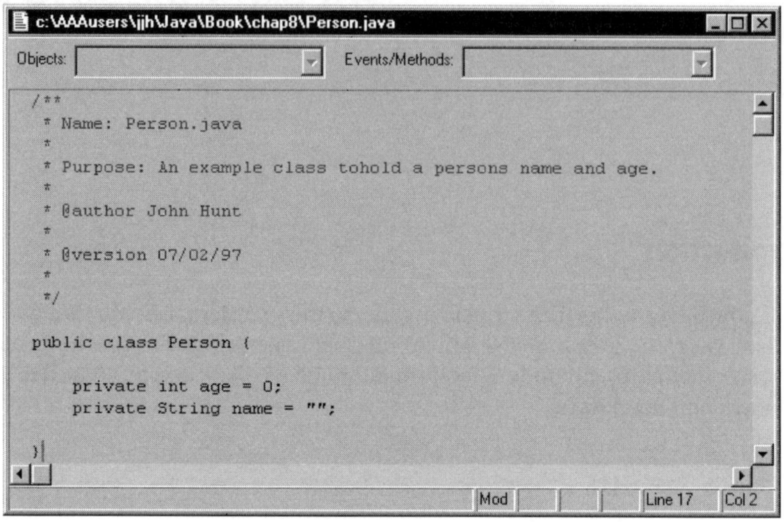

Fig. 8.1 The class Person in a Visual Café editor.

8.3 Defining a Method

We first define the main method. We then define a constructor which initializes the instance variables in the appropriate manner.

8.3.1 The main Method

Every Java application must have at least one main method where the execution begins. This method creates a new instance of the class and sends it the message birthday:

```
public static void main (String args []) {
   Person p = new Person();
   p.birthday();
}
```

Note that this method *must* be defined within the scope of the class! This is essentially the same as in Chapter 6, so we do not re-analyze it.

8.3.2   The Constructor

As was explained in Chapter 6, a constructor allows parameters to be passed into a class when a new instance is created. However, we are keeping things simple here and relying on the default constructor (which is called with no parameters). The definition of this constructor is presented below:

```
public Person () {
   System.out.println("In Person constructor");
   age = 33;
   name = "John Hunt";
}
```

This constructor prints out a message to the console and then initializes age (as the integer 33) and name (the string "John Hunt"). Once this method has executed, control returns to the point at which the instance was created (in our case, to the main method).

At this point your class definition should resemble that in Figure 8.2. Note that the instance variable definitions do not need to be at the start of the class.

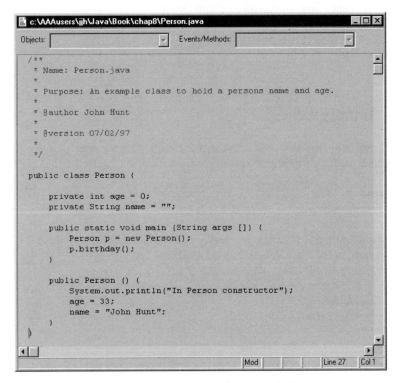

Fig. 8.2 The Person class with some methods.

8.3.3 The Accessor Methods

Now we can define some methods for accessing the instance variables. These are sometimes called *getter* methods. The two methods to be defined are getAge and getName.

The getAge method is defined as a public method (i.e. it is available outside the class) that returns the value of the instance variable age (which is specifically of type int):

```
public int getAge () {
   return age;
}
```

The getName method has exactly the same format, except that it returns an instance of String:

```java
public String getName () {
    return name;
}
```

8.3.4 The Updater Method

We are now going to define a method which can update the value of the age instance variable. Such a method is known as an updater or *setter* method. This method is again public but it does not return any value and is said to return void. It takes one parameter (of type int) called newAge. Note the way that the method names and the variable names start with a lower-case letter, but subsequent words start with a capital letter.

```java
public void setAge (int newAge) {
    age = newAge;
}
```

8.3.5 The birthday Method

Having defined the methods that access the private instance variables (notice that nothing outside the class can modify these variables), we now define a method called birthday:

```java
public void birthday () {
    int oldAge, newAge;
    oldAge = getAge();
    System.out.println("Happy birthday " + getName());
    System.out.print("You were " + oldAge);
    System.out.print(" but now you are ");
    newAge = oldAge + 1;
    setAge(newAge);
    System.out.println(age);
}
```

This last method prints out a birthday greeting and increments the person's age. It uses the other methods to change the current value of the instance variable age and to print a meaningful message to the user. This type of programming is known as variable-free programming and is considered good style. For the moment just accept that system.out.println causes output to be generated in the command window.

8.4 Creating an Instance

You should now execute the Java application you have created. You do this by running the byte code compiled from the file Person.java on the virtual machine. The result of compiling and running this application in Windows is presented in Figure 8.3.

Executing the byte code on the virtual machine causes an instance of Person to be created, the constructor to be called automatically and the message birthday to be sent to the new instance.

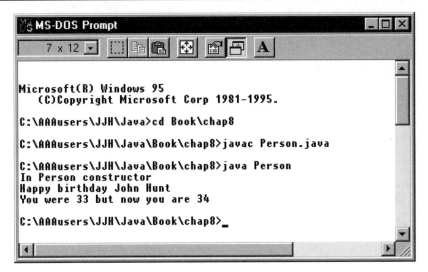

Fig. 8.3 Running the Person application.

Once you have done this and are happy with what is happening, try to change the method definitions or add a new instance variable called address and define the appropriate methods for it. The complete Person class definition is presented below.

```java
public class Person {
  private int age = 0;
  private String name = "";
  public static void main (String args []) {
    Person p = new Person();
    p.birthday();
  }
  public Person () {
    System.out.println("In Person constructor");
    age = 33;
    name = "John Hunt";
  }
  public int getAge () {
    return age;
  }
  public void setAge (int newAge) {
    age = newAge;
  }
  public String getName () {
    return name;
  }
  public void birthday () {
    int oldAge, newAge;
    oldAge = getAge();
    System.out.println("Happy birthday " + getName());
    System.out.print("You were " + oldAge);
```

```
        System.out.print(" but now you are ");
        newAge = oldAge + 1;
        setAge(newAge);
        System.out.println(age);
    }
}
```

Part **3**
Java and Object Orientation

Chapter *9*

Classes, Inheritance and Abstraction

9.1 Introduction

In this chapter, we consider some of the language features you saw in the last section of the book from an object-oriented point of view. This chapter discusses how you should use classes and what you should, and should not, use them for. It considers how you should use inheritance, abstraction and subclasses and highlights the use of constructors. It also tries to explain the use of (the oft misunderstood) main method.

9.2 Classes Revisited

The following is an incomplete example which illustrates many of the features found in class definitions. It is presented as a reminder without further explanation.

```
public class Person {
  // Define a class variable
  public static int numberCreated = 0;
  // Define an instance variable
  public String name = " ";

  // Define a class method
  public static void incrementNumberCreated() {
    numberCreated = numberCreated + 1;
  }

  // Define an instance method
  public void setName(String aName) {
    name = aName;
  }
  ...
}
```

Notice that the keyword **static** illustrates that the following element is on the class side (as opposed to the instance side).

9.2.1 What Are Classes For?

In some object-oriented languages, classes are merely templates used to construct objects (or instances). In these languages, the class definition specifies the structure of the object and a separate mechanism is often used to create the object using this template.

In some other languages (for example Smalltalk-80), classes are objects in their own right; this means that they can not only create objects, they can also hold data, receive messages and execute methods just like any other object. Such object-oriented systems tend to have what is called a rich meta-model built upon the use of metaclasses. A metaclass is a special class whose sole instance is a class.

An object is an instance of something, so if a class is an object, it must be an instance of something. In the meta-model, a class is an instance of a metaclass. It should be noted that the metaclass concept is probably one of the most confusing parts of the whole of Smalltalk. This is partly due to the names used, but also because almost all of it is hidden from the developer. The developer is therefore only vaguely aware of it (if at all) during development.

Java adopts a position halfway between the two camps. That is, it has a weak meta-model in which classes can respond to messages and to requests for class variable values. However, Java does not provide the full power of the Smalltalk meta-model, since that is confusing and most developers never need to use it. This results in a simpler, cleaner and easier to understand model.

Thus, in Java, classes are not objects (in the true sense of the word), but are unique within a program and can:

- create instances
- be inherited by subclasses (and can inherit from existing classes)
- implement interfaces
- have class methods
- have class variables
- define instance methods
- define instance variables
- be sent messages

Objects (or instances), on the other hand, can:

- be created from a class
- have instance variables
- be sent messages
- execute instance methods
- have many copies in the system (all with their own data)

Thus a class is more than just a template for an object; it can also hold data and provide class specific behaviour. However, if you are confused by most of the above, remember: a class's two primary roles are to define instances and to allow inheritance.

9.2.2 Class-Side Methods

It may at first seem unclear what should normally go in an instance method as opposed to what should go in a class (or static) method when defining a new class. After all, they are both defined in the class. However, it is important to remember that one defines the behaviour of the instance and the other the behaviour of the class (it is a pity that these methods are both designated by the keyword static, as it is not obvious to the new programmer what static actually means). Class-side methods should only perform one of the following roles:

- *Instance creation* This role is very important as it is how you can use a class as the root of an application. It is common to see main methods which do nothing other than create a new instance of the class. For example:

```
public class Account {
   double balance = 0.0;

   public static void main (String args []) {
      Account account = new Account();
   }

   ... remainder of class definition ...
```

  If you define such a method, but the class is not the root of the application, it is ignored. This makes it a very useful way of providing a test harness for a given class.
- *Answering inquiries about the class* This role can provide generally useful objects, frequently derived from class variables. For example, they may return the number of instances of this class that have been created.
- *Instance management* In this role, class-side methods control the number of instances created. For example, a class only allows a single instance to be created. Instance management methods may also be used to access an instance (e.g. randomly or in a given state).
- *Documentation* Methods for documentation can be very useful.
- *Examples* Occasionally, class methods are used to provide helpful examples which explain the operation of a class. This is good practice.
- *Testing* Class-side methods can be used to support the testing of an instance of a class. You can use them to create an instance, perform an operation and compare the result with a known value. If the values are different, the method can report an error. This is a very useful way of providing regression tests.
- *Support for one of the above roles*

Any other tasks should be performed by an instance method.

9.2.3 A Class or an Instance

In some situations, you may only need to create a single instance of a class and reference it wherever it is required. A continuing debate ponders whether it is worth creating such an instance or whether it is better to define the required behaviour in class methods and reference the class (which, after all, can be sent messages and have its class variables accessed). Invariably the answer to this is no, for the following reasons:

- Such an approach breaks the object-oriented model. Although this approach has been adopted by numerous Java authors, it is not object-oriented and suggests that the programmer has not fully embraced the object-oriented model.
- The creation of an instance has a very low overhead. This is a key feature in Java and it has received extensive attention.
- You may require more than one instance at some time in the future. If you implement all the code on the class side, you will have to move the methods to the instance side of the class.

- You may be tempted to treat the class as a global reference. This suggests that the implementation has been poorly thought out. It is unfortunate that a number of facilities provided by the Java system classes seem to support this use of a class as a global reference. For example, you can convert a numeric string into an integer using the parseInt class-side method of the class Integer:

```
Integer.parseInt("100");
```

This is essentially a way of making the parseInt method globally available. It is better to define the method on the class String and call it something like toInteger. If you do so, you can send any string a message requesting that it convert itself into an integer, rather than sending the Integer class such a request.

9.3 Inheritance in Classes

Inheritance is achieved in Java using the extends keyword (as was discussed in Chapter 6). Java is a single inheritance system, so a Java class can only inherit from a single class, which can, of course, implement zero or more interfaces. The following class definition builds on the class Person presented earlier:

```java
public class Student extends Person {
  private String subject = "Computer Science";
  public String getSubject() {
    return subject;
  }
}
```

This class extends the class Person by adding a new instance variable, subject, and a method to access it.

9.3.1 The Role of a Subclass

A subclass modifies the behaviour of its parent class. This modification should refine the class in one or more of these ways:

- Changes to the external protocol: the set of messages to which instances of the class respond.
- Changes in the implementation of the methods: the way in which the messages are handled.
- Additional behaviour which references inherited behaviour.

If a subclass does not provide one or more of the above, then it is incorrectly placed. For example, if a subclass implements a set of new methods, but does not refer to the instance variables or methods of the parent class, then the class is not really a subclass of the parent (it does not extend it).

For example, consider the class hierarchy illustrated in Figure 9.1. A generic (probably abstract) root class has been defined. This class defines a Conveyance which has doors and fuel (both with default values) and a method, startUp, that starts the engine of the conveyance.

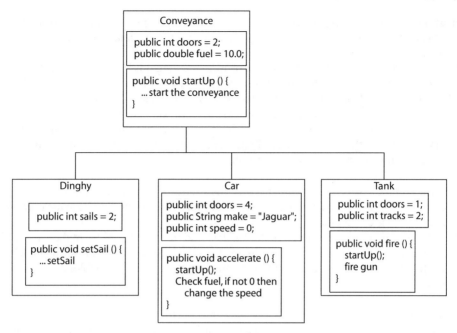

Fig. 9.1 Subclasses.

Three subclasses of Conveyance have also been defined: Dinghy, Car and Tank. Two of these subclasses are appropriate, but one should probably not inherit from Conveyance. We shall consider each in turn to determine their suitability.

The class Tank overrides the number of doors inherited, uses the startUp method within the method fire, and provides a new instance variable. It therefore matches all three of our criteria.

Similarly, the class Car overrides the number of doors and uses the method startUp. It also uses the instance variable fuel within a new method accelerate. It also, therefore, matches our criteria.

The class Dinghy defines a new instance variable sails and a new method setSail. As such, it does not use any of the features inherited from Conveyance. However, we might say that it has extended Conveyance by providing this instance variable and method. We must then consider the features provided by Conveyance. We can ask ourselves whether they make sense within the context of Dinghy. If we assume that a dinghy is a small sail-powered boat, with no cabin and no engine, then nothing inherited from Conveyance is useful. In this case, it is likely that Conveyance is misnamed, as it defines some sort of a motor vehicle, and the Dinghy class should not have extended it.

The exceptions to this rule are subclasses of Object. This is because Object is the root class of all classes in Java. As you must create a new class by subclassing it from an existing class, you can subclass from Object when there is no other appropriate class.

9.3.2 Capabilities of Classes

A subclass or class should accomplish one specific purpose; it should capture only one idea. If more than one idea is encapsulated in a class, you may reduce the chances for reuse, as well as contravene the laws of encapsulation in object-oriented systems. For example, you may have merged two concepts together so that one can directly access the data of another. This is rarely desirable.

Breaking a class down costs little but may produce major gains in reusability and flexibility. If you find that, when you try to separate one class into two or more classes, some of the code needs to be duplicated for each class, then the use of abstract classes can be very helpful. That is, you can place the common code into an abstract superclass to avoid unnecessary duplication.

The following guidelines may help you to decide whether to split the class with which you are working. Look at the comment describing the class (if there is no class comment, this is a bad sign in itself). Consider the following points:

- Is the comment short and clear? If not, is this a reflection on the class? Consider how the comment can be broken down into a series of short clear comments. Base the new classes around those comments.
- If the comment is short and clear, do the class and instance variables make sense within the context of the comment? If they do not, then the class needs to be re-evaluated. It may be that the comment is inappropriate, or the class and instance variables are inappropriate.

Look at the instance variable references (i.e. look at where the instance variable access methods are used). Is their use in line with the class comment? If not, then you should take appropriate action.

9.3.3   Restricting a Subclass

You can restrict the ability of a subclass to change what it inherits from its superclass. Indeed, you can also stop subclasses being created from a class. This is done using the keyword `final`. This keyword has different meanings depending on where it is used:

```
public final class LaserPrinter extends Printer {
```

No element of this class can be extended, so no subclass of `LaserPrinter` can be created.

```
public final int maximumMemory = 128;
```

The instance variable `maximumMemory` cannot have its value changed. It is a bit like specifying that a variable is a constant. You can also apply the keyword `final` to class variables.

```
public final void handshake() {
```

This states that this method cannot be overridden in a subclass. That is, a subclass cannot redefine `handshake()`; it must use the one that it inherits. You can also specify class methods as `final`.

Restricting the ability to overwrite part of, or all of, a class is a very useful feature. It is particularly important where the correct behaviour of the class and its subclasses relies on the correct functioning of particular methods, or the appropriate value of a variable, etc. A class is normally only specified as `final` when it does not make sense to create a subclass of it. These situations need to be analyzed carefully to ensure that no unexpected scenarios are likely to occur.

9.4 Abstract Classes

An abstract class is a class from which you cannot create an object. It is missing one or more elements required to create a fully functioning instance. In contrast, a non-abstract (or concrete) class leaves nothing undefined and can be used to create a working instance. You may wonder what use an abstract class is. The answer is that you can group together elements which are to be shared among a number of classes without providing a complete implementation. In addition, you can force subclasses to provide specific methods ensuring that implementers of a subclass at least supply appropriately named methods. You should therefore use abstract classes when:

- You wish to specify data or behaviour common to a set of classes, but which are insufficient for a single instance.
- You wish to force subclasses to provide specific behaviour.

In many cases, the two situations go together. Typically, the aspects of the class to be defined as abstract are specific to each class, while what has been implemented is common to all classes. For example, consider the following class (based loosely on the Conveyance class presented above):

```
public abstract class Conveyance {
  private int doors = 2;
  private double fuel = 5.0;
  private boolean running = false;
  public void startUp() {
    running = true;
    consumeFuel();
    while (fuel > 0) {
      consumeFuel();
    }
  }
  abstract void consumeFuel();
}
```

This abstract class definition means that you cannot create an instance of Conveyance. Within the definition of Conveyance, we can see that the startUp method is defined, but the method consumeFuel is specified as abstract and no method body is provided. Any class which has one or more abstract methods is necessarily abstract (and must therefore have the keywords abstract class). However, a class can be abstract without specifying any abstract methods.

Any subclass of Conveyance must implement the consumeFuel method if instances are to be created from it. Each subclass can define how much fuel is consumed in a different manner. The following PetrolCar class provides a concrete class which builds on Conveyance:

```
public class PetrolCar extends Conveyance {
  public static void main (String args []) {
    PetrolCar p = new PetrolCar();
    p.startUp();
  }
  public void consumeFuel () {
    fuel = fuel - 1.0;
    System.out.println(fuel);
```

```
    }
  }
```

The result of executing this class is illustrated below:

```
C:>java PetrolCar
4.0
3.0
2.0
1.0
0.0
```

We can also define a DieselCar class in which the fuel consumption rate is lower, for example:

```java
public class DieselCar extends Conveyance {
  public static void main (String args []) {
    DieselCar d = new DieselCar();
    d.startUp();
  }
  public void consumeFuel () {
    fuel = fuel - 0.5;
    System.out.println(fuel);
  }
}
```

However, if all you wish to do is to specify that a set of methods should be defined by a subclass, then you may well be better off defining an interface. Interfaces never contain method bodies, nor do they declare instance variables; thus it is clearer that all you intend to do is to specify a particular protocol to be defined by those classes which implement the interface (see Chapter 6).

9.5 Constructors and Their Use

Constructors should only be used to initialize an instance of a class in an appropriate manner and you should attempt to place all the initialization code in as few constructors as possible. For example, if there is only one initialization process, but different numbers or combinations of parameters can be passed to the constructors, then you should define a single root constructor. The root constructor should represent the constructor with the most parameters. You should then define convenience constructors with fewer parameters. These constructors call the root constructor using default values for the parameters which are not provided. For example:

```java
public class Account {
  private double balance = 0.0;
  private String name = "";

  Account(double amount, String person) {
    balance = amount;
    name = person;
  }
```

```
Account (String person) {
  this(0.0, person);
}

Account () {
  this(0.0, "man with no name");
}
}
```

In this example, the three constructors each allow different amounts of information to be provided. However, the actual initialization only takes place within one method. Thus any changes to the way in which the initialization process is performed are localized to this one method.

An annoying feature of Java is that subclasses of Account do **not** inherit these constructors and must define their own.

9.6 The main Method

The main method should not be used to define the application program. This tends to happen when people move from C or C++ to Java, since in C the main function is exactly where the main functionality is placed. It is, therefore, unfortunate that the name main is used for this method. The main method should only ever do a very few things:

- Create an instance of the class within which it is defined. It should never create an instance of another class. If it does then you are not thinking in an object-oriented manner.
- Send the newly created instance a message so that it initializes itself.
- Send the newly created instance a message that triggers off the application's behaviour.

The PetrolCar and DieselCar classes are good examples of this. Both classes create a new instance (of the class) and send it the message startUp. Nothing else happens in the main method; all the work is done in the instance methods.

There is one situation in which you may break this rule. That is where the class you are defining is not intended to be the root class of the application. This class would not normally possess a main method and, if you define one, it is ignored when the class is used within a larger application (or applet). Therefore you can use the main method to provide a test harness for the class. If you do not delete this main method, then it is available to those who modify or update the class at a later date. It can also act as a simple regression test.

Chapter 10

Encapsulation and Polymorphism

10.1 Introduction

This chapter discusses the encapsulation and polymorphic features of Java. It illustrates how the encapsulation facilities can allow quite fine-grained control over the visibility of elements of your programs. The concept of packages is also discussed, along with some concrete examples. The polymorphic nature of Java concludes the chapter.

10.2 Encapsulation

In Java, you have a great deal of control over how much encapsulation is imposed on a class and an object. You achieve it by applying modifiers to classes, instance and class variables and methods. Some of these modifiers refer to the concept of a package. For now, accept that a package is a group of associated classes.

10.2.1 Class Modifiers

You can change the visibility of a class by using a modifier keyword before the `class` keyword in the class definition, for example:

```
public class Person {...}
```

A public class is defined within its own file and is visible everywhere. A class that is local to a particular package has no modifier. It can be defined within a file containing other classes. At most, one of the classes in a file may be a public class.

10.2.2 Variable Modifiers

The amount of encapsulation imposed by a class is at the discretion of the programmer. You can allow complete access to everything within the class, or you can impose various levels of restrictions. In particular, you can control how much access another class has to the instance and class variables of a class. You do this by using a modifier keyword before the type of the variable, for example:

```
public static int MAX_VALUE = 100;
protected String name = "John Hunt";
private int count = 0;
```

Table 10.1 The effect of a variable or method modifier.

`public`	Visible everywhere (the class must also be public)
no modifier	Visible in current package
`protected`	Visible in current package and in subclasses in other packages
`private`	Visible only to current class

Table 10.1 lists the modifiers and their meanings. Generally it is a good idea to impose as much encapsulation as possible. Thus everything should be hidden unless it has to be visible to other classes, in which case you should allow the minimum amount of visibility.

Notice that `protected` is weaker than using no modifier! You should use no modifier in preference to protected.

10.2.3 Method Modifiers

You can also limit the access of other classes to methods. You do this by using a modifier keyword before the return type of the method. The modifiers are the same as for variables:

```
public void setName(String name) {...}
private static int countInstances() {...}
protected final Object findKey() {...}
```

10.3 Packages

You can bring a set of related classes together in a single compilation unit by defining them all within one file. By default, this creates an implicit (unnamed) package; classes can access variables and methods which are only visible in the current package. However, only one of the classes can be publicly visible (the class with the same name as the file). A much better approach is to group the classes together into an explicit, named package.

Packages are encapsulated units which can possess classes, interfaces and sub-packages. Packages are extremely useful:

- They allow you to associate related classes and interfaces.
- They resolve naming problems which would otherwise cause confusion.
- They allow some privacy for classes, methods and variables which should not be visible outside the package. You can provide a level of encapsulation such that only those elements which are intended to be public can be accessed from outside the package.

The JDK provides a large number of packages. In general, you use these packages as the basis of your programs.

10.3.1 Declaring a Package

An explicit package is defined by the `package` keyword at the start of the file in which one or more classes (or interfaces) are defined:

```
package benchmarks;
```

Package names should be unique to ensure that there are no name conflicts. Java imposes a naming convention, by which a package name is made up of a number of components separated by a full stop. These components correspond to the location of the files. Thus if the files in a particular package are in a directory called benchmarks, within a directory called tests, then the package name is given as:

```
package tests.benchmarks;
```

Notice that this assumes that all files associated with a single package are in the same directory. It also assumes that files in a separate package will be in a different directory. Any number of files can become part of a package; however, any one file can only specify a single package.

All components in the package name are relative to the contents of the CLASSPATH variable. This environment variable tells the Java compiler where to start looking for class definitions. Thus, if the CLASSPATH variable is set to C:\jjh\java then the following path is searched for the elements of the package:

```
c:\jjh\java\tests\benchmarks
```

All the class files associated with the tests.benchmarks package should be in the benchmarks directory.

10.3.2 An Example Package

As an example, the files for the book.chap10.lights package are stored within a directory called lights, within a directory called chap10, within the book directory. The lights directory contains three classes which make up the contents of the lights package: Light, WhiteLight and ColoredLight. The header for the Light.java file contains the following code:

```
package book.chap10.lights;
import java.awt.*;
public abstract class Light extends Panel {...}
```

The WhiteLight.java and ColoredLight.java files are similar, for example:

```
package book.chap10.lights;
import java.awt.*;
public class ColoredLight extends WhiteLight {. . .}
```

The directory containing the lights package is listed below:

```
C:\AAAusers\JJH\Java\Book\chap10\lights>dir

COLORE~1 JAV       428 09/04/97  16:01 ColoredLight.java
LIGHT~1  CLA       695 09/04/97  15:55 Light.class
WHITEL~1 JAV       505 09/04/97  15:54 WhiteLight.java
LIGHT~1  JAV       634 09/04/97  15:54 Light.java
LIGHT              632 09/04/97  15:50 Light
WHITEL~1 CLA       631 09/04/97  15:55 WhiteLight.class
COLORE~1 CLA       655 09/04/97  16:01 ColoredLight.class
         7 file(s)          4,180 bytes
         2 dir(s)      89,227,264 bytes free
```

The CLASSPATH variable includes the path C:\AAAusers\JJH\Java, so the package specification, book.chap10.lights, completely specifies the files.

10.3.3 Accessing Package Elements

There are two ways to access an element of a package. One is to name the element in the package fully. For example, we can specify the Panel class by giving its full designation:

```
public abstract class Light extends java.awt.Panel {...}
```

This tells the Java compiler exactly where to look for the definition of the class Panel. However, this is laborious if we refer to the Panel class a number of times.

The alternative is to import the Panel class, which makes it available to the package within which we are currently working:

```
import java.awt.Panel;
public abstract class Light extends Panel { . . . }
```

However, in some situations, we wish to import a large number of elements from another package. Rather than generate a long list of import statements, we can import all the elements of a package at once using the * wildcard. For example:

```
import java.awt.*;
```

This imports all the elements of the java.awt package into the current package. Notice that this can slow down the compilation time considerably (although it has no effect on the run-time performance). Also note that this only imports the contents of the java.awt package – it has no effect on the java.awt.event package (or any other packages within java.awt.<packagename>).

10.3.4 An Example of Using a Package

The lights package described above has been used within a class outside the package. This class uses the ColoredLight class. It therefore imports it into the current package. For example:

```
import java.awt.Frame;
import java.awt.event.WindowListener;
import book.chap10.lights.ColoredLight;

public class LightsGUI extends Frame implements
        WindowListener {
  public static void main (String args []) {
    Frame f = new LightsGUI();
  }

  public LightsGUI () {
  ...
    add("Center", new ColoredLight(true));
  ...
```

```
    }
    ...
}
```

Do not worry too much about what this class does (it draws a circle on a window), just notice that it has to import three classes from three separate packages in order to use Frame, WindowListener and ColoredLight.

10.4 Polymorphism

Polymorphism is the ability to send the same message to completely different objects, all of which respond to that message in their own way. Java's polymorphic abilities are derived from its use of dynamic (or late) binding. In addition, the same method name can be used with different parameters to allow apparently the same method to be declared a number of times within the same class.

10.4.1 Dynamic or Late Binding

Dynamic or late binding refers to the way in which Java decides which method should be run. Instead of determining the method at compile time (as a procedural language might), it determines it at run time. That is, it looks to see what class of object has received the message and then decides which method to run. As this decision is made at run time, there is some run-time overhead. However, there is also greater flexibility. For example, consider the following classes:

```java
public class Vehicle {

    public void drive() {
        System.out.println("Drive a vehicle");
    }
}

public class Car extends  Vehicle {

    public void drive() {
        System.out.println("Drive a car");
    }
}
```

We can use these two classes within a test harness, as follows:

```java
public class Example {

    public static void main(String args []) {

        Vehicle v = new Vehicle();
        Car c = new Car();
        v.drive();
        c.drive();
```

```
        v = c;
        v.drive();

    }
}
```

When this application is executed, the version of drive defined in the class Car is called twice, whereas the version in the superclass Vehicle is called only once:

```
C:\Book\chap10>java Example
Drive a vehicle
Drive a car
Drive a car

C:\Book\chap10>
```

The variable v was declared to be of type Vehicle. When it was assigned the instance of Car and it received the message drive, it responded with the Car version of drive, which was was chosen at run time (based on the object held by v).

10.4.2 Method Selection

When the Java system selects a method in response to a message, it does so using three things:

- the class of the receiving object
- the name of the method
- the class (and order) of the parameters

The third element means that you can define two methods in the same class with the same name, but with different parameters. The system works out which method you want to call at run time by examining the parameters:

```
public class Lorry extends Vehicle {

    public void load (int i) {
        System.out.println("Loading integers " + i);
    }

    public void load (String s) {
        System.out.println("Loading strings " + s);
    }
}
```

This class, Lorry, has two methods called load, both of which take a single parameter. However, the parameters are of different types. This means that the Java system can distinguish between the two methods and thus no conflict arises. For example:

```
public class LorryExample {

    public static void main (String args []) {
        Lorry l = new Lorry();
```

```
        l.load(10);
        l.load("John");
    }
}
```

In this application, we use both versions of the load method, with the following result:

```
Loading integers 10
Loading strings John
```

You can also use this approach to provide class constructors.

Chapter 11

Inner Classes and Reflection

11.1 Introduction

One of the new features introduced back in version 1.1 of the JDK was inner classes. These are classes defined with the scope of an outer (or top-level) class. These inner classes can be defined within the main body of a class, within a block of statements or (anonymously) within an expression. This chapter introduces inner classes and considers where and when they should be used.

This chapter also briefly introduces the reflection API before providing an example of using an inner class to provide a way of generalizing reusable software.

11.2 What Are Inner Classes?

Inner classes are classes that exist inside other, top-level, classes. They possess very specific properties, which include being:

- defined within the scope of an existing class, or a method inside an existing class
- able to access the outer class's instance and class variables (except nested classes, which are explained later in this chapter)
- able to access an outer class's "this" variable (by prefixing it with the name of the outer class). This does not apply to nested classes
- able to be an interface specification
- able to have default, private, protected or public visibility
- able to be anonymous (that is not be explicitly named)
- abstract

There are also a number of limitations on non-nested inner classes compared with their outer (top-level) class relatives. They:

- cannot be instantiated without reference to their encompassing class
- only have meaning inside their outer class

For example, in the following class, Employee, two inner classes are defined that are used to represent an address and a wage. Thus the structure of the class is as illustrated in Figure 11.1.

The source code for the class, and its two inner classes, is presented below:

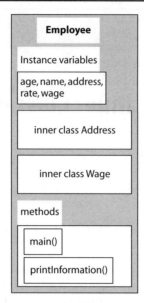

Fig. 11.1 The structure of the Employee class.

```java
public class Employee {
  int age = 0;
  public String name = "Bob";
  double rate = 12.45;
  Address address;
  Wage wage;
  public Employee (String aName, int number,
      String aStreet, String aCity,
      double ratePerHour, int hours) {
    name = aName;
    rate = ratePerHour;
    address = new Address(number, aStreet, aCity);
    wage = new Wage(hours);
  }

  // Inner class -------------------------------------
  class Address {
    int number = 0;
    String street = "";
    String city = "";
    Address (int num, String aStreet, String aCity) {
      number = num;
      street = aStreet;
      city = aCity;
    }
    void printDetails() {
      System.out.println(number + " " + street +
          " , " + city);
    }
  }
```

```
// Inner class -------------------------------------
class Wage {
  int hoursWorked = 0;

  Wage (int hours) {
    hoursWorked = hours;
  }
  void printDetails() {
    System.out.println("Pay packet = " +
    hoursWorked * rate);
  }
}

public static void main (String args []) {
  Employee e = new Employee("John", 33, "High Street",
    "Bath", 2.45, 36);
  e.printInformation();
}

public void printInformation() {
  System.out.println("\nFor Employee: " + name);
  address.printDetails();
  wage.printDetails();
}
}
```

The result of executing this application is:

```
C:>java Employee

For Employee: John
33 High Street , Bath
Pay packet = 88.2
```

The rate variable referenced by the printDetails method of the Wage class refers to an instance variable in the encapsulating class Employee. Thus, inner classes can access variables and methods from the enclosing class.

In many ways, the top-level class can act as an object package containing zero or more inner classes. This is particularly useful for component-oriented development. In addition, the ability to define a particular piece of code that can be created and passed to where it is needed, is very important. For example, C provides function pointers while Smalltalk uses block objects (objects that represent code). Java provides the inner class and anonymous inner classes in particular.

11.3 Types of Inner Class

11.3.1 Nested Top-Level Classes

A nested top-level class or interface is exactly like a normal outer class, except that it has been placed within an existing class. Such classes are declared static and must be declared within an existing outer class (although they can be nested up to any depth). Such classes are grouped together within an outer class for convience and may be treated like any normal class (although they must be referenced either via their outer class or imported directly using the import statement – import outerClassName.innerClassName;). That is, these classes may be referenceable by objects outside the top-level class (depending upon their visibility). Instances can be created from them (assuming they are not interfaces or abstract classes) and they can inherit from any appropriate class (but not from their own outer class). They cannot access the outer class's instance variables.

11.3.2 Member Inner Classes

These are the sort of classes illustrated in the Employee example above. They are classes which are defined within the scope of an existing class but outside any method.

11.3.3 Method Level/Local Inner Classes

These are classes which are defined within a method. They have the scope of the enclosing block; thus they may only be visible for part of a method's execution. They can access the enclosing class(es) and any local final variables and parameters. An example of a method level class is illustrated below:

```java
public class Test extends Frame {

    public Test() {
        setUpWindowHandler();
        ...
    }

    public void setUpWindowHandler() {

        // --- method level/local inner class
        class Handler extends WindowAdapter {
            public void windowClosing(WindowEvent e) {
                System.exit(0);}
            }
        }

        Handler h = new Handler();
        addWindowListener(h);
    }

}
```

In this example, the method setUpWindowHandler first declares a local class Handler which impelements a single method windowClosing(WindowEvent). Once it has done this it declares a variable h to hold a new instance of the Handler class. It then passes this as a parameter to the method addWindowListener. The class Handler cannot be instantiated outside the scope of this method (although an instance of Handler can be used outside the method, as this example shows).

11.3.4 Anonymous Inner Classes

Anonymous inner classes are classes which are generated and instantiated on the fly. An interface or existing class (which may be abstract) is used as the template of the new anonymous class. The anonymous class then defines a new behaviour required and is immediately instantiated. No programmatic reference to the anonymous class is maintained for the programmer and no further instances of the class can be created (except via method such as `clone()`). For example:

```
ActionListener handler =
  new ActionListener {
    public void actionPerformed(ActionEvent event) {
      System.out.println("An event occurred");}};
```

This example creates a class based on the `ActionListener` interface which requires that the `actionPerformed(ActionEvent)` method is implemented. This anonymous class implements that method within the outer curly brackets. It is therefore a concrete implementation of `ActionListener` and can be used anwhere that the `ActionListener` interface is specified.

As you can see from this example, anonymous classes can produce very compact code. However, it can become obscure to read, so care needs to be taken with its use.

11.4 How and When Should I Use Inner Classes?

11.4.1 As Helper Classes

Inner classes are often used as helper classes to perform some specific function (such as implementing a particular action), to implement some generic features (such as an interface to be used thoughout the outer class but nowhere else) or to provide a particular view on to some data (by providing an iterator or enumerator etc.). In general they are not used as a "cheap" way of packing a whole set of classes together and only need to reference the top-level class. However, it is worth noting that this is a programming idiom which could be used.

11.4.2 As Event Handlers

A very common use of an inner class is with the AWT. An inner class can be used to implement a particular listener or to subclass a particular adapter. This has the benefit of separating out the control aspect of the interface from the display elements. It also means that the event handler inner class can inherit from a different class to the encompassing class. For example, in the following code, the outer class inherits from the class `Frame`, but the inner class inherits from the class `WindowAdapter` (thus we do not have to provide null implementation methods for the event handlers we do not wish to use in the `WindowListener` interface):

```
import java.awt.*; import java.awt.event.*;
public class Hello extends Frame {
  public static void main (String args []) {new Hello(args[0]);}
  public Hello (String label) {
    add(new Label(label));
    addWindowListener(new WindowHandler());
```

```
      pack();
      setVisible(true);
    }
    // ---- inner class event handler
    private class WindowHandler extends WindowAdapter {
      public void windowClosing(WindowEvent e) {System.exit(0);}
    }
  }
```

11.4.3 As Anonymous Event Handlers

Anonymous inner classes can also be used to provide a similar facility to the above. The resulting code is far less readable (and for large anonymous classes can be very difficult to follow). However, for classes that are only ever going to be used once, they may have a role to play. For example, if we convert the above into an anonymous class then the resulting source code might look like:

```
import java.awt.*; import java.awt.event.*;

public class Hello extends Frame {
  public static void main (String args []) { new Hello(args[0]);}
  public Hello (String label) {
    add(new Label(label));
    addWindowListener(new WindowAdapter () {
      public void windowClosing(WindowEvent e) {
        System.exit(0);
      }}});
    pack();
    setVisible(true);
  }}
```

As you can see from this, the anonymous class has been embedded into the call to addWindowListener(). This is a common style that you will find used in many situations. However, it renders the code far from clear – unless you are expecting an inner class at this point. Indeed, I have come across inner classes which span pages like this – which makes it very difficult to fathom what is going on!

You should therefore be careful of liberally sprinkling your code with inner classes (particularly anonymous inner classes), as if they are not properly documented, the source code can become hard to follow. Note that as of JDK 1.1.* the javadoc facility does not pick up on inner classes and cannot therefore provide a way of documenting them!

11.4.4 Laying Out a Java Class With Inner Classes

You should try to follow these guidelines when laying out a Java class which contains named inner classes:

- Try to avoid mixing variables, methods and inner classes when laying out the class – this will only lead to confusion. Instead, group variable declarations together, methods together and inner classes together. You don't need to worry about which comes first, as the Java compiler is a multiple pass compiler which will sort out forward references.

- Remember that the built-in make facility may miss inner classes referenced in other classes. You may therefore find that when you recompile you do not get the expected behaviour.
- Don't use outer class as a cheap global "database". One temptation is to treat the outer class as a global blackboard onto which you can write global data (thus providing a limited scope global database). This is not good programming style and may jeopardize future development.

11.4.5 Inner class guidelines

This section provides some guidelines on the definition and implementation of inner classes:

- Make an inner class private by default. That way you will stop the outer class merely being a "cheap" package. If you have to make the inner classes non-private then at least you must make this decision explicitly.
- Use nested level inner classes for separate but related objects.
- Use member inner classes as helper classes which support a particular functionality or abstraction.
- Use method-based inner classes for local shared functionality
- Use method-based inner classes carefully.
- Avoiding using lots of anonymous classes - they are confusing and difficult to maintain
- Be careful how you document inner classes.

11.5 The Reflection API

The Java Reflection API (implemented by the `java.lang.reflect` package) allows access to information about Java classes and objects. It greatly simplifies the task of building tools such as inspectors, debuggers, component builders and test support tools because it gives the tools access to information about the methods and their visibility, the class and instance variables, the constructors etc.

If your security policy allows it, then the Reflection API (also sometimes referred to as introspection) can be used to:

- obtain class or instance information
- construct new class instances and new arrays
- access and modify class and instance variables
- invoke methods on classes and instances

The Reflection API provides new classes based on the class `Class`:

- *Field* represents a field in a class or instance. It allows you to obtain information about the field and to access or modify the data held by the field.
- *Method* represents a method in a class or instance. It allows you to obtain information about the method's parameters, return type and checked exceptions. It also provides an `invoke` method which is used to execute the actual method in a class or on an object.
- *Constructor* represents a class constructor. You can use it to obtain information about a constructor's parameter. It can also create a new instance of the associated class using the represented constructor.

The Reflection API also extends the class Class. The new methods give information about a class or instance and return a field, method or constructor instance, for example, getField, getMethod, getConstructor, getFields, getMethods and getConstructors. For example, the following code, which implements a class called Inspector, uses the class Class to obtain various items of information about a given class. For each class it obtains information about the constructors, interfaces, methods and variables the class defines. It also finds out which class it inherits from.

```java
import java.lang.reflect.*;
import java.util.*;

public class Inspector {

    private Vector constructors = new Vector();
    private Vector classMethods = new Vector();
    private Vector classVariables = new Vector();
    private Vector instanceMethods = new Vector();
    private Vector instanceVariables = new Vector();
    private String name = "";
    private Class superClass;
    private Class cls;
    private Vector interfaces = new Vector();

    public Inspector(String classname) {
        int mod;
        name = classname;
        try {
            System.out.println("Loading class : " + classname);
            cls = Class.forName(classname); // Loads the class object
            System.out.println("Class load successful");

            // Find the superclass
            setSuperClass(cls.getSuperclass());
            // Find the constructors
            Constructor cons[] = cls.getDeclaredConstructors();
            if (cons != null) {
                for (int i = 0; i < cons.length; i++) {
                    addConstructor(cons[i]);
                }
            }
            // Find the interfaces
            Class ints[] = cls.getInterfaces();
            if (ints != null) {
                for (int i = 0; i < ints.length; i++) {
                    addInterface(ints[i]);
                }
            }
            // Find the methods declared in this class
            // and distinguish between the instance and
            // class methods.
            Method methods[] = cls.getDeclaredMethods();
```

```
      if (methods != null) {
        Method m;
          for (int i = 0; i < methods.length; i++) {
            m = methods[i];
            mod = m.getModifiers();
            if (Modifier.isStatic(mod)) {
              addClassMethod(m);
            } else {
            addInstanceMethod(methods[i]);
            }
          }
        }
      // Find the variables of the class and
      // distinguish between instance and class
      Field fields[] = cls.getDeclaredFields();
      if (fields != null) {
        Field f;
        for (int i = 0; i < fields.length; i++) {
          f = fields[i];
          mod = f.getModifiers();
          if (Modifier.isStatic(mod)) {
            addClassVariable(f);
          } else {
            addInstanceVariable(fields[i]);
          }
        }
      }
    } catch (java.lang.ClassNotFoundException e) {
      System.out.println("Error loading " + cls);
    }
  }

  public void addClassMethod(Method meth) {
    classMethods.addElement(meth);
  }

  public void addClassVariable (Field field ) {
    classVariables.addElement(field);
  }

  public void addConstructor(Constructor cons) {
    constructors.addElement(cons);
  }.

  public void addInstanceMethod(Method meth) {
    instanceMethods.addElement(meth);
  }

  public void addInstanceVariable (Field field ) {
    instanceVariables.addElement(field);
  }
```

```java
  public void addInterface(Class anInterface) {
    interfaces.addElement(anInterface);
  }

  public String getName( ) {
    return name;
  }

  public Class getSuperClass() {
    return superClass;
  }

  public void setSuperClass(Class superClass) {
    this.superClass = superClass;
  }

  /**
   * Returns a String that represents the value of this object.
   */
  public String toString() {
    StringBuffer result = new StringBuffer("Class details for " +
                                          name + "\n");
    if (superClass != null) {
      result.append("\tSuperclass: " + getSuperClass() + "\n");
    }

    if (!constructors.isEmpty()) {
      result.append("Constructors: \n");
      Enumeration e = constructors.elements();
      while (e.hasMoreElements()) {
        result.append("\t" + e.nextElement() + "\n");
      }
    }

    if (!interfaces.isEmpty()) {
      result.append("Interfaces: \n");
      Enumeration e = interfaces.elements();
      while (e.hasMoreElements()) {
        result.append("\t" + e.nextElement() + "\n");
      }
    }

    if (!classVariables.isEmpty()) {
      result.append("Class Variables \n");
      Enumeration e = classVariables.elements();
      while (e.hasMoreElements()) {
        result.append("\t" + e.nextElement() + "\n");
      }
    }

    if (!classMethods.isEmpty()) {
```

```java
      result.append("Class Methods \n");
      Enumeration e = classMethods.elements();
      while (e.hasMoreElements()) {
        result.append("\t" + e.nextElement() + "\n");
      }
    }

    if (!instanceVariables.isEmpty()) {
      result.append("Instance Variables \n");
      Enumeration e = instanceVariables.elements();
      while (e.hasMoreElements()) {
        result.append("\t" + e.nextElement() + "\n");
      }
    }

    if (!instanceMethods.isEmpty()) {
      result.append("Instance Methods \n");
      Enumeration e = instanceMethods.elements();
      while (e.hasMoreElements()) {
        result.append("\t" + e.nextElement() + "\n");
      }
    }

    return result.toString();
  }

  // Main method for Inspector application
  public static void main(java.lang.String[] args) {
    if (args.length < 1) {
      System.out.println("Usage java Inspector <fully qualified class
name>");
        System.exit(1);
    }
    Inspector insp = new Inspector(args[0]);
    System.out.println(insp);
  }
}
```

Note that we had to wrap much of the code directly involved with reflection in a try catch block. This is because a number of the reflection methods throw the ClassNot-FoundException if the specified class cannot be loaded. The results of running the Inspector on itself are presented below:

```
C:\jjh\JAVA\practioners\chap11>java Inspector Inspector
Loading class : Inspector
Class load successful
Class details for Inspector
        Superclass: class java.lang.Object
Constructors:
        public Inspector(java.lang.String)
Class Methods
```

```
        public static void Inspector.main(java.lang.String[])
Instance Variables
        private java.util.Vector Inspector.constructors
        private java.util.Vector Inspector.classMethods
        private java.util.Vector Inspector.classVariables
        private java.util.Vector Inspector.instanceMethods
        private java.util.Vector Inspector.instanceVariables
        private java.lang.String Inspector.name
        private java.lang.Class Inspector.superClass
        private java.lang.Class Inspector.cls
        private java.util.Vector Inspector.interfaces
Instance Methods
        public void Inspector.addClassMethod(java.lang.reflect.Method)
        public void Inspector.addClassVariable(java.lang.reflect.Field)
        public void
Inspector.addConstructor(java.lang.reflect.Constructor)
        public void Inspector.addInstanceMethod(java.lang.reflect.Method)
        public void
Inspector.addInstanceVariable(java.lang.reflect.Field)
        public void Inspector.addInterface(java.lang.Class)
        public java.lang.String Inspector.getName()
        public java.lang.Class Inspector.getSuperClass()
        public void Inspector.setSuperClass(java.lang.Class)
        public java.lang.String Inspector.toString()
```

Chapter **12**

Data Structures

12.1 Introduction

Classes and objects merely package code and data together; you must still decide how to represent and maintain that data, for example in a list, as a tree, as part of a hash table or ordered in some manner. This chapter discusses how data structures are created and manipulated in Java. We consider a number of classes in the java.util package, namely Dictionary, Hashtable, Vector and Stack. We also consider how arrays are implemented in Java. The chapter concludes by considering automatic memory management. Note that an extended set of collections classes were added in Java 2 (SDK 1.2) onwards. These are discussed in some detail in Chapter 13.

12.2 Data Structure Classes

Figure 12.1 illustrates the relationships between the root class Object, the data structure classes and the Clonable and Serializable interfaces which they implement. The boxes indicate classes and the ovals indicate an interface.

The root class, Object, is defined in the package java.lang. The other classes are all defined in the java.util package. Dictionary is an abstract class, which cannot be used to create instances. The other three classes are all concrete classes, which can create instances.

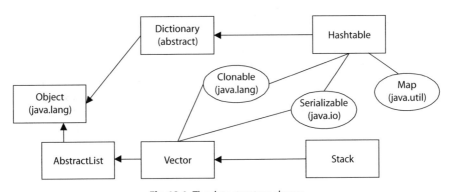

Fig. 12.1 The data structure classes.

12.3 The Abstract Class `Dictionary`

A `Dictionary` is a set of associations between a key and a value. It is an abstract subclass of `Object`. It is also the superclass of `Hashtable`. The elements in a `Dictionary` are unordered, but each has a definite name or *key*. Thus a `Dictionary` can be regarded as an unordered collection of object values with external keys (Table 12.1).

Table 12.1 The dictionary protocol.

`get(Object aKey)`	Returns the value associated with a Key.
`put(Object aKey, object aValue)`	Puts a Value into a dictionary with the external key a Key.
`keys()`	Responds with an enumeration of keys from the receiver.
`elements()`	Answers with an enumeration of the values in the receiver.
`remove (Object aKey)`	Removes the key (and its corresponding value) from the dictionary.
`size()`	Returns the number of keys in the receiver.

Notice that the key and the value must be objects (that is, you cannot use a primitive type, such as `int`, although you can use an integer object). Enumerations are explained in the next chapter.

12.4 The `Hashtable` Class

This is a concrete subclass of the abstract `Dictionary` class. It implements a simple hash table, such as that found in some other languages (e.g. Common LISP) or in libraries available for other languages (e.g. C). The great advantage of Java is that everyone has the same type of `Dictionary`. In Pascal or C, almost everyone has to invent their own or purchase a library to get the same functionality. This, of course, leads to problems of consistency between implementations.

You create an instance of a hash tables using the `Hashtable` method with the parameters specified in Table 12.2.

Table 12.2 The hash table constructor parameters.

no parameters	Creates a new empty hash table with a default initial capacity of 101.
`int initialCapacity`	Creates a new empty hash table of size initial Capacity. The load factor is 75% by default.
`int initialCapacity float loadFactor`	Creates a new hash table of size initial Capacity and the specified load factor.

The load factor is the point at which the hash table should grow and be rehashed. The load factor should be a real number between 0.0 and 1.0. When the number of entries is greater than the product of the load factor and the current capacity, the size of the hash table is increased and then it is rehashed. The new size of the hash table is twice the original size plus 1.

Here is a simple `Hashtable` example you might like to type in and try out. You must save it into a file called `Example.java`. You must also explicitly import the class `Hashtable` as it is defined in a separate package called `java.util`.

```
import java.util.Hashtable;

public class Example {
```

```
    public static void main (String args []) {
        Example e = new Example();
        e.example();
    }

    public void example () {
        Hashtable x = new Hashtable();
        x.put("jjh", "John");
        x.put("msw", "Myra");
        x.put("dec", "Denise");
        System.out.println(x.get("dec"));
        System.out.println(x.get("jjh"));
    }
}
```

In addition to the methods defined in Dictionary, Hashtable also provides the instance protocols shown in Table 12.3. The Hashtable class assumes that the key objects in the table implement the hashCode and the equals methods. In addition, for efficiency, the size of the hash table should be a prime number larger than the actual size required. For example, if the table is intended to hold 100 keys, then it should be created with a default size of 151.

Table 12.3 The hash table instance protocol.

clear()	Empties the hash table.
clone()	Returns a "shallow" copy of the table (the table is duplicated, but the key and value references remain the same).
contains (Object aValue)	Returns true if the table contains the value.
containsKey (Object aKey)	Returns true if the table contains the key.
rehash()	Rehashes the table into a larger table.
toString()	Returns a string representation of the table.

Notice that, by default, all hash tables return an object (i.e. an instance of the class Object). It is therefore necessary to cast the returned object into the correct class. For example, if the values in a hash table are strings then it is necessary to execute the following code:

```
    result = (String)aHashtable.get(aKey);
```

12.5 The Vector Class

The Vector class (Tables 12.4 and 12.5) is a concrete class which provides a similar facility to a linked list (or list structures in Lisp and Ordered Collections in Smalltalk) for objects. You can add elements to a vector, remove elements from it, check to see if an element is in it and process

Table 12.4 The vector constructor parameters.

no parameters	Creates an empty vector with a default size (10 in the JDK)
int initialCapacity	Creates an empty vector of size initialCapacity
int initialCapacity int capacityIncrement	creates an empty vector of size initialCapacity and sets the growth increment to capacityIncrement

Table 12.5 The vector instance protocol.

addElement (Object object)	Adds the object to the end of the vector
clone()	Returns a duplicate of this vector. As the vector only holds references to the elements it holds, the elements themselves are not cloned
contains (Object element)	Returns true if the element is held in the vector
copyInto (Object anArray[])	Copies the vector elements into the array. The array must be at least large enough to hold all the vector elements
elementAt (int index)	Returns the element at the specified index
elements()	Returns an enumeration of the elements in the vector
firstElement()	Returns the first element in the vector without removing it from the vector
indexOf (Object element)	Returns the position of the first element matching the parameter within the vector
indexOf (Object element, int index)	Returns the position of the first element matching the parameter starting at the position specified by index
insertElementAt (Object object, int index)	Inserts the object at the position specified by index. If an object exists at that position, all objects with this and higher indexes are shifted up one position
isEmpty()	Returns true if the vector holds no objects
lastElement()	Returns the last element in the vector
lastIndexOf (Object element)	Returns the position of the last occurrence of the element in the receiving vector
removeAllElements()	Deletes all elements from the vector
removeElement (Object element)	Deletes the specified element from the vector. Returns true if it is successful and false if the element was not a member of the receiving vector
removeElementAt (int index)	Removes the element held at the position indicated by the index
setElementAt (Object object, int index)	Replaces the element at the index with the new object

all the elements in it. In addition, the vector grows such that it possesses enough space to hold the elements within it. It is essentially an array of objects which can grow. You can access elements by their position in the vector. Notice that a vector of four elements is numbered 0 to 3. A vector cannot hold one of the primitive types such as int or boolean. Instead, they must be wrapped within a class such as Integer or Boolean.

The methods which return the objects held within the vector always return objects of type Object (just as for hash tables). They must then be cast into the appropriate type. The following code presents a simple example of using a vector:

```java
import java.util.*;
public class VectorDemo {
    Vector names = new Vector(3, 2);

    public static void main (String argv []){
        VectorDemo v = new VectorDemo();
        v.example();
    }
```

```
    public void example () {
       names.addElement("John");
       names.addElement("Denise");
       names.addElement("Phoebe");
       System.out.println("The capacity is " +
               names.capacity());
       System.out.println("The size is " +
               names.size());
       names.insertElementAt("David", 2);
       System.out.println("The capacity is now " +
               names.capacity());
       System.out.println("The size is now " +
               names.size());
       System.out.println("The last element is " +
               names.lastFlement());
    }
}
```

The result of compiling and executing the VectorDemo is presented below:

```
C:>java VectorDemo
The capacity is 3
The size is 3
The capacity is now 5
The size is now 4
The last element is Pheobe
```

Vectors try to control the amount of storage they require by using the current capacity and two instance variables capacityIncrement and elementCount. The capacity indicates the current maximum capacity of the vector, the capacityIncrement determines the amount by which the vector grows in size once the current size (indicated by elementCount) exceeds the capacity.

To improve performance, the Vector class allows you to increase the size of the vector if you are about to add a large number of objects or to trim it down to size if the vector has grown larger than is currently needed (Table 12.6). Notice the difference between ensureCapacity and setSize.

Table 12.6 Vector management protocol.

capacity()	Returns the number of elements currently held in the vector
ensureCapacity(int minimumCapacity)	Increases the amount of space available in the vector to that specified by the parameter minimumCapacity. If the capacity of the vector is greater than that specified no change is made
setSize(int newSize)	Sets the number of elements that are currently held in the vector. If the new size is greater than the number of elements, then null values are added; if the number of elements exceeds the new size, those elements at positions newSize and greater are deleted
size()	Returns the number of elements held by the receiving vector
trimToSize()	Reduces the capacity of the vector to the current size. This frees up any unused storage space previously obtained by the vector

12.6 The Stack Class

The class Stack (Table 12.7), a subclass of Vector, provides a basic stack object with the required last in, first out behaviour. It provides a single constructor, Stack, which creates a new empty stack.

Table 12.7 Stack instance protocol.

empty()	Returns true if the stack has no elements
peek()	Returns the object at the top of the stack, without removing it from the stack
pop()	Returns the object from the top of the stack and removes it from the stack
push(Object object)	Places the object on the top of the stack
search (Object object)	Returns the position of the object on the stack (or −1 if the object is not in the stack)

12.7 A Queue Class

You can easily define a Queue class in Java using the Vector class. Queues have a first in, first out behaviour, so you can use the addElement, firstElement and removeElement methods:

```
import java.util.Vector;

public class Queue extends Vector {
  public final void add (Object object) {
    addElement(object);
  }
  public final Object peek () {
    return firstElement();
  }
  public final Object next () {
    Object result = firstElement();
    removeElement(result);
    return result;
  }
}
```

This class defines three new methods: add(Object object), peek and next. The add and peek methods are very straightforward, using the addElement and firstElement methods defined in Vector. The next method is not complex but has to use the firstElement method to obtain the object at the front of the queue so that it can remove this object and then return it.

12.8 Enumeration

Any object which is an instance of a class that implements the Enumeration interface produces a list of the elements it contains. You can access the list elements one at a time. The classes Hashtable and Vector (along with the collection classes above) implement the Enumeration interface. You can access the elements contained in instances of these classes iteratively. This is an extremely useful feature as any programmer who has used Lisp, Smalltalk or POP11 knows.

The elements method obtains an enumeration of an object's contents. The enumeration can then be accessed using the nextElement method, which returns successive elements from the list. The hasMoreElements method determines whether any further elements remain in the enumeration. This enumeration interface definition is presented below:

```
public interface java.util.Enumeration {
   public abstract boolean hasMoreElements();
   public abstract Object nextElement();
}
```

You can use such an enumeration to apply the same message to all elements of a Vector (or collection). For example, to apply the printself message to all elements of a vector, we could write:

```
for (Enumeration e = aVector.elements() ;
   e.hasMoreElements() ; ) {
   temp = e.nextElement();
   temp.printself();
}
```

This approach will be used in the next chapter to print out the contents of instances of Set and SortedCollection.

12.9 Arrays

Arrays in Java are objects, like most other data types. Like arrays in any other language, they hold elements of data in an order specified by an index. They are zero-based arrays, as in C, which means that an array with 10 elements is indexed from 0 to 9.

To create a new array, you must specify the type of array object and the number of elements in the array. The number of elements is specified by an integer between square brackets. As an array is an instance, it is created in the usual way using the new operation:

```
new String[10];
```

This creates an array capable of holding 10 string objects. We can assign such an array instance to a variable by specifying that the variable holds an array. You do this by indicating the type of the array to be held by the variable along with the array indicator. Notice that we do not specify the number of array locations which are held by the array variable:

```
String names [];
String [] names;
```

Both of the above formats are legal; you should use the one with which you are more comfortable. Personally, I always use the former.

We now create an array and assign it to our variable:

```
String names [] = new String [4];
```

There is a short-cut way to create and initialize an array:

```
String names [] = {"John", "Denise", "Phoebe", "James"};
```

This creates an array of four elements containing the strings "John", "Denise", "Phoebe" and "James". We can change any of these fields by specifying the appropriate index and replacing the existing value with a new string:

```
names [3] = "Isobel";
```

The above statement replaces the string "James" with the string "Isobel". Merely being able to put values into an array would be of little use; we can access the array locations in a similar manner:

```
System.out.println("The name in position 2 is " + names[1]);
```

The above statement results in the following string being printed:

```
The name in position 2 is Denise
```

As arrays are objects we can also obtain information from them. For example, to find out how many elements are in the array we can use the instance variable length:

```
names.length
```

Arrays are fixed in length when they are created, whereas vectors can change their length. To obtain the size of an array, you can access the instance variable length, but you must use a method, size, to determine the current size of a vector.

Arrays can be passed into and out of methods very simply by specifying the type of the array, the name of the variable to receive the array and the array indicator.

12.9.1 Arrays of Objects

The above examples have focused on arrays of Strings; however, you can also create arrays of any type of object, but this process is a little more complicated (it is actually the exactly the same for strings, but some of what is happening is hidden from you). For example, assuming we have a class Person; then we can create an array of Persons:

```
Person [] p = new Person[4];
```

It is important to realize what this gives you. It provides a variable p which can hold a reference to an array object of Persons. At present this array is empty and *does not* hold references to any instances of Person. Note that this indicates that the array is actually an array of references to the instances "held" in the array as opposed to an array of those instances. This illustrated in the first part of Fig 12.2. To actually make it hold instances of Person we must add each person instance to the appropriate array location. For example:

```
p[0] = new Person();
p[1] = new Person();
p[2] = new Person();
p[3] = new Person();
```

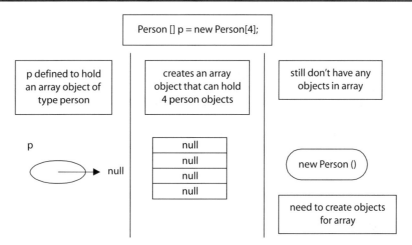

Fig. 12.2 Creating an array of objects.

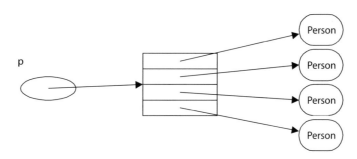

Fig. 12.3 The complete array structure.

This is illustrated in the last part of Figure 12.2 and in Figure 12.3. Thus the creation of an array of objects is a three-stage process:

1. Create a variable which can reference an array of the appropriate type of object.
2. Create the array object.
3. Fill the array object with instances of the appropriate type.

12.9.2 Basic Type Arrays

It should be noted that an array of basic types is exactly that. It is not an array of references to the basic types. Thus an array of basic types is simpler and the generation of such an array produces an array containing the specified value or the default (zero) values, for example:

```
int totals [] = {0, 2, 5, 1, 7};
```

12.9.3 Multi-Dimensional Arrays

As in most high-level languages, multi-dimensional arrays can be defined in Java. This is done in the following manner:

```
String f [] [] = { {"John", "Denise", "Phoebe"},   {"Paul", "Fiona",
"Andrew"}};
```

However, it is instructive to consider what this actually means. It states that a string array f can hold references to other string arrays which in turn can hold actual string objects. Thus if we create these arrays and objects for the Person class then we would:

1. Define the variable p as holding a reference to an array of arrays:

    ```
    Person p [][];
    ```

2. Create the multi-dimensional array:

    ```
    p = new Person[2][];
    ```

    Note we have to specify the first dimension as it is necessary to allocate enough space for the required references. We do not have to specify the second dimension as this can be specified in the subsequent array object creation messages.
3. Create the sub-arrays:

    ```
    p[0] = new Person[2];
    p[1] = new person[2];
    ```

    We are now ready to add instances to the two-dimensional array; for example:

    ```
    p[0][0] = new person("John");
    ```

As you can see from this last example, multi-dimensional arrays are accessed in exactly the same way as single-dimensional arrays with one index following another (note that each is within its own set of square brackets - [ ]). That is, you can access this two-dimensional array by specifying a particular position within the array using the same format:

```
System.out.println(matrix[2][2]);
```

It is also possible to have ragged arrays, as the second dimension is made up of separate array object. For example, the following code defines a two-dimensional array in which the first row has four elements and the second has three.

```
String f [] [] = { {"John", "Denise",
                    "Phoebe", "Adam"},
                  {"Paul", "Fiona", "Andrew"}};
```

Of course the way that multi-dimensional arrays are implemented in Java means that you can easily implement any number of dimensions required.

12.9.4 The main Method

At this point you are ready to review the parameter passed into the main class method. As a reminder, it always has the following format:

```
public static void main (String args []) {
  ...
}
```

From this you can see that the parameter passed into the main method is an array of strings. This array holds any command line arguments passed into the program.

We now have enough information to write a simple program which parses the main method command line arguments:

```
public class ParseInput {
  public static void main (String args [] ) {
    if (args.length == 0) {
      System.out.println("No arguments");
    }
    else {
      for (i = 0; i < args.length; i++) {
        System.out.println("Argument number"
          + i + " is " + args[i]);
      }
    }
  }
}
```

This is a very simple program, but it provides the basics for a command line parser. Do not worry if you do not understand the syntax of the whole program; we cover if statements and for loops later in the book.

Arrays in Java are passed into methods by value (Figure 12.4). However, as they only hold a reference to the objects they contain, if those objects are modified internally, the array outside the method is also modified. This can be the cause of extreme frustration when trying to debug programs. Arrays can also be returned from methods:

modifiers static-specifier **type** [] methodName (...)

public String [] returnNames () {
  ...
}

As an example of an array-based application, consider the following class ArrayDemo, which calculates the average of an array of numbers. This array is created in the main method and is passed into the processArray method as a parameter. Within this method, the values of the

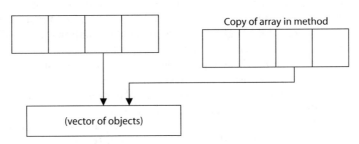

Fig. 12.4 Passing an array into a method.

array are added together and the total is divided by the number of elements in the array (i.e. its length):

```java
public class ArrayDemo {
  public static void main (String args []) {
    ArrayDemo d = new ArrayDemo();
    int anArray [] = {1, 4, 7, 9};
    d.processArray(anArray);
  }
  public void processArray (int myArray []) {
    int i, total = 0, average = 0;

    for (i = 0; i < (myArray.length); ++i){
      total = total + myArray[i];
    }
    average = total / myArray.length;
    System.out.println("The average was " + result);
  }
}
```

12.10 Memory Management

12.10.1 Why Have Automatic Memory Management?

Any discussion of data structures in Java needs to consider how Java handles memory. One of the many advantages of Java over languages such as C++ is that it automatically manages memory allocation and reuse. It is not uncommon to hear C++ programmers complaining about spending many hours attempting to track down a particularly awkward bug only to find it was a problem associated with memory allocation or pointer manipulation. Similarly, a regular problem for C++ developers is that of memory creep, which occurs when memory is allocated but is not freed up. The application either uses all available memory or runs out of space and produces a run-time error.

Most of the problems associated with memory allocation in languages such as C++ occur because programmers must not only concentrate on the (often complex) application logic but also on memory management. They must ensure that they allocate only the memory which is required and deallocate it when it is no longer required. This may sound simple, but it is no mean feat in a large complex application.

An interesting question to ask is "Why do programmers have to manage memory allocation?". There are few programmers today who would expect to have to manage the registers being used by their programs, although 20 or 30 years ago the situation was very different. One answer to the memory management question, often cited by those who like to manage their own memory, is that "it is more efficient, you have more control, it is faster and leads to more compact code". Of course, if you wish to take these comments to their extreme, then we should all be programming in assembler. This would enable us all to produce faster, more efficient and more compact code than that produced by Pascal, C++ or Java.

The point about high-level languages, however, is that they are more productive, introduce fewer errors, are more expressive and are efficient enough (given modern computers and compiler technology). The memory management issue is somewhat similar. If the system automatically handles the allocation and deallocation of memory, then the programmer can concentrate on the application logic. This makes the programmer more productive, removes problems due to poor memory management and, when implemented efficiently, can still provide acceptable performance.

12.10.2 Memory Management in Java

Java provides automatic memory management. Essentially, it allocates a portion of memory as and when required. When memory is short, it looks for areas which are no longer referenced. These areas of memory are then freed up (deallocated) so that they can be reallocated. This process is often referred to as "garbage collection".

The Java Virtual Machine (JVM) uses an approach known as *mark and sweep* to identify objects which can be freed up. The garbage collection process searches from any root objects, i.e. objects from which the main method has been run, marking all the objects it finds. It then examines all the objects currently held in memory and deletes those objects which are not marked. It is at this point that an object's finalize method is executed.

A second process invoked with garbage collection is memory compaction. This involves moving all the allocated memory blocks together so that free memory is contiguous rather than fragmented.

12.10.3 When Is Garbage Collection Performed?

The garbage collection process runs in its own thread. That is, it runs at the same time as other processes within the JVM. It is initiated when the ratio of free memory versus total memory passes a certain point.

You can also explicitly indicate to the JVM that you wish the garbage collector to run. This can be useful if you are about to start a process which requires a large amount of memory and you think that there may be unneeded objects in the system. You can do this in one of two ways:

```
System.gc();
Runtime.getRuntime().gc();
```

However, calling System.gc is (allegedly) only an indication to the compiler that you would like garbage collection to happen. There is no guarantee that it will run. This is not made clear from the JDK documentation:

> Runs the garbage collector. Calling this method suggests that the Java Virtual Machine expend effort toward recycling unused objects in order to make the memory they currently occupy available for quick reuse. When control returns from the method call, the Java Virtual Machine has made its best effort to recycle all unused objects.

This explanation is misleading as it says that it "runs the garbage collector"!

12.10.4 Checking the Available Memory

You can find out the current state of your system (with regard to memory) using the Runtime environment object. This object allows you to obtain information about the current free memory, total memory etc.:

```java
public class MemoryStatus {

    public static void main (String args []) {
        MemoryStatus s = new MemoryStatus();
        s.testMemory();
    }

    public void testMemory() {

        Runtime rt = Runtime.getRuntime();
        long freeMemory = rt.freeMemory();
        long totalMemory = rt.totalMemory();

        System.out.println("Total memory is " +
            totalMemory + " and free memory is " +
                freeMemory);
        System.gc();
        freeMemory = rt.freeMemory();
        System.out.println("Total memory is " +
            totalMemory + " and free memory is now " +
                freeMemory);
    }
}
```

12.11 Exercise: Vectors

The aim of this exercise is to give you a chance to use the very useful class Vector. This class is a growable array which can be used as a linked list structure or as an array.

What You Should do

Your task is to implement a set data structure using an array.

A set is a data structure which will only hold a single instance of a particular type of object. That is, it will only hold a single instance of the string "john".

The class Set should define the following methods:

- add(Object) – Add an object to the set if it is not already present.
- remove(Object) – Remove an object from the set if it is already in the set.
- elements() – Return an enumeration of the elements in the Set (see the class Vector and the interface Enumeration).

Testing Your Set Class

You should test your newly defined class Set on the following application:

```java
public class Test {
    public static void main (String args []){
        Set s = new Set();
        s.add("John");
```

```
        s.add("Paul");
        s.add("John");
        s.add(new Button("Exit"));
        s.add(new Button("Exit"));
        Enumeration e = s.elements();
        while (e.hasMoreElements()) {
          System.out.println(e.nextElement());
        }
      }
    }
```

What is the result of running this program? Did it have any surprises for you?

Hints

1. You will need to import java.util.Vector into the file defining your class Set.
2. Define a class Set which contains a Vector (you can't subclass Vector!).
3. You should use the equals(Object) method to determine whether one object is the same as another.

Take advantage of the elements() method defined in Vector.

12.12 Summary

In this chapter you have encountered the various data structure classes which form the corner-stone of most implementations: Dictionary, Hashtable, Vector and Stack. If you come from a Lisp-style language, things like Vectors should not have seemed too strange. However, if you come from languages such as C, Pascal or Ada, you may well have found the idea of a vector quite bizarre. Stick with it, try it out, implement some simple programs using it and you will soon find that it is easy to use and extremely useful. You will very quickly come to wonder why every language does not have the same facility!

12.13 Further Reading

Almost any good book on Java includes a detailed discussion of the classes used to construct data structures. However, particularly good references can be found in Cornell and Horstmann (1997).

Chapter 13

The Collections API

13.1 Introduction

In Java 2 SDK 1.2 Sun introduced a new set of collection classes. A collection, according to JavaSoft, is a single object representing a group of objects (such as Java's familiar Vector class). That is they are a *collection* of other objects. Collections may also be referred to as containers (as they contain other objects). These collection classes are used as the basis for data structures.

The new collection classes extended the facilities provided by the utility classes Vector and Hashtable. These classes are called by names such as HashSet, ArraySet, LinkedList etc. Some of the collection classes, for example, ArrayList, provide functionality similar existing data structure classes such as the Vector class, but have been optimized for performance. Like Vector and Hashtable the collection classes can only hold objects; thus if you wish to hold the basic types within them, you need to wrap the basic type in the appropriate object wrapper. The Collections API is implemented as part of the java.util package.

13.2 What Is in the Collections API?

The collection classes and interfaces in SDK 1.2 are collectively referred to as the Collections API. A *collection* is a group of objects (these objects are called the *elements* of the collection). Collections are the Java mechanism for building data structures of various sorts; it is therefore important to become familiar with the collection API and its functionality.

Interface Collection is the root of all collections in the API. Figure 13.1 summarizes the Collections API in Java. Some of the classes illustrated are abstract classes on which others build. In fact, the collection class hierarchy (Figure 13.2) is a classic example of the use of interfaces and abstract classes and how they can be used to group together functionality as well as

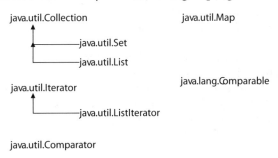

Fig. 13.1 The interfaces defined in the Collections API.

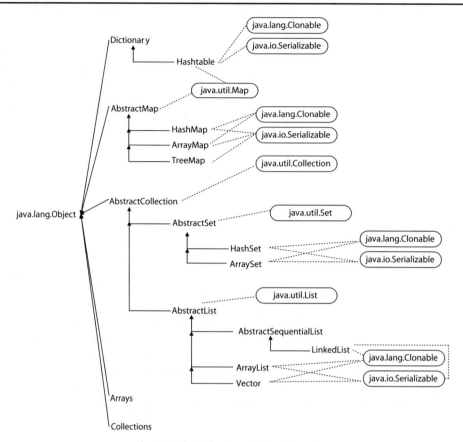

Fig. 13.2 The Collections API class hierarchy.

indicate what is expected of subclasses. Now might be a good time to stop and examine the collection API itself.

The Collections API can be divided up in the following manner:

- *Collection Interfaces* There are four collection interfaces which represent the core types of collections supported by the Collections API. These interfaces are Collection, Set, List and Map. We will look in more detail at these interfaces later.
- *Abstract Implementations* These provide the abstract root classes for the collection hierarchy. They specify the behaviour which must be implemented by subclasses which provide the features of a Set, a List etc.
- *Concrete Implementations* These are general-purpose implementations of the core collection interfaces.
- *Anonymous Implementations* These are classes which the developer does not instantiate, but which are returned by *static* factory methods in the classes Collections and Arrays. They are intended to enable pre-Collections API data structures to be converted into collections efficiently and effectively. They allow legacy APIs that return arrays to inter-operate with new APIs that expect collections.
- *Infrastructure* This grouping includes new interfaces for iteration and ordering as well as two new exceptions.

- *Array Sorting and Searching* As JavaSoft admit, the `Arrays` class static methods for sorting and searching arrays is not really part of the Collections API. However, they are being provided in JDK 1.2 for the first time and they are useful in manipulating array-based data structures.

Just as with the older utility data structure classes, the basic operations that are performed by the collection data structures include adding and removing elements, determining the size of the collection, querying the presence or absence of elements and iterating over the elements.

13.3 Collection Interfaces

The interfaces that comprise the collection hierarchy are designed to allow manipulation of collections in an implementation-independent fashion. This should allow for interoperability among unrelated APIs and applications that take collections as input or return them as output. This should reduce the effort required to design, implement, maintain and understand such APIs and applications. The collection API should also help in the production of reusable software. The interfaces which form the basis of the Collections API are:

- `Collection`. This interface is the root of most of the Collections API. The only classes which do not implement this interface are the map-oriented classes (these are `Hashtable`, `HashMap`, `ArrayMap` and `TreeMap`).
- `Set`. This interface represents the set data type. `Set` contains all the elements put into them, in any order. Duplicates are not kept; adding equal objects many times results in only one such object in the `Set`. This interface extends the `Collection` interface.
- `List`. This interface defines an Ordered Collection data type (also known as a sequence). An ordered collection is a collection where the ordering is given by the order in which elements were added. This interface again extends the `Collection` interface.
- `Map`. A map is an association between pairs of objects. One object often acts as the key to the other object (referred to as the value).

If you wish to define your own collection classes, then implementing one of these interfaces could be your starting point. The details of these interface are presented below.

13.3.1 Collection

The `Collection` interface is the interface which acts as the root of (almost) all collection classes. It defines the methods which all collections (except `Map` type collections) must implement. Note that some of the implementing classes may decide that the implementation should throw an `UnsupportedOperationException` to indicate that they should not be used with this type of collection.

The interface defines methods for adding an element to a collection, accessing elements in a collection, removing an element from a collection and indicating the size of the collection. It also provides facilities which allow an iterator to be returned (these are similar to enumerations in JDK 1.1). The `toArray()` method also allows the collection to be converted into an array.

Any object can be stored into any collection (however, again, implementations of a particular collection may limit the type of object they hold). This means that a collection can be a very flexible way of holding other objects. Typically, collections are used as data structures;

however, they can also be used as temporary holding places for groups of calculations, results, classes etc.

The Collection interface defines the following (abstract) methods:

- add(Object) Ensures that this Collection contains the specified element (optional operation).
- addAll(Collection) Adds all of the elements in the specified Collection to this Collection (optional operation).
- clear() Removes all of the elements from this Collection (optional operation).
- contains(Object) Returns true if this Collection contains the specified element.
- containsAll(Collection) Returns true if this Collection contains all of the elements in the specified Collection.
- equals(Object) Compares the specified Object with this Collection for equality.
- hashCode() Returns the hash code value for this Collection.
- isEmpty() Returns true if this Collection contains no elements.
- iterator() Returns an Iterator over the elements in this Collection.
- remove(Object) Removes a single instance of the specified element from this Collection, if it is present (optional operation).
- removeAll(Collection) Removes from this Collection all of its elements that are contained in the specified Collection (optional operation).
- retainAll(Collection) Retains only the elements in this Collection that are contained in the specified Collection (optional operation).
- size() Returns the number of elements in this Collection.
- toArray() Returns an array containing all of the elements in this Collection.

You may note that some of the above methods are labelled "optional". This denotes that some implementations may not perform one or more of these operations. If they are called they should throw a run-time exception, the previously mentioned UnsupportedOperationException. This means that collection implementations must specify in their documentation which optional operations they support.

JavaSoft has introduced several terms to aid in this specification:

- Collections that do not support any modification operations (such as add, remove, clear) are referred to as unmodifiable. Collections that are not unmodifiable are referred to modifiable.
- Collections that additionally guarantee that no change in the Collection will ever be observable via "query" operations (such as iterator, size, contains) are referred to as immutable. Collections that are not immutable are referred to as mutable.
- Lists that guarantee that their size will remain constant even though the elements may change are referred to as fixed-size. Lists that are not fixed-size are referred to as variable-size.

Some implementations may restrict what elements (or in the case of maps, keys and values) may be stored. Possible restrictions include requiring elements to:

- be of a particular type
- be comparable to other elements in the collection
- be non-null
- obey some arbitrary predicate

If a programmer attempts to add an element that violates an implementation's restrictions, then that collection should generate a run-time exception. Under normal circumstances this should be one of:

- `ClassCastException`
- `IllegalArgumentException`
- `NullPointerException`

In addition, if a programmer tries to remove or test for such an element, then one of these exceptions may again be raised. However, this is not enforced and as such, depending on the implementation, no exception may be raised.

JavaSoft also state that all general-purpose Collection implementation classes should provide two "standard" constructors: a void (no arguments) constructor, which creates an empty `Collection`, and a constructor with a single argument of type `Collection`, which creates a new `Collection` with the same elements as its argument. In effect, the latter constructor allows the user to copy any `Collection`, producing an equivalent `Collection` of the desired implementation type. Similarly, all general-purpose `Map` implementations should provide a void (no arguments) constructor and a constructor that takes a single argument of type `Map`. There is no way to enforce these recommendations (as interfaces cannot contain constructors) but all of the general-purpose `Collection` and `Map` implementations in the JDK 1.2 comply with this guideline.

13.3.2 Set

The interface `Set` is basically the same as the interface `Collection`, with the exception that it does not allow duplicates. That is, it is only possible to hold a single reference to an object in a set.

13.3.3 List

A list is an ordered collection of elements . That is, a list has a very specific sequence to the elements it contains. That order is determined by the order in which objects are added to the ordered collection/`List` instance. An implementation of the `List` interface can hold any type of object. Implementations of the `List` interface can be used in situations where the order in which the objects were added to the instance must be preserved. In general, `List` implementations will allow duplicate objects (although any particular implementation may reject duplicates and thus throw a run-time exception). They may allow null objects, although again any particular implementation may decide to reject null values.

There is a range of order-related messages which allow objects to be added and accessed with reference to the order in the `List` instance. For example, it is possible to access an object at a particular location, to find the positon of an object or the last position of an object using methods such as `get(int)`, `set(int Object)`, `indexOf(Object)`, `indexOf(Object, int)` and `lastIndexOf(Object)`. Note that like arrays and `Vectors`, `Lists` are zero-based; thus the first location in a `List` is position zero. In addition this interface inherits all the methods defined in the `Collection` interface.

To process `Lists` it would certainly be possible to iterate over the elements of the `List` using a standard for loop and the `get(int)` method. However, the time taken to access a particular object is linear with respect to its position in the list. It is therefore more efficient to use one of the `Iterator` access methods provided by a `List`. List provides a special `Iterator`, called a `ListIterator`, that allows element insertion and replacement, and bidirectional access in addition to the normal `Iterator` operations. Two `Iterator` access methods are provided. One returns an iterator for the whole `List` while the second returns an iterator that starts at a specified position in the List.

The methods defined in this interface (in addition to those inherited from `Collection`) are:

- addAll(int, Collection) Inserts all of the elements in the specified Collection into this List at the specified position (optional operation).
- get(int) Returns the element at the specified position in this List.
- indexOf(Object) Returns the index in this List of the first occurrence of the specified element, or –1 if the List does not contain this element.
- indexOf(Object, int) Returns the index in this List of the first occurrence of the specified element at or after the specified position, or –1 if the element is not found.
- lastIndexOf(Object) Returns the index in this List of the last occurrence of the specified element, or –1 if the List does not contain this element.
- lastIndexOf(Object, int) Returns the index in this List of the last occurrence of the specified element at or before the specified position, or –1 if the List does not contain this element.
- listIterator() Returns a ListIterator of the elements in this List (in proper sequence).
- listIterator(int) Returns a ListIterator of the elements in this List (in proper sequence), starting at the specified position in the List.
- remove(int) Removes the element at the specified position in this List (optional operation).
- removeRange(int, int) Removes from this List all of the elements whose index is between fromIndex, inclusive and toIndex, exclusive (optional operation).
- set(int, Object) Replaces the element at the specified position in this List with the specified element (optional operation).

13.3.4 Map

A Map is a set of associations, each representing a key–value pair. The elements in a Map may be unordered, but each has a definite name or *key*. Although the values may be duplicated, keys cannot. In turn, a key can *map* to at most one value. Some Map implementations, like TreeMap and ArrayMap, make specific guarantees as to their order; others, like HashMap, do not.

The Map protocol allows the keys to be viewed, the values to be viewed or the keys to be used to access the values. JavaSoft have stated that all general-purpose Map implementation classes should provide two "standard" constructors: a void (no arguments) constructor which creates an empty Map, and a constructor with a single argument of type Map, which creates a new Map with the same key–value mappings as its argument. In effect, the latter constructor allows the user to copy any Map, producing an equivalent Map of the desired class.

- clear() Removes all mappings from this Map (optional operation).
- containsKey(Object) Returns true if this Map contains a mapping for the specified key.
- containsValue(Object) Returns true if this Map maps one or more keys to the specified value.
- entries() Returns a Collection view of the mappings contained in this Map.
- equals(Object) Compares the specified Object with this Map for equality.
- get(Object) returns the value associated with aKey.
- hashCode() Returns the hash code value for this Map.
- isEmpty() Returns true if this Map contains no key–value mappings.
- keySet() answers with a Set of keys from the receiver.
- put(Object key, Object value) Puts value into a dictionary with the external key key.
- putAll(Map) Copies all of the mappings from the specified Map to this Map (optional operation).
- remove(Object) Removes the mapping for this key from this Map if present (optional operation).

- `size()` Returns the number of key–value mappings in this Map.
- `values()` answers with a `Collection` of the values in the receiver. Note that values are not necessarily unique (hence they are returned as a `Collection` rather than as a `Set`).

13.3.5 Comparisons

In order to sort a collection, the objects within the collection either need to be `Comparable` or they need to be able to be compared using a `Comparator`. `Comparable` and `Comparator` are two interfaces which can be implemented so that collections and classes can be sorted.

- `public interface Comparable`. This interface defines the `compareTo(Object)`. This method should allow one object to be compared to another. The result of this comparison is referred to as the natural ordering of the objects. Arrays of `Objects` that implement this interface can be sorted automatically by `List.sort`. The interface assumes that concrete implementations of this interface will implement the `int compareTo(Object o)` method such that the method return negative if the receiver is less than the object passed to the metrhod, zero if they are equal and positive if the receiver is greater. Note many of the classes in the JDK now implement this interface.
- `public interface Comparator`. This interface defines a comparison function, which imposes a total ordering on some collection of `Objects`. Comparators can be passed to a sort method (such as `Arrays.sort`) to allow precise control over the sort order. The `Comparator` interface specifies one method: the `static int compare(Object, Object)` method. This method assumes that the result returned is negative if the first object is less than the second, zero if they are equal and a positive number if the first is greater than the second.

13.4 Abstract Implementations

A set of abstract classes are provided which implement the Collections API interfaces. These classes are `AbstractCollection`, `AbstractSet`, `AbstractList`, `AbstractSequentialList` and `AbstractMap`. They provide basic implementations for many of the methods specified in their associated interfaces (note the naming convention). The documentation provided with each class in the JDK 1.2 release indicates which methods need to be implemented for a concrete class to be implemented. We shall consider each of these classes below.

13.4.1 `AbstractCollection`

The `AbstractCollection` class provides a skeleton implementation of a `Collection`. This implementation represents what is often referred to as a bag or multiset. Abstractly, a `Bag` can be considered to be any collection of objects, which can be of any class; these objects are the elements of the `Bag`. It is a general placeholder for collections of objects. There is no order assumed. It is the most general form of collection available in Java.

If you are confused by this description of a bag, think of it as a shopping bag. At a supermarket, you pick objects up from the shelves and place them in your shopping bag. For example, you pick up a pint of milk, a box of corn flakes, a packet of biscuits, three bags of potato crisps, and a few bananas (see Figure 13.3).

Each of the objects in the bag is a different type of thing, with different characteristics etc. There is no particular order to them: they will have moved about in the bag while you were shopping and while you brought them home. When you reach into the bag at home to remove

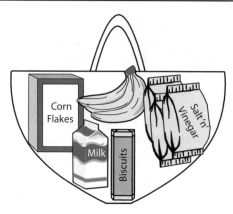

Fig. 13.3 A shopping bag.

the objects, the order in which they come out will not be predictable. If you think of a bag collection in these terms then you will not be far off the mark.

To create a concrete implementation of a Bag (or any other collection class) from the AbstractCollection class it is necessary to implement the following methods:

- public Iterator iterator() Returns an Iterator over the elements contained in this Collection. This object must implement the hasNext and next methods.
- public int size() Returns the number of elements in this Collection.

In addition, if the collection is to be modifiable, the subclass must implement the add(Object) method. This is because in the AbstractCollection class this method throws an UnsupportedOperationException. Note that the methods equals(Object) and hashCode() are inherited from Object.

13.4.2 AbstractSet

This abstract class is a direct subclass of AbstractCollection. It implements the Set interface. The only methods which are defined in this class are the methods equals(Object) and hashCode(). The equals(Object) method checks to see that the two objects are sets, that they have the same size and that all the objects in the set are equal. Note that it is assumed that the addition methods will conform to the Set constraint that duplicates are not allowed.

13.4.3 AbstractList

This abstract class provides a skeleton implementation of the List interface. Many methods are inherited from its direct superclass AbstractCollection. However, it defines methods such as add(int, Object), indexOf(Object) and indexOf(Object, int) from the interface definition so that the basic structure of a List (orderedCollection) is provided. It uses an array to hold the data internally. The data structure used is optimized for random access. If sequential access is to be the most commonly used form of access, then the AbstractSequentialList class should be subclassed.

To create a concrete List collection class a subclass must implement the following methods:

- get(int) This returns the object held at the specified position.
- size() This returns the number of elements held in the collection.

In addition, if the List collection is modifiable the subclass must implement the set(int, Object) method. The default implement will throw the UnsupportedOperationException. The assumption is also made that the List collection is of fixed size. This means that if the subclass is to be "growable" (that is can grow in size if necessary) then the subclass must also override the add(int, Object) and remove(int) methods. Note that it is not necessary to override the add() method. This is because the add method actually calls the add(int, Object) method using the size() method to generate the position index.

13.4.4 AbstractSequentialList

This is essentially the same as the AbstractList class from which it inherits except that the data structure and its access methods have been optimized for sequential access rather than random access. This means that it that it implements the "random access" methods (get(int index), set(int index, Object element), set(int index, Object element), add(int index, Object element) and remove(int index)) on top of List's listIterator, instead of the other way around.

To create a concrete subclass of this class, that subclass must implement:

- public abstract ListIterator listIterator(int index) Returns a ListIterator of the elements in this List (in proper sequence).
- public abstract int size() Returns the number of elements in this List.

In addition, for an unmodifiable List, the programmer should implement the listIterator's hasNext, next, hasPrevious, previous and index methods. For a modifiable List the programmer should also implement the listIterator's set method. For a variable-size list the programmer should additionally implement the listIterator's remove and add methods. Remember that the get, set and remove methods all use the list's listInterator.

13.4.5 AbstractMap

This abstract class provides a basic implementation for the Map interface. To create a concrete implementation of a map a subclass must implement:

- public abstract Collection entries() This method is expected to return a collection of all the key–value pairs in the map. It is expected to reflect the current state of the map; thus any changes made to the map should be reflected in the collection. Note that this collection is not expected to support the add or remove methods, and its Iterator should not support the remove method.

In addition, if a modifiable Map is to be defined, then the concrete subclass should override this class's put method (which otherwise throws an UnsupportedOperationException), and the Iterator returned by entries().iterator() must also implement its remove method.

13.5 Concrete Implementations

As stated earlier in this chapter these classes are general-purpose implementations of the core collection interfaces. They all inherit from appropriate abstract classes and thus provide good examples of how to create concrete versions of the various concepts such as lists and sets. The

Table 13.1 Concrete collection classes.

HashSet	Implements a Set
ArraySet	Intended for small sets (faster creation and iteration than HashSet)
ArrayList	An unsynchronized Vector
LinkedList	A doubly-linked List which may provide better performance if insertion and deletion occur frequently
Vector	As in JDK 1.1. Included for legacy applications
HashMap	An unsynchronized Hashtable
ArrayMap	Intended for small hashtables (faster creation and iteration than HashMap)
TreeMap	A balanced binary tree implementation of the Map interface. Unlike Hashtable, imposes an ordering on its elements
Hashtable	As in JDK 1.1. Included for legacy applications

classes are summarised in Table 13.1. All the new classes (that is those other than Hashtable and Vector) are unsynchronized as this greatly improves their performance. They can be synchronized by using a synchonizing wrapper which can be obtained using the appropriate Collection class static method. For example, to generate a synchronized version of a collection class you can use the static method Collection.synchronizedCollection(Collection c).

As the concrete collectionclasses implement the appropriate associated interfaces we will not list the complete set of methods for each class. Instead, we will only look at the new classes and consider the inheritance relationships between the classes and what constructors they provide. In some cases an example of using that class is also provided.

13.5.1 HashSet

This class is a direct subclass of the AbstractSet class. It implements the Set interface as well as the java.lang.Clonable and java.io.Serializable interfaces.

The HashSet class provides the following constructors:

- HashSet() Constructs a new, empty HashSet; the backing HashMap has default capacity and load factor. The default capacity and load factor for a HashMap are 101 and 75%.
- HashSet(Collection) Constructs a new HashSet containing the elements in the specified Collection.
- HashSet(int) Constructs a new, empty HashSet; the backing HashMap has the specified initial capacity and default load factor (75%).
- HashSet(int, float) Constructs a new, empty HashSet; the backing HashMap has the specified initial capacity and the specified load factor.

For example, consider the following simple Test class. This class creates a simple set and adds four strings to it (one of which is a duplicate):

```java
import java.util.*;

public class Test {
  public static void main(String args []) {
    HashSet set = new HashSet(10);
    set.add("John");
    set.add("Denise");
```

```
    set.add("Phoebe");
    set.add("John");
    Iterator it = set.iterator();
    while (it.hasNext()) {
      System.out.println(it.next());
    }
  }
}
```

Note that an iterator is used to process all the elements in the set. Iteration over collections is described in more detail later in this chapter. The result of executing this class is:

```
C:>java Test
John
Phoebe
Denise
```

13.5.2 ArraySet

This class is a direct subclass of the AbstractSet class. It implements the Set interface as well as the java.lang.Clonable and java.io.Serializable interfaces. It is intended for use with small sets which are likely to be frequently modified. It will give *extremely* poor performance for large sets.

The ArraySet class provides the following constructors:

- ArraySet() Constructs a new, empty ArraySet; the backing ArrayList has default initial capacity (10) and capacity increment (0). If the increment is zero then the size of the ArrayList is doubled each time the current capacity is exceeded.
- ArraySet(Collection) Constructs a new ArraySet containing the elements in the specified Collection.
- ArraySet(int) Constructs a new, empty ArraySet; the backing ArrayList has the specified initial capacity and default capacity increment.

13.5.3 ArrayList

This is a concrete subclass of the AbstractList class. It is a resizable list collection. Essentially this is an unsynchronized Vector. Like a Vector, it has an initial capacity and an increment. Again like Vector its default capacity is 10 and its default increment is zero. If the increment is zero then the size of the ArrayList doubles each time the capacity is exceeded. Also like Vector it possesses methods to manipulate its size, such as ensureCapacity(int), trimToSize() and size().

The ArrayList class provides the following constructors:

- ArrayList() constructs an array list with a capacity of 10 and an increment of 0.
- ArrayList(Collection) Constructs an ArrayList containing the elements of the specified Collection, in the order they are returned by the Collection's iterator. The increment is defaulted to zero.
- ArrayList(int) Constructs an empty ArrayList with the specified initial capacity and the default increment.

- ArrayList(int, int) Constructs an empty ArrayList with the specified initial capacity and capacity increment.

As an example, consider the following Test class modified to use an ArrayList. This class creates a simple set and adds four strings to it (one of which is a duplicate):

```java
import java.util.*;

public class Test {
    public static void main(String args []) {
        ArrayList list = new ArrayList(10);
        list.add("John");
        list.add("Denise");
        list.add("Phoebe");
        list.add("John");
        Iterator it = list.iterator();
        while (it.hasNext()) {
            System.out.println(it.next());
        }
    }
}
```

The results obtained from running this example are illustrated below:

```
C:>java Test
John
Phoebe
Denise
John
```

Note that ArrayList allows duplicates.

13.5.4 LinkedList

The LinkedList class is a concrete subclass of the AbstractSequentialList class. It provides a doubly linked list implementation of the List interface. This class is particularly good for sequential access oriented operations and for insertions and deletions. It provides the following constructors:

- LinkedList() Constructs an empty LinkedList.
- LinkedList(Collection) Constructs a LinkedList containing the elements of the specified Collection, in the order they are returned by the Collection's iterator.

The LinkedList class also provides the following additional methods for adding objects to the front and back of a list:

- addFirst(Object) Inserts the given element at the beginning of this List.
- addLast(Object) Appends the given element to the end of this List.

In turn it also provides the following additional access methods:

- getFirst() Returns the first element in this List.
- getLast() Returns the last element in this List.

The following deletion methods are also defined:

- removeFirst() Removes and returns the first element from this List.
- removeLast() Removes and returns the last element from this List.

13.5.5 HashMap

This class is a concrete subclass of the AbstractMap class. It is essentially an unsynchronized HashTable. As with the HashTable class it possesses a default capacity and loading factor. In HashMap these are 101 and 75% respectively. The constructors provided by HashMap are:

- HashMap() Constructs a new, empty HashMap with a default capacity of 101 and load factor of 75%.
- HashMap(int) Constructs a new, empty HashMap with the specified initial capacity and default load factor.
- HashMap(int, float) Constructs a new, empty HashMap with the specified initial capacity and the specified load factor.
- HashMap(Map) Constructs a new HashMap with the same mappings as the given Map.

An example of using a HashMap is provided below:

```java
import java.util.*;

public class MapTest {
    public static void main(String args []) {
        HashMap table = new HashMap(10);
        table.put("John", "C47");
        table.put("Denise", "D57");
        table.put("Phoebe", "A12");
        table.put("Isobel", "E56");
        System.out.println("Johns office is " + table.get("John"));
    }
}
```

The result of executing this class is:

```
c:> java MapTest
Johns office is C47
```

13.5.6 ArrayMap

This is a concrete subclass of AbstractMap. It is intended for small, but fast, hash tables. It is implemented on top of an ArrayList and overrides the entries(), clone() and put(key, value) methods. In an ArrayMap the key and value pairs are guaranteed to be in the order in which they were inserted. If a key–value pair is removed and a mapping for the same key is inserted at a later time, the mapping goes to the end of the map.

It provides the following constructors:

- ArrayMap() Constructs a new, empty ArrayMap; the backing ArrayList has default initial capacity and capacity increment.
- ArrayMap(int) Constructs a new, empty ArrayMap; the backing ArrayList has the specified initial capacity and default capacity increment.
- ArrayMap(Map) Constructs a new ArrayMap containing the mappings in the specified Map.

13.5.7 TreeMap

This class is a concrete subclass of the AbstractMap class and implements a binary tree as the data structure for holding the mappings from keys to values. The binary tree is ordered on the keys and thus guarantees that the key–value pairs are in key order. This class thus provides guaranteed log(n) time cost for the containsKey, get, put and remove operations.

It provides the following constructors:

- TreeMap() Constructs a new, empty TreeMap, sorted according to the key's natural sort method.
- TreeMap(Comparator) Constructs a new, empty TreeMap, sorted according to the given comparator.
- TreeMap(Map) Constructs a new TreeMap containing the same mappings as the given Map, sorted according to the key's natural sort method.

13.6 The Collections Class

The Collections class is a general utility class of the Collections API. It provides many very useful (static) methods which can be used to wrap collections in a syncrhonized wrapping, to search and sort collections, to find the minimum or maximum value in a collection and create unmodifiable versions of modifiable collections. Note that this class provides no instance-side methods – all the methods are static.

The following list sumarises the set of methods available:

- binarySearch(List, Object) Performs a binary search on the list for the specified object.
- binarySearch(List, Object, Comparator) Performs a binary search on the list for the specified object using the specified comparator.
- enumeration(Collection) Returns an enumeration object for the specified collection.
- max(Collection) Returns the object which is returns the maximum value for the normal comparison methods for its elements.
- max(Collection, Comparator) Returns the maximum element of the given Collection, according to the order induced by the specified Comparator.
- min(Collection) Returns the object which returns the minimum value for the normal comparison methods for its elements.
- min(Collection, Comparator) Returns the minimum element of the given Collection, according to the order induced by the specified Comparator.
- nCopies(int, Object) Generates a list containing the specified number of copies of the object. This list is immutable.
- sort(List) Sorts the specified List into ascending order, according to the natural comparison method of its elements.

- `sort(List, Comparator)` Sorts the specified `List` according to the order induced by the specified `Comparator`.
- `subList(List, int, int)` Generates a sublist consisting of the elements of the specified list between the first and second indexes. The first index is inclusive the second index is exclusive.
- `synchronizedCollection(Collection)` Returns the collection wrapped in a synchronization wrapper.
- `synchronizedList(List)` Returns the `List` wrapped in a synchronization wrapper.
- `synchronizedMap(Map)` Returns the `Map` wrapped in a synchronization wrapper.
- `synchronizedSet(Set)` Returns the `Set` wrapped in a synchronization wrapper.
- `unmodifiableCollection(Collection)` Returns a version of the collection which is unmodifiable.
- `unmodifiableList(List)` Returns a version of the list which is unmodifiable.
- `unmodifiableMap(Map)` Returns a version of the map which is unmodifiable.
- `unmodifiableSet(Set)` Returns a version of the set which is unmodifiable.

13.7 Iteration Over Collections

Just as with the classes `Vector` and hashtable it is possible to iterate over the contents of any of the collection classes. In JDK 1.1 implementations of the `Enumeration` interface were used to perform this iteration. In JDK 1.2 iterators are used. The change in name is intended to indicate that iterators are more powerful and are meaningful (in that a number of the methods have changed their name to be more obvious). For example, the `hasMoreElements()` method of `Enumeration` is replaced by `hasNext()` as the method `next()` is used to access the next element in the iteration. It is also possible to modify the collection underlying the iteration, while the iteration is in progress. In time it is expected that the `Iterator` will replace the `Enumeration`.

The `Iterator` interface is one of two interfaces (the `ListIterator` is the other) which provide for iteration. This interface defines the following (abstract) methods which are implemented by any concrete iterator:

- `hasNext()` This returns `true` if there is at least one more element to process.
- `next()` Returns the next element in the collection to process. Note to access the first element in the iteration, the method `next()` must first be called.
- `remove()` This method deletes the last element returned by the method `next()` from the underlying collection.

The `Iterator` interface has a direct sub-interface, the `ListIterator` interface. This interface extends the concept of iterators to allow much greater manipulation of the underlying collection as well as the ability to process elements of the iteration in either direction (i.e. backwards as well as forwards).

The `ListIterator` interface defines the following (abstract) methods which are implemented by any concrete `ListIterator`:

- `add(Object)` Adds the `Object` to the underlying list. The object is added at the current point in the iteration. Thus a subsequent call to `next()` would return this object.
- `hasNext()` Returns `true` if there is at least one more element to return using the `next()` method.

- hasPrevious() Returns true if there is at least one more element to return using the previous() method.
- next() Returns the next element in the collection to process. Note to access the first element in the iteration, the method next() must first be called.
- nextIndex() Returns the index of the element that would be returned by a subsequent call to next.
- previous() returns the element before the current element in the iteration.
- previousIndex() Returns the index of the element that would be returned by a subsequent call to previous.
- remove() Removes from the List the last element that was returned by next() or previous().
- set(Object) Replaces the last element returned by next or previous with the specified element.

13.8 Array Sorting and Searching

The Arrays class provides a set of utility methods for sorting and searching arrays as well as for converting arrays to lists. There are a wide range of sorting and searching methods for different basic data types (such as byte, short, long etc.) as well as for objects (reference types). The search methods are all of the format binarySearch(<array of type>, <data of type>) for example binarySearch(byte[], byte). In turn the sorting methods are all of the format sort(<array of type>), for example sort(short[]). For arrays of type Object, an additional sorting method is provided in which the type of comaprator to be used can be specified (sort(Object [], comparator)). The toList method takes an array of type Object and returns a list.

13.9 Choosing a Collection class

It can sometimes be confusing for those new to the Collections API to decide which collection class to use. Some make the mistake of always using an array (because it is similar to the constructs that they are used to). However, this is failing to understand the way one should work with collections (data structures) in Java. To this end the decision tree of Figure 13.4 may be of use.

The most commonly used collection classes are HashSet, ArrayList, HashMap and LinkedList.

13.10 Summary

It is likely that, just as in Smalltalk, these classes will become the most used classes in Java. The various collection API interfaces and classes will form the basis of the data structures you build and will be the cornerstone of most of your implementations. For those of you coming from a Lisp-style language these concepts won't have seemed too strange. However, for those of you coming from languages such as C, Pascal or Ada you may well have found the ideas of a bag and a set quite bizarre. Stick with them, try them out, implement some simple programs using them

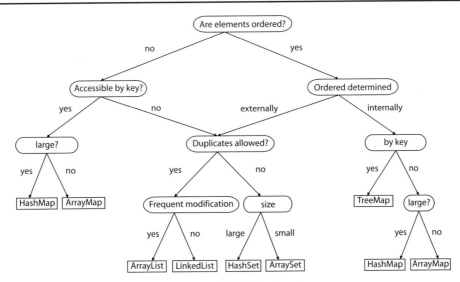

Fig. 13.4 Selecting which Collection class to use.

and you will soon find that they are easy to use and extremely useful. You will very quickly come to wonder why every language doesn't have the same facilities!

Part **4**

Further Java

Chapter 14

Control and Iteration

14.1 Introduction

This chapter introduces control and iteration in Java. In Java, as in many other languages, the mainstays of the control and iteration processes are the `if` and `switch` statements and the `for` and `while` loops.

14.2 Control Structures

14.2.1 The `If` Statement

The basic format of an `if` statement in Java is the same as that in C. A test is performed and, depending on the result of the test, a statement is performed. A set of statements to be executed can be grouped together in curly brackets {}. For example:

```java
if (a == 5)
   System.out.println("true")
else
   System.out.println("false");

if (a == 5) {
   System.out.print("a = 5");
   System.out.println("The answer is therefore true");
}
else {
   System.out.print("a != 5");
   System.out.println("The answer is therefore false");
}
```

Of course, the `if` statement need not include the optional `else` construct:

```java
if (a == 5) {
   System.out.print("a = 5");
   System.out.println("The answer is therefore true");
}
```

You must have a boolean in a condition expression, so you cannot make the same equality mistake as in C. The following code always generates a compile time error:

```
if (a = 1) {
    ...
}
```

Unfortunately, assigning a boolean to a variable results in a boolean (all expressions return a result) and thus the following code is legal, but does not result in the intended behaviour (the string "Hello" is always printed on the console):

```
public class Test {
    public static void main (String args []) {
        boolean a = false;
        if (a = true)
            System.out.println("Hello");
} }
```

You can construct nested if statements, as in any other language:

```
if (count < 100)
    if (index < 10)
        {...}
    else
        {...}
else
    {...}
```

However, it is easy to get confused. Java does not provide an explicit if-then-elseif-else type of structure. In some languages, you can write:

```
if (n < 10)
    print ("less than 10");
else if (n < 100)
    print ("greater than 10 but less than 100");
else if (n < 1000)
    print ("greater than 100 but less then 1000");
else
    print ("greater than 1000");
```

This code is intended to be read as laid out above. However, if we write it in Java, it should be laid out as below:

```
if (n < 10)
    print ("less than 10");
else if (n < 100)
        print ("greater than 10 but less than 100");
    else if (n < 1000)
            print ("> than 100 but < 1000");
        else
            print ("> than 1000");
```

This code clearly has a very different meaning (although it may have the same effect). This can lead to the infamous "dangling else" problem. Another solution is the `switch` statement. However, as you will see, the `switch` statement has significant limitations.

14.2.2 The Conditional Operator

Java has inherited the conditional operator from C. This has both good and bad points. It is good because it is a very concise and efficient way of performing a test and carrying out one of two operations. It is bad because its terse nature is not clear to non-C programmers. However, it is a part of the language and all Java programmers must understand it.

The Java conditional operator has three operands which are separated by two symbols in the following format:

```
boolean expression ? true expression : false expression
```

The boolean expression determines whether the true or false expression is evaluated. For example, the following expression prints the maximum of two numbers:

```
m >= n ? System.out.println(m) : System.out.println(n);
```

The conditional operator, unlike an `if` statement, returns a value. It can therefore be used in an assignment statement. For example, we can assign the larger of two numbers to a third variable:

```
x = m >= n ? m : n;
```

Notice that this is becoming less readable (unless you are an experienced C programmer, in which case you would argue that it is obvious!).

14.2.3 The `switch` Statement

The conditional operator is not the only control statement that Java inherits from C; it also inherits the (flawed) C switch statement. This is a multi-way selection statement (similar to the case or select statement of some other programming languages). The structure of the switch statement is basically:

```
switch (expression) {
  case label1 :
    ...
    break;
  case label2 :
    ...
    break;
  ...
  default: ...
}
```

The expression returns an integer value and the case labels represent the possible values produced by the expression. Each case label is followed by one or more statements which are executed until a break (or return) statement is encountered. A switch statement may include a default statement which is executed if none of the case labels match the integer in the expression.

The switch statement has two major flaws. The first flaw is the need to "break" out of each case block. This is a major problem that has led to many software bugs. For example, in December 1989 the long-distance telephone service in the USA was disrupted by a software problem in the AT&T electronic switching systems. The problem was allegedly traced to the misuse of a break statement in a C program. The inclusion of such a feature has serious implications for the construction of high-integrity software.

The second major flaw is the inability of the switch statement to deal with anything other than integer comparisons (or types that can be converted to ints, such as byte, char or short). Note that this means you cannot use long, double or any type of object in such a comparison. Therefore there are many situations in which it would be far easier to write the following code:

```java
switch (student.getMark() ) {
   case > 70 ...
   ...
}
```

Instead, you must convert the tested value into an integer and then test the integers explicitly:

```java
public class Grades {

   public static void main (String argv[]) {
      Grades g = new Grades();
      g.classify(60);
   }

   public void classify(int aNumber) {
      int temp = 0;
      System.out.println("The grade mark is " +
            aNumber);

      temp = aNumber / 10;

      switch (temp) {
         case 4 : System.out.println("Pass"); break;
         case 5 : System.out.println("2.2"); break;
         case 6 : System.out.println("2.1"); break;
         case 7 : case 8: case 9: case 10 :
            System.out.println("1st"); break;
         default : System.out.println("Fail");
      }
   }
}
```

The result of running this application is illustrated in Figure 14.1.

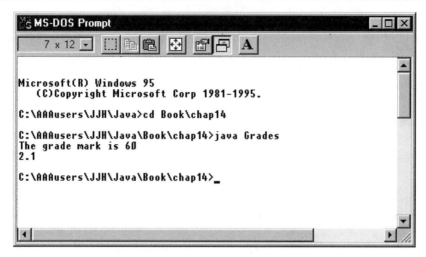

Fig. 14.1 The result of running the Grades application.

14.3 Iteration

Iteration in Java is accomplished using the for, while and do-while statements. Just like their counterparts in other languages, these statements repeat a sequence of instructions a given number of times.

14.3.1 for Loops

A for loop in Java is very similar to a for loop in C. It is used to step a variable through a series of values until a given test is false. Many languages have a very simple for loop, for example:

```
for i = 1 to 10 do
   ...
endfor;
```

In this construct, you do not need to specify the end condition, nor how the variable i is incremented; in Java, you must specify both :

```
for (initial-expression; test; increment-expression)
statement
```

This has the disadvantage of making the for construct more complicated, but it does offer a great deal of control. One point to note with this for loop is that the boolean test expression indicates the condition that must hold while the loop is repeated. That is, it is a *while true* loop, rather than an *until true* loop. An example for loop is presented below:

```
for (n = 1; n <= 10; n = n + 1)
System.out.println(n);
```

This loop assigns n the initial value 1. While n <= 10, it executes the println method and increments the value of n. We can repeat more than one statement, if we enclose them in curly brackets { }.

As in C, you can use a comma-delimited list to initialize and increment (decrement) several variables in a for loop. The expressions separated by commas are evaluated from left to right:

```
for (i = 0, j = 10; i < 10; i++, j--)
System.out.println (i + " : " + j);
```

14.3.2 while Loops

The while loop exists in almost all programming languages. In most cases, it has a basic form such as:

```
while (test expression)
statement
```

This is also true for Java. The while expression controls the execution of one or more statements. If more than one statement is to be executed then the statements must be enclosed in curly brackets {}:

```
n = 1;
while (n <= 10) {
   System.out.println(n);
   n++;
}
```

The above loop tests to see if the value of n is less than or equal to 10, and then prints the current value of n before incrementing it by one. This is repeated until the test expression returns false (i.e. n > 11).

You must assign n an initial value before the condition expression. If you do not provide an initial value for n, it defaults to null and the comparison with a numeric value raises an exception.

14.3.3 do Loops

In some cases, we want to execute the body of statements at least once; you can accomplish this with the do loop construct:

```
do
   statement
while (test expression);
```

This loop is guaranteed to execute at least once, as the test is only performed after the statement has been evaluated. As with the while loop, the do loop repeats until the condition is false. You can repeat more than one statement by bracketing a series of statements into a block using curly brackets {}:

```
n = 10;
do {
   System.out.println(n);
   n--;
} while (n > 0);
```

The above do loop prints the numbers from 10 down to 1 and terminates when n = 0.

14.3.4 An Example of Loops

As a concrete example of the for and while loops, consider the following class. It possesses a method which prints numbers from 0 to 1 less than the MaxValue class variable:

```java
public class Counter {
  // A class variable
  public static int MaxValue = 10;

  public static void main (String argv[]) {
    Counter c = new Counter();
    c.count();
  }

  public void count() {
    int i;
    System.out.println("----- For -------");
    for (i = 0; i < MaxValue; ++i) {
      System.out.print(" " + i);
    }
    System.out.println(" ");
    System.out.println("----- While -------");
    i = 0;
    while (i < MaxValue) {
      System.out.print(" " + i);
      ++i;
    }
    System.out.println(" ");
    System.out.println("--------------------");
  }
}
```

The result of running this application should be:

```
>java Counter
----- For -------
 0 1 2 3 4 5 6 7 8 9
----- While -------
 0 1 2 3 4 5 6 7 8 9
--------------------
```

14.4 Recursion

Recursion is a very powerful programming idiom found in many languages. Java is no exception. The following class illustrates how to use recursion to generate the factorial of a number:

```java
public class Factorial {

  public static void main (String argv[]) {
    Factorial f = new Factorial();
    System.out.println(f.factorial(5));
  }

  public int factorial (int aNumber) {
    System.out.println(aNumber);
    if (aNumber == 1)return 1;
    else return aNumber + factorial(--aNumber);
  }
}
```

The result of running this application is illustrated in Figure 14.2.

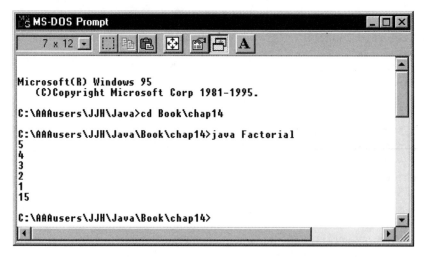

Fig. 14.2 Running the factorial application.

14.5 Summary

You now know virtually everything about Java, the language. You have learned the basics of the language, including conditional and iteration statements. You are now ready to consider a much larger application in Java.

Chapter 15

An Object-Oriented Organizer

15.1 Introduction

This chapter presents a detailed example application constructed using the data structure classes. The application is intended as an electronic personal organizer. It contains an address book, a diary (or appointments section) and a section for notes. The remainder of this chapter describes one way of implementing such an organizer. At the end of the chapter, there is a programming exercise.

15.2 The Organizer Class

This application involves more than one class and has a more complex architecture than anything you have seen so far (see Figure 15.1). It also illustrates another important concept in object orientation, that of an object within an object. These are often referred to as *part-of* hierarchies, i.e. one object is *part-of* another. This should not be confused with the class hierarchy, which is a *kind-of* hierarchy.

Fig. 15.1 The structure of the anOrganizer object.

An instance of the Organizer class contains three other objects. These objects are held in the instance variables addressBook, appointments and notes. The instances within addressBook and appointments are Hashtable objects, while the notes instance variable holds a Vector object.

15.3 The Class Definition

The purpose of the Organizer class is to provide some of the facilities of a personal organizer. The class definition is illustrated below. We shall build this definition up throughout the chapter:

```java
import java.util.*;

public class Organizer {

    // Instance variable definitions
    private Hashtable addressBook = new Hashtable();
    private Hashtable appointments = new Hashtable();
    private Vector notes = new Vector();
    ...
    // all methods go here
    ...
}
```

We have defined the class and its instance variables. Notice that we have made the instance variables private. This ensures that objects outside the Organizer class cannot access the variables directly; they must access the information via specified interfaces. Also notice that we have imported the java.util package, as we are using both the Hashtable and Vector classes. In addition, we have initialized the instance variables so that they hold the appropriate objects.

15.4 The Updating Protocol

Now we define the methods for the *updating* protocol. That is, we define all the methods associated with adding new information to the organizer.

The addNote method adds a new note to the notes instance variable. It is an extremely simple method that requires no additional explanation:

```java
public void addNote(String aNote) {
    notes.addElement(aNote);
}
```

The addAddress method adds a new address to the addressBook. It first checks to see whether the name provided is already in the address book. If it is, an error message is generated; otherwise the name and address are added to the book. Notice that we use another instance method addressFor (part of the accessing protocol) to determine whether the addressee is already present; if not, it returns the result null (you can use the null value instead of any object, in this case, a string). The addAddress method is illustrated below:

```java
public void addAddress(String name, String location) {
    String alreadyThere;
    alreadyThere = addressFor(name);
    if (alreadyThere == null) {
        addressBook.put(name, location);
        System.out.println("Added " + name +
```

```
            " to the address book");
   }
   else
      System.out.println("An entry for " + name +
            " is already present");
}
```

The method for adding a new appointment is essentially the same as the addAddress method:

```
public void newAppointment(String anAppointment,
         String aDate) {
   String alreadyThere;
   alreadyThere = appointmentFor(aDate);
   if (alreadyThere == null) {
      appointments.put(aDate, anAppointment);
      System.out.println("Added " + anAppointment +
            " for " + aDate);
   }
   else
      System.out.println("An entry for " + aDate +
            " is already present");
}
```

15.5 The Accessing Protocol

Next, we define the methods associated with obtaining information from the organizer. That is, we define all the methods used to access information within the instance variables.

The addressFor method retrieves an address from the address book. Although the return type of the method is String, it can also return a null value. Also, notice that we must cast the result obtained from the hash table addressBook to a String:

```
public String addressFor(String name) {
   String address;
   address = (String) addressBook.get(name);
   if (address == null)
      System.out.println("No address for " + name);
   return address;
}
```

The appointmentFor method retrieves an appointment from the appointments instance variable. It is essentially the same as the addressFor method:

```
public String appointmentFor(String aDate) {
   String appointment;
   appointment = (String) appointments.get(aDate);
   if (appointment == null)
      System.out.println("No appointment for " + aDate);
   return appointment;
}
```

Finally, the printNotes method displays all the notes which have been made in the organizer:

```
public void printNotes() {
  String item;
  System.out.println("\n\t Notes");
  System.out.println("\t-------\n");
  for (Enumeration enum = notes.elements();
       enum.hasMoreElements(); ) {
    item = (String) enum.nextElement();
    System.out.println(item);
  }
}
```

The above method uses special characters, known as escape characters, which help to control the printed text. The characters \t and \n indicate a tab and a line feed, respectively.

15.6 The main Method

Once you have defined all the methods, you are ready to use your organizer. The Organizer class is not intended as an application in its own right. Instead it is intended to be used with other classes as part of a larger application. However, it is good Java style to provide a main method. In a class which is not expected to be the top-level class in an application, this method can provide a test harness which illustrates typical use of the class. When the class is used as part of a larger application the main method is ignored. The main method in the Organizer class has been used in just such a way:

```
public static void main (String args [] ) {
  Organizer organizer = new Organizer();
  System.out.println("Adding test information\n");
  organizer.addAddress("John", "Room 47");
  organizer.addAddress("Myra", "Room 42");
  organizer.newAppointment("Meeting with MEng",
                    "10/10/97");
  organizer.addNote("I must do all my work");
  System.out.println("\nNow performing tests\n");
  System.out.println("Johns address is " +
                  organizer.addressFor("John"));
  System.out.println("Appointments for 10/10/97 are "
                  + organizer.appointmentFor("10/10/97"));
  organizer.printNotes();
}
```

This method shows how the organizer can be used. It creates a new organizer and adds some entries to it (see Figure 15.2).

Try your organizer out in a similar way. Extend its functionality. For example, provide a way of deleting an address or replacing it with a new one.

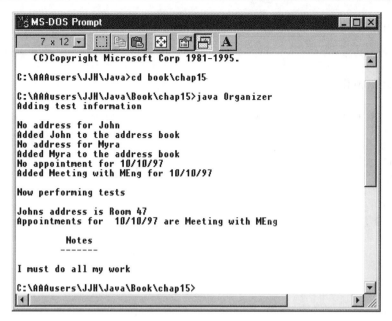

Fig. 15.2 Running the organizer as an application.

15.7 Exercise – the Financial Manager Project

In the remainder of this book, you develop a small project which provides the basic functionality of a Financial Manager application:

1. Add a deposit to a current account for a specified amount.
2. Make a payment (withdrawal) from a current account for a specified amount.
3. Get the current balance of a current account.
4. Print a statement of all payments and deposits made, in the order in which they happened, to the Transcript.

Create a subclass of Object (for example, FinancialManager) to hold the current balance and handle deposits and withdrawals. You should be able to specify the user's name and initial balance to the constructor. Use a Vector class to hold the statement. Create a test class with a main method that resembles the following code:

```
public class Test {
  public static void main (String args []) {
    FinancialManager fm =
        new FinancialManager("John", 0.0);
    fm.deposit(25.00);
    fm.withdraw(12.00);
    fm.deposit(10.00);
    fm.deposit(5.00);
    fm.withdraw(8.00);
    System.out.println("The current balance is " +
                       fm.balance());
```

```
      fm.statement();
   }
}
```

The output from this Test class is:

```
The current balance is 20.0
Statement:
Deposit  0.0
Deposit  25.0
Withdraw 12.0
Deposit  10.0
Deposit  5.0
Withdraw 8.0
```

Chapter 16

Streams and Files

16.1 Introduction

This chapter discusses the second most used class hierarchy in Java: the Stream classes. The Stream classes are used (amongst other things) for accessing files. The stream classes can be found in the java.io package.

Notice that the Stream classes and hierarchies are quite large and complex. You should therefore not worry if you are unable to grasp the facilities provided by all the classes (or indeed how they relate to each other). This chapter does not attempt to provide a complete description of the classes; rather, it tries to offer a taste of what Streams can do and why they are provided. You should refer to the Java online reference material for further details.

16.2 Streams

16.2.1 What Is a Stream?

Streams are objects which serve as sources or sinks of data. At first this concept can seem a bit strange. The easiest way to think of a stream is as a conduit of data flowing from or into a pool. Some streams read data straight from the "pool" and some streams read data from other streams. These streams then do some "useful" processing of the data and are referred to as "filter" streams. Figure 16.1 illustrates this idea. In this figure the initial stream reads data from the data source, the BufferedInputStream, then buffers the data-reading process for efficiency; then the DataInputStream converts the low-level bytes into meaningful data types.

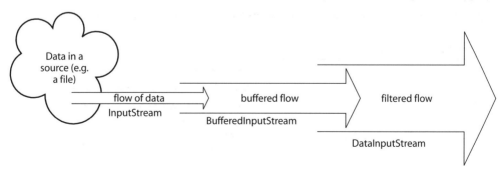

Fig. 16.1 Filter streams.

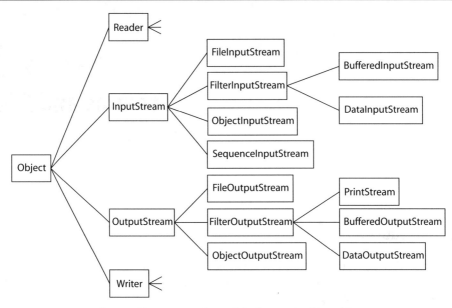

Fig. 16.2 The structure of part of the Stream class hierarchies.

There are a number of types of stream in the Java system, and each has a wide range of uses. Figure 16.2 illustrates part of the structure of the Stream class hierarchy. The abstract InputStream and OutputStream classes are the root classes of the stream hierarchies. Below them are stream classes for reading, writing, accessing external files etc.

A stream may be input only (InputStream) or output only (OutputStream); it may be specialized for handling files (FileInputStream); and it may be an internal stream (which acts as a source or sink for data internal to the system) or an external stream (which is the source or sink for data external to the system). A string is a typical example of an internal source or sink, whereas a file is a typical example of an external source or sink.

Typically, a stream is connected to an external device or a collection of data. If a stream is connected to an external device (for example, a file), then it acts as an interface to that device. It allows messages to be sent to and received from the external device object, enabling it to accomplish various activities including input and output. If a stream is connected to a collection (such as a string) it acts as a way to process the contents of the collection. In both cases, the stream views the source (or sink) of the data as being able to provide (or receive) a data item on request.

Tables 16.1–16.4 list the methods and classes used by input and output streams.

Table 16.1 InputStream class methods.

close()	Closes the receiving input stream and releases resources
read()	Answers the next byte of data in the receiver stream
read(byte b [])	Reads bytes of data into the array from the receiver
read(byte b [], int offSet, int length)	Reads bytes of data into the array, starting at offSet and finishing at offSet plus length

Table 16.2 OutputStream class methods.

close()	Closes the receiving output stream and releases resources
flush()	Flushes the output stream such that any buffered output is written
write (int b)	Writes a byte, b, to the receiving stream
write (byte b [])	Writes the contents of the array, b, to the receiving stream
write(byte b [], int offSet, int length)	Writes all data elements of the array, b, to the receiver stream starting at offSet and finishing at offSet plus length

Table 16.3 The input stream classes.

FileInputStream	Reads data from a file
FilterInputStream	Superclass of all classes that filter input streams
ObjectInputStream	Reads data and objects from a file (used with a FileInputStream)
SequenceInputStream	Enables several input streams to be linked serially
BufferedInputStream	Buffers input to reduce number of reads
DataInputStream	Reads primitive Java data types from an underlying input stream

Table 16.4 The output stream classes.

FileOutputStream	Writes data to a file
FilterOutputStream	Superclass of all classes that filter output streams
ObjectOutputStream	Saves data and objects to a file (used with a FileOutputStream)
BufferedOutputStream	Buffers writing to an underlying stream for efficiency
PrintWriter	Handles output of non-byte data
DataOutputStream	Writes primitive data types to an output stream

16.2.2 Readers and Writers: Character Streams

Specialist class hierarchies (Figure 16.3) intended for reading and writing character streams form part of the java.io package and return characters (rather than bytes).

Versions 1.0 and 1.0.2 did not contain such classes. They have been introduced because they simplify the task of writing programs that are not dependent on a specific character encoding. They make it easier to write a program that works with ASCII, Unicode etc., which is important if you are developing systems which might be used in different parts of the world, using different encodings to represent features of different languages. By default, Java uses Unicode, an international standard character encoding.

The Reader classes convert bytes from a byte input stream into characters in Java's Unicode representation. In turn, the Writer classes convert characters into bytes and then write those bytes to a byte output stream. Typically, you do not use these classes directly. You instantiate them and use them in conjunction with an object, such as a stream tokenizer.

The Reader class (Table 16.5) is the abstract root class for all streams that read characters. Its subclasses must override the read(char[], int, int) and close methods, at least. However, most subclasses override other methods and provide functionality.

The Writer class (Table 16.6) is the abstract root class for all streams that write characters. Subclasses of this class must override the write(char[], int, int), flush and close methods, at least. They may also override other methods and provide additional methods.

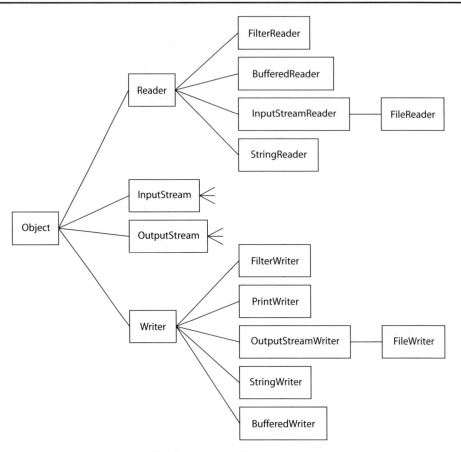

Fig. 16.3 The Reader and Writer hierarchies.

Table 16.5 The Reader class protocol.

close()	Closes a stream
read()	Reads a single character
read(char charBuffer [])	Reads characters into an array
read(char charBuffer [], int offSet, int length)	Reads characters into a portion of an array, starting at offSet and up to offSet plus length
ready()	Indicates whether the stream is ready to be read from

Table 16.6 The Writer class protocol.

close()	Closes the stream, flushing it first
flush()	Flushes the stream by writing buffered characters to the byte stream, which is also flushed
write(int character)	Writes a single character
write (char charBuffer [])	Writes out an array of characters
write (char charBuffer [], int offSet, int length)	Writes a portion of an array of characters, starting at offSet and finishing at offSet plus length
write(String string)	Writes a string to a stream
write(String string, int offSet, int length)	Writes a portion of a string starting at offSet and finishing at offSet plus length

Table 16.7 The Reader classes.

BufferedReader	A stream that provides for the efficient buffering of characters being read
FilterReader	Abstract class for reading filtered character streams
StringReader	A character stream whose source is a string
InputStreamReader	A stream that translates bytes into characters according to a specified character encoding
FileReader	Convenience class for reading character files

The constructors of the FileReader class (Table 16.7) assume that the default character encoding and the default byte buffer size are appropriate. You can specify these values yourself by constructing an InputStreamReader on a FileInputStream.

The constructors of the FileWriter class (Table 16.8) assume that the default character encoding and the default byte buffer size are acceptable. To specify these values yourself, construct an OutputStreamWriter on a FileOutputStream.

Table 16.8 The Writer classes.

BufferedWriter	A class that provides for the efficient buffering of characters being written
FilterWriter	Abstract class for writing filtered character streams
StringWriter	A character stream whose sink is a string
OutputStreamReader	A class that translates characters into bytes according to a specified character encoding
FileWriter	Convenience class for writing character files
PrintWriter	A class that prints formatted representations of objects to a text output stream

16.2.3 Stream Tokenizers

The StreamTokenizer class takes an input stream and parses it into "tokens" that are read one at a time. You can control the parsing process, enabling identifiers, numbers, quoted strings and various comment styles (including C and C++ style comments) to be parsed. You can also tell a stream tokenizer to ignore line terminators or to return identifiers in lower case.

A stream tokenizer provides the next available token in response to the nextToken message. The result may be a string or a number from the underlying streams. This process can be repeated until the nextToken message returns the value TT_EOF, indicating that the end of the file has been reached. The stream tokenizer allows a much higher level of response from the system than is possible using the byte or character input streams. This saves you a lot of work (although it may at first seem very confusing).

16.2.4 Using the IO Classes

You may have noticed that the reading and writing classes do not look that friendly! However, streams are often combined to provide the required functionality. This section looks at reading and writing basic types such as int, reading strings via readers and writing them via writers. It also looks at using a tokenizer to read both.

Reading and Writing Basic Types

To read and write basic types we need to convert the basic bytes read by the actual data source reading streams into ints, floats, doubles, shorts, longs and booleans etc. To do this we need

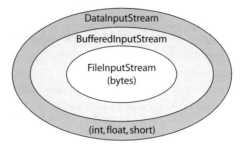

Fig. 16.4 Reading basic types.

to use a DataInputStream wrapped around appropriate lower level streams. This is illustrated in Figure 16.4. In this diagram a low-level data-reading FileInputStream reads data from a file. This data is passed to a BufferedInputStream (for efficiency) and then on to a DataInputStream in order to convert it to the appropriate type.

The actual source code that implements this structure is presented below:

```
DataInputStream dis =
   new DataInputStream(
     new BufferedInputStream(
       new FileInputStream("data.txt")));
int i = dis.readInt();
dis.close();
```

To write basic data types out to a file you use a similar approach. Essentially instead of an input stream type class you use an output stream type class. Thus to write the data to the file data.txt you would write:

```
DataOutputStream dos =
   new DataOuputStream(
     new BufferedOutputStream(
       new FileOuputStream("data.txt")));
dos.writeInt(32);
dos.close();
```

Reading and Writing Strings

Reading and writing strings is, as has been stated, complicated by the need to translate between the ASCII character set and the Unicode character set used within Java. However, the Reader and Writer classes provide facilities for this, and thus you should always use these classes when reading and writing strings.

As with reading basic data types, you need to have a low-level byte-reading stream to allow you to obtain data from the data source (for example a file). An example of such a stream is of course the FileInputStream. This can be wrapped inside an InputStreamReader that will convert the bytes into Unicode characters within String objects. You could read from this reader directly; however, using a BufferedReader is both more efficient and simpler to use. This is illustrated in Figure 16.5.

In the case of reading strings from files the operation is thought to be common enough that a short cut has been povided for the FileInputStream and InputStreamReader constructs via the FileReader class. Thus we can write:

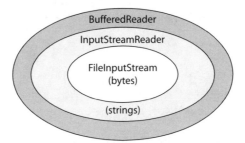

Fig. 16.5 Reading basic types.

```
BufferedReader br = new BufferedReader(
  new InputStreamReader(
    new FileInputStream("text.txt")));
```

or

```
BufferedReader br = new BufferedReader(
  new FileReader("text.txt"));
```

In either case we can then write:

```
String st = br.readLine();
br.close();
```

So why have we told you about both approaches? The answer is that a FileReader class only works when reading text from files. However, there are other sources of text, such as sockets and the keyboard. For example, to read in strings from the keyboard you could write:

```
BufferedReader reader = new BufferedReader(
  new InputStreamReader(System.in));
s = reader.readLine();
while (s != null) {  // Is it the end of the input stream?
  System.out.println("Read: " + s);
  s = reader.readLine();
}
```

Notice that to change this code to read from a file all you would need to change is where the InputStreamReader obtains its data from. Instead of indicating the input stream associated with the System class (i.e. the keyboard) you could have specified a FileInputStream!
Writing strings to files can be accomplished using Writer classes. For example to create a BufferedWriter to a file you can write:

```
BufferedWriter bw =
  new BufferedWriter(
    new FileWriter("text.txt"));
```

However, for writing strings out we have another Writer class that is extremely useful: the PrintWriter class. This class provides a very high level interface for writing strings. A

PrintWriter can be created by wrapping a BufferedWriter within a PrintWriter, for example:

```
PrintWriter pw =
  new PrintWriter(
    new BufferedWriter(
      new FileWriter("text.txt")));
```

You can now use methods such as println and print to write strings to files (just as you have been doing when writing strings to the command line). For example:

```
pw.println("The string to read back in");
pw.close();
```

Also note that we have used a FileWriter, as this is convenient. We could also have used a OutputStreamWriter wrapped around an appropriate byte-writing output stream (such as a FileOutputStream).

Using a Tokenizer

Figure 16.6 illustrates one way of reading characters (as opposed to bytes) from a file. It uses a character stream in combination with other objects to obtain the data in the file. We shall endeavour to consider each of the objects involved separately and to explain what they do and why the objects all work together.

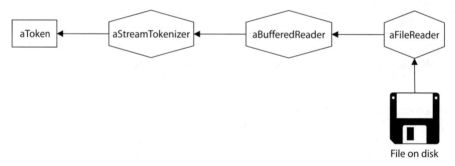

File on disk

Fig. 16.6 Reading strings and numbers from a file.

The FileReader class (a subclass of InputStreamReader) defines an object that translates the bytes from a file into a character stream. This is advisable, as character streams are potentially more efficient than byte streams (partly due to the way in which the byte-oriented streams were originally implemented in Java).

Character streams are often used in collaboration with an instance of BufferedReader. This class processes text from a character input stream (such as FileReader), buffering characters to provide for the efficient reading of characters, strings and lines. You can override the default buffer size. Notice that each request to the buffered reader causes a corresponding request to be made to the underlying character reader. In object-oriented terms, the character reader object is responsible for reading individual characters on request. The buffered reader object is responsible for buffering such requests for efficiency.

Next, a stream tokenizer reads individual tokens. The result may be a string or a number from the underlying streams.

The following source code illustrates how to use these classes:

```
inputFile = new FileReader("input.data");
reader = new BufferedReader(inputFile);
tokens  = new StreamTokenizer(reader);

while ((next = tokens.nextToken()) != tokens.TT_EOF) {
  switch (next) {
    case tokens.TT_NUMBER: {
      aNumber = (int) tokens.nval;
      ...
    }
    default : {
      aString = tokens.sval;
      ...
    }
  }
}
inputFile.close();
```

16.3 Files

16.3.1 Accessing File Information

To access a file, you must first have a filename to work with. A filename is created by one of the constructors of the File class (Table 16.9).

Table 16.9 File class constructors.

File (String path)	Creates an instance that represents the file with the given path
File (String path, String name)	Creates an instance that represents the file with the given path and name
File (File dir, String name)	Creates an instance that represents the file in the given directory and with the given name

The File class also defines a number of class variables which provide information on the platform's directory separator characters:

```
File.separator
```

You may wish to check to see whether a file exists before attempting to access it (to be sure there is something to read from or to make sure you do not overwrite an existing file; see Table 16.10). You do this with the exists message, which returns true if the file is present and false if it is not.

A File object can be used with a FileReader or FileWriter constructor to build a stream between a file and an application.

16.3.2 The FileReader Class Constructors

- FileReader(String fileName) takes a string which defines the file.
- FileReader(File file) takes an instance of a file.

Table 16.10 File messages.

canRead()	Tests whether the specified file can be read
canWrite()	Tests whether the specified file can be written
delete()	Deletes the specified file
getParent()	Returns the parent directory of the file
getPath()	Returns the pathname of the file
isDirectory()	Tests whether the file is a directory
isFile()	Tests whether the file is a "normal" file
lastModified()	Returns the time that the file was last modified
list()	Returns a list of the files in the directory specified by this File object
list (FileFilter filter)	Returns a list of the files in the directory that satisfy the specified filter
mkdir()	Creates a directory whose pathname is specified by the receiver
mkdirs()	Creates a directory and any necessary parent directories
renameTo(File)	Renames the file to have the pathname given by the File argument
toString()	Returns a string representation of the object

These contructors both throw FileNotFoundException.

16.3.3 The FileWriter Class Constructors

- FileWriter(String fileName) creates a stream to the specified file.
- FileWriter(String fileName, boolean append) creates a stream to the specified file.
- FileWriter(File file) creates a stream to the file specified by the instance of the class File.

These contructors throw IOException.

16.3.4 The BufferedReader Class Constructors

- BufferedReader(Reader reader) creates a buffering character input stream that uses a default size of input buffer.
- BufferedReader(Reader reader, int size) creates a buffering character input stream that uses an input buffer of the specified size.

16.3.5 The BufferedWriter Class Constructors

- BufferedWriter(Writer writer) creates a buffered character output stream that uses a default size of output buffer.
- BufferedWriter(Writer writer, int size) creates a buffered character output stream that uses an output buffer of the specified size.

16.3.6 The StreamTokenizer Class

The constructors available for StreamTokenizer include:

- StreamTokenizer(Reader reader) creates a tokenizer that parses the given character stream.
- StreamTokenizer(InputStream inputStream) creates a tokenizer that parses the specified input stream.

The StreamTokenizer protocol includes:

- nextToken obtains the next token in the input stream.
- ttype indicates the type of the token just parsed. This can be a string (TT_WORD), a number (TT_NUMBER), the end of the line (TT_EOL) or the end of the file (TT_EOF).
- sval holds the current string (if ttype indicates a string).
- nval holds the current number (if ttype indicates a number).

16.3.7 The PrintWriter Class Constructors

The constructors available for the PrintWriter class include:

- PrintWriter(OutputStream outputStream) creates a new PrintWriter from an existing OutputStream.
- PrintWriter(OutputStream outputStream, boolean autoflush) creates a new PrintWriter, with or without automatic line flushing, from an existing OutputStream.
- PrintWriter(Writer writer) creates a new PrintWriter on a writer object.
- PrintWriter(Writer writer, boolean autoflush) creates a new PrintWriter, with or without automatic line flushing, on a writer object.

A PrintWriter object responds to a variety of printing messages including all the print and println methods used with the System.out stream.

16.3.8 Handling File IO Errors

Java knows that IO operations (such as accessing a file) can lead to exceptions being raised. For example, if you read from a file which does not exist, then an exception is raised and your system is left in an unstable state with streams open.

Java does not allow you to do nothing with an exception. You must either handle the exception or delegate responsibility for handling it. The next chapter considers how you can handle, generate and define exceptions. In this chapter, we merely consider how to delegate responsibility for the exception.

You delegate responsibility for an exception by specifying in a method header that the method should throw an exception of a particular class (or subclass) back up the execution stack:

```
public void example () throws IOException {
   ...
}
```

The IOException is the root of all exceptions raised during IO operations. In this case, every IOException, and all subclasses of IOException, are passed out of the method example.

16.4 Accessing a File

This section presents a simple application, FileDemo, which illustrates how the contents of a file can be accessed. The application uses the classes described earlier in this chapter, including FileReader, BufferedReader and StreamTokenizer.

Notice that it uses a separate Grades class to determine the grade that should be allocated for a given mark. It is common object-oriented style to place a large chunk of functionality into a class in its own right. This may at first seem very procedural; however, Grades provides a particular type of operation which may be used in different situations and in different classes, and it makes most sense to provide it as a reusable component.

```java
import java.io.*;
import java.util.*;

public class FileDemo {

    Vector records = new Vector();

    public static void main (String argv[])
            throws IOException {
        FileDemo d = new FileDemo();
        d.loadData("input.data");
    }
    public void loadData (String filename)
            throws IOException {
        // Define local variables
        FileReader inputFile;
        Reader reader;
        StreamTokenizer tokens;
        Grades g = new Grades();
        String aString;
        int aNumber, next;

        // Set up link to file and token reader.
        inputFile = new FileReader(filename);
        reader = new BufferedReader(inputFile);
        tokens  = new StreamTokenizer(reader);

        System.out.println("-------------------------");
        // Read contents of file using nextToken.
        while ((next = tokens.nextToken()) != tokens.TT_EOF) {
            switch (next) {
                // Check to see the type of token returned
                // TT_WORD indicates a string
                case tokens.TT_NUMBER: {
                    aNumber = (int) tokens.nval;
                    g.classify(aNumber);
                    records.addElement(new Integer(aNumber));
                    System.out.println("--------------------");
                    break;
                }
                default : {
                    aString = tokens.sval;
                    System.out.println(aString);
                }
            }
```

```
      }
      // Now close the file
      inputFile.close();
   }
}
```

The sample data file input.data contains:

```
"Bob" 45 "Paul" 32 "Peter" 76 "Mike" 29 "John" 56
```

The result of executing this application is illustrated in Figure 16.7.

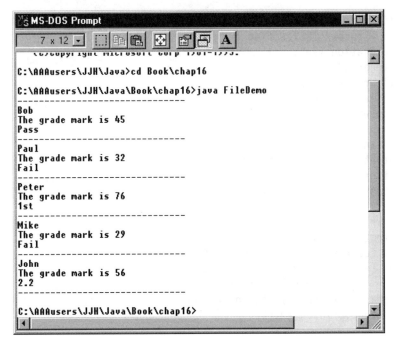

Fig. 16.7 Running FileDemo.

16.5 Creating a File

As a contrast, the FileOutDemo application illustrates how output can be written to a file. Notice that connecting to a file for output is essentially the same as connecting to a file for input. The primary difference is that instead of using a StreamTokenizer, we use a PrintWriter. This class is really the same class as FileDemo with two new methods: printGrades and writeData. The following code presents only the new or changed parts of the class definition:

```
public class FileOutDemo {
   public static void main (String argv [])
         throws IOException {
      FileOutDemo f = new FileOutDemo();
      f.printGrades();
```

```
    }

    public void printGrades () throws IOException {
        loadData("input.data");
        writeData("output.data");
    }

    public void loadData (String filename)
            throws IOException {
        ... as for FileDemo ...
    }

    public void writeData(String filename)
            throws IOException {
        Enumeration item;
        Integer aMark;
        FileWriter outputFile;
        BufferedWriter writer;
        PrintWriter output;

        // Link a stream to the file
        outputFile = new FileWriter(filename);
        writer = new BufferedWriter(outputFile);
        output = new PrintWriter(writer);

        // Write data to the file
        output.println("The file contains " +
            records.size() + " records");
        for (item = records.elements();
                item.hasMoreElements();){
            aMark = (Integer) item.nextElement();
            output.println(aMark);
        }

        // Lastly don't forget to close the file
        output.close();
    }
}
```

The result of executing this application is presented in Figure 16.8.

16.6 Input From the Console

As was mentioned earlier you can obtain input from the user via the console using an InputStream. This is similar to generating output to the console. The global object System possesses both an output and an input stream. The output stream has been used extensively in the examples throughout this book. The input stream can be used to obtain information from the user. This is illustrated in the following very simple working example application:

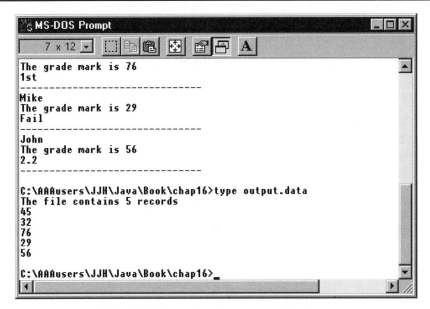

Fig. 16.8 Running the FileOutDemo application.

```java
import java.io.*;
public class TestReader {
  public static void main (String args [])
        throws IOException {
    TestReader t = new TestReader();
    t.printMenu();
  }
  public void printMenu() throws IOException {
    char ch;
    System.out.println("The options available are:");
    System.out.println(" 1. File");
    System.out.println(" 2. Exit");
    System.out.print("Please make a selection: ");
    ch = (char)System.in.read();
    System.out.println("\n The input was " + ch);
  }
}
```

The result of executing the above application is illustrated in Figure 16.9.

16.7 Summary

In this chapter, you have encountered streams and their use in file input and output. Many simple Java applications and applets do not access files. However, if you need to store information or share it between applications, then you need to interact with the host file system. You

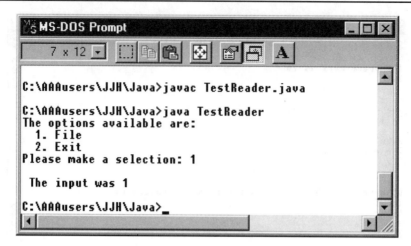

Fig. 16.9 Running the TestReader application.

have now seen the basic facilities available, and should spend some time exploring the stream and file facilities available in Java.

Chapter *17*
Serialization

17.1 Introduction

If you save object information without serialization, then you can only save the ASCII version of the data held by the object. You need to reconstruct the data into objects when you read the text file, which means that you have to indicate that certain data is associated with certain objects and that certain objects are related. This is very time-consuming and error-prone. It is also very unlikely that the ASCII data written out by someone else is in the right format for your system.

This was the only way of creating persistent data in the JDK versions 1.0 and 1.0.2. However, in JDK version 1.1 serialization was introduced to simplify this operation.

Serialization allows you to store objects directly to a file in a compact and encoded form. You do not need to convert the objects or reconstruct them when you load them back in. In addition, everyone else who uses serialization can read and write your files. This is useful not only for portability but also for sharing objects.

The name, serialization, comes from situations which can arise when saving more than one related object to a file. For example, in Figure 17.1, four objects are related by references and are held by another object Family (within a vector).

If, when we want to save the whole family to file, we merely save each object independently, we also have to save copies of the objects that they reference. In the above example, we would end up with multiple copies of Phoebe. If we can determine whether an object has already been saved to disk, then we can record a reference to the previously saved object, so that the original structure can be restored at a later date. This reference is referred to as a serial number (hence the name serialization).

Each object is stored to disk with its own serial number. If an object has been stored, then a reference to its serial number is included with any object which references it. For example, if

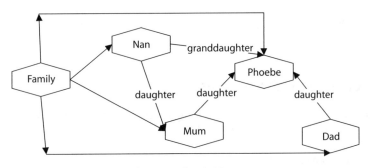

Fig. 17.1 Related objects.

Phoebe has serial number 1 then, when Mum, Dad or Nan are saved, they merely record that they reference the object with serial number 1.

17.1.1 Saving Objects

To save an object to file, you use the ObjectOutputStream class. However, an Object-OutputStream must use a stream, such as FileOutputStream, to write data into a file:

```
FileOutputStream file = new FileOutputStream("data");
ObjectOutputStream output = new ObjectOutputStream(file);
output.writeObject(family);
file.close();
```

The above code results in all the objects held by family being saved to the file data using serialization. This illustrates that, although you may find the concepts confusing, serialization is easy to work with.

17.1.2 Reading Objects

To read objects which have been saved to file back into an application, you need to use the ObjectInputStream class. You must also use an input stream, such as FileInputStream, to read the (byte) data from the file:

```
FileInputStream file = new FileInputStream("data");
ObjectInputStream input = new ObjectInputStream(file);
Family family = (Family) input.readObject();
file.close();
```

Notice that you must cast the object retrieved by the readObject method into the appropriate class (just as with vectors and hash tables).

17.2 The ObjectOutputStream Class

The ObjectOutputStream class defines a single constructor which creates an Object-OutputStream that writes to the specified OutputStream:

```
ObjectOutputStream(OutputStream output) throws IOException
```

The ObjectOutputStream class provides the protocol shown in Table 17.1.

17.3 The ObjectInputStream Class

The ObjectInputStream class defines a single constructor which creates an Object-InputStream that reads from the specified InputStream:

```
ObjectInputStream(InputStream input)
        throws IOException, StreamCorruptedException
```

Table 17.1 The protocol for the `ObjectOutputStream` class.

`close()`	Closes the stream
`flush()`	Flushes the stream
`write(byte b[])`	Writes an array of bytes
`write(byte b[], int offSet, int length)`	Writes a sub array of bytes
`write(int anInt)`	Writes a byte
`writeBoolean (boolean bool)`	Writes a boolean
`writeByte(int anInt)`	Writes an 8 bit byte
`writeBytes (String string)`	Writes a string as a sequence of bytes
`writeChar (int character)`	Writes a 16 bit character
`writeChars (String string)`	Writes a string as a sequence of characters
`writeDouble (double aDouble)`	Writes a 64 bit double
`writeFloat (float aFloat)`	Writes a 32 bit float
`writeInt(int anInt)`	Writes a 32 bit int
`writeLong(long aLong)`	Writes a 64 bit long
`writeObject (Object object)`	Writes the specified object
`writeShort(int aShort)`	Writes a 16 bit short

The `ObjectInputStream` class defines the protocol shown in Table 17.2.

Table 17.2 The protocol for the `ObjectInputStream` class.

`close()`	Closes the input stream
`read()`	Reads a byte of data
`read(byte charBuffer[], int offSet, int length)`	Reads into an array of bytes
`readBoolean()`	Reads in a boolean
`readByte()`	Reads an 8 bit byte
`readChar()`	Reads a 16 bit char
`readDouble()`	Reads a 64 bit double
`readFloat()`	Reads a 32 bit float
`readInt()`	Reads a 32 bit int
`readLine()`	Reads a line that has been terminated by a \n, \r, \r\n or EOF
`readLong()`	Reads a 64 bit long
`readObject()`	Read an object from the receiver
`readShort()`	Reads a 16 bit short
`readUnsignedByte()`	Reads an unsigned 8 bit byte
`readUnsignedShort()`	Reads an unsigned 16 bit short

17.4 The `Serializable` Interface

Any class whose objects are to be used as part of a serializable application must implement the `Serializable` interface (if you examine the diagrams in the appendices, you can see that many classes, such as Vector, implement the Serializable interface). The serialization interface is a flag indicating that a class can be serialized. It means that user-defined classes can also be serialized without the need to define any new methods. All the instance variables of an object are written onto the output stream automatically. When the object is restored the instance variable information is automatically restored.

17.5 The transient Keyword

It is also possible to indicate that a particular instance variable should not be serialized using the transient keyword. This indicates to the serialization system that the instance variable should be ignored. This is useful for information that is not "persistent" and should not be saved along with the object or for data that cannot be serialized (for example instances of the class Thread cannot be serialized). To do this you can define an instance variable thus:

```
private transient int current;
```

17.6 The Externalizable Interface

In some situations, you may need to implement the methods specified by the Externalizable interface. For example, you may not need to save the information held in all the instance variables, but only one or two variables from a set of 20. This would minimize the size of the serialized objects on disk. A user-defined class can define the readObject and writeObject methods. The Externalizable interface definition for these two methods is:

```
private void writeObject(java.io.ObjectOutputStream out)
    throws IOException
private void readObject(java.io.ObjectInputStream in)
    throws IOException, ClassNotFoundException;
```

The writeObject method must write onto the output stream, out, the information required to restore the object. In turn, the readObject method is expected to read that information back into an object, setting instance variables as appropriate from the in stream. In either case, you should use the write or read methods defined on the appropriate streams to handle the instance variable data.

If you are confused by what these methods do, then think of it this way: "These methods define what information is saved to the file or restored from the file, for a particular class of object".

If you try to save an object which is not serializable, then the NotSerializableException is thrown. This exception identifies the class of the non-serializable object.

Notice that the way in which you define how an object can be saved to a file or restored from a file is classic object orientation. That is, the object itself defines how it should be saved to a file. The parameter to writeObject is the stream which is linked to the file, but the stream does not decide what is written.

17.7 A Simple Serialization Application

This section describes a very simple application which creates a set of person objects and a family object, and implements relationships as illustrated in Figure 17.1. The Family class defines how members are added to the family and how the writeObject and readObject methods are implemented (notice that we did not need to define these, as the objects could have been serialized automatically). Finally, the Person class defines the functionality of person objects (such as how to add daughters and granddaughters) and how to implement readObject and writeObject.

17.7.1 The Person Class

The Person class implements the Serializable interface by defining the methods writeObject and readObject.

An additional method, toString, is used by the output stream to print a textual representation of the object.

```
import java.io.*;
public class Person implements Serializable {
  private String title;
  private Person daughter;
  private Person granddaughter;
  public Person(String string) {title = string;}
  public String name () {return title;}

  public void addDaughter(Person person) {
    daughter = person;
  }

  public void addGrandDaughter(Person person) {
    granddaughter = person;
  }

  public String toString() {
    String result;
    result = "Person: " + title;
    if (daughter != null)
      result = result + " : daughter " +
          daughter.name();
    if (granddaughter != null)
      result = result + " granddaughter " +
          granddaughter.name();
    return result;
  }
}
```

17.7.2 The Family Class

The definition of the Family class is considerably simpler than the Person class as all it does is act as an interface to a vector. As vectors already know how to save their contents to a file, we merely need to write the whole vector to the output stream. When we come to read the objects back in from a file we can read the whole vector in one go (remembering to cast the result returned by readObject to Vector).

```java
import java.util.Vector;
import java.util.Enumeration;
import java.io.*;
public class Family implements Serializable {

  private Vector members = new Vector();

  public void addFamilyMember(Person person) {
    members.addElement(person);
  }

  public void printFamily() {
    Person member;
    for (Enumeration e = members.elements();
           e.hasMoreElements() ; ) {
      member = (Person)e.nextElement();
      System.out.println(member);
    }
  }

  private void writeObject(ObjectOutputStream out)
          throws IOException {
    out.writeObject(members);
  }

  private void readObject(ObjectInputStream in)
      throws IOException, ClassNotFoundException {
    members = (Vector)in.readObject();
  }
}
```

17.7.3 The Test Class

The Test class provides a test harness for the serializable classes. The setUpAndSave method instantiates a family object and constructs a set of person objects as illustrated in Figure 17.1. It then saves this structure to a file called family.data. The data is not saved into any instance variables and is not passed between this method and the load method. The load method loads objects in from the family.data file.

```java
import java.io.*;

public class Test {

  public static void main (String args [])
      throws IOException, ClassNotFoundException {
```

```
        Test t = new Test();
        t.setUpAndSave();
        t.load();
    }

    public void setUpAndSave() throws IOException {
        Family family = new Family();
        Person nan = new Person("Nan");
        Person dad = new Person("Dad");
        Person mum = new Person("Mum");
        Person phoebe = new Person("Phoebe");
        dad.addDaughter(phoebe);
        mum.addDaughter(phoebe);
        nan.addGrandDaughter(phoebe);
        nan.addDaughter(mum);
        family.addFamilyMember(dad);
        family.addFamilyMember(mum);
        family.addFamilyMember(nan);
        family.addFamilyMember(phoebe);

        family.printFamily();
        System.out.println("\nSaving family to object file");
        FileOutputStream file =
                new FileOutputStream("family.data");
        ObjectOutputStream output =
                new ObjectOutputStream(file);
        output.writeObject(family);
        file.close();
        System.out.println("Family saved");
    }

    public void load() throws IOException,
            ClassNotFoundException {
        System.out.println("\nLoading new family from file");
        FileInputStream file =
                new FileInputStream("family.data");
        ObjectInputStream input =
                new ObjectInputStream(file);
        Family family = (Family) input.readObject();
        file.close();
        System.out.println("New family loaded\n");
        family.printFamily();
    }
}
```

Figure 17.2 shows that the same information is printed in both methods. The serialization process was a success! One copy of each object is stored to the file, and each subsequent reference to that object is replaced with a serial number (see Figure 17.3).

Fig. 17.2 Running the serialization example.

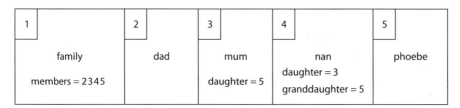

Fig. 17.3 The file structure for the Family application.

17.8 Exercise – Using Files With the Financial Manager

This application builds on the one started in Chapter 15. The Financial Manager application keeps a record of deposits and withdrawals from a current account. It also keeps an up-to-date balance and allows statements to be printed.

A problem with the version in Chapter 15 is that there is no way of permanently storing the account information. As soon as the FinancialManager object is destroyed (or the reference to it is lost), then all the information associated with it is also lost. This exercise extends the existing application so that it can:

- save the current statement to a file
- load an existing statement from a file

You must provide two new interfaces, one to load a file and one to save a file. These files contain a formatted version of the information held in the statement. If you were to use a text file then the format might be:

```
<type of action> <amount> newline
```
For example:
```
deposit 24.00
withdraw 13.00
```

It is significantly easier to use serialization, as it makes accessing the contents of the file much easier. You must check to see that the file exists before loading it.

If you are successful, then the following main method should give the same result from both FinancialManager objects.

```
public class Test {

    public static void main (String args []) {
        FinancialManager fm = new FinancialManager();
        fm.deposit(25.00);
        fm.withdraw(12.00);
        fm.deposit(10.00);
        fm.deposit(5.00);
        fm.withdraw(8.00);
        System.out.println("The current balance is " +
                fm.balance();
        fm.statement();
        fm.save("account1");

        FinancialManager anotherFM = new FinancialManager();
        anotherFM.load("account1");

        System.out.println("\n");
        anotherFM.statement();
        System.out.println("The loaded balance is " +
                anotherFM.balance());
    }
}
```

The result of running this Test class is shown below:

```
C:\Book\chap17\finance>java Test
The current balance is 20.0
Statement:
Deposit  0.0
Deposit  25.0
Withdraw 12.0
Deposit  10.0
Deposit  5.0
Withdraw 8.0

Statement:
Deposit  0.0
Deposit  25.0
Withdraw 12.0
Deposit  10.0
```

```
Deposit  5.0
Withdraw 8.0
The loaded balance is 20.0
```

17.9 Summary

In this chapter you have encountered object input and output streams and their use in storing and retrieving objects from file. This is another way of sharing information (in this case, objects) between applications. It also provides a way of providing object persistence. You should now spend some time exploring the object input and output stream facilities available in your Java system.

Chapter 18

Observers and Observables

18.1 Introduction

This chapter introduces the perform mechanism (also referred to as notification) which provides an alternative way to send messages. It then presents a practical discussion of the dependency mechanism.

18.2 The Notification Mechanism

There are a number of different relationships between objects in an object-oriented system. We have already considered several of these earlier in this book:

- Inheritance (class to class relationships)
- Instantiation (class to instance relationships)
- *Part-of* or contains (instance to instance relationships)

However, there is another important relationship supported by many object-oriented languages, such as Smalltalk and Java. This is the dependency or notification relationship, where the state or behaviour of one object is dependent on the state of another object. Figure 18.1 indicates that there is a set of dependency relationships between the objects A to F. Object A is dependent on some aspect of objects B and D. In turn object B is dependent on some aspect of object C and so on.

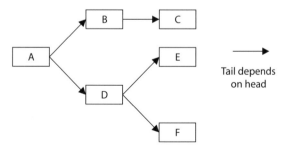

Fig. 18.1 Dependency between objects.

18.2.1 Why Do We Want Dependency?

The reasons for dependency are all down to *change*. We wish to communicate the fact that an object has changed its value to another object which may be interested in either the fact of the change or the new value effected by the change. The dependency mechanism provides a way of communicating such events in a generic implementation-independent manner.

An obvious question is "Why not just get the object to send messages to those interested in it?". The answer is that if you know the objects that are interested, then you can send messages to them. However, if all you know is that at some time, at a later date, some object may need to know something about the state of an object (but you do not know what that other object might be) then you cannot arrange to send messages to it.

The dependency mechanism allows any object whose class is a subclass of Observable to act as the source of a dependency. Any object that implements the Observer interface can act as the dependent object.

We do not need to know what might be interested in the object. We merely need to know that it might be involved in a dependency relationship. The (hidden) dependency mechanism takes care of informing the unknown objects about the updates.

18.2.2 How Does Dependency Work?

The dependency mechanism is implemented in the class Observable within the java.util package. This class is a direct subclass of Object, so any class can inherit from Observable and thus take part in a dependency relationship.

In Java terminology, the head of the dependent relationship (i.e. the object on which other objects depend) is referred to as the observable object, while the dependent object is referred to as the observer object. The observable object allows other objects to observe its current state. An observable object can have zero or more observers, which are notified of changes to the object's state by the notifyObservers method.

You can browse the Observable class to explore the dependency mechanism. The basic implementation, inherited from Observable, associates a vector of other objects with the observable object. This vector holds the objects which are dependent on the object (collectively, these objects are known as the object's observers). For example, in Figure 18.2, the object ObjectA has two observers ObjectB and ObjectC. The links to the dependent objects are held by ObjectA in a list of observers called obs. ObjectA cannot access this vector as it is private to the Observable class. However, it can obtain the number of observers using the countObservers method.

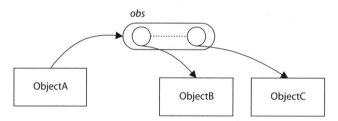

Fig. 18.2 An object and its observers.

18.2.3 Constructing Dependencies

The addObserver message adds an object to a dependency list. For example, we can construct the above dependencies:

```
ObjectA.addObserver(ObjectB);
ObjectA.addObserver(ObjectC);
```

Duplicates cannot be held in the list of observers. If you attempt to add an object to the list of observers more than once, it is only recorded once (and thus is only told of changes once).

An observable object holds a vector of objects which depend on it, but an object cannot access information about the objects on which it depends. For example, there are no references from ObjectB or ObjectC back to ObjectA in Figure 18.2. This may seem a bit strange at first; however, once you understand how the dependency mechanism works, as realized by the Observable class and the Observer interface, you will see why things are this way round.

You can remove dependencies once they have been created. The following code removes ObjectB from the observer list of ObjectA:

```
ObjectA.deleteObserver(ObjectB);
```

18.2.4 A Simple Dependency Example

We develop further the following very simple dependency example during the chapter. It creates two objects and a dependency between them. The objects are instances of the classes DataObject and ObserverObject, which are direct subclasses of Observable and Object, respectively. Place the classes in appropriate .java files (i.e. DataObject.java and ObserverObject.java).

```java
import java.util.Observable;
public class DataObject extends Observable {
}
```

The update method is explained below. It is merely used here to allow the ObserverObject to implement the Observer interface:

```java
import java.util.Observer;
import java.util.Observable;

public class ObserverObject implements Observer {
  public void update(Observable o, Object arg){
    System.out.println("Object " + o + " has changed");
  }
}
```

We now have two classes which can take part in a dependency relationship. To illustrate how objects of these classes can be related, define the following class in a file called TestHarness.java. Although, in general, I do not condone using separate objects to illustrate how other objects work, in this case it ensures that you understand that the dependency relationships are handled automatically via the inherited facilities.

```java
public class TestHarness {
  public static void main(String args []) {
    TestHarness t = new TestHarness();
    t.test();
  }
  public void test () {
    DataObject temp1 = new DataObject();
    ObserverObject temp2 = new ObserverObject();
    temp1.addObserver(temp2);
```

```
        System.out.println(temp1.countObservers());
    }
}
```

The result of `println` is the value 1, although our `DataObject` class is empty! From the point of view of the `DataObject` class, dependency is an invisible mechanism which works behind the scenes. Of course, this is not really the case. The dependency mechanism has been inherited from `Observable` and is implemented via message sends and method executions just like any behaviour provided by an object.

18.2.5 Making Dependency Work for You

We have now considered how to construct a dependency relationship. We want this relationship to inform the dependent objects that a change has occurred in the object on which they depend.

To do this we use two sets of methods. One set, the "changed" methods, states that something has changed. The other set, the "update" methods, is used to state what type of update is required.

Figure 18.3 illustrates the sequence of messages which are sent in response when an object changes. That is, when `ObjectA` is sent the `setChanged` and `notifyObservers` messages (usually by itself) all its observers are sent an update message. From the point of view of `ObjectA`, much of this behaviour is hidden; in fact, so much so that a point of confusion relates to the sending of one message (the `notifyObservers` message) and the execution of another method (the `update` method). A programmer defining Objects A, B and C:

- sends one (or more) `setChanged` messages to `ObjectA`
- sends a `notifyObservers` message to `ObjectA`
- defines an `update` method in `ObjectB` and `ObjectC`

The confusion stems from the need to send one message but define another. However, if you think about how you are linking into the existing dependency framework, it can make more sense. The change message is a message to the dependency mechanism asking it to notify the object's dependants about a change. The dependency mechanism is inherited and is generic across applications, but system developers cannot know when the change message should be sent – that is application-specific. It is, therefore, the application developer's responsibility to send the change messages. For example, you may only want dependants to be told of certain changes, such as updates to one field on an input screen.

Similarly, there is no way that the system developers can know how the dependants should update themselves. The update message could display the new value produced by the originating object, perform some calculation, or access a database. As the update methods are

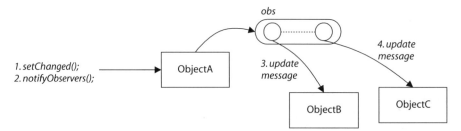

Fig. 18.3 The dependency mechanism in action.

defined in an interface, they do nothing; they are abstract methods. Nothing is said anywhere in the system about what an observer should do when the object changes.

In the simple example above, we need to specify what ObjectB and ObjectC should do when ObjectA changes. This requires defining update methods (as we did very briefly in the ObserverObject example presented earlier).

18.2.6 The "Changed" Methods

There are three messages which inform an object that it has changed and should notify its observers:

- setChanged() indicates to the observable object that something has happened which should be passed onto any observers next time they are notified of a change. It is very useful to separate out specifying that something has changed from the actual notification action. You can determine that observers must be notified at one point in an object's execution (when data is entered), but trigger the notification at another point (at the end of some execution cycle). Interestingly, the Smalltalk dependency mechanism does not provide this flexibility.
- notifyObservers() informs the observers that something has changed (but not what the change was). It calls the notifyObservers(Object object) method with a null parameter.
- notifyObservers(Object object) notifies the observers that something has changed and what the change was. This is done by sending the update message to the objects in the obs vector. The update method takes two parameters: the current object and the object passed into the notifyObservers method. It assumes that the change can be represented as an object, so if the change results in the number 24, it must be wrapped in an Integer object.

The first point to note about the changed messages is that they are sent to the object which has changed in some way. They inform the object that it has changed and that this change should be passed on to any observers. The changed messages do not effect the change or notify the observers.

The notifyObservers messages triggers off the update part of the dependency mechanism. The only difference between the messages relates to the amount of information provided. The simplest notification message (and the one with the least information) is the notifyObservers() message. This can be useful when you want to make sure that the dependants assume nothing about the object to which the change is happening.

The way these messages are implemented is that the setChanged method sets a boolean flag, changed, to true. This flag is examined by the notifyObservers(Object) method; if the flag is set to true, it notifies the objects in the obs vector that they need to update themselves and resets the changed flag to false. If the changed flag is already false, it does nothing.

18.3 The Observer Interface

The Observer interface defines the abstract update method which must be implemented by objects which wish to take part in a dependency:

```
public interface Observer {
  void update(Observable observable, Object arg);
}
```

As with all interfaces, any concrete class that implements this interface must provide the body of the update method. Any class implementing this interface can be guaranteed to work with the notification methods used in an observer object.

The first parameter passed to this method is the observable object. If ObjectA is sent a setChanged message followed by a notifyObservers message, then ObjectB and ObjectC are sent the update message with the first parameter set to ObjectA.

The value of the arg parameter depends on the version of notifyObservers which was sent to ObjectA. If no parameters were sent, then the value of arg is null. If one parameter was sent, arg holds the parameter. This means that the developer can decide how much information the observer object can work with.

18.4 Extending the Dependency Example

This section provides an example of how the dependency mechanism works. We use the DataObject and ObserverObject classes defined in Section 18.2.4.

The first thing we do is to define some instance variables (age, name and address), a constructor and an updater, age, in DataObject:

```java
import java.util.Observable;

public class DataObject extends Observable {
    String name = "";
    int age = 0;
    String address = "";

    public DataObject (String aName,
        int years, String anAddress) {
        name = aName;
        age = years;
        address = anAddress;
    }

    public void age (int years) {
        age = years;
        setChanged();
        notifyObservers("age");
    }

    public String toString() {
        return "(DataObject: " + name + " of " + address
                + " who is " + age + ")";
    }
}
```

The updater method, age, which sets the age instance variable, also informs itself that it has changed (using setChanged) and that this fact should be passed onto its dependants (using notifyObservers("age")). This is a typical usage of the notifyObservers message. That is, it informs the notification mechanism about the type of change which has taken place. It also illustrates good style: it informs this object about the change which has taken place. It is very poor style to have an object send an instance of DataObject the message age, followed by the changed messages. It implies that something outside the DataObject decides when to inform its observers.

Next we define how an instance of ObserverObject responds to the change in a DataObject; we define an update method:

```java
import java.util.Observer;
import java.util.Observable;
public class ObserverObject implements Observer {
  public void update(Observable o, Object arg){
    if (arg == "age")
      System.out.println("Object " + o +
            " has changed its " + arg);
    else
      System.out.println("Don't know how to handle
            changes to " + arg);
  }
}
```

As this is just a simple example, all it does is print a string on the console that reports the change. We use the TestHarness class we defined earlier to try out this simple example. We use the new DataObject constructor to create the observable object and the age updater to change the observable object's age:

```java
public class TestHarness {

  public static void main(String args []) {
    TestHarness t = new TestHarness();
    t.test();
  }

  public void test () {
    DataObject temp1 =
          new DataObject("John", 33, "C47");
    ObserverObject temp2 = new ObserverObject();
    temp1.addObserver(temp2);
    System.out.println(temp1.countObservers());
    temp1.age(34);
  }
}
```

The result of executing this class is illustrated below:

```
C:\AAAusers\JJH\Java\Book\chap18>java TestHarness

1
Object (DataObject: John of C47 who is 34) has changed its age

C:\AAAusers\JJH\Java\Book\chap18>
```

The ObserverObject has been informed of the change of age, although we did not define a method to do this directly.

In the simple example presented above, you should note (and understand) the following points:

- `DataObject` does not have a reference to, nor does it know anything about, an `ObserverObject`.
- The `ObserverObject` does not reference a `DataObject` internally.
- The link between `temp1` and `temp2` is external to both objects.

It can be difficult to debug and maintain relationships which have been implemented using the dependency mechanism (as the message chain is partly hidden). Therefore, you should exercise care in its use.

18.5 Exercise – Dependency and the Financial Manager

Try to modify the `FinancialManager` example by adding a monitor class to send the user a message if the bank balance dips below a certain threshold.

18.6 Summary

This chapter has introduced the dependency mechanism in Java as implemented by the `Observable` class and `Observer` interface. This relationship is quite complex, but the user interface classes make extensive use of it and you should gain some experience with it.

Part 5

Graphical Interfaces and Applets

Chapter **19**

Graphic Programming Using the Abstract Window Toolkit

19.1 Introduction

This chapter describes how to create graphical displays using the standard JDK windowing and graphical classes. It does not cover the construction of graphical user interfaces, which are discussed in the next chapter.

In this chapter we consider windows in Java, how you create them and how you can draw and write in them. Such windows can be used to display graphs, images, text, lines and shapes (such as boxes and circles).

19.2 Windows as Objects

In Java, almost everything is an object; it is said to be a pure object-oriented language. This issue was considered earlier, but some of the implications may well have passed you by. Windows and their contents are also objects; when you create a window, you create an object which knows how to display itself on the computer screen. You must tell it what to display, although the framework within which the associated method (paint) is called is hidden from you. You should bear the following points in mind during your reading of this chapter and the next; they will help you understand what you are required to do:

- You create a window by instantiating an object.
- You define what the window displays by creating subclasses of system-provided classes (such as Panel).
- You can send messages to the window to change its state, perform an operation, and display a graphic object.
- The window object can send messages to other objects in response to user (or program) actions.
- Everything displayed by a window is an object and is potentially subject to all of the above.

This approach may very well contrast with your previous experience. In many other windowing systems, you must call the appropriate functions in order to obtain a window, providing default behaviour either by pointers to functions, or by associating some event with a particular function. You also determine what is displayed in the window by calling various functions on the window.

In the object-oriented world, you define how a subclass of the windowing classes responds to events, for example what it does in response to a request to paint itself. All the windowing functionality and window display code is encapsulated within the window itself.

19.3 Windows in Java

Of course the above description is a little simplistic. It ignores the issue of how a window is created, initialized and displayed, and how its contents are generated. In Java, these are handled by the classes Frame, Component and Container (or their subclasses).

- *Frames* provide the basic structure for a window: borders, a label and some basic functionality (e.g. resizing).
- *Components* are graphical objects displayed in a frame. Some other languages refer to them as widgets. Examples of components are lines, circles, boxes and text.
- *Containers* are special types of component which are made up of one or more components (or containers). All the components within a container (such as a panel) can be treated as a single entity.

Windows have a component hierarchy which is used (amongst other things) to determine how and when elements of the window are drawn. The component hierarchy is rooted with the frame, within which components and containers can be added. Figure 19.1 illustrates a component hierarchy for a window with a frame, two containers (subclasses of Panel, which is itself a direct subclass of Container) and a few basic components.

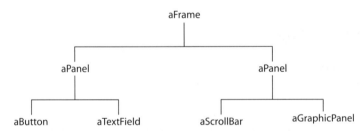

Fig. 19.1 The component hierarchy for a sample window.

When the Java Virtual Machine (JVM) needs to redraw the window displayed by the above hierarchy, it starts with the highest component (the frame) and asks it to redraw itself. It then works down the hierarchy to the bottom components, asking each to redraw itself. In this way each component draws itself before any components that it contains. This process is handled by the windowing framework. The user generally only has to redefine the paint method to change the way in which a component is drawn.

19.4 The Abstract Window Toolkit

The Abstract Window Toolkit (AWT) is a generic, platform-independent, windowing system. It allows you to write graphical Java programs which have (almost) the same look and feel, whatever the host platform. For example, the graphical applications presented within this section of the book have been written on a Windows 95 PC and a Solaris 2.5 Sun. This is because these are the machines available to me, and depending on the time of day, I may be working on one or the other. I do not need to worry about the host environment, only about the AWT.

This is, of course, not a new idea. The VisualWorks development environment for Smalltalk, from ParcPlace-Digitalk, has had such a system since the early 1990s. However, that does not reduce its usefulness. Such toolkits greatly reduce the problems which software vendors often face when attempting to deliver their system on different platforms. Indeed, a small software house with which I am involved is moving to Java primarily because of the benefits that the AWT offers.

The AWT is made up of a number of associated packages that provide the Java side of the windowing environment. At some point, these facilities must be converted into calls to the host windowing system; however, such operations are extremely well hidden from the Java programmer, who does not need to know anything about them. The following packages comprise the AWT:

- `java.awt` is the main AWT package, which provides the primary classes with which most Java programmers become familiar: `Frame,Component,Container,Button,Menu,Label`, and many more.
- `java.awt.image` provides classes which allow graphic images (such as those in GIF or JPEG formats) to be manipulated and displayed.

`java.awt.peer` defines a set of interfaces which are used when creating peer objects. Peers are objects which allow the functionality of an interface to remain the same, even though the way in which the interface is displayed changes.

`java.awt.event` is the AWT event model, introduced in JDK 1.1, and is catered for by classes defined within this package. This is another package with which all Java programmers who use graphics are likely to become familiar.

`java.awt.datatransfer` provides three classes and a number of interfaces which support mechanisms to transfer data using cut, copy and paste style operations and clipboards. In JDK 1.1, however, this package only provides a Clipboard API; the Drag-and-Drop API associated with this package is in the following releases.

The package with which we are concerned in this chapter is the `java.awt` package. Figure 19.2 presents the primary classes used in graphics programming and their relationships. In the figure, ovals indicate interface definitions and rectangles represent classes. For further information on the primary classes you should consult the online documentation provided with your toolkit.

19.5 The Component Class

The `Component` class, an abstract subclass of `Object`, defines the basic functionality for all graphic components in the AWT. As all graphic elements are objects, it is their responsibility to determine what their visual effect should be. It is also their responsibility to draw (and redraw) themselves and to respond to actions. For example, although a button may be told that it should be disabled, it is the button's responsibility to decide how to illustrate this to the user (perhaps "greyed-out", or not to display at all). The point is that the button component decides this. The `Component` class defines many methods, some of which are listed below:

- `paint(Graphics)` paints the component.
- `repaint()` repaints the component.

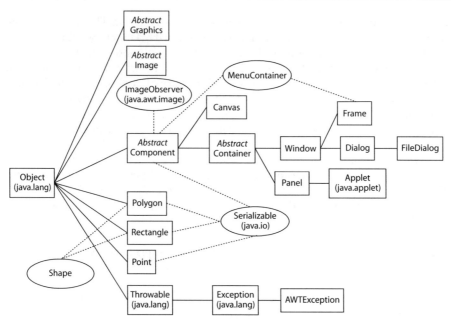

Fig. 19.2 Part of the java.awt package.

- setVisible(boolean) shows the component if the flag is true or hides it if the flag is false.
- isVisible() checks whether the Component is visible.

The following methods are associated with the component size, shape and location on the display:

- setBounds(int, int, int, int) reshapes the component to the specified bounding box.
- setBounds(Rectangle) reshapes the component to the specified bounding box.
- getBounds() returns the current bounds.
- getMaximumSize() returns the maximum size.
- getMinimumSize() returns the minimum size.
- getPreferredSize() returns the preferred size.
- getSize() returns the current size.
- setSize(Dimension) resizes the component to the specified dimension.
- setSize(int, int) resizes the component to the specified width and height.
- getLocation() returns the current location of this component.
- getLocationOnScreen() returns the current location of this component in the screen's coordinate space.
- contains(int, int) checks whether this component contains the specified (x, y) location, relative to the coordinate system.
- contains(Point) checks whether this component contains the specified point, relative to the coordinate system of this component.

In many situations, you want to be able to modify the background and foreground colours associated with a component. You can use the following methods :

- getBackground()
- setBackground(Color)
- setForeground(Color)
- getForeground()

The class also defines methods associated with the cursor and font being used:

- getCursor() gets the cursor set on this component.
- setCursor(Cursor) sets the cursor image to a predefined cursor.
- getFont() gets the font of the component.
- setFont(Font) sets the font of the component.

Finally, there are a number of component related methods:

- getName() gets the name of the component.
- getParent() gets the parent of the component.
- isShowing() checks if this Component is showing on screen.
- isValid() checks if this Component is valid.
- setName(String) sets the name of the component to the specified string.

19.6 The Container Class

The Container class is a direct subclass of Component. It allows one or more components (or containers) to be handled as a unit. Conceptually, it means that a group of component objects can be treated as a single (composite) object for certain operations. It possesses a single constructor, Container(), which creates a new instance of a container.

The protocol for the Container class contains a large number of methods for adding and removing components, for redrawing the display and for handling events. This last issue is not covered in this chapter.

- add(Component) adds the specified component to the container.
- getComponentAt(int, int) locates the component that contains the x, y position in the receiver.
- getComponentAt(Point) locates the component that contains the specified point.
- getComponentCount() returns the number of components in this panel.
- getComponents() gets all the components in this container.
- remove(Component) removes the specified component from this container.
- removeAll() removes all the components from this container.

This class also includes methods for dealing with the maximum, minimum and preferred sizes of the component. These are important when resizing the window and for enabling the layout manager to generate (reasonably) good displays on different platforms:

- getMaximumSize() returns the maximum container size.
- getMinimumSize() returns the minimum container size.
- getPreferredSize() returns the preferred container size.

Finally, the Container class also allows you to specify a layout manager. A layout manager handles how components should be laid out in a window. For example, they may be laid out according to a grid, or they may just fill the space available as effectively as possible. Layout managers are discussed in detail in Chapter 21.

- `setLayout(LayoutManager)` sets the layout manager.
- `getLayout()` gets the layout manager.

19.7 The Panel Class

The `Panel` class (a direct subclass of `Container`) defines a generic container which uses a layout manager to determine where to place components. The `Panel` class provides the following constructors:

- `Panel()` creates a new panel. The default layout for all panels is `FlowLayout`. This is the simplest way of laying out components.
- `Panel(LayoutManager layout)` creates a new panel with the specified layout manager.

This class is used extensively to create containers for components.

19.8 The Frame Class

The `Frame` class defines an object which provides the outer rectangular box of a window. It is a direct subclass of the `Window` class, which defines windows which have no borders or menus. The `Frame` class includes the window borders, the title and associated buttons (such as the minimize, maximize and close buttons). Within this outer frame the rest of the window can be drawn.

An example of using the `Frame` class to create a very simple window object is presented below. It inherits from the `Frame` class, which provides all the basic facilities it requires, and from the `Component` class, which sets the size of the window (`setSize(200, 100)`) and its visibility (`setVisible(true)`):

```java
import java.awt.*;

public class SimpleExample extends Frame {
  public SimpleExample (String name) {
    super("Hello : " + name);
    setSize(200, 100);
    setVisible(true);
  }

  public static void main (String argv []) {
    SimpleExample win = new SimpleExample(argv [0]);
  }
}
```

You can execute this code to produce the window displayed in Figure 19.3 by providing a parameter which forms part of the window label:

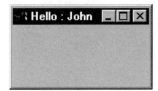

Fig. 19.3 A basic frame window.

```
c:>java SimpleExample John
```

You must close the window by killing the Java process because we have not defined what happens when the Exit button is pressed.

The Frame class provides two constructors:

- Frame() constructs a new unlabelled window that is initially invisible.
- Frame(String title) constructs a new, initially invisible window with the specified title as its label.

The Frame class defines an extensive set of class-side variables which indicate different types of cursor, including CROSSHAIR_CURSOR, DEFAULT_CURSOR, HAND_CURSOR, MOVE_CURSOR, TEXT_CURSOR and WAIT_CURSOR. The Frame protocol provides the following methods:

- getTitle() returns the receiving window object's current label.
- isResizable() returns true if the user can resize the receiving window object.
- setIconImage(Image) sets the image to display when the receiving window is iconized.
- setResizable(boolean) allows the programmer to indicate whether the receiving window should be resizeable or not.
- setTitle(String) sets the title for the receiving window to the specified title.

19.9 The Graphics Class

The abstract Graphics class, a direct subclass of Object for all graphics contexts, allows an application to draw components on various devices or onto off-screen images.

A graphics context is an object which works with windows to display graphical objects (determining how the graphic object should be rendered). You should never need to create a graphics context, as this part of the AWT framework is hidden from most programmers. However, you need to know how to use a graphics context.

In the paint(Graphics) method, you normally send messages to the specified graphics context to tell it what to display (e.g. a string, an image, a line or a rectangle; see Table 19.1). The context can translate what is being displayed, clip an area or perform logical operations.

Filled versions of many of these are also available, for example:

- fill3DRect(int x, int y, int width, int height, boolean raised)
- fillArc(int x, int y, int width, int height, int startAngle, int arcAngle)
- fillLine(int x1, int y1, int x2, int y2)
- fillOval(int x, int y, int width, int height)
- fillPolygon(int[] xPoints, int[] yPoints, int nPoints)

Table 19.1 The Graphics protocol – drawing methods.

clearRect(int x, int y, int width, int height)	Fills the specified rectangle with the current background colour
copyArea(int x, int y, int width, int height, int deltax, int deltay)	Copies an area of the component
draw3DRect(int x, int y, int width, int height, boolean raised)	Draws a 3-D highlighted outline of the specified rectangle
drawArc(int x, int y, int width, int height, int startAngle, int arcAngle)	Draws the outline of an arc covering the specified rectangle
drawLine(int x1, int y1, int x2, int y2)	Draws a line between the specified points
drawOval(int x, int y, int width, int height)	Draws the outline of an oval covering the specified rectangle
drawPolygon(int[] xPoints, int[] yPoints, int nPoints)	Draws the outline of a polygon, defined by arrays of coordinates
drawPolygon (Polygon polygon)	Draws the outline of a polygon, defined by the specified object
drawRect(int x, int y, int width, int height)	Draws the outline of the specified rectangle
drawRoundRect(int x, int y, int width, int height, int arcWidth, int arcHeight)	Draws the outline of the specified rounded corner rectangle

- fillPolygon(Polygon polygon)
- fillRect(int x, int y, int width, int height)
- fillRoundRect(int x, int y, int width, int height, int arcWidth, int arcHeight)

You can also draw characters and strings, and display images on a drawing context (Table 19.2).

Table 19.2 The Graphics protocol – characters, strings and images.

drawChars(char[] buf, int offset, int count, int x, int y)	Draws the specified characters using the current font and colour
drawString(String string, int x, int y)	Draws the specified String using the current font and colour
DrawImage(Image image, int x, int y, Color bgcolor, ImageObserver observer)	Draws as much of the specified image as is currently available at the specified coordinate (x, y) with the given solid background colour
drawImage(Image image, int x, int y, ImageObserver observer)	Draws as much of the specified image as is currently available at the specified coordinate (x, y)
drawImage(Image image, int x, int y, int width, int height, Color bgcolor, ImageObserver observer)	Draws as much of the specified image as has already been scaled to fit inside the specified rectangle with the given solid background colour
drawImage(Image image, int x, int y, int width, int height, ImageObserver observer)	Draws as much of the specified image as has already been scaled to fit inside the specified rectangle

Translation and clipping operations are also supported:

- translate(int x, int y) translates the origin of the graphics context to the point (x, y) in the current coordinate system.
- clipRect(int x1, int y1, int x2, int y2) intersects the current clip with the specified rectangle.
- setClip(int x1, int y1, int x2, int y2) sets the current clip to the rectangle specified by the given coordinates.

- getClip() returns a Shape object representing the current clipping area.
- setClip(Shape shape) sets the current clipping area to an arbitrary clip shape. Takes as a parameter any object whose class implements the Shape interface.
- getClipBounds() returns the bounding rectangle of the current clipping area.

You can also obtain and change the current drawing colour and font:

- getColor() gets the current colour.
- getFont() gets the current font.
- setColor(Color color) sets the current colour as specified.
- setFont(Font font) sets the font for all subsequent text rendering operations.

Finally, logical graphical operations are also supported:

- setPaintMode() sets the logical pixel operation function to the Paint, or overwrite, mode.
- setXORMode(Color color) sets the logical pixel operation function to the XOR mode, which alternates pixels between the current colour and a the specified XOR alternation colour.

19.10 A Worked Graphical Application

We will work through a very simple application which uses a Frame and a Panel to illustrate the ideas presented in this chapter. The aim of the application is to create a graphical window which displays a string, draws a rectangle around that string and draws some coloured lines (see Figure 19.4).

Fig. 19.4 A simple graphic application.

This graphic application is constructed from two classes: ExampleFrame and Example-Panel. In order to emphasize that they are two completely separate classes, whose instances work together to generate the above window, I have defined them both as public classes (and they must therefore be defined in separate .java files).

19.10.1 The ExampleFrame Class

The ExampleFrame class is a concrete class which directly inherits from the Frame class. This class does four main things:

- Creates a bordered window by calling the super constructor (super(label)).

- Places a canvas on the window using the add method.
- Sets the size of the window and displays the window using the setSize() and setVisible(true) methods.
- Registers itself as the object which should handle any window events which occur. This allows us to provide a way of terminating the window once it is created (see the next chapter for further detail).

The construction of the frame is quite straightforward. Of course, if we add more panels to the window, then it could get substantially more complex. The source code for the ExampleFrame class is defined in the file ExampleFrame.java:

```java
import java.awt.*;
import java.awt.event.*;
public class ExampleFrame extends Frame
        implements WindowListener {
  public static void main (String args []) {
    ExampleFrame exampleFrame =
          new ExampleFrame("Graphics Example");
  }

  public ExampleFrame (String label) {
    // Call the super constructor to add the label
    super(label);
    // Create and add the canvas to the frame
    add(new ExamplePanel());
    // Set the window size to that required
    setSize(150, 100);
    // Display the window
    setVisible(true);
    // Set up a listener for the window
    addWindowListener(this);
  }

  public void windowClosed(WindowEvent event) {}
  public void windowOpened(WindowEvent event) {}
  public void windowDeiconified(WindowEvent event) {}
  public void windowIconified(WindowEvent event) {}
  public void windowActivated(WindowEvent event) {}
  public void windowDeactivated(WindowEvent event) {}

  public void windowClosing(WindowEvent event) {
    System.exit(0);
  }
}
```

The ExampleFrame class also implements an interface called WindowListener. This interface specifies a set of methods (which must, of course, be defined by the implementing class) which specify how to handle various events which occur in the window. The only method of interest is the windowClosing method, which executes whenever the window's Close button is activated. We can use this to provide a more controlled way of closing a window than that used in the earlier frame example. We send the exit message, with the parameter 0, to the System object to terminate the application.

Note that we could have chosen to extend the WindowAdapter class. This is a class that implements the WindowListener interface and provides implementations for all the methods in that interface. However, these implementations do nothing. The advantage is that you only have to implement the one method of interest to you rather than provide five methods which do nothing. The down side is that Java only provides for single inheritance; thus if you have already extended a class you cannot also extend the WindowAdapter class. One way round this is to use an inner class as the handler for the WindowEvents, thus allowing the outer class to extend, for example, the Frame class and the inner event handler to extend the WindowAdapter class.

19.10.2 The ExamplePanel Class

The ExamplePanel class, a subclass of Panel, defines what should be displayed by the application. It is, if you like, the drawing surface displayed within the window frame. This class defines a single method, paint(Graphics g), which defines the operations that display the contents of the window. In this case, it draws a string, places a rectangle around the string and then displays a set of red and blue lines. To ensure that any methods using paint do not have problems with colours, it resets the original colour before terminating. The methods used to change the colour and draw the string, the rectangle and the lines are all defined by the Graphics class. The source code for this class is defined in the file ExampleCanvas.java:

```java
import java.awt.*;

public class ExampleCanvas extends Canvas {
    String string = "Hello John";

    // This method is automatically executed whenever
    // Java requires the window to be displayed.
    public void paint (Graphics g) {
        int i;

        // Get original colour
        Colour originalColour = g.getColour();

        // Write some text into the window
        g.drawString(string, 40, 20);
        g.drawRect(35, 8, (string.length() * 7), 14);

        // Now draw some lines
        for (i = 20 ; i < 50; i = i + 3) {

            // Set the colour of the line and draw it
            if ((i % 2) == 0)
                {g.setColour(Colour.blue);}
            else
                {g.setColour(Colour.red);};
            g.drawLine(25, (70 - i), 100, (5 + i));
        }
        // Restore original colour
```

```
        g.setColour(originalColour);
    }
}
```

19.11 Further Reading

The current AWT documentation provided by the JDK tells you much about the methods provided by a particular class, but little about how to use them. However, there are very many books available which describe the Java AWT.

Cornell and Horstmann (1997) has two very good chapters on the AWT, covering most aspects of interest to the casual developer. An excellent book dedicated to the AWT is Geary and McClellan (1997). This book provides detailed coverage of the AWT and 30 additional components which build on the AWT components. These additional components are referred to as the Graphic Java Toolkit (GJT).

In addition, you should make extensive use of the online documentation provided by your system. A number of the toolkit vendors, such as Symantec and Microsoft, provide additional graphic classes which can be extremely useful (although they may tie your future development to these toolkits).

Chapter **20**

User Interface Programming

20.1 Introduction

In the last chapter you saw how to create a window and place a panel on it that allows you to draw graphic objects (lines, rectangles etc.). However, today's graphical user interfaces (GUIs) go far beyond this, allowing buttons, input and output fields, selection lists, menus etc. The Abstract Window Toolkit (AWT) provides many classes which directly support these types of facilities. As Java is a pure object-oriented language, a button is an object, a menu is an object, a text field is an object and so is a selection list. Thus to create a GUI in Java, you create the window and instances of the facilities you require; then you add these instances to the window instance. You use the Frame and Panel classes, just as you did in the previous chapter, to display such GUI component objects.

Of course life is not quite as simple as this; you need to take into account how the various components in the window should be laid out, what the window should do in response to an event (such as a user clicking a button) and how to terminate the window cleanly. In the last chapter, you briefly saw part of this when the WindowListener interface was used to catch the windowClosing event.

In this chapter, we consider how events can be caught and handled and the range of GUI facilities provided by the AWT. In the next chapter we look at how to lay out components in a window.

20.2 The Event Delegation Model

Version 1.1 of JDK introduced a new event model into Java. This event model is much cleaner than the previous approach and should result in simpler, clearer and more maintainable code. However, partly due to the introduction of new terminology, many find the new model confusing. This is typically because they have already become familiar with the previous approach or they are familiar with how language *X* did it.

20.2.1 The Philosophy Behind the Event Model

When trying to understand the event model in Java there are a few things you should remember. You must not forget that you are generating objects (including windows, components in windows, and events), which themselves generate other objects or send messages. You must, therefore, construct objects which work within this framework.

The way in which Java handles input to a user interface is part of a concept which was called the Model–View–Controller (MVC) architecture in Smalltalk. This concept states that it is a good idea to separate the application program (the model) from the user display (the view) and from the object which controls what happens on the display (the controller) (see Hunt (1997)).

This means that different interfaces can be used with the same application, without the application knowing about it (see Figure 20.1). The intention is that any part of the system can be changed without affecting the operation of the other parts. For example, the way that the graphical interface displays the information can be changed without modifying the actual application or the textual interface. Indeed, the application need not know what type of interface is connected to it.

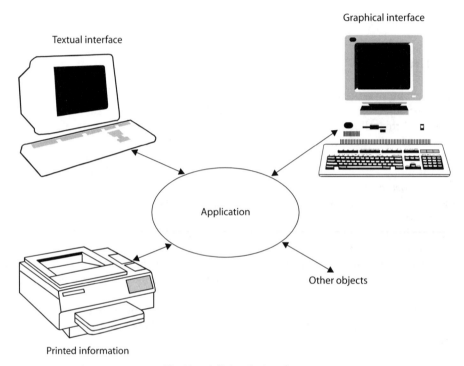

Fig. 20.1 Splitting the interface.

The MVC architecture aims to separate the user interface from the underlying information model to enable:

- Reusability of application and user interface components
- Separate development of the application and user interface
- Inheritance from different parts of the class hierarchy
- Control style classes which provide common features separately from how those features are displayed

To achieve the MVC architecture, Java provides two facilities:

- The observer/observable model which allows application programs and user interfaces to be loosely coupled
- Listeners which act as controllers handling various events

Listeners are objects which "listen" for a particular event and then react to it. For example, when a button is clicked by the user, the listener is notified and decides what action to take. This approach is known in Java as an *Event Delegation Model* because the responsibility for handling an event, which occurs in one object, is held by another object.

20.2.2 A Partial Example

A user constructs a GUI application by defining the graphic objects to be displayed, adding them to the display and associating them with a listener object. The listener object then handles the events which are generated for that object. This requires the user interface class (typically a subclass of Frame) to implement one or more interfaces which ensure that the window responds to the correct events from the JVM infrastructure. For example, if we want a window to respond to an action on a frame button, such as the Close button, then the window must implement the WindowListener interface:

```
public class SimpleGUI extends Frame implements WindowListener{
  protected Button exitButton;

  ... display construction code ...

  public void windowClosed(WindowEvent event) {}
  public void windowOpened(WindowEvent event) {}
  public void windowDeiconified(WindowEvent event) {}
  public void windowIconified(WindowEvent event) {}
  public void windowActivated(WindowEvent event) {}
  public void windowDeactivated(WindowEvent event) {}
  public void windowClosing(WindowEvent event) {
    System.exit(0);
  }
}
```

The WindowListener interface defines the set of window methods listed above. When an event occurs, the appropriate message is sent to the object along with the initiating event, which can then be handled in the appropriate manner. In this case, we have only defined the windowClosing method using the exit(int) method defined on the System object.

In the above example, we also wish to create a button which is displayed on the interface and allows the user to exit without using the border frame buttons (some window managers on Unix do not provide a Close Window frame button). To do this, we create a button and a listener for the action on the button:

```
exitButtonController = new ExitButtonController(this);
exitButton = new Button(" Exit ");
exitButton.addActionListener(exitButtonController);
```

This code creates a listener object, ExitButtonController, and a labelled button. It then adds the exitButtonController as the listener for the button. The ExitButtonController class provides a single instance method actionPerformed which initiates the System.exit(0) method.

The resulting class and instance structures are illustrated in Figure 20.2. As you can see from this diagram, the separation of interface and control is conceptually very clean.

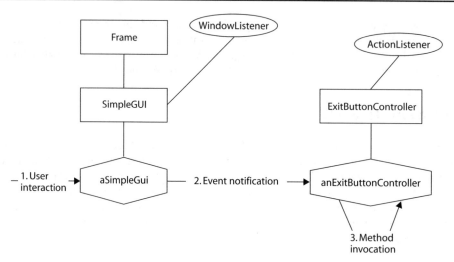

Fig. 20.2 The class and object diagram using the event delegation model.

The ExitButtonController class definition is presented below. You do not have to call such a class "controller", you can equally call it an ExitButtonEventListener. However, the listeners are the interface definitions. By choosing a different name, we make it clear that we are talking about the classes which provide the execution control.

```
class ExitButtonController implements ActionListener {
    protected Frame view;
    public ExiButtonController (Frame win) {
        view = win;
    }
    public void actionPerformed(ActionEvent event) {
        System.exit(0);
    }
}
```

Notice that the ExitButtonController class does not inherit from any particular class (other than Object). It implements the ActionListener interface. Listeners are defined as classes which implement various interfaces. This should not be a surprise, as the listener objects must decide what to do with particular events on an application specific basis: there is little the system-provided class could do. Instead, the interfaces ensure that the implementing classes provide the protocol required by the Java event delegation model.

20.2.3 The Listener Interfaces

There are a number of interfaces associated with the event delegation model defined in the package java.awt.event. Table 20.1 presents the listener interfaces, the methods which are triggered in response to events and the objects which originate the events. Using this table, you can see that if you wish to handle an action on a button, list or text field you must define an object which implements the ActionListener. This interface defines a single method actionPerformed(). Your listener class must therefore define this method.

Table 20.1 The listeners used with the event delegation model.

Interface	Triggered methods	Originating object
`ActionListener`	`actionPerformed (ActionEvent)`	`Button, List, MenuItem, TextField`
`ItemListener`	`itemStateChanged (ItemEvent)`	`Checkbox, CheckboxMenuItem, Choice`

`WindowListener`
The argument to these methods is
`WindowEvent`
	`windowClosing`
	`windowOpened`
	`windowIconified`
	`windowDeiconified`
	`windowClosed`
	`windowActivated`
	`windowDeactivated`
		`Dialog, Frame`

`ComponentListener`
The argument to these methods is
`ComponentEvent`
	`componentMoved`
	`componentHidden`
	`componentResized`
	`componentShown`
		`Dialog, Frame`

`AdjustmentListener`	`adjustmentValueChanged` `(AdjustmentEvent)`	`Scrollbar`
`ItemListener`	`itemStateChanged` `(ItemEvent)`	`Checkbox, CheckboxMenuItem, Choice, List`
`MouseMotionListener`	`mouseDragged(MouseEvent)` `mouseMoved(MouseEvent)`	`Canvas, Dialog, Frame, Panel, Window`

`MouseListener`	`mousePressed(MouseEvent)`
	`mouseReleased(MouseEvent)`
	`mouseEntered(MouseEvent)`
	`mouseExited(MouseEvent)`
	`mouseClicked(MouseEvent)`
		`Canvas, Dialog, Frame, Panel, Window`

`KeyListener`	`keyPressed(KeyEvent)`
	`keyReleased(KeyEvent)`
	`keyTyped(KeyEvent)`
		`Component`

`TextListener`	`textValueChanged(TextEvent)`	`TextComponent`

20.3 GUI Component Classes

The components defined by the AWT which support the range of facilities commonly found on a GUI are relatively limited. Anyone who has used tools such as Delphi, Visual C++ or VisualWorks will probably be disappointed. This situation will change over time, however the facilities provided by release 1.1 of the JDK are those indicated in Figure 20.3. The only elements not illustrated in this diagram are the `Dialog` and `FileDialog` classes. The most commonly used of these classes are discussed briefly below. The remaining classes are summarized at the end of this section.

20.3.1 The `Button` Class

The `Button` class defines a labelled button component. Such buttons, typically, are rectangular in shape, have a textual label and cause a method to execute when the user selects the button. The `Button` class defines two constructors and two listener methods:

- `Button()` constructs a button with no label.
- `Button(String)` constructs a button with the specified label.

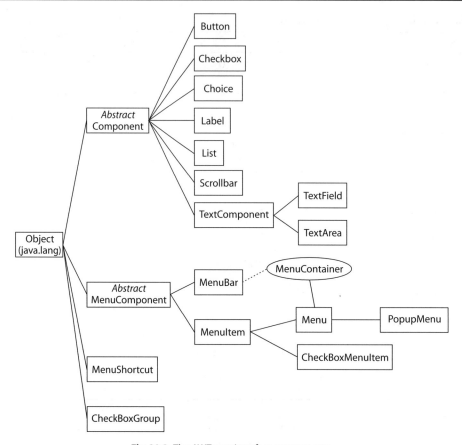

Fig. 20.3 The AWT user interface components.

- addActionListener(ActionListener) adds the specified listener to receive action events from this button.
- removeActionListener(ActionListener) removes the specified listener so it no longer receives events from this button.

The method protocol includes:

- setLabel(String) which sets the button label
- getLabel() which returns the current button label

20.3.2 The Checkbox Class

A checkbox object is a graphical component which comprises a label, a toggle and a state. The state can be either true or false, which is represented graphically by a selected or unselected checkbox (see Figure 20.4). This application is defined in a class RadioTest, which is based on the SimpleGUI class presented in this chapter. A checkbox can be part of a group within which only one checkbox can be selected. Such groups are often known as radio buttons.

The Checkbox class defines a number of constructors:

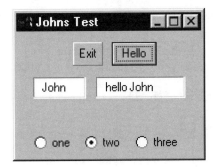

Fig. 20.4 Using checkboxes.

- Checkbox() constructs a checkbox with an empty label.
- Checkbox(String) constructs a checkbox with the specified label.
- Checkbox(String, boolean) constructs a checkbox, with the specified label, set to a specified state.
- Checkbox(String, boolean, CheckboxGroup) constructs a checkbox with the specified label, set to the specified state, and in the specified checkbox group. There is also a version of this constructor which swaps the order of the state and group.

The method protocol for the Checkbox class includes methods to access the label associated with the checkbox item:

- getLabel() returns the label of the checkbox.
- setLabel(String) sets this label of the checkbox.

The Checkbox class possesses methods to obtain and set the state of the checkbox item:

- getState() returns the boolean state of the Checkbox.
- setState(boolean) sets the Checkbox to the specified boolean state.

Two methods enable you to set the checkbox group:

- getCheckboxGroup() returns the checkbox group containing the receiver.
- setCheckboxGroup(CheckboxGroup) sets the checkbox group of the receiver.

There are also two methods to set and delete a listener object:

- addItemListener(ItemListener) adds the specified item listener to receive item events from this checkbox.
- removeItemListener(ItemListener) removes the specified item listener so that it no longer receives item events from this checkbox.

20.3.3 The CheckboxGroup Class

The CheckboxGroup class creates an object which associates a set of checkboxes in a radio button relationship. Only one checkbox within a group may be set to true at any one time.
The CheckboxGroup class has a single constructor which creates a new instance.

The method protocol for this class includes:

- `getSelectedCheckbox()` which returns the currently selected checkbox
- `setSelectedCheckbox(Checkbox)` sets the current choice to the specified checkbox

An example of constructing a set of checkboxes and a checkbox group is presented below:

```
CheckboxGroup g = new CheckboxGroup();
add(one = new Checkbox("one", g, false));
add(two = new Checkbox("two", g, true));
add(three = new Checkbox("three", g, false));
```

This is, essentially, the source code used to generate the checkbox group displayed in Figure 20.4.

20.3.4 The Label Class

The Label class is used to construct a textual label for display within a window. It is an output only field which can be modified dynamically. It possesses three class variables which specify the alignment of the text within the label:

- CENTER
- LEFT
- RIGHT

The Label class defines three constructor methods:

- Label() constructs an empty label.
- Label(String) constructs a new label with the specified string.
- Label(String, int) constructs a new label with the specified string of text and alignment.

The Label class provides methods for getting and setting the label and its alignment:

- getText() gets the text of this label.
- setText(String) sets the text for this label to the specified text.
- getAlignment() gets the current alignment of this label.
- setAlignment(int) sets the alignment for the receiving label.

20.3.5 The TextComponent Class

TextComponent is a generic class which provides a component that allows you to edit text. It is of primary importance because it is the direct superclass of TextField and TextArea. These classes inherit some of the features of a TextComponent. In particular, it defines the listener methods:

- addTextListener(TextListener) adds the specified text event listener to handle events generated by the receiver.
- removeTextListener(TextListener) removes the specified text event listener so that it no longer handles events from the receiver.

This class also defines methods which allow you to specify whether the text can be edited, what the text is and which part of the text is selected:

- `setEditable(boolean)` sets the specified boolean to indicate whether or not the receiver can be edited by the user. If it is false, the `TextComponent` is read only.
- `setText(String)` sets the text displayed by the receiver.
- `getSelectedText()` returns the selected text contained in the receiver.

20.3.6 The `TextField` Class

This class manages the display (and editing) of a single line of text. It is a direct subclass of `TextComponent` and adds the following constructors:

- `TextField()` constructs a new empty `TextField`.
- `TextField(int)` constructs an empty `TextField` with the specified number of columns.
- `TextField(String)` constructs a new `TextField` initialized with the specified text.
- `TextField(String, int)` constructs a new `TextField` initialized with the specified text and columns.

`TextField` also defines some additional method protocols:

- `addActionListener(ActionListener)` links the receiving object to an action listener.
- `setColumns(int)` sets the number of columns in the receiver.

20.3.7 The `TextArea` Class

This class, also a direct subclass of `TextComponent`, provides a graphical component for displaying and editing multiple lines of text.

It defines a number of class variables which indicate the number of scrollbars required:

- `SCROLLBARS_BOTH`
- `SCROLLBARS_HORIZONTAL_ONLY`
- `SCROLLBARS_NONE`
- `SCROLLBARS_VERTICAL_ONLY`

The `TextArea` class provides five constructors:

- `TextArea()` constructs a new `TextArea`.
- `TextArea(int, int)` constructs an empty `TextArea` with the specified number of rows and columns.
- `TextArea(String)` constructs a `TextArea` which displays the specified text.
- `TextArea(String, int, int)` constructs a `TextArea` with the specified text and number of rows and columns.
- `TextArea(String, int, int, int)` constructs a `TextArea` with the specified text, number of rows and columns, and scrollbar visibility.

The `TextArea` class provides a large number of methods, including:

- `append(String)`, which appends the given text to the end
- `insert(String, int)`, which inserts the string into the receiver at the specified point

- setColumns(int), which sets the number of columns for the receiver
- setRows(int), which sets the number of rows for the receiver

20.4 Additional AWT Classes

There are a number of other classes with which you should become familiar (Table 20.2). Additional documentation for all these classes is available online within the java.awt package documentation.

Table 20.2 Other AWT classes.

Class	Description
Choice	Provides a choice button which presents a number of selections. The label shows the current choice
List	Provides single (and multiple) selection lists
Scrollbar	Allows a variable's value to be modified within a range. They can be used with a canvas to provide a scrollable region (you may also use a ScrollPane, new in JDK 1.1)
MenuBar	Provides an object which generates a platform-dependent representation of a window's menu bar
MenuItem	Generates an option on a menu
Menu	Defines a menu on a menu bar
PopupMenu	Defines a dynamically generated and displayed menu which can pop up at a specific point within a window. (This class was new in JDK 1.1.)
Dialog	Generates a simple window which receives data from a user. They can be modal or non-modal
FileDialog	Defines a file selection dialog appropriate to the current platform, thus removing the need for the user to write different dialogs for each platform. It is a modal dialog

Chapter *21*

Managing Component Layout

21.1 Introduction

A layout manager is an object which works with a graphical application and the host platform to determine the best way to display the objects in the window. The programmer does not need to worry about what happens if a user resizes a window, works on a different platform or (if you are developing applets) uses a Web browser.

Layout managers help to produce portable, presentable user interfaces. There are a number of different layout managers which use different philosophies to handle the way in which they lay out components: `FlowLayout`, `BorderLayout`, `GridLayout`, `GridBagLayout` and `CardLayout` (for notebook style interfaces).

21.2 The FlowLayout Manager

This is the simplest layout manager. It lays the components out in a row across a window. When there is no more space left, it starts on the next row, and so on until no more space is left. The display in Figure 21.1 could be generated using a `FlowLayout` object.

Fig. 21.1 Using a flow layout manager.

The class which generated this application is presented below (the buttons do not actually do anything):

```
import java.awt.*;

public class FlowLayoutExample extends Frame {

  public static void main (String argv []) {
    FlowLayoutExample f = new FlowLayoutExample();
```

```
    }

    public FlowLayoutExample () {
      setTitle("FlowLayout Example");

      setLayout(new FlowLayout(FlowLayout.LEFT));

      add(new Button("One"));
      add(new Button("Two"));
      add(new Button("Three"));
      add(new Button("Four"));

      setSize(150, 100);
      setVisible(true);
    }
}
```

Most of what this Frame subclass does should be familiar to you by now. It sets the label for the frame, creates some buttons and adds them to the window, sets the frame size and whether it should be visible or not. However, it also creates a FlowLayout manager which is initialized using left alignment (the default alignment is "center"). The layout manager object determines where within the window frame the components are placed.

The FlowLayout class defines three class variables which indicate the type of alignment required:

- CENTER
- LEFT
- RIGHT

The FlowLayout class defines three constructors:

- FlowLayout() constructs a flow layout with a centred alignment and a default 5-unit horizontal and vertical gap.
- FlowLayout(int) constructs a flow layout with the specified alignment and a default 5-unit horizontal and vertical gap.
- FlowLayout(int, int, int) constructs a new flow layout with the specified alignment and horizontal and vertical gaps.

Although the FlowLayout class does define instance methods, they are not normally used by the user.

21.3 The BorderLayout Manager

The BorderLayout class defines a layout manager which has a concept of four outer points and a central point (labelled North, East, South, West and Center). This window is divided up as illustrated in Figure 21.2. Of course, you do not have to place components at all available locations. If you omit one (or more) locations, the others stretch to fill up the space. The border layout is the default layout for frames and panels.

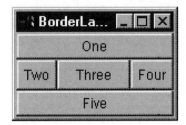

Fig. 21.2 Using a border layout manager.

To add components to a window which has a border layout manager, you use a version of the add method which takes a position indicator (such as "South") as well as the component to add. For example, we can change the FlowLayout example to work with borders and produce the display in Figure 21.2.

```
public class BorderLayoutExample extends Frame {
    ... as before
    public BorderLayoutExample () {
        setTitle("BorderLayout Example");
        setLayout(new BorderLayout());
        add("North", new Button("One"));
        add("West", new Button("Two"));
        add("Center", new Button("Three"));
        add("East", new Button("Four"));
        add("South", new Button("Five"));
        ... as before
    }
}
```

The BorderLayout class defines five class variables:

- CENTER
- EAST
- NORTH
- SOUTH
- WEST

It also defines two constructors:

- BorderLayout() constructs a border layout with no gaps between the components.
- BorderLayout(int, int) constructs a border layout with the specified gaps.

21.4 The GridLayout Manager

The GridLayout manager defines a two-dimensional grid onto which components are added. The default order of addition is from left to right and top to bottom. Figure 21.3 shows an exam-

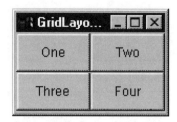

Fig. 21.3 Using a grid layout manager.

ple of using a 2×2 grid. It was created by defining a grid layout manager and then adding the four buttons:

```
public class GridLayoutExample extends Frame {
  ... as before
  public GridLayoutExample () {
    setTitle("GridLayout Example");
    setLayout(new GridLayout(2, 2));
    add(new Button("One"));
    add(new Button("Two"));
    add(new Button("Three"));
    add(new Button("Four"));
    ... as before
  }
}
```

The GridLayout class defines the following constructors:

- GridLayout() creates a grid layout with one column per component, in a single row.
- GridLayout(int, int) creates a grid layout with the specified rows and columns.
- GridLayout(int, int, int, int) creates a grid layout with the specified rows, columns, and horizontal and vertical gaps.

21.5 The GridBagLayout Manager

The GridBagLayout manager is a powerful and flexible layout manager which is more complex to use than the other layout managers. This layout manager uses a dynamically created grid to lay components out. However, a component can stretch across more then one column and row, the columns and rows may not be of equal size, and they do not need to be filled in order.

The GridBagLayout class provides a single constructor, GridBagLayout(), and a number of instance methods which help control the way in which components are laid out.

To position a component object, a GridBagLayout object uses a GridBagConstraints object, which specifies constraints on how to position a component (for example, its initial x and y location, width and height), how to distribute the component objects, and how to resize and align them.

The display in Figure 21.4 was constructed using a GridBagLayout object and a GridBagConstraint object.

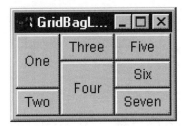

Fig. 21.4 Using a grid bag layout manager.

The class definition that uses this layout manager is a little more complex than that for the previous layout managers:

```java
import java.awt.*;

public class GridBagLayoutExample extends Frame {

  private GridBagLayout layout;
  private GridBagConstraints constraints;

  public static void main (String argv []) {
    GridBagLayoutExample f = new GridBagLayoutExample();
  }

  public GridBagLayoutExample () {
    // Create the layout manager and
    //the constraint object
    layout = new GridBagLayout();
    constraints = new GridBagConstraints();

    // Set layout characteristics
    constraints.weightx = 1.0;
    constraints.weighty = 1.0;
    constraints.fill = GridBagConstraints.BOTH;
    setTitle("GridBagLayout Example");
    setLayout(layout);

    // Add the buttons
    addButton(0, 0, 1, 2, "One");
    addButton(0, 2, 1, 4, "Two");
    addButton(1, 0, 1, 1, "Three");
    addButton(1, 1, 1, 4, "Four");
    addButton(2, 0, 1, 1, "Five");
    addButton(2, 1, 1, 1, "Six");
    addButton(2, 2, 1, 1, "Seven");

    setSize(150, 100);
    setVisible(true);
  }
```

```
    private void addButton(int x, int y, int w, int h,
            String s) {
    Button button = new Button(s);
    constraints.gridx = x;
    constraints.gridy = y;
    constraints.gridwidth = w;
    constraints.gridheight = h;
    layout.setConstraints(button, constraints);
    add(button);
    }
}
```

There are two parts to the layout features used in this class: the layout constraints and the positioning of the components. The general layout principles are controlled by a GridBag-Constraint object. You must set out the instance variables as shown in Table 21.1.

Table 21.1 The instance variables of a GridBagConstraint object.

fill	Determines how to resize a component that is smaller than the display area:
	NONE do not resize (the default)
	HORIZONTAL fill the display area horizontally, but do not
	            change the height
	VERTICAL fill the display area vertically, but do not change
	            the width
	BOTH fill the display area entirely

ipadx ipady	Specify how much to pad out the component (beyond its minimum size).
insets	Specifies the space between the component and the edges of its display area.
anchor	Determines where to place a component that is smaller than the display area: CENTER (the default) NORTH SOUTH NORTHEAST SOUTHEAST NORTHWEST SOUTHWEST EAST WEST
weightx weighty	Determine how to distribute space; this is important for specifying resizing behaviour. Unless you specify a weight for at least one component in a row (weightx) and column (weighty), all the components clump together in the centre of their container. When the weight is zero (the default), any extra space is put between the grid of cells and the edges of the container

The grid coordinates of a component are determined by instance variables on the constraints object:

- gridx,gridy together specify the top left of the component's display area. The top-left cell has address (gridx=0, gridy=0).
- gridwidth,gridheight together specify the number of cells in a row and column in the component's display area. The default value is 1.

Once these constraints have been set, you must associate them with a particular component (or container). In the above class, each button is associated with a set of constraints for the layout manager using the setConstraints() method.

Finally, the component is added to the layout manager using the add(component) method. We did not have to create a new GridBagConstraint object for each button; instead, we reset the positioning instance variables of a single constraint object.

21.6 The CardLayout Manager

This is a layout manager for a container that contains several "cards". Only one card is visible at a time and the user can flip through the cards. It possesses two constructors:

- CardLayout() creates a card layout with gaps of size zero.
- CardLayout(int, int) creates a card layout with the specified gaps.

The primary methods in this class are:

- first(Container), which flips to the first card
- last(Container), which flips to the last card
- next(Container), which flips to the next card

21.7 A Simple GUI Example

In this section we present a very simple GUI class. An instance of this class generated the window displayed in Figure 21.5. This application performs the following functions:

- Displays the string "hello John" in a text box in response to the user clicking on the Hello button.
- Exits the application in response to the user clicking on the Exit button.

Fig. 21.5 A simple graphical application.

It combines the layout managers presented in this chapter with the components introduced in the previous one. It also makes use of the event delegation model introduced in the last chapter.

The structure of this interface is essentially the same as that presented in Figure 21.2. The main difference is that the controller class is called SimpleController and it handles two button events: the Exit button and the Hello button.

The class SimpleGUI should not contain any surprises for you. It creates a new panel onto which it adds two buttons. These buttons use a listener object to handle the events generated. The window itself acts as a window listener, enabling it to handle operations such as closing the window. In addition, it uses a border layout to position buttons on the panel, as well as the panel, text field and label on the frame.

```
import java.awt.*;
import java.awt.event.*;
public class SimpleGUI extends Frame implements WindowListener{
```

```java
protected Button exitButton, helloButton;
protected TextField field1;
private SimpleController controller;
public static void main (String args []) {
  Frame f = new SimpleGUI();
}

public SimpleGUI () {
  setTitle("Johns Simple GUI");
  controller = new SimpleController(this);

  // Set up panel for buttons (using a flow layout)
  Panel b = new Panel();
  b.setLayout(new FlowLayout(FlowLayout.CENTER));

  exitButton = new Button("Exit");
  exitButton.addActionListener(controller);
  b.add(exitButton);

  helloButton = new Button("Hello");
  helloButton.addActionListener(controller);
  b.add(helloButton);

  // Add the button panel to the frame
  add("North", b);

  // Create a non-editable text field and add that
  field1 = new TextField(10);
  field1.setEditable(false);
  add("Center", field1);

  // Put a label in the frame
  Label label = new Label("(c) 1997: John Hunt");
  add("South", label);

  // Make the frame handle window events
  addWindowListener(this);

  // Resize and show the window
  setSize(160, 110);
  setVisible(true);;
}

public void windowClosed(WindowEvent event) {}
public void windowOpened(WindowEvent event) {}
public void windowDeiconified(WindowEvent event) {}
public void windowIconified(WindowEvent event) {}
public void windowActivated(WindowEvent event) {}
public void windowDeactivated(WindowEvent event) {}
public void windowClosing(WindowEvent event) {
  System.exit(0);
```

```
      }
  }

    class SimpleController implements ActionListener {
      SimpleGUI view;

      public SimpleController (SimpleGUI win) {
        view = win;
      }

      public void actionPerformed(ActionEvent event) {
        // You can get the source object of an event
        Object source = event.getSource();

        // You can then compare the event source with
        // actual objects.
        if (source == view.exitButton)
          System.exit(0);
        else if (source == view.helloButton)
          view.field1.setText("hello John");
      }
  }
```

You could have a different controller for each button. In such a situation, you do not need to test to see which button generated an event (thus eliminating the if statement that selects the action). This is a more object-oriented approach and it is used in the next chapter.

Chapter *22*

Putting the Swing into Java

22.1 Introduction

We have already mentioned the Java Foundation Classes (JFC), Swing and post-Java 2 SDK 1.2 releases in this book. However, many of you won't be sure of the relationships between Swing, JFC and the JDK; nor indeed of what Swing actually provides. This chapter cuts through the hype and shows you what Swing will mean for you.

22.2 Swing, the JFC and the JDK

Let us start by talking about Swing. What is it? It has been stated that the overall goal of the Swing project was "to build a set of extensible GUI components to enable developers to more rapidly develop powerful Java front ends for commercial applications" (see `http://java.sub.com/products/jfc/swingdoc-static/swing_arch.html`). That's all well and good, but what does it mean to you and me? In real terms, it means that Swing provides a set of graphical components which allow user interfaces to be constructed which provide commercial quality (and functionality) with the minimum of effort. For example, many users are now familiar with the idea of brief reminders being displayed when they leave their cursor over a button for a short period. In Swing, these are referred to as tooltips and are simple and straightforward to implement. Prior to Swing, however, the equivalent functionality would have to have been provided by developers themselves catching mouse events, waiting a period of time and then popping up a small window with the tooltip displayed inside it. None of this would have been trivial.

What else does Swing provide? Firstly, all components in Swing are 100% pure Java (referred to as lightweight). This means that the windows should look the same whatever platform they are on and should be easier to maintain (for Sun). As all graphical components are "lightweight", their appearance is controlled purely by the Java code (without the need for platform-dependent peers – as in JDK 1.0 and 1.1). In Swing, a separate user interface "view" component performs the actual rendering of the component on the screen. This allows different views to be plugged in. This in turn allows the idea of different "look and feels". This means that it should be possible for a Windows developer to select the Motif look and feel and see what the interface would look like on that platform. It also means that it is easier to deploy the same software on different platforms, but with interfaces that match the interface manager on that particular platform. This separation of view from the actual component is based on a modified version of the Model–View–Controller architecture (described later).

Swing also provides a greatly increased set of facilities for graphical user interfaces, including trees, icons on buttons, dockable menus bars, menus with icons, borders and improved support for fonts and colours.

So does this mean that the AWT (The Abstract Window Kit) of version 1.0 and 1.1 of Java is being thrown out of the window? Not exactly – the AWT will still be available and systems can be constructed using both the AWT and Swing (although there are some limitations). However, as the AWT knows nothing about different "look and feels" and mixes both lightweight (pure Java) and heavyweight (native) components, any AWT windows may not be consistent with the Swing windows. From the point of view of the developer, it makes little sense to continue to use the AWT when all of the AWT's facilities (and more) are replicated in Swing. Indeed, much of what an AWT developer already knows will go a long way towards helping to get started with Swing, as will be shown by this chapter.

So that's Swing, but what is its relationship to the JFC and the Java 2 platform? Essentially, Swing is a core component of the JFC, along with Java2D, Accessibility and Drag and Drop. It is the largest element of the JFC (as it stands now) and will therefore be taken by many to equate to the JFC. Indeed, one insider has said that it is "spelt JFC but pronounced Swing". However, as can be seem from the above list, this is not the case. As this chapter is about Swing we will not digress into Java2D, the Accessibility API or Drag and Drop, except to say that each is a significant development with Java2D being a major improvement over the basic facilities in previous versions of the Java. For Java 3D see Palmer (2001).

Where does that leave the Java 2 SDK 1.2 (and more recent releases, including 1.4)? Swing is now a very well established part of the Java 2 platform. With each successive release of the Java 2 SDK it has been refined, with the Java 2 SDK 1.4 providing even more enhancements. It is likely that with each successive release of Java 2, Swing will progress further and further – at least let us hope so.

22.3 What Is the MVC?

We have already said that Swing is based on a modified version of the Model–View–Controller (MVC) architecture. So what is the MVC? The MVC is not a new idea (it originated in Smalltalk), but the concept has been used in many places. The intention of the MVC architecture is the separation of the user display from the control of user input and from the underlying information model as illustrated in Figure 22.1 (Krasner and Pope, 1988). This is often referred to as model-driven programming (i.e. the separation of GUIs from the data that they present). There are a number of reasons why this is useful:

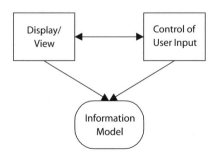

Fig. 22.1 The Model–View–Controller architecture.

- reusability of application and/or user interface components
- ability to develop the application and user interface separately
- ability to inherit from different parts of the class hierarchy
- ability to define control style classes which provide common features separately from how these features may be displayed

This means that different interfaces can be used with the same application, without the application knowing about it. It also means that any part of the system can be changed without affecting the operation of the other. For example, the way that the graphical interface (the look) displays the information could be changed without modifying the actual application or how input is handled (the feel). Indeed, the application need not know what type of interface is currently connected to it at all. Prior to Swing it was certainly possible to build GUIs based on the MVC in Java (Hunt, 1997). However, Swing makes the concept of separating the data from the display and control fundamental to its operation.

22.4 Swinging the MVC Into Action

Swing uses a modified version of the traditional Model–View–Controller architecture. This is because in practice the view and the controller need to be tightly bound. Indeed, in Smalltalk it was common to find that many classes in the view hierarchy had associated classes in the controller hierarchy, and that if you used one particular view, then you had to use the associated controller. For myself, I have found that I have moved to defining my controllers as inner classes to my views, so that while I am separating them logically, they are directly tied together. This is essentially the conclusion which the Swing development team came to. Thus in Swing there is a model object (for holding the data) and a UI object for managing the view and the control. For example, even a `Button` has a separate model: in the case of the class `javax.swing.JButton`, any model used must implement the `javax.swing.ButtonModel` interface.

However, even this description fails to capture a subtlety introduced by Swing – "UI delegates". In order to allow different look and feels to be plugged in, each view controller combination actually has a "UI delegate" associated with it. It is the UI delegate which actually draws the component, although it is the component itself which is responsible for handling the display and user input (see Figure 22.2).

In Figure 22.2, the data-specific Model is separated from the `JComponent` (the root of many of Swing's GUI components) which possesses both the view and the controller. In turn, the controller uses a separate UI delegate to actually draw the component in a window. Thus Swing provides leverage for both model-driven programming and pluggable look and feels.

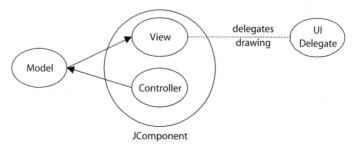

Fig. 22.2 The modified MVC in Swing.

So what does this mean for the developer? Does it mean that to use a button you must first create a model of the data displayed by a button? No: in the case of simple components such as buttons and labels, when you construct the GUI component an appropriate model is created automatically. However, for more complex GUI components, such as trees, you first need to create the model (in terms of `DefaultMutableTreeNodes`) and then instantiate the `JTree` GUI component on top of it. The `JTree` GUI component then displays the information held in the model.

22.5 Transitioning to Swing

In the remainder of this chapter we will look at how to convert a relatively simple AWT-based application to a Swing-based one. The application we shall use provides a very simplistic picture tool. However, it possesses many of the features which will be of interest to Java developers. We shall first look at how this application is implemented in the AWT and then at what changes we need to make to move it over to Swing. In reality you will probably just build the application in Swing from the start. However, as we have already learnt about the AWT in Chapter 19 we will use this as the starting point in this chapter.

22.5.1 The `SimpleGallery` Application

The `SimpleGallery` application allows a user to display GIF or JPEG images. It is intended as a simple personal image viewer. It does not include any zoom facility, nor does it allow for editing of the images. The simple AWT-based gallery application is illustrated in Fig. 22.3. This figure shows a GIF image (my daughter at 4 months old!). Users can load images, resize the window and exit the application. The program is implemented by two classes, `SimpleGallery` and `PicturePanel`, within the gallery package. Listing 22.1 presents the `SimpleGallery` class.

Fig. 22.3 The `SimpleGallery` application.

Listing 22.1 `SimpleGallery`

```
package gallery;

import java.awt.*;
import java.awt.event.*;

public class SimpleGallery extends Frame {
  PicturePanel picturePanel;
  public static void main(String args []) {
    new SimpleGallery("Simple Gallery");
  }

  public SimpleGallery(String label) {
    super(label);
    // registers window handler
    addWindowListener(new WindowHandler());
    // creates and adds button panel
    Panel panel = new Panel();
    ButtonPanelController bpc = new ButtonPanelController();
    Button b = new Button("Load");
    b.addActionListener(bpc);
    panel.add(b);
    b = new Button("Exit");
    b.addActionListener(bpc);
    panel.add(b);
    add("North", panel);
    // Creates and adds picture panel to main frame
    picturePanel = new PicturePanel();
    ScrollPane pane = new ScrollPane(ScrollPane.SCROLLBARS_ALWAYS);
    pane.add(picturePanel);
    add("Center", pane);

    pack();
    setVisible(true);
  }

  // Inner class to handle window events
  class WindowHandler extends WindowAdapter {
    public void windowClosing(WindowEvent event) {
      System.exit(0);
    }
  }

  // Inner class to handle button events
  class ButtonPanelController implements ActionListener {
    public void actionPerformed(ActionEvent event) {
      String cmd = event.getActionCommand();
      if (cmd.equals("Load")) {
        FileDialog fd = new FileDialog(SimpleGallery.this, "Select
Image", FileDialog.LOAD);
```

```
            fd.setVisible(true); picturePanel.setImageFilename(fd.getFile());
        } else {
          System.exit(0);
        }
      }
    }
  }
}
```

This class is not particularly complex, nor indeed does it make use of many AWT facilities. As such it is representative of a wide spectrum of interfaces. It possesses a main frame, to which are added to sub-panels, one containing two buttons and one containing an instance of a drawing panel. It also possesses two inner classes which handle the events generated when users click on the buttons or the window frame's buttons. These are presented as inner classes as they provide access to the encompassing object (e.g. SimpleGallery.this refers to the object containing the ButtonPanelController). In particular, the ButtonPanelController class uses the FileDialog class to present the user with a selection box from which to select the appropriate GIF or JPEG file.

The PicturePanel class is a little more complex. This class must load a GIF or JPEG image from a file and display it within the drawing area of the panel. This class is listed in Listing 22.2.

Listing 22.2 The PicturePanel class.

```
package gallery;

import java.awt.*;
import java.awt.image.*;

public class PicturePanel extends Panel implements ImageObserver {
  private String imageFilename;
  private Image image;

  // Repaint the panels display whenever the graphics have been
  // corrupted or a new image is to be displayed
  public void paint(Graphics gc) {
    // Note drawImage returns immediately.
    // An image observer is required to determine
    // when the image has been fully loaded (see
    // imageUpdate().
    if (image != null)
      gc.drawImage(image, 1, 1, this);
  }

  // Specifies the image to load and then triggers the loading of the
  // image
  public void setImageFilename(String filename) {
    imageFilename = filename;
    loadImage();
  }

  // Load the image using the appropriate toolkit for the current
  // platform
```

```java
    private void loadImage() {
    try {
      Toolkit toolkit = Toolkit.getDefaultToolkit();
      image = toolkit.getImage(imageFilename);
    } catch(Exception e) {System.out.println("Problem loading image");}
  }

  /**
   * This method is used to determine whether the
   * image being displayed has been fully loaded or
   * not. If it returns true then the image still
   * requires more information. If it returns false
   * then the image has been successfully loaded
   * or an error has occurred.
   */
  public boolean imageUpdate(Image img,
    int infoflags,
    int x,
    int y,
    int width,
    int height) {
    if (ImageObserver.PROPERTIES == infoflags) return true;
    else if (ImageObserver.ERROR == infoflags) {
      System.out.println("Error in image - image display aborted");
      return false;
    } else return true;
  }

  // Need to specify the size of the panel
  public Dimension getPreferredSize() {return new Dimension(400, 400);}
}
```

The PicturePanel class is made more complex due to the way in which it must load the image from a file. As Java was originally intended for use with the Internet, it allows an image to be loaded in parts. Thus any object which tries to load an image must monitor the loading process to determine when it has finished. This is done by implementing the ImageObserver interface and thus the imageUpdate method. This is further complicated by the need to use a platform-specific toolkit to actually load the image in the first place. Once the image is loaded it is quite simple to actually draw it in the panel by redefining the paint(Graphics) method to execute the drawImage() method on the graphics context passed to it. The paint(Graphics) method is executed whenever part (or all) of the display is corrupted, or whenever the repaint() method is called.

22.6 A Swinging Gallery

We are now ready to port this application to Swing. So where do we start? The first thing is to convert classes such as Frame, Button and Panel to their Swing equivalents. In general the graphical components in Swing are prefixed by a J; thus the Swing version of a Button is JButton etc. Table 22.1 presents some comparisons.

Table 22.1 Mapping AWT to Swing components.

AWT name	Swing name	AWT name	Swing name
Button	JButton	CheckBox	JCheckBox
Frame	JFrame	ScrollBar	JScrollBar
Panel	JPanel	Label	JLabel
Menu	JMenu	List	JList
TextField	JTextField	TextArea	JTextArea

You should be careful of merely assuming that the Swing versions of components will be exactly the same as the AWT versions. In general they provide more functionality. In some cases they have changed their names because their functionality has changed so much (for example, FileDialog is now JFileChooser). In other cases new classes have been introduced to provide a better way of implementing features. For example, to generate a radio button in the AWT a developer uses a CheckBox object within a checkbox group; in Swing we now have the JRadioButton class.

So far so good – we have now changed all the Buttons, Panels and Frames to become JButton, JPanel and JFrame. Next we need to obtain the top-level JFrame's content pane. For example, this is done in Listing 22.3 in the following manner: Container pane = getContentPane(). This is new. You never had to get hold of a frame's content pane in the AWT. Indeed, did a frame have a content pane in the AWT? So what is this content pane? In Swing, JFrame, JDialog and JApplet are top-level containers. These top-level containers provide the framework within which other (lightweight) components can draw themselves. This framework is implemented by the content pane. Without a content pane , lightweight components such as JButton and JLabel could not be drawn. Thus lightweight components must be drawn within some form of top-level container (or within a component which is eventually drawn within a top-level container). Effectively, the content pane is the link to the host platform: it is a heavyweight AWT component (in fact an instance of Container) which can render itself on the host platform's windowing system.

Once you have got hold of the JFrame's content pane, you must then make sure that all the components displayed within the window are added to the content pane and not the JFrame. For the gallery application (now named SwingGallery) the structure of the application is therefore that illustrated in Figure 22.4.

For the main SwingGallery class, we can now start to think about taking advantage of some of the new features of Swing to improve the look and feel of our application. For example, we can add icons to our buttons. This is very easy to do: the ImageIcon class can be used to create an image which can be used as an icon for a button. One of the constructors for this class takes a string specifying the location of the image to use (for example, ImageIcon buttonIcon = new ImageIcon("load.gif");). Now we need to modify the constructor used to create the actual button so that the newly created icon is passed to it as one of its parameters (such as JButton b = new JButton("Load", buttonIcon);), and that is all there is to it. We can also add keyboard short-cuts using setAcceleratorKey(char) (or setMnemonic(char) if you are using the Swing release rather than the JDK 1.2 – setMnemonic was omitted from that release by accident!). Finally, we can also add tooltips to buttons using the setToolTip(String) method (for example, b.setToolTipText("Loads a picture");).

For the SwingGallery we have now completed the porting process. However, we can have some fun by adding the option to use different look and feels. This can be done by defining two radio buttons which will select either the basic look and feel or a Motif-style look and feel and adding them to a button group. The associated RadioButtonHandler then loads into

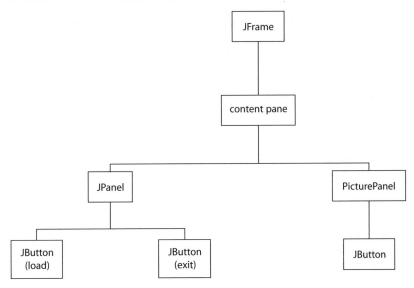

Fig. 22.4 The structure of the SwingGallery GUI.

UIManager whichever look and feel has been selected (for example, UIManager. setLookAndFeel("com.sun.java.swing.plaf.motif.MotifLookAndFeel");). Essentially, this will cause the Swing components to change their UI delegates to ones which draw, in this case, Motif-style components. To ensure that all components update their display, one of the Swing utility facilities is used (for example SwingUtilities.updateComponentTreeUI();). Thus to change the whole display's look and feel we only need to write a few lines of Java. Note that this process may throw an exception if an unavailable look and feel has been specified. The specification of the SwingGallery class is presented in Listing 22.3.

Listing 22.3 The SwingGallery class.

```
package swing.gallery;

import java.awt.Container;
import java.awt.event.*;
import javax.swing.*;
import javax.swing.border.*;

  // Now need to make class a subclass of JFrame
  public class SwingGallery extends JFrame {
    PicturePanel picturePanel;
    public static void main(String args []) {
      new SwingGallery("Swing Gallery");
    }

  public SwingGallery(String label)
    { super(label);

      // Need to get the JFrames content pane
      Container pane = getContentPane();
      addWindowListener(new WindowHandler());
```

```
// Now use a JPanel instead of Panel (can set a border)
JPanel p = new JPanel();
p.setBorder(BorderFactory.createEtchedBorder());

ButtonPanelController bpc = new ButtonPanelController();
// Now use JButtons instead of Button which can take an icon
ImageIcon buttonIcon = new ImageIcon("load.gif");
JButton b = new JButton("Load", buttonIcon);
// Can now set a keyboard short-cut and tooltips
b.setKeyAccelerator('l');
b.setToolTipText("Loads a picture");
b.addActionListener(bpc);
p.add(b);

b = new JButton("Exit");
b.setKeyAccelerator('x');
b.setToolTipText("Exits from application");
b.addActionListener(bpc);
p.add(b);

// VERY IMPORTANT: Now add the panel to the content pane
pane.add("North", p);

picturePanel = new PicturePanel();

// Now use a JScrollPane
JScrollPane scrollPane = new JScrollPane(picturePanel,
    ScrollPaneConstants.VERTICAL_SCROLLBAR_ALWAYS,
    ScrollPaneConstants.HORIZONTAL_SCROLLBAR_ALWAYS
);

pane.add("Center", scrollPane);

// Some extra bits to show some of Swings look and feel
// Illustrate use of different look and feel using radio buttons
JCheckBox motifButton = new JCheckBox("Motif");
motifButton.setActionCommand("motif");
motifButton.setToolTipText("Selects the Motif look and feel");
JCheckBox basicButton = new JCheckBox("Basic", true);
basicButton.setActionCommand("basic");
basicButton.setToolTipText("Selects the Basic look and feel");
RadioButtonHandler rbh = new RadioButtonHandler(this);
motifButton.addItemListener(rbh);
basicButton.addItemListener(rbh);

ButtonGroup buttonGroup = new ButtonGroup();
buttonGroup.add(motifButton);
buttonGroup.add(basicButton);

p = new JPanel();
p.setAlignmentX(LEFT_ALIGNMENT);
```

```
    p.setBorder(new BevelBorder(BevelBorder.RAISED));

    p.add(motifButton);
    p.add(basicButton);
    pane.add("South", p);

    pack();
    setVisible(true);
  }

  // Inner class to handle window events
  class WindowHandler extends WindowAdapter {
    public void windowClosing(WindowEvent event) {
      System.exit(0);
    }
  }

  // Inner class to handle button events
  class ButtonPanelController implements ActionListener {
    public void actionPerformed(ActionEvent event) {
      String cmd = event.getActionCommand();
      if (cmd.equals("Load")) {
        // Now need to use Swing file dialog
        JFileChooser fd = new JFileChooser(".");
        fd.setPrompt("Select Image");
        fd.showDialog(SwingGallery.this);
        String filename = (fd.getSelectedFile()).getName();
        picturePanel.setImageFilename(filename);
      } else {
        System.exit(0);
      }
    }
  }

  // New inner class to handle radio button look and feel options
  class RadioButtonHandler implements ItemListener {
    private JFrame frame;
    public RadioButtonHandler (JFrame frame) {this.frame = frame;}
    public void itemStateChanged(ItemEvent event) {
      String lookAndFeel;
      String option = ((JCheckBox)event.getItem()).getActionCommand();
      if (option.equals("motif")) {lookAndFeel =
          "com.sun.java.swing.plaf.motif.MotifLookAndFeel";
      } else {lookAndFeel =
          "com.sun.java.swing.plaf.basic.BasicLookAndFeel";}
      // This is where the look and feel gets set
      try {
        UIManager.setLookAndFeel(lookAndFeel);
        SwingUtilities.updateComponentTreeUI(frame);
        frame.pack();
      } catch (Exception exc) {
```

```
            System.err.println("could not load LookAndFeel: " +
      lookAndFeel);
            }
          }
        }
      }
```

We now need to look at the `PicturePanel` class. In Swing we can make this class much simpler. Of course we need to change references to `Panel` to `JPanel`; however, we can now use the `JButton` class to display the image and the `ImageIcon` class to load it. Thus our `JPanel` merely creates a `JButton` object using only an `Image` (i.e. no string label) and adds it to itself. When a new image is to be displayed a new `JButton` object is created with the new image. The Swing version of the `PicturePanel` class is presented in Listing 22.4.

Listing 22.4 The Swing version of `PicturePanel`

```
package swing.gallery;

import javax.swing.*;

// Now make this a subclass of JPanel
public class PicturePanel extends JPanel {
  private String imageFilename;
  private JButton image;
  public void setImageFilename(String filename) {
    imageFilename = filename;
    loadImage();
  }

  // Use a button with the image as an icon - a lot easier
  private void loadImage() {
    if (image != null) remove(image);
      ImageIcon picture = new ImageIcon(imageFilename);
      image = new JButton(picture);
      add(image);
    }
  }
```

The result of running our new Swing-based application is presented in Figure 22.5, using both the basic and Motif look and feels.

22.7 Things to Remember

This section briefly summarises some of the things you need to remember when you are porting an AWT interface to Swing (or writing a Swing interface from scratch):

1.   You need to get hold of the top-level component's content pane before you can add anything to it. You can do this using the `getContentPane()` method.

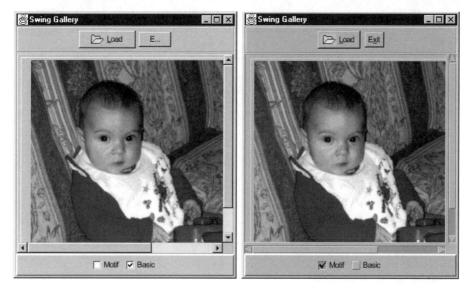

Fig. 22.5 The SwingGallery application (in basic and Motif).

2. All Swing components have an associated model. For buttons and labels etc. this model is created for you; for more complex components you need to create it before creating the GUI component (on it).
3. You need to be careful about mixing lightweight Swing components with heavyweight AWT components. This can cause problems with the use of different look and feels as well as when refreshing displays.
4. We have ignored whole areas of Swing in this chapter. For example, the buttons in the SwingGallery application might well have been better implemented as a dockable menu bar (see javax.swing.JToolBar).
5. You will need to import Swing from different places depending on whether you are using Swing with JDK 1.1 or JDK 1.2.
6. Swing has not been fully released yet and as such is subject to change and possesses a number of undesirable "features".

22.8 Online References

- The JDK 1.2: http://java.sun.com/
- The Swing Connection: http://java.sun.com/products/jfc/swingdoc-current/doc/index.html
- The JFC Home Page: http://java.sun.com/products/jfc/index.html
- The Java Tutorial: Using the JFC "Swing" Release: http://java.sun.com/docs/books/tutorial/index.html

Chapter 23

A GUI Case Study

23.1 Introduction

In this chapter, we consider how to construct an object-oriented graphical application. Many people use languages such as C++ to develop the graphical user interface (GUI) of their system, but then resort to C for the remainder of the system. However, in many cases these people do not construct the GUI in an object-oriented manner. They use the facilities available, but tend to pack everything together. In this chapter, we attempt to consider how a GUI can be constructed using a tried and tested object-oriented approach.

We shall construct the Account application shown in Figure 23.1. This application allows users to keep track of their current account balance using two buttons which indicate whether the amount input should be treated as a deposit or a withdrawal. The amount is entered by the user into the first text field and the current balance is displayed in the second text field. The user can exit from the application in a controlled manner using the Exit button.

Fig. 23.1 The GUI for the Account application.

To construct this application, we use a number of concepts which have been introduced over the last few chapters:

- The Model–View–Handler architecture
- Event listeners (via the Java event delegation model)
- Dependency via observers and observables
- Frames, panels and layout managers

If you have read the last few chapters, none of the above should be a surprise to you. However, you may not be clear on how they may be used within a "real" application.

23.1.1 The Model–View–Handler Architecture

The Model–View–Handler (MVC)[1] architecture separates the interface objects (the views) from the objects which handle user input (the Handlers) from the application (the model). It has already been described in the Swing chapter. However, it is an architecture which you can usefully employ when constructing your own graphical applications.

Figure 23.2 illustrates the overall structure of the Account application. Notice that there are direct links between the interface (or view) object and the Handler objects. However, although the interface and the Handler objects have links to the application (anAccount), the application knows nothing about the interface or the Handlers. This means that it is independent of the interface and its Handlers and can be associated with various different interfaces. Any of the elements can be modified without the need to change the others.

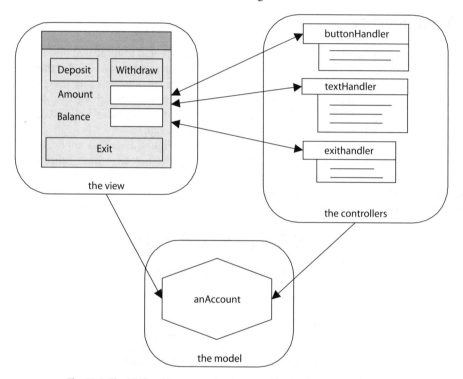

Fig. 23.2 The MVC architecture as implemented by the Account application.

Figure 23.3 illustrates the system interaction. It shows the various messages sent when a user clicks on the deposit button. You should notice the following points:

- Neither the display nor the Handler holds the balance. It is obtained from the account whenever it is needed.
- The Handler relies on the event delegation model to determine that it should do something.
- When the Handler asks the model to change it does not tell the display. The display finds out about the change through the dependency mechanism.

---

1   Note that the abbreviation MVC is used here, but in this case we are calling the controllers Handlers as they handle events – MVC was developed before Java, so some of the terminology differs.

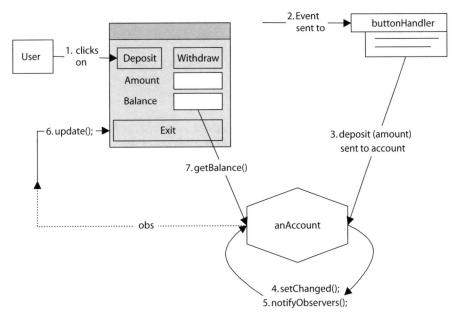

Fig. 23.3 Interaction in the MVC.

- The account is unaware that the message deposit(amount) comes from the Handler. Any object can send a deposit message and the account still informs its dependants about the change.

23.1.2 Event Listeners

In this system, the Handlers are registered as event listeners for the input elements on the interface. The buttonHandler deals with inputs associated with the Deposit and Withdraw buttons. The fieldHandler deals with inputs to the amount field (when the user presses the Return key). Finally, the exitHandler deals with inputs associated with the Exit button.

23.1.3 Observers and Observables

Although Figure 23.2 illustrates that there is no direct link from the account object to the interface, the dependency mechanism can inform any object interested in the state of the account object, that a change has occurred. Thus, the interface object can register itself as an observer of the account object. When a deposit or withdrawal is made, the account object informs its observers (including the interface object) that its balance has changed and they should update themselves. The account object does not have to know about the interface object.

23.1.4 Frames, Panels and Layout Managers

The interface object is made up of a number of objects such as a frame, a number of panels and graphic components (buttons and text fields). Layout managers control the way in which these objects are arranged within the window frame. The exit button Handler can be used without any modification from previous examples. The abstract buttonHandler class is a reusable class for any object acting as a Handler within an MVC architecture; it is the superclass of the buttonPanelHandler class.

23.2 The Class Structure

In this section, we consider each of the classes defined as part of the Account application. The instance structure is considered in the next section. The classes are:

- AccountInterface
- WindowHandler
- ButtonHandler
- TextHandler
- ExitButtonHandler
- ButtonPanelHandler
- ButtonPanel
- TextPanel
- Account

The Account class and the AccountInterface class are the only public classes. All the other GUI classes are defined within the same file as the AccountInterface class.

23.2.1 The AccountInterface Class

This is the root class of the whole application. It is the only class with a main method and thus represents the entry point for the application. The AccountInterface class is a direct subclass of Frame and it implements the WindowListener and Observer interfaces (see Figure 23.4). It defines a constructor which builds up the window to be displayed to the user by instantiating the buttonPanel, the TextPanel and a button component. It also registers as an observer of the account object, sets the size of the window and makes itself visible.

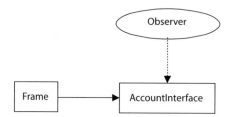

Fig. 23.4 The AccountInterface class.

Instances of this class only hold references to the text fields (which need to be accessed and updated), the exit button and its Handler, and the account object. The other objects are expected to maintain references to the accountInterface object so that they can obtain information from it. You do not need to provide an explicit link from the accountInterface to these objects as they receive information via the event delegation mechanism (i.e. they are event listeners associated with the window). This buffers the accountInterface from changes in the other objects.

The accountInterface class also defines an instance method, update, which defines how instances of this class should respond when the account object reports a change. In this case, the response is that the current balance, held by the account object, is displayed in the second balance text field.

```java
public class AccountInterface extends JFrame implements Observer {
  protected TextPanel textPanel;
  protected Account account = new Account(0.0);

  public static void main (String args []) {
    Frame f = new AccountInterface();
  }

  public AccountInterface () {
    super("Bank Account");

    /* Get the JFrames content pane */
    Container pane = getContentPane();

    /* Add the interface as an observer of the account */
    account.addObserver(this);

    /* Create the Toolbar object and its Handler */
    JToolBar toolbar = new JToolBar();
    toolbar.add(new ButtonPanel(this));
    pane.add("North", toolbar);

    /* Next set up the text panel */
    textPanel = new TextPanel();
    pane.add("Center", textPanel);

    /* Now add the exit button and its handler */
    Button exitButton = new Button(" Exit ");
    exitButton.addActionListener(new ExitButtonHandler(this));
    pane.add("South", exitButton);

    /* Finally add the listener for the whole window */
    addWindowListener(new WindowHandler());

    /* Now set the size of the window and make it visible */
      pack();
      setVisible(true);
  }

    /* The update method is called whenever an observed object (in this
  case the account wishes to notify an observer that a change had occurred
  */
    public void update (Observable o, Object arg) {

      textPanel.balanceField.setText(account.stringBalance());
  }
}
```

23.2.2 The WindowHandler class

This class handles window events. It is a direct subclass of the WindowAdapter, which is a convience class that provides null implementations of all the methods specified in the WindowListener interface. This means that it is only necessary to implement the windowClosing() method, as the remaining methods are provided as a null body implementation in the superclass.

```
class WindowHandler extends WindowAdapter {
  public void windowClosing(WindowEvent event) {
    System.exit(0);
  }
}
```

23.2.3 The JPanel Classes

There are two JPanel classes used in this application (see Figure 23.5). They inherit from the JPanel class and define what should be displayed on an area of the window. The ButtonPanel class defines two button components. The TextPanel class defines two labels and two text fields.

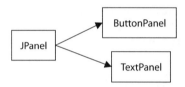

Fig. 23.5 The JPanel classes.

Both classes create instances of Handler classes which define what should happen when a user provides some input (either via the mouse or as text). The Handler classes are described in the next subsection. Note that the ButtonPanel is displayed within a JToolBar which provides a dockable toolbar for the application (Figure 23.6).

 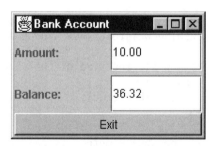

Fig. 23.6 The dockable toolbar used with the application.

The ButtonPanel *Class*

The ButtonPanel class definition uses elements from the Swing package and the java.awt and java.awt.event packages (as do most of the remaining classes):

```
class ButtonPanel extends JPanel {
  public ButtonPanel (AccountInterface win) {
    ButtonPanelHandler panelHandler =
            new ButtonPanelHandler(win);

    JButton button = new JButton("Deposit");
    button.addActionListener(panelHandler);
    add("East", button);
    button = new JButton("Withdraw");
    button.addActionListener(panelHandler);
    add("West", button);
  }
}
```

When this class is instantiated, it first creates a listener for the two buttons, ButtonPanelHandler. It then creates the buttons and places them within the panel (the flow layout manager is the default for panels). This class assumes nothing about the container within which it is used. Thus it can be used in many different situations, with different containers and different applications. This illustrates one of the advantages of making part of the display an object.

The TextPanel *Class*

The TextPanel class provides a similar facility for textual elements of the display. It defines four graphic components which are displayed in a two-by-two grid. The text fields handle the amount (inputField) and the current balance (balanceField). Note that it creates a separate Handler (TextHandler) to handle events and makes this Handler the listener for the inputField:

```
class TextPanel extends JPanel {
  protected JTextField inputField, balanceField;

  public TextPanel () { TextHandler panelHandler = new TextHandler(this);

    setLayout(new GridLayout(2, 2, 5, 5));

    add(new JLabel("Amount: "));
    inputField = new JTextField(8);
    inputField.addActionListener(panelHandler);
    add(inputField);

    add(new JLabel("Balance: "));

    balanceField = new JTextField(8);
    add(balanceField);
  }
}
```

23.2.4 The Handler Classes

The Handler classes provide the actions to be performed when specified events occur. They do this by implementing the ActionListener interface (see Figure 23.7).

There is one abstract superclass, ButtonHandler. The concrete ExitButtonHandler, ButtonPanelHandler and TextHandler classes are used in conjunction with the panel objects (or the exit button component).

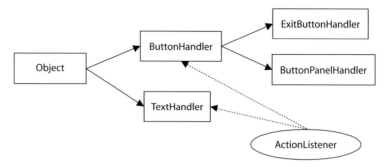

Fig. 23.7 The Handler classes.

The ButtonHandler *Class*

This is an abstract superclass for all classes which handle events generated by buttons (or containers which possess buttons). It is abstract because it does not attempt to define the actionPerformed method specified by the ActionListener interface. It defines one instance variable, view, and one constructor which initializes the instance variable. The instance variable provides a link between a view and the event handler (this is why Swing modifies the MVC so that the view and controller are part of the Swing component).

```
abstract class ButtonHandler implements ActionListener {
  protected AccountInterface view;
  public ButtonHandler (AccountInterface win) {
    view = win;
  }
}
```

The ExitButtonHandler *Class*

This class is a concrete subclass of ButtonHandler. It specifies the action to be performed when the user presses the Exit button. In this case, the message exit is sent to the system object and the application terminates.

```
class ExitButtonHandler extends ButtonHandler {

  public ExitButtonHandler(AccountInterface win) {
    super(win);
  }

  public void actionPerformed(ActionEvent event) {
    System.exit(0);
  }
}
```

Note that the actionPerformed method does not perform any checks on the event or determine the button pressed. This is because it is only ever called when the button pressed event is triggered. This is a very clean and simple way of specifying what should happen when a button is pressed. We can create a unique Handler class for each button. The disadvantage of this approach is the proliferation of classes (and .class) files that it produces. An alternative approach is presented by the ButtonPanelHandler class. The approach that you take depends on personal preference and the nature of the application.

The ButtonPanelHandler *Class*

This class deals with events on both the Deposit and Withdraw buttons. This means that it must determine which button was pressed. It does this by sending the getActionCommand message to the event object. This method returns the action command associated with the button pressed. By default the action command is the label of the button. The method can then compare the action command string with the string "Withdraw" to determine which action to actually perform.

Text fields always return a string. You must convert the string into a numeric form (in this case, a double) to use it with the deposit and withdraw methods. The class method valueOf (defined on class Double) is used to create an instance of Double. The actual value is then obtained by sending this object the doubleValue message.

Once the input amount has been obtained, an if statement sends either the withdraw or the deposit message to the account held by the top-level view (hence the need to provide a link to the AccountInterface object).

```
class ButtonPanelHandler extends ButtonHandler {
  public ButtonPanelHandler(AccountInterface win) {
    super(win);
  }
  public void actionPerformed(ActionEvent event) {
    String cmd = event.getActionCommand();
    double amount;
    // Converts the numerical strings in the text input field to a double
    amount =
      (Double.valueOf(view.textPanel.inputField.getText())).doubleValue();
    // Depending on which button is pressed, the amount is either
    // deposited or withdrawn
    if (cmd.equals("Withdraw"))
      view.account.withdraw(amount);
    else
      view.account.deposit(amount);
  }
}
```

The TextHandler *Class*

This class handles the events generated for the inputField. An event is generated when the user presses Return while the cursor is within the text field. When this happens a message is printed on the console. It is an extremely simple event listener, but it illustrates that event listeners need not be complex.

```java
class TextHandler implements ActionListener {
  protected TextPanel panel;
  public TextHandler (TextPanel aPanel) {
    panel = aPanel;
  }
  public void actionPerformed(ActionEvent event) {
    System.out.println("Input is " +
        (panel.inputField.getText()));
  }
}
```

23.2.5 The Account Class

The Account class defines the application used with the GUI. It is a very simple application which maintains a numeric value of type double (the current account balance). It uses two methods to add or subtract amounts from this balance (deposit and withdraw, respectively). The dependency mechanism is used to inform objects observing account instances that a change has taken place.

```java
import java.util.Observable;

public class Account extends Observable {
  private double balance = 0.0;

  public Account (double initialBalance) {
    setBalance(initialBalance);
  }

  private void setBalance (double anAmount) {
    balance = 0.0;
    deposit(anAmount);
  }

  public void deposit (double anAmount) {
    balance += anAmount;
    setChanged();
    notifyObservers();
  }

  public void withdraw (double anAmount) {
    balance -= anAmount;
    setChanged();
    notifyObservers();
  }

  public String stringBalance () {
    return String.valueOf(balance);
  }
}
```

Note that the setBalance(double) method ensures that, when the balance is set, the same notification takes place as when an amount is deposited. Also note that the current balance is returned as a string. This is a convenience method for objects working with the account object.

23.3 The Instance Structure

Figure 23.8 presents the instance structure of the GUI. As you can see from this diagram, this application's user interface is extremely object-oriented. Not only are the graphical components objects (buttons, labels and text fields), but the elements which handle events on the objects are also objects.

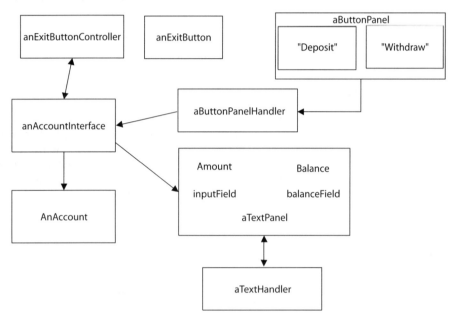

Fig. 23.8 The instance structure of the application.

The Exit button Handler has been reused from the examples presented in the previous two chapters. This illustrates one of the benefits of this approach: the reusability of interface components. In addition, the application code (represented by the account object) is independent of the interface and its event handlers (Handlers). If this was a real application, we might well have very many classes representing the application rather than just the single class presented above.

23.4 Exercise – A GUI for the Financial Manager

As an exercise you should try to construct a GUI for the financial manager application. You can either start from scratch or build on the simple application presented above.

23.5 Summary

You should not have found anything surprising in this chapter, as we have covered all of the aspects before. However, you may not have visualized them working together in the way presented here. Remember that the aim of this chapter has been to apply object-oriented techniques to the construction of the GUI, in the same way that we apply them to the construction of the application.

You can write a Java program which is not object-oriented. The same is true of the user interface aspects of Java. In the case of the example, you could place all of the application within a single Account Interface class, which would hold the application code, the window definition and the event-handling code.

However, the less object-oriented you make the interface part of your application, the less reusable, the less robust to change and the less effective it becomes. You lose the following advantages:

- reusability of parts of the system
- the ability to inherit from different parts of the class hierarchy
- modularity of system code
- resilience to change
- encapsulation of the application

Although these issues might not be a problem for an application as simple as that presented here, for real-world systems they are certainly significant. I hope that you are now aware of the benefits of adopting the MVC architecture and will try to adopt this approach in your own systems. Of course, you may find that the resulting system appears overly complex at first. However, if you persevere with it, the approach will become second nature.

23.6 Further Reading

One place to read about the concepts behind the MVC architecture is within the Smalltalk community. Smalltalk explicitly uses the MVC architecture to promote object-oriented reusable interfaces. A good place to start is with an article in the *Java Report*, Sevareid (1997), which provides an excellent introduction to the event delegation model.

Chapter *24*

The Lowdown on Layouts, Borders and Containers

24.1 Introduction

An important issue in Java for graphical applications is "how best to create the displays I want". An easy option is to ignore concepts such as nesting containers, the use of layout managers and borders and opt for a null layout and explicitly position components yourself (and indeed this is often the default presented to developers by many IDEs). However, for portability reasons, as well as long-term maintenance, developers should exploit the facilities available within Swing. These facilities are based around the use of containers (such as JPanel and Box), layout managers (which actually lay the components out within a container and were discussed in Chapter 21) and Borders (which can provide additional visual control). In the remainder of this chapter these three key concepts are explored.

24.2 Containers in Swing

There are a wide range of containers available within the Swing set, the most common of which are illustrated in Figure 24.1. Some of these have AWT versions that were described earlier in this book. Each type of container can contain one or more components (ideally JComponents

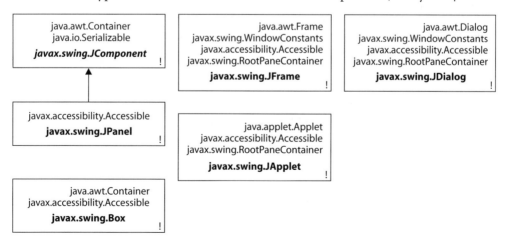

Fig. 24.1 The core container classes in Swing.

257

for Swing). As JPanels and Boxes are types of component this means that a container can also hold one or more JPanels and Boxes. The exact number depends on the layout currently being used within the components. This is because a container does not directly determine where the components within it will be positioned. Nor indeed do the components themselves in Java (note that it is possible to override this behaviour, but it is not advisable). This is because different platforms may use different fonts, different styles (for components such as buttons) and different resolutions. Ideally we want our graphical Java application to look the same on each platform. Thus a separate component, referred to as a layout manager, is responsible for working with containers and the components (or the containers that it holds) to determine how the components should be positioned. Layout managers will be covered in more detail later.

Most graphical Java applications will have GUIs that are comprised of multiple containers with a top-level container. Examples of top-level containers are JFrame, JDialog and JApplet. These top-level containers can act as the root of an application (whereas containers such as JPanel and Box cannot). Note that a JFrame and a JDialog cannot be placed inside any other container.

The containers JPanel and Box are very similar in that they are able to hold one or more components (or containers) and can be placed inside any container. However, a box is limited to using a BoxLayout, whereas a JPanel, although possessing a FlowLayout by default, can use any layout manager.

24.3 Layouts for Containers

Swing uses the layout managers first defined for the AWT with the addition of the BoxLayout and OverlayLayout. The core layouts used in most applications are presented in Figure 24.2. The AWT-based layouts were covered in Chapter 21 and the reader is directed there for details of these layouts; the BoxLayout and OverlayLayout will be covered in a little more detail here.

24.3.1 The FlowLayout Manager

This is the simplest layout manager. It lays the components out in a row across a window. When there is no more space left, it starts on the next row, and so on until no more space is left. The display in Figure 24.3 was generated using a FlowLayout object. The FlowLayout class defines three class variables that indicate the type of alignment required: CENTER, LEFT and RIGHT.

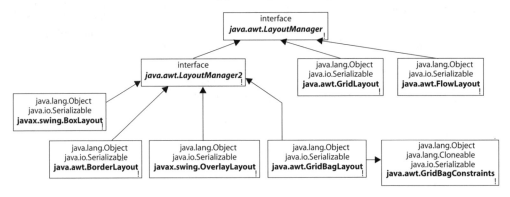

Fig. 24.2 The layout managers used with Swing containers.

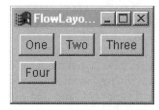

Fig. 24.3 Using a flow layout manager.

FlowLayout is the default layout for JPanels. The FlowLayout honours the height and width of the components it contains.

24.3.2 The BorderLayout Manager

The BorderLayout class defines a layout manager that has a concept of four outer points and a central point (labeled North, East, South, West and Center). This window is divided up as illustrated in Figure 24.4. Of course, you do not have to place components at all available locations. If you omit one (or more) locations, the others stretch to fill up the space (except Center, which depends on the size of the window in which the BorderLayout is being used). The border layout is the default layout for JFrame and JApplet. The border layout honours the height of the components in the North and South regions (but forces them to fill the region horizontally). In turn it honours the width of the components in the East and West regions (but forces them to fill the available vertical space). The Center component is forced to fill the remaining space (thus its preferred width and height are ignored).

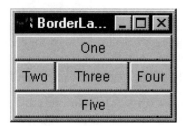

Fig. 24.4 Using a border layout manager.

24.3.3 The GridLayout Manager

The GridLayout manager defines a two-dimensional grid onto which components are added. The default order of addition is from left to right and top to bottom.

The GridLayout class defines the following constructors:

- GridLayout() creates a grid layout with one column per component, in a single row.
- GridLayout(int, int) creates a grid layout with the specified rows and columns.
- GridLayout(int, int, int, int) creates a grid layout with the specified rows, columns, and horizontal and vertical gaps.

The GridLayout forces all the components in the grid to be the same size. This size is determined by the largest component in the grid.

24.3.4 The GridBagLayout Manager

The GridBagLayout manager is a powerful and flexible layout manager that is more complex to use than the other layout managers. This layout manager uses a dynamically created grid to lay components out. However, a component can stretch across more then one column and row, the columns and rows may not be of equal size, and they do not need to be filled in order.

To position a component object, a GridBagLayout object uses a GridBagConstraints object, which specifies constraints on how to position a component (for example, its initial x and y location, width and height), how to distribute the component objects, and how to resize and align them.

24.3.5 BoxLayout

The BoxLayout is similar to a flow layout except that it can lay out components in either the x or the y direction (that is, either the horizontal or vertical). It is therefore more flexible than the FlowLayout (which to some extent it supersedes). In addition, the BoxLayout also honours a component's x and y alignment properties as well as its minimum size. In many cases a box layout negates the need for a GridBagLayout, and as it is much easier to use this is a major benefit. You can either use a BoxLayout with a Box container (where it is the default) or you can use it with a container such as a JPanel. If you do this you will need to override the default layout manager for the container. This can be done using either the constructor or the setLayout(Layout) method. For example:

```
JPanel p = new JPanel();
LayoutManager l = new BoxLayout(p, BoxLayout.Y_AXIS);
p.setLayout(l);
```

Note that the BoxLayout constructor takes the container to be managed as one of the parameters. This is because there is a bidirectional link between the container and the box layout manager (whereas with AWT layout managers the link is only from the container to the manager).

An example of using multiple box layouts with five different panels inside a frame is presented in Figure 24.5.

As was mentioned earlier, the BoxLayout honours the x and y alignment of the component's container within the container. This means that the alignment properties of the components can be used to control their exact positioning within the container. The exact effect of these alignment properties depends on the orientation of the BoxLayout; for example, if the orientation is in the y-axis, then the orientation properties will align the components to the left, centre or right of the available area. The example presented in Figure 24.6 illustrates two box layouts

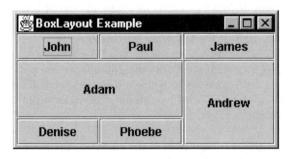

Fig. 24.5 Using multiple panels with multiple BoxLayouts.

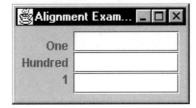

Fig. 24.6 Using two panels with two BoxLayouts, with right- and left-aligned components.

being used: one in which the components are right-aligned and one in which they are left-aligned. The code for this example is presented in Listing 24.1.

Listing 24.1 Aligning components.

```java
import javax.swing.*;
import java.awt.*;
import java.awt.event.*;

public class BoxSample extends JFrame {

  public static void main(String args[]) {
    JFrame frame = new BoxSample2("Alignment Example");
  }

public BoxSample2(String title) {
    super(title);

    JPanel p1 = new JPanel();
    BoxLayout layout1 = new BoxLayout(p1, BoxLayout.Y_AXIS);
    p1.setLayout(layout1);

    String [] labels = {"One", "Hundred", "1"};
    for (int i=0; i<labels.length; i++) {
      JLabel b1 = new JLabel(labels[i]);
      b1.setAlignmentX(Component.RIGHT_ALIGNMENT);
      p1.add(b1);
    }

    JPanel p2 = new JPanel();
    BoxLayout layout2 = new BoxLayout(p2, BoxLayout.Y_AXIS);
    p2.setLayout(layout2);
    for (int i=0; i<3; i++) {
      JTextField tf = new JTextField(10);
      tf.setAlignmentX(Component.LEFT_ALIGNMENT);
      p2.add(tf);
    }

    JPanel p3 = new JPanel();
    p3.add(p1);
```

```
    p3.add(p2);
    Container contentPane = getContentPane();
    contentPane.add(p3);
    pack();
    setVisible(true);
    }
}
```

24.3.6 OverlayLayout

The overlay layout manager handles components that in some way overlap. That is where part of one component lies on top of another component. Like BoxLayout, it is the *x* and *y* alignment properties that determine the exact location of the components in the layout. Their order then defines which components appear in front of which other components.

24.4 Borders in Swing

A border is a JComponent property; that is, all JComponents have a border and support the setBorder and getBorder accessor methods. By default, a component does not have a border (that is, the border property has the value null, i.e. getBorder() == null). Instead, the default border used is appropriate to the current state of the component. For example, a button will have a different border if it is being depressed than if it is out of focus. It is possible to change the border of a component (and thus override this default behaviour) using the setBorder method. It is still possible to reset a components border back to null, but in order to have the system provide the appropriate border automaticaly it is necessary to call updateUI() for the component.

There are eight predefined borders (defined in javax.swing.border). These are listed below:

- EmptyBorder
- EtchedBorder
- LineBorder
- BevelBorder
- SoftBevelBorder
- TitledBorder
- MatteBorder
- CompoundBorder

The eighth, CompoundBorder, can contain any of the other seven or another instance of a CompoundBorder thus allowing any level of nesting (and thus a wide range of presentations). The full class hierarchy for the border classes is presented in Figure 24.7.

All eight borders extend the AbstractBorder class that implements the Border interface. The border interface contains three methods: paintBorder, getBorderInsets and isBorderOpaque.

paintBorder(Component c, Graphics g, int x, int y, int width, int height) is the key method in this interface. This is the method used to actually draw the border. This method often uses the insets to determine the area around the component (that the border is being

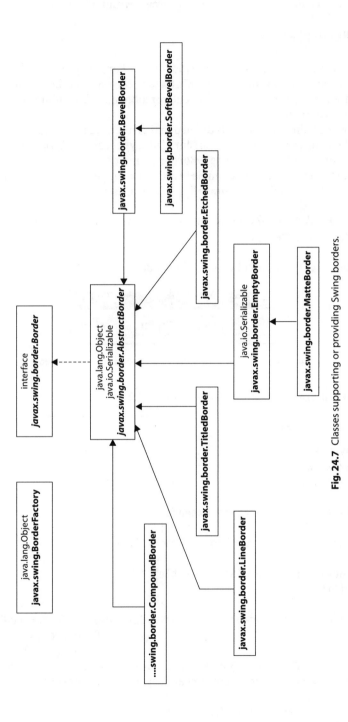

Fig. 24.7 Classes supporting or providing Swing borders.

drawn around). If the border is opaque then the border should fill the whole area left around the component. Note that a border can only be drawn within the inset areas.

24.4.1 The BorderFactory

A convenience factory class (javax.swing.BorderFactory) is provided that allows default borders to be created simply and easily. This factory class also caches borders, as the same border instance can be used around different components (thus minimizing memory and performance overheads).

There are over 20 different methods defined in this interface that are used to create various different borders, such as createBevelBorder(int type), createCompoundBorder(Border outside, Border inside), createEmptyBorder() and createEtchedBorder().
The methods in this factory are quite simple to use. For example, to create a simple beveled border with an outer line in red and an inner line in green, use:

```
Border b = BorderFactory.createBevelBorder(BevelBorder.LOWERED,
Color.red, Color.green);
```

Figure 24.8 illustrates this border being used with both a label and a button:

Fig. 24.8 Using two BevelBorders: one raised and one lowered.

The source for this example is presented in Listing 24.2.

Listing 24.2 Beveled borders.

```
import javax.swing.*;
import javax.swing.border.*;
import java.awt.*;

public class BevelBorderFrame extends JFrame {
  public static void main(String args[]) {
    JFrame frame = new BevelBorderFrame("Bevel Border Frame");
  }
  public BevelBorderFrame(String title) {
    super(title);

    Border b = BorderFactory.createBevelBorder(BevelBorder.LOWERED,
                                               Color.red,
                                               Color.green);
    Border raisedBorder = BorderFactory.createRaisedBevelBorder();
    Border loweredBorder = BorderFactory.createLoweredBevelBorder();

    JLabel l1 = new JLabel("Raised");
    l1.setBorder(raisedBorder);
    JLabel l2 = new JLabel("Custom");
    l2.setBorder(b);
```

```
    JButton button = new JButton("Button");
    button.setBorder(b);
    JLabel l3 = new JLabel("Lowered");
    l3.setBorder(loweredBorder);

    Container contentPane = getContentPane();
    contentPane.setLayout(new FlowLayout());
    contentPane.add(l1);
    contentPane.add(l2);
    contentPane.add(button);
    contentPane.add(l3);
    pack();
    setVisible(true);
  }
}
```

24.4.2 Empty Borders

An EmptyBorder can literally be an empty border, or it can be a border that contains some "padding", although in both cases an empty border has no visual presentation (such as a line or pattern). An empty border can therefore be used to help in laying out components within a panel or frame.

An EmptyBorder has two constructors and two factory methods to go with these constructors – in fact this is a general rule: if there is a constructor for a Border class there will often be a factory method for that constructor. Note, however, that you should try to use the factory methods over the constructors for the benefits noted above.

Listing 24.3 presents two examples of an empty border: one with some padding and one without. To illustrate the effect of these borders, three labels with default borders surround the two empty bordered labels. Figure 24.9 illustrates the use of these borders. Note that label "four" has a large amount of space to the left and right of it. Also note that this window was packed (that is the window determined its minimum size itself) and thus the height is determined by the amount of space around the fourth label.

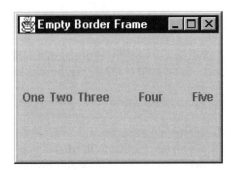

Fig. 24.9 Using EmptyBorders, one with padding.

Listing 24.3 An empty border.

```
import javax.swing.*;
import javax.swing.border.*;
import java.awt.*;
```

```
public class EmptyBorderFrame extends JFrame {
  public static void main(String args[]) {
    JFrame frame = new EmptyBorderFrame("Empty Border Frame");
  }
  public EmptyBorderFrame(String title) {
    super(title);

    Border b1 = BorderFactory.createEmptyBorder();
    int top = 50; int left = 25;
    int bottom = 50; int right = 25;
    Border b2 = BorderFactory.createEmptyBorder(top, left, bottom,
right);

    JLabel l1 = new JLabel("One");
    JLabel l2 = new JLabel("Two");
    l2.setBorder(b1);
    JLabel l3 = new JLabel("Three");
    JLabel l4 = new JLabel("Four");
    l4.setBorder(b2);
    JLabel l5 = new JLabel("Five");

    Container contentPane = getContentPane();
    contentPane.setLayout(new FlowLayout());
    contentPane.add(l1);
    contentPane.add(l2);
    contentPane.add(l3);
    contentPane.add(l4);
    contentPane.add(l5);
    pack();
    setVisible(true);
  }
}
```

24.4.3 LineBorder class

The line border provides a coloured line of a thickness configurable by the client code. Again there are factory methods that can be used to create this border, including:

```
Border b = BorderFactory.createLineBorder(Color.red, 5);
```

This would create a line border in which the line was drawn in red and of 5 pixels thickness. Note that there are two factory methods for black and gray borders. If you wish to create a lined border with round corners you will need to use the LineBorder(Color color, int thickness, boolean roundedCorners) constructor, as there is no factory method for this constructor.

24.4.4 BevelBorder and SoftBevelBorder

The BevelBorder has already been presented in Listing 24.1. It is a border that can be used to present either a raised or lowered effect around a component. A SoftBevelBorder is very similar except that it "softens" the edges of the border.

24.4.5 EtchedBorder

An EtchedBorder is another variation on the Bevel Border. This time, it provides a border that
appears to have a raised or sunken line around the component. This is illustrated in Figure
24.10 and Listing 24.4.

Fig. 24.10 Using two EtchedBorders: one lowered and one raised.

Listing 24.4 An EtchedBorder.

```java
import javax.swing.*;
import javax.swing.border.*;
import java.awt.*;

public class EtchedBorderFrame extends JFrame {
  public static void main(String args[]) {
    JFrame frame = new EtchedBorderFrame("Etched Border Frame");
  }

  public EtchedBorderFrame(String title) {
    super(title);
    Border b1 = BorderFactory.createEtchedBorder();
    Border b2 = BorderFactory.createEtchedBorder(EtchedBorder.RAISED);

    JLabel l1 = new JLabel("One");
    l1.setBorder(b1);
    JLabel l2 = new JLabel("Two");
    JLabel l3 = new JLabel("Two");
    l3.setBorder(b2);

    Container contentPane = getContentPane();
    contentPane.setLayout(new FlowLayout());
    contentPane.add(l1);
    contentPane.add(l2);
    contentPane.add(l3);
    pack();
    setVisible(true);
  }
}
```

24.4.6 The MatteBorder class

A MatteBorder has two different varieties. It can be used to draw a coloured line around a
component with different thicknesses to each side (something not possible in a line border). It
can also be used to create a border based on an icon. In this second example, the icon is repeat-

edly drawn around the component to form the border. The icon could be either an `ImageIcon` or a user-defined object that implements the icon interface.

24.4.7 The `TitledBorder`

This is a very useful border that allows you to place a title on a border. The title can be placed in six different positions (above the bottom, above the top, below the bottom, below the top line, placed on the bottom line, and placed on the top – default). It is also possible to indicate how you wish the title to be justified in its particular position. These justification positions are center, left, right and default (which is the same as left). Figure 24.11 illustrates the use of a title border with a number of different title positions. These can either be specified when the border is created or by using setter methods (such as `setTitleJustification`). Note to avoid unnecessary screen redraws this should have been done before the border is displayed.

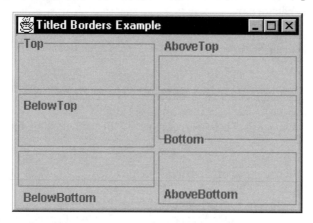

Fig. 24.11 Multiple title borders with different title positions.

However, `TitledBorders` can get a great deal more complex as they can actually contain another border. For example, to create a title border with multiple headings you can create one title border on top of another, as illustrated in Listing 24.5 and Figure 24.12.

Fig. 24.12 Placing two headings on a border.

Listing 24.5 Double title border.

```
import javax.swing.*;
import javax.swing.border.*;
import java.awt.*;

public class DoubleTitleFrame extends JFrame {
    public static void main(String args[]) {
        JFrame frame = new DoubleTitleFrame("Double Title Example");
```

```
    }
    public DoubleTitleFrame(String title) {
        super(title);
        TitledBorder b1 = BorderFactory.createTitledBorder("Top");
        b1.setTitlePosition(TitledBorder.TOP);
        TitledBorder b2 = new TitledBorder (b1, "Bottom", TitledBorder.RIGHT,
            TitledBorder.BOTTOM);

        JLabel l = new JLabel("Label");
        l.setBorder(b2);
        Container contentPane = getContentPane();
        contentPane.add(l, BorderLayout.CENTER);
        pack();
        setVisible(true);
    }
}
```

With a title border it is also possible to use a different type of visual effect for the actual border. For example, a matte border could be used to draw a line of variable with or a border based on an icon. Other aspects that can be changed for a titled border are the font used, the colour used for the title text and the actual border line colour.

24.4.8 CompoundBorder class

A compound border is a border made up of two existing borders (either of which could also be a compound border) and combines them to create a single border object. As a Swing component is only allowed to have a single border object associated with it, this is a very god way to create effects based on multiple borders that can then be added to any Swing component.

An example of using two borders might be when an empty border (containing some padding) is used with a line border to ensure that additional spacing is placed around the component and the line border etc. This is illustrated in Figure 24.13, where the first label has a simple line border and the second label has a compound border with an empty border (with padding) inside a line border. Listing 24.6 presents the code for this example.

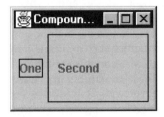

Fig. 24.13 Using a compound border to place space around a label inside its border.

Listing 24.6 Compound borders.

```
import javax.swing.*;
import javax.swing.border.*;
import java.awt.*;

public class CompoundBorderFrame extends JFrame {
```

```java
  public static void main(String args[]) {
    JFrame frame = new CompoundBorderFrame("Compound Border Example");
  }
  public CompoundBorderFrame(String title) {
    super(title);

    Border b1 = LineBorder.createBlackLineBorder();

    JLabel l1 = new JLabel("One");
    l1.setBorder(b1);

    Border b2 = BorderFactory.createEmptyBorder(25, 10, 25, 50);
    Border b3 = new CompoundBorder(b1, b2);
    JLabel l2 = new JLabel("Second");
    l2.setBorder(b3);

    Container contentPane = getContentPane();
    contentPane.setLayout(new FlowLayout());
    contentPane.add(l1);
    contentPane.add(l2);
    pack();
    setVisible(true);
  }
}
```

24.5 Using Panels, Layouts and Borders

The first thing to remember here is that a panel is a type of component. Thus it is possible to place a border around a panel that contains a number of components. For example, it might be necessary to place a titled border around a panel containing a set of radio buttons.

The next thing to notice is that the panels themselves can possess a range of different layouts, including FlowLayout (the default), BoxLayout and GridLayout. Of course, a Box component (which is very similar to a JPanel but can only use a BoxLayout) can also be used. Thus, depending on the type of layout used with a panel or box, we can obtain different results.

This can be taken further, as containers such as panels can contain not only components but other containers as well. Thus a box may contain a number of panels that contain components (or further containers). Each of these containers may have their own layout and their own border.

Finally, the components contained in the containers can also have their own borders. Thus by combining different containers with different components and different layouts, sophisticated displays can be generated. An example is presented in Figure 24.14.

24.6 Planning a Display

The above discussion means that it is extremely important in Java to plan out how you are going to generate your display. This usually means designing the display first – something which

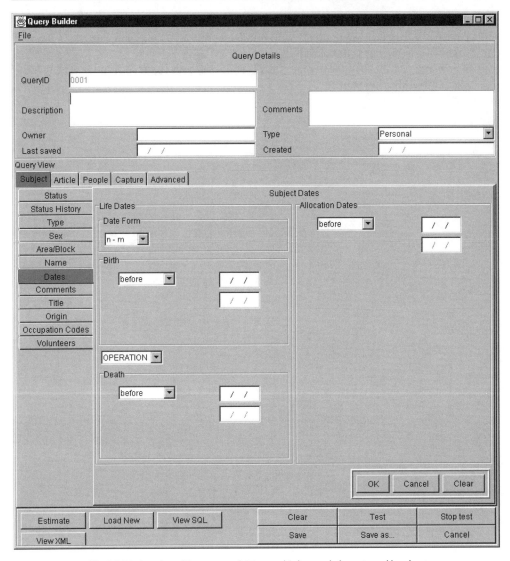

Fig. 24.14 A real-world screen exploiting multiple panels, layouts and borders.

sadly is often neglected. This display should then be analyzed to determine the combination of containers, layouts, borders and components required to create the desired effect. Some prototyping and experimentation may be required during this stage, as actions such as resizing displays may cause a beautiful display to become a sow's ear!

Of course a GridBagLayout could always be used, but such an approach requires just as much analysis and design and may result in a display which is less resilient to change and future enhancement!

24.7 Online References

- The Swing Connection: http://java.sun.com/products/jfc/tsc/index.html

- The JFC Home Page: `http://java.sun.com/products/jfc/index.html`
- The Java Tutorial: Using the JFC "Swing" Release: `http://java.sun.com/docs/books/tutorial/uiswing/index.html`
- Swing Tutorial: `http://developer.java.sun.com/developer/onlineTraining/GUI/AWTLayoutMgr/index.html`

Chapter 25

Combining Graphics and GUI Components

25.1 Introduction

This chapter aims to bring together the graphic elements described earlier in the book with the user interface components (such as buttons and layout managers) from the last few chapters. It presents a case study of a drawing tool akin to tools such as Visio, xfig and MacDraw.

25.2 The SwingDraw Application

The SwingDraw application allows a user to draw diagrams using squares, circles, lines and text. The user can also select, resize and reposition any of these graphic objects. At present, no delete option is provided (although this would be a simple addition). SwingDraw is implemented using the Swing set of components as defined in the 1.0.2 release of Swing. This means that buttons with icons, menus with icons, dockable menu bars and different look and feels can be used. This application was implemented using this release of Swing and release 1.1.6 of the JDK.

When users start the SwingDraw application, they see the interface shown in Figure 25.1. It has a menu bar across the top, a dockable toolbar below the menu bar and a scrollable drawing area below. The first button clears the drawing area. The second and third buttons are not implemented but are intended to allow a user to load and save drawings. The next four buttons set the drawing mode, which determines whether a line, a square, a circle or text is added when the mouse is clicked in the drawing area. The final button allows the user to exit the application. These buttons are duplicated on the applications menus (as illustrated in Fig. 25.2).

Once a graphic component has been added to the drawing, the user can select it by clicking on the component with the mouse. The selected component is redrawn in red and is surrounded by four small boxes. The user can then move it around (no resize function is provided).

25.3 The Structure of the Application

The interface is made up of a number of elements (see Figure 25.3): the menu bar, the panel of buttons across the top of the window, a scroll pane containing the drawing panel, and the window frame (implemented by the SwingDraw class).

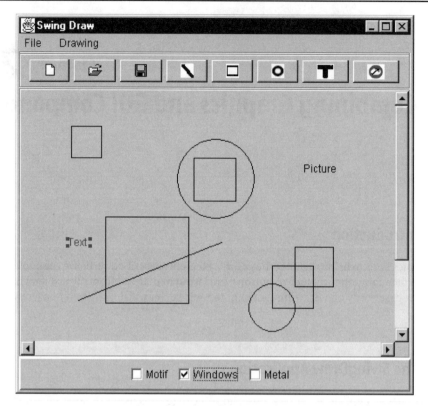

Fig. 25.1 The SwingDraw application.

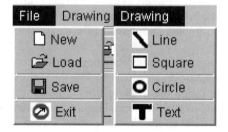

Fig. 25.2 The File and Drawing menus.

Figure 25.4 shows the same information as Figure 25.3, but as a containment hierarchy, which means that one object is contained within another. In Figure 25.4, the lower level objects are contained in the higher level objects. It is important to visualize this, as the majority of Java interfaces are built up in this way, using layout managers. Note that the DrawToolBar object actually contains another object called ButtonPanel. It is the ButtonPanel that holds the various buttons.

Figure 25.5 illustrates the inheritance structure between the classes used in the SwingDraw application. This class hierarchy is typical of an application which incorporates user interface features with graphical elements. For example, there is a subclass of Frame within the main Draw application class. The Model–View–Controller structure has a controller class (DrawingController), a model subclass (Drawing) and a view class (DrawingPanel).

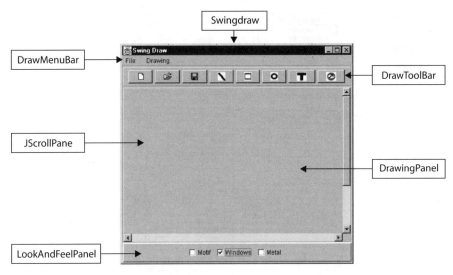

Fig. 25.3 The objects in the SwingDraw interface.

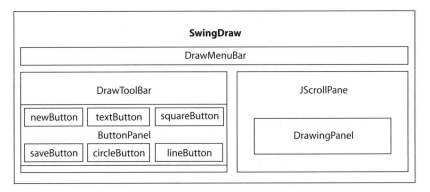

Fig. 25.4 The containment hierarchy of the SwingDraw interface.

There are four types of drawing object: `Circle`, `Line`, `Square` and `TextFigure`. The only difference between these classes is what is drawn on the graphics context representing the view. The `Figure` class, from which they all inherit, defines the common attributes used by all objects within a `Drawing` (e.g. x and y location and size).

The `ButtonPanel` and `ButtonPanelController` classes display the buttons and deal with user interactions.

Although exceptions are not introduced until Chapter 25, the `Drawing` class uses an exception whenever the user adds a component which it does not know about. Exceptions are well suited for such a scenario and it is a good example of how they should be used.

The final class in the SwingDraw application is the `TextDialog` class. Dialogs are modal windows which the user must handle before continuing. This is, therefore, a good way of obtaining the text to be displayed.

In Figure 25.5, the classes in bold are part of the draw package which defines the SwingDraw application. The other classes are extended by the SwingDraw classes. Solid lines indicate the extension of a parent class (shown to the left of the subclass). Additional classes are used with

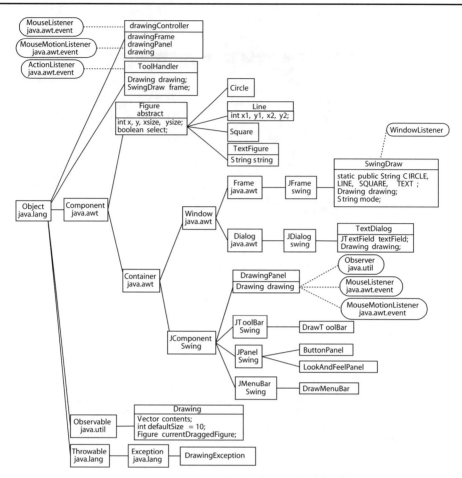

Fig. 25.5 Inheritance in SwingDraw.

the application but are not presented in this figure (for example, Vector and Button). Also note that interfaces are presented in oval boxes and dashed lines indicate the implementation of an interface.

However, the inheritance hierarchy is only part of the story for any object-oriented application. Figure 25.6 shows how the objects relate to one another within a working application. The SwingDraw application object does not possess any links to the objects displayed within it. This is because the user interacts with the application via the event delegation model; individual controllers handle user interaction and the observer–observable mechanism refreshes the drawing display. This separates the interface from the drawing elements and the button action elements of the application.

JScrollPane is an AWT class which handles scrolling panels. As SwingDraw does not manipulate the scrolling panel from within the application, it does not need to maintain a reference to this object.

The Drawing, DrawingPanel and DrawingController classes exhibit the classic MVC structure. The view and the controller classes (DrawingPanel and DrawingController) know about each other and the drawing, whereas the drawing knows nothing about the view or the controller. The view is notified of changes in the drawing through the dependency mechanism implemented through the observer–observable class and interface.

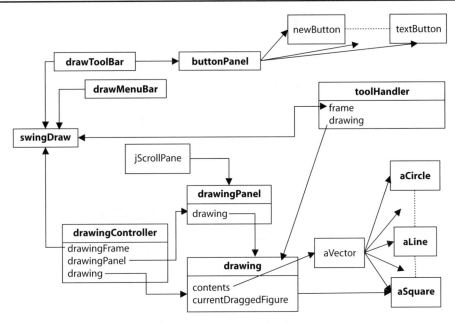

Fig. 25.6 The object relationships.

Drawing is a relatively simple model which merely records a set of graphical objects in a Vector. These can be any type of object and can be displayed in any way. It is the objects themselves which determine what they look like when drawn.

25.4 The Interactions Between Objects

We have now examined the physical structure of the application, but not how the objects within that application interact. In many situations this can be extracted from the source code of the application (with varying degrees of difficulty). However, in the case of an application such as SwingDraw, which is made up of a number of different interacting components, it is useful to describe the system interactions explicitly.

The diagrams illustrating the interactions between the objects use the following conventions:

- a solid arrow indicates a message send
- a dashed arrow indicates an instance creation
- a square box indicates a class
- a round box indicates an instance
- a name in brackets indicates the type of instance
- numbers indicate the sequence of message sends

These diagrams are based on the mechanism diagrams described by Rumbaugh *et al.* (1991) and discussed in more detail in Part 7.

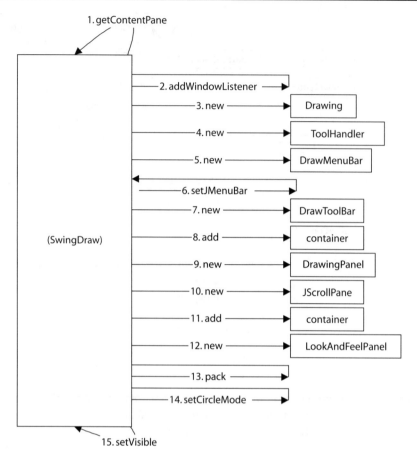

1. getContentPane

2. addWindowListener

3. new → Drawing

4. new → ToolHandler

5. new → DrawMenuBar

6. setJMenuBar

7. new → DrawToolBar

8. add → container

9. new → DrawingPanel

10. new → JScrollPane

11. add → container

12. new → LookAndFeelPanel

13. pack

14. setCircleMode

(SwingDraw)

15. setVisible

Fig. 25.7 The actions performed by the SwingDraw constructor.

25.4.1 The Draw Constructor

When the SwingDraw application is initiated, the main method in the SwingDraw class is executed. This method creates an instance of the class SwingDraw, executing the SwingDraw constructor. The operations performed by the constructor are summarized in Figure 25.7.

The constructor sets up the environment for the application. It creates the drawing object, its panel (and as part of this operation its controller), and the toolbar and its menu bar, as well as the drawing itself. It also makes itself the listener for window events and sets the default drawing mode to "circle". It also sets its size (using pack()) and then makes itself visible.

25.4.2 Changing the Type of Graphic Object

One interesting thing to look at is what happens when the user selects one of the buttons in the button panel held in the toolbar panel.

The button panel is an object into which each of the buttons has been placed (user interfaces in Java tend to be built up from components and types of container in a hierarchical manner; see Figure 25.3). The toolController handles the events generated (as part of the event delegation model which we saw earlier in the book). When an event is generated the

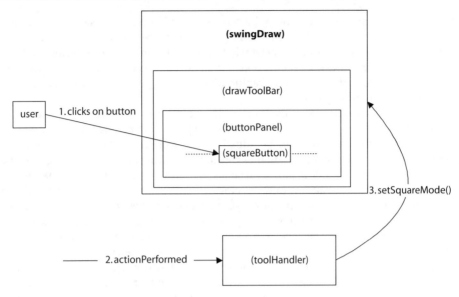

Fig. 25.8 Changing the graphic object.

actionPerformed method of the toolController sends the drawing object the appropriate set*Mode method.

Figure 25.8 shows what happens when the user clicks on the Square button. The setSquareMode method sets the mode variable of the drawing object to the string "Square". The mode values are defined as class variables: "Line", "Circle", "Square" and "Text". The same effect would result if the user selected on the of the Drawing menu options (i.e. the actionPerformed(ActionEvent) method of the toolHandler would be executed).

25.4.3 Adding a Graphic Object

A user adds a graphic object to the drawing displayed by the drawingPanel by pressing the mouse button. We do not distinguish between the mouse buttons , although it can be done quite simply by using the getModifiers method and comparing the result with the class variables button1_Mask, button2_Mask and button3_Mask.

Figure 25.9 illustrates what happens when the user presses and releases a mouse button over a blank part of the drawing area to create a new component.

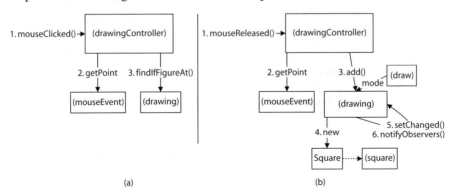

Fig. 25.9 Adding a graphic component.

When the user presses the mouse button, a mouseClicked message is sent to the drawingController, which decides what action to perform in response (see Figure 25.9(a)). In SwingDraw, it obtains the cursor point at which the event was generated by sending a getPoint message to the mouseEvent. If a graphic object is already at this location, it is highlighted. In this case, we assume that there is no graphic object at the current cursor location and it becomes the start point of a new object.

When the user releases the mouse button, the mouseReleased message is sent to the drawingController (see Figure 25.9(b)). The drawing controller finds the new cursor location (the end point of the object to be added) by sending the getPoint message to the mouseEvent object. It then sends an add message to the drawing object, specifying the type of object (determined by the mode instance variables). The drawing object creates a new instance of the appropriate class and adds it to the vector held in its contents field. Then the drawing object sends itself the setChanged and notifyObservers messages so that its dependants can be informed of the change. The dependency mechanism sends the update message to the drawingPanel, which sends itself a repaint message. The paint method then asks each of the graphic objects to draw itself on the graphics context (i.e. the screen).

This section has outlined the most difficult part of constructing a graphical view – working out what is sent where, by what and when. The thing to remember is that you are slotting your application-specific code into a number of generic frameworks, in particular, the observer–observable dependency mechanism, the event delegation model and the hierarchical construction of interfaces. At this stage it is often much easier to look at what someone else has done and use it as the basis of what you require, although it is still important to become familiar with these frameworks and their use.

25.4.4 Moving a Graphic Object

A user moves a graphic object by clicking the mouse button, dragging the mouse and releasing the button (see Figure 25.10). This application must handle the button pressed, mouse dragged and button released events.

Figure 25.10(a) illustrates the interactions which occur when the mouse is clicked over a graphic object. Essentially, it is the same as in Figure 25.9, except that the object is sent the message select. This changes the state of the graphic object, which alters its display. By default, an object displays with a solid black line. When it is selected, it displays with a red line and a small red box at each corner.

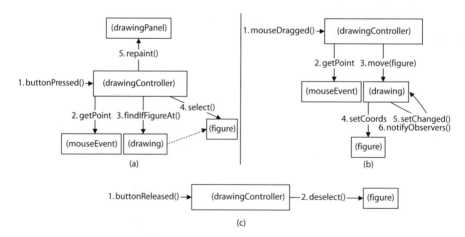

Fig. 25.10 Moving a graphic component.

Figure 25.10(b) illustrates what happens as the mouse is dragged. A move message (with the figure as parameter) is sent to the drawing object, which uses the setCoords method to change the figure's position. The setChanged and notifyObservers messages are then used to inform observers of the drawing that something has changed. The update method of the drawingPanel executes and the window is repainted.

When the mouse button is released (Figure 25.10(c)), the currently selected figure is deselected.

25.5 The Classes

This section presents the classes in the SwingDraw application. As these classes build on concepts already presented in the last few chapters, they will be presented in their entirety with annotations highlighting specific points of their implementations. If you find any aspect of a class confusing, refer to the chapter discussing the related issue.

25.5.1 The SwingDraw Class

The SwingDraw class provides the main window for the application.

```java
package swingdrawing;

import java.awt.*;
import java.awt.event.*;
import javax.swing.*;

public class SwingDraw extends JFrame {

  protected static String CIRCLE = "Circle", SQUARE = "Square",
      LINE = "Line", TEXT = "Text";

  private Drawing drawing;
  protected String mode;

  public static void main(String args []) {
    new SwingDraw("Swing Draw");
  }

  public SwingDraw(String label) {
    super(label);

    // Need to get the JFrames content pane
    Container pane = getContentPane();

    // Set the window handler so that the window can be closed
    addWindowListener(new WindowHandler());

    // Create the drawing data model
    drawing = new Drawing();
```

```
    // Create the handler to be used by the toolbar and the menubar
    ToolHandler toolHandler = new ToolHandler(this, drawing);

    // Build up the menu structure. Note the method used to
    // set the menu for the frame is setJMenuBar and not setMenuBar
    // (which is inherited from Frame).
    setJMenuBar(new DrawMenuBar(toolHandler));

    // Now build the toolbar across the top of the window
    pane.add("North", new DrawToolBar(toolHandler));

    // Now build the drawing area which forms the majority of the
    // interface. Note that the view (the drawingPanel) is itself
    // displayed within a JScrollPane so that a scrollable drawing area
    // is provided.
    JScrollPane scrollPane = new JScrollPane(new DrawingPanel(this,
      drawing), ScrollPaneConstants.VERTICAL_SCROLLBAR_ALWAYS,
      ScrollPaneConstants.HORIZONTAL_SCROLLBAR_ALWAYS
    );

    pane.add("Center", scrollPane);

    // Illustrate use of different look and feel using radio buttons
    pane.add("South", new LookAndFeelPanel(this));

    // Initialize the size of the window, set the current mode
    // and make the window visible.
    pack();
    setCircleMode();
    setVisible(true);
  }

  public void setSquareMode () {
    mode = SwingDraw.SQUARE;
  }

  public void setCircleMode () {
    mode = SwingDraw.CIRCLE;
  }

  public void setLineMode () {
    mode = SwingDraw.LINE;
  }

  public void setTextMode() {
    mode = SwingDraw.TEXT;
  }

  // Inner class to handle window events
  class WindowHandler extends WindowAdapter {
    public void windowClosing(WindowEvent event) {
```

```
      System.exit(0);
    }
  }
}
```

25.5.2 The DrawMenuBar class

The DrawMenuBar class is a subclass of the JmenuBar class which defines the contents of the menu bar for the SwingDraw application. It does this by creating two JMenu objects and adding them to the menu bar. Each JMenu implements a drop-down menu from the menu bar. The createMenuItem() method is used to create the individual menu items to be displayed on each menu. This method takes a string and an ActionListener and creates a menu item with an icon based on the string (which is also used as the menu label).

```java
package swingdrawing;

import java.awt.event.*;
import javax.swing.*;

public class DrawMenuBar extends JMenuBar {

  public DrawMenuBar (ActionListener handler) {

    // Now create the File menu
    JMenu menu = new JMenu("File");
    menu.add(createMenuItem("New", handler));
    menu.add(createMenuItem("Load", handler));
    menu.addSeparator();
    menu.add(createMenuItem("Save", handler));
    menu.addSeparator();
    menu.add(createMenuItem("Exit", handler));
    // Add this menu to the menu bar itself
    add(menu);

    // Now create the drawing style menu
    menu = new JMenu("Drawing");
    menu.add(createMenuItem("Line", handler));
    menu.add(createMenuItem("Square", handler));
    menu.addSeparator();
    menu.add(createMenuItem("Circle", handler));
    menu.addSeparator();
    menu.add(createMenuItem("Text", handler));
    // Add menu to menu bar itself
    add(menu);
  }

  private JMenuItem createMenuItem(String label, ActionListener
      handler) {
    JMenuItem mi = new JMenuItem(label);
    mi.setHorizontalTextPosition(JButton.RIGHT);
    mi.setIcon(new ImageIcon(label + ".gif"));
```

```
        mi.addActionListener(handler);
        return mi;
    }
}
```

25.5.3 The DrawToolBar and ButtonPanel Classes

The DrawToolBar class is a subclass of JtoolBar. This allows the DrawToolBar to act like a dockable toolbar. It contains a single object, which is the ButtonPanel. The ButtonPanel class, a subclass of JPanel, handles the display of the buttons. It simplifies the construction of the user interface. A simple flow manager places the buttons on the panel and the whole panel is added to the SwingDraw application window using a border manager. Note that the method createButton takes an ActionListener and two strings. It then creates a JButton which displays an icon whose file is based on the label passed to it and which includes tooltips. Note that this means that it would be relatively straightforward to internationalize the creation of the buttons.

```
package swingdrawing;

import javax.swing.*;
import java.awt.event.ActionListener;

/**
 * Provides a tool bar using a ButtonPanel class
 */
public class DrawToolBar extends JToolBar {
  public DrawToolBar(ActionListener handler) {
    add(new ButtonPanel(handler));
  }
}

/**
 * Defines a set of buttons with icons in a panel.
 * At present the buttons are hard coded, but could be
 * loaded from a preferences file.
 */
class ButtonPanel extends JPanel {
  ButtonPanel (ActionListener handler) {
    add(createButton(handler, "New", "Creates new drawing"));
    add(createButton(handler, "Load", "Loads a drawing"));
    add(createButton(handler, "Save", "Saves a drawing"));
    add(createButton(handler, "Line", "Sets line mode"));
    add(createButton(handler, "Square", "Sets square mode"));
    add(createButton(handler, "Circle", "Sets circle mode"));
    add(createButton(handler, "Text", "Sets text mode"));
    add(createButton(handler, "Exit", "Exits from application"));
  }

  private JButton createButton(ActionListener handler,
      String cmd,
      String tips) {
```

```
      ImageIcon icon = new ImageIcon(cmd + ".gif");
      JButton button = new JButton(icon);
      // Need to set the action command for this button as
      // no text label has been provided.
      button.setActionCommand(cmd);
      button.setToolTipText(tips);
      button.addActionListener(handler);
      return button;
   }
}
```

25.5.4 The ToolHandler Class

The ToolHandler class defines, in the actionPerformed method, what happens when each of the buttons in the ButtonPanel is pressed or the menu options in the DrawMenuBar selected. The response of most buttons is to call a method on another object (primarily to set the drawing object mode).

```
   package swingdrawing;

   import java.awt.event.ActionListener;
   import java.awt.event.ActionEvent;

   class ToolHandler implements ActionListener {
      SwingDraw drawFrame;
      Drawing drawing;
      ToolHandler (SwingDraw draw, Drawing d) {
         drawFrame = draw;
         drawing = d;
      }
      public void actionPerformed(ActionEvent event) {
         String cmd = event.getActionCommand();
         if (cmd.equals("New")) {
            drawing.newDrawing();
         } else if (cmd.equals("Save")) {
            System.out.println("Save: Not implemented");
         } else if (cmd.equals("Load")) {
            System.out.println("Load: Not implemented");
         } else if (cmd.equals("Line"))
            drawFrame.setLineMode();
         else if (cmd.equals("Square"))
            drawFrame.setSquareMode();
         else if (cmd.equals("Circle"))
            drawFrame.setCircleMode();
         else if (cmd.equals("Text"))
            drawFrame.setTextMode();
         else {
            System.exit(0);
         }
      }
   }
}
```

25.5.5 The Drawing Class

The Drawing class is a subclass of Observable (so that it can act as the source of a dependency relationship). The instance variable, currentDraggedFigure, indicates a figure whose size is determined by the user dragging the cursor. It is not a particularly good way to implement this function, but it does keep things simple.

```java
package swingdraw;

import java.util.*;
import java.awt.*;

public class Drawing extends Observable {
  private Vector contents = new Vector();
  private int defaultSize = 10;
  private Figure currentDraggedFigure = null;

  public void add (String comp, Point point1,
         Point point2, int size, String string) {
    Figure fig;
    if (currentDraggedFigure != null){
      contents.removeElement(currentDraggedFigure);
      currentDraggedFigure = null;
    }
    try {
      if (comp == Draw.SQUARE)
        fig = new Square(point2, size);
      else if (comp == Draw.CIRCLE)
        fig = new Circle(point2, size);
      else if (comp == Draw.LINE)
        fig = new Line(point1, point2);
      else if (comp == Draw.TEXT)
        fig = new TextFigure(point2, string);
      else
        throw new DrawingException("Unknown figure: "
          + comp);
      contents.addElement(fig);
      setChanged();
      notifyObservers();
    }
    catch (DrawingException e) {
      System.out.println("Unknown figure");
    }
  }

  public void move(Figure fig, Point point) {
    fig.setCoords(point.x, point.y);
    setChanged();
    notifyObservers();
  }
```

```
  public void addDraggedFigure (String comp,
          Point point, Point endPoint, int  size) {
    if (currentDraggedFigure != null)
      contents.removeElement(currentDraggedFigure);
      currentDraggedFigure = null;
      add(comp, point, endPoint, size, null);
      currentDraggedFigure =
          (Figure) contents.lastElement();
  }

  public void remove (Object object) {
    contents.removeElement(object);
    setChanged();
    notifyObservers();
  }

  public Enumeration elements () {
    return contents.elements();
  }

  public Figure findIfFigureAt(Point point) {
    Enumeration e = contents.elements();
    Figure fig;
    while (e.hasMoreElements()) {
      fig = (Figure)e.nextElement();
      if (fig.contains(point))
        return fig;
    }
    return null;
  }

  public void newDrawing () {
    contents = new Vector();
    setChanged();
    notifyObservers();
  }
}
```

25.5.6 The DrawingPanel Class

The DrawingPanel class is a subclass of the Panel class. It provides the view for the drawing data model. This uses the classical MVC architecture and has a drawing (data model), a drawingPanel (the view) and a drawingController (the controller).

Note that it is a subclass of JComponent. This is because JPanel produced undesired bevhiour in the 1.0.2 release of Swing in this application.

The DrawingPanel instantiates its own DrawingController to handle mouse events. This class could really be an inner class of the DrawingPanel; however, for clarity in this example it is left as a top-level class.

```java
package swingdraw;

import java.awt.*;
import java.util.*;
import javax.swing.*;

public class DrawingPanel extends JComponent implements Observer {

   private Drawing drawing;

   DrawingPanel (JFrame frame, Drawing d) {
      drawing = d;
      drawing.addObserver(this);

      // Create the controller associated with this DrawingPanel
      DrawingController controller = new DrawingController(frame, this,
drawing);
      addMouseListener(controller);
      addMouseMotionListener(controller);
   }

   // Changes name from paint to paintComponent
   public void paintComponent(Graphics g) {
      Figure afig;
      Enumeration e = drawing.elements();
      while (e.hasMoreElements()) {
         afig = (Figure)e.nextElement();
         afig.paint(g);
      }
   }

   /**
    * Defines the dimensions of the drawing panel
    */
   public Dimension getPreferredSize() {
      return new Dimension(400, 400);
   }

   /* Observer methods */

   public void update(Observable object, Object arg) {
      repaint();
   }
}
```

The getPreferredSize method returns a dimension which indicates the size that we would like the panel to be. This method is required so that the layout managers can determine the optimum layout for the interface.

25.5.7 The DrawingController Class

The DrawingController class provides the control class for the MVC architecture used with the drawing (model) and DrawingPanel (view) classes. In particular, it handles the mouse events in the DrawingPanel.

It implements the MouseListener and MouseMotion-Listener interfaces which catch the mouse events. We also define a number of other mouse event methods (such as mouseEntered and mouseExited).

```java
package swingdrawing;

import java.awt.*;
import java.awt.event.*;
import javax.swing.JFrame;

public class DrawingController
    implements MouseListener, MouseMotionListener {
  Figure fig;
  Draw drawingFrame;
  DrawingPanel drawingPanel;
  Drawing drawing;
  Point startPoint;
  int xDiff = 0, yDiff = 0;
  Cursor oldCursor;
  DrawingController (Draw draw, DrawingPanel drawPanel,
          Drawing drawModel) {
    drawingFrame = draw;
    drawingPanel = drawPanel;
    drawing = drawModel;
  }

  /* Mouse listener methods */
  public void mouseClicked(MouseEvent e) {}
  public void mousePressed(MouseEvent e) {
  Figure figUnderCursor = drawing.findIfFigureAt(e.getPoint());
  if (figUnderCursor != null){
    fig = figUnderCursor;
    fig.select();
    startPoint = null;
    drawingPanel.repaint();
  }
  else
    startPoint = e.getPoint();
  }

  public void mouseReleased(MouseEvent e) {
    String s = "";
    if (startPoint != null) {
      if (drawingFrame.mode == Draw.TEXT) {
        TextDialog d =
          new TextDialog(drawingFrame, drawing);
```

```
              d.setVisible(true);
              s = d.getString();
            }
          Point currentPoint = e.getPoint();
          Point endPoint = getPoint(currentPoint);
          drawing.add(drawingFrame.mode,
              startPoint,
              endPoint,
              Math.max(xDiff, yDiff),
              s);
        }
        else {
          fig.deselect();
          fig = null;
          drawingPanel.repaint();
        }
    }

    public void mouseEntered(MouseEvent e) {
      oldCursor = drawingPanel.getCursor();
      drawingPanel.setCursor(new
            Cursor(Cursor.CROSSHAIR_CURSOR));
    }

    public void mouseExited (MouseEvent e) {
      drawingPanel.setCursor(oldCursor);
    }
    /* Mouse Motion Listener methods */

    public void mouseDragged(MouseEvent e) {
      if ((startPoint != null) &&
            (drawingFrame.mode != Draw.TEXT))
        drawing.addDraggedFigure(drawingFrame.mode,
              startPoint,
              getPoint(e.getPoint()),
              Math.max(xDiff, yDiff));
      else if (fig != null)
        drawing.move(fig, e.getPoint());
      }

    public void mouseMoved(MouseEvent e) {}
      private Point getPoint (Point currentPoint) {
      if (drawingFrame.mode == Draw.LINE)
        return currentPoint;
      else if (startPoint.equals(currentPoint))
        return currentPoint;
      else {
        xDiff = Math.abs(startPoint.x - currentPoint.x);
        yDiff = Math.abs(startPoint.y - currentPoint.y);
        if ((xDiff < 10) && (yDiff < 10))
          return currentPoint;
```

```
      else {
        Point newPoint =
        new Point(Math.min(startPoint.x,
          currentPoint.x),
          Math.min(startPoint.y,
              currentPoint.y));
        return newPoint;
      }
    }
  }
}
```

25.5.8 The LookAndFeelPanel Class

The LookAndFeelPanel class creates a panel which contains check boxes to indicate the type of look and feel to be used by the SwingDraw application. At present three look and feels are supported, "motif", "windows" and "metal". The class creates the appropriate JCheckBox to be used to select different look and feels and places within ButtonGroup. It then adds them to itself so that when it is displayed the buttons will appear. The createJCheckBox method is used to create each check box object. Note the metal look is the default selection. The RadioButtonHandler class is used to respond to the itemStateChanged method which is called when a different check box is selected.

```
package swingdrawing;

import java.awt.*;
import java.awt.event.*;
import javax.swing.*;
import javax.swing.border.*;

public class LookAndFeelPanel extends JPanel {
  private static String Motif = "Motif";
  private static String Windows = "Windows";
  private static String Metal = "Metal";

  public LookAndFeelPanel(JFrame frame) {
    RadioButtonHandler rbh = new RadioButtonHandler(frame);
    ButtonGroup buttonGroup = new ButtonGroup();
    JCheckBox motifButton = createRadioButton(rbh, Motif,
      "Selects the Motif look and feel", buttonGroup);
    JCheckBox windowsButton = createRadioButton(rbh, Windows,
      "Selects the Windows look and feel", buttonGroup);
    JCheckBox metalButton = createRadioButton(rbh, Metal,
      "Selects the Metal look and feel", buttonGroup);
    metalButton.setSelected(true);

    // Now configure the look of this panel and add the buttons
    setAlignmentX(LEFT_ALIGNMENT);
    setBorder(new BevelBorder(BevelBorder.RAISED));
    add(motifButton);
    add(windowsButton);
```

```
      add(metalButton);
   }
   private JCheckBox createRadioButton(ItemListener handler,
        String label,
        String tips,
        ButtonGroup group) {
     JCheckBox button = new JCheckBox(label);
     button.setActionCommand(label);
     button.setToolTipText(tips);
     button.addItemListener(handler);
     group.add(button);
     return button;
   }
   // Inner class to handler itemlistener events
   class RadioButtonHandler implements ItemListener {
     private String motif =
"com.sun.java.swing.plaf.motif.MotifLookAndFeel";
     private String windows =
"com.sun.java.swing.plaf.windows.WindowsLookAndFeel" ;
     private String metal =
"com.sun.java.swing.plaf.metal.MetalLookAndFeel";
     private JFrame frame;
     public RadioButtonHandler (JFrame frame) {
        this.frame = frame;
     }
     public void itemStateChanged(ItemEvent event) {
        String lookAndFeel;
        String option = ((JCheckBox)event.getItem()).getActionCommand();
        if (option.equals(Motif)) {
          lookAndFeel = motif;
        } else if (option.equals(Windows)) {
          lookAndFeel = windows;
        } else {
          lookAndFeel = metal;
        }
        try {
          UIManager.setLookAndFeel(lookAndFeel);
          SwingUtilities.updateComponentTreeUI(frame);
          frame.pack();
        } catch (Exception exp) {
          System.err.println("Could not load LookAndFeel: " + lookAndFeel);
        }
     }
   }
}
```

25.5.9 The DrawingException Class

This is a very simple class which is a minimal extension of the Exception class. It explicitly catches the DrawingException if it is raised in the Drawing class.

```
package swingdraw;

public class DrawingException extends Exception {
  DrawingException (String message) {
    super(message);
  }
}
```

25.5.10 The Figure Class

The Figure class (an abstract superclass and a subclass of Component) captures all the elements which are common to graphic objects which are displayed within a drawing. The x and y instance variables define the cursor position when the mouse is clicked; the xsize and ysize instance variables define the size of the object.

```
package swingdraw;

import java.awt.*;

public abstract class Figure extends Component {
  int x, y, xsize, ysize;
  boolean selected = false;

  Figure () {
    this(1, 1);
  }

  Figure (Point point, int size) {
    this(point.x, point.y, size);
  }
  Figure (Point point, int aSize, int bSize) {
    this(point.x, point.y, aSize, bSize);
  }
  Figure (int a, int b) {
    this(a, b, 10);
  }
  Figure (int a, int b, int c) {
    x = a;
    y = b;
    xsize = c;
    ysize = c;
  }
  Figure (int a, int b, int c, int d) {
    x = a;
    y = b;
    xsize = c;
    ysize = d;
  }

  public void setCoords (int a, int b) {
    x = a;
```

```
    y = b;
  }

  public void setFigureSize(int x) {
    xsize = x;
    ysize = x;
  }

  public Point getStartPoint() {
    return new Point(x, y);
  }

  public boolean contains (int a, int b) {
    boolean result = false;
    if ((a >= x) && (a <= (x + xsize)))
      if ((b >= y) && (b <= (y + ysize)))
        result = true;
    return result;
  }

  public boolean contains (Point point) {
    return contains(point.x, point.y);
  }

  /** The subclasses of this class are expected to
    extend the method paint   */
  public void paint(Graphics g) {
    displayFigure(g);
  }
  public void drawselectededBoxes (Graphics g) {
    g.fillRect(x - 2, y - 2, 4, 4);
    g.fillRect(x - 2, (y + ysize), 4, 4);
    g.fillRect((x + xsize), y - 2, 4, 4);
    g.fillRect((x + xsize), (y + ysize), 4, 4);
  }

  public void displayFigure (Graphics g) {
    if (selected){
      g.setColor(Color.red);
      drawselectededBoxes(g);
    }
    else
      g.setColor(Color.black);
  }

  public void selected () {
    selected = true;
  }

  public void deselected () {
    selected = false;
```

```
   }
}
```

The constructors provided by this class allow an instance of Figure to be generated in a number of different ways. The constructors which take fewer parameters are convenience constructors for those taking larger numbers of parameters. This focuses the functionality into one or two places.

25.5.11 The Square Class

This is a subclass of Figure that specifies how to draw a rectangle in a drawing. It extends the paint method inherited from Figure.

```
package swingdraw;

import java.awt.*;

class Square extends Figure {
  Square(Point p, int s) {
    super(p, s);
  }
  public void paint (Graphics g) {
    super.paint(g);
    g.drawRect(x, y, xsize, ysize);
  }
}
```

25.5.12 The Circle Class

This is another subclass of Figure. It extends the paint method by drawing a circle:

```
package swingdraw;

import java.awt.*;

class Circle extends Figure {
  Circle (Point p, int aSize) {
    super(p, aSize);
  }
  public void paint (Graphics g) {
    super.paint(g);
    g.drawOval(x, y, xsize, ysize);
  }
}
```

25.5.13 The Line Class

This is another subclass of Figure. It is more complex, as the way in which a line is selected and moved differs from that inherited from Figure.

```java
package swingdraw;

import java.awt.*;

class Line extends Figure {
  int x1, y1, x2, y2;
  Line(Point p1, Point p2) {
    x1 = p1.x;
    y1 = p1.y;
    x2 = p2.x;
    y2 = p2.y;
  }
  public void paint (Graphics g) {
    super.paint(g);
    g.drawLine(x1, y1, x2, y2);
  }
  public void drawSelectedBoxes(Graphics g) {
    g.fillRect(x1 - 2, y1 - 2, 4, 4);
    g.fillRect(x2 - 2, y2 - 2, 4, 4);
  }

  public void setEndPoint(int a, int b) {
    x2 = a;
    y2 = b;
  }
  public void setEndPoint(Point point) {
    setEndPoint(point.x, point.y);
  }
  public void setStartPoint(int a, int b) {
    x1 = a;
    y1 = b;
  }
  public void setStartPoint(Point point) {
    setStartPoint(point.x, point.y);
  }
  public void setCoords(int a, int b) {
    if ((a > (x1 - 10)) && (a < (x1 + 10)))
      if ((b > (y1 - 10)) && (b < (y1 + 10)))
        setStartPoint(a, b);
    if ((a > (x2 - 10)) && (a < (x2 + 10)))
      if ((b > (y2 - 10)) && (b < (y2 + 10)))
        setEndPoint (a, b);
  }
  public Point getStartPoint() {
    return new Point(x1, y1);
  }
  public Point getEndPoint() {
    return new Point(x2, y2);
  }
  public boolean contains (int a, int b) {
    if ((a > (x1 - 10)) && (a < (x1 + 10)))
```

```
        if ((b > (y1 - 10)) && (b < (y1 + 10)))
          return true;
      if ((a > (x2 - 10)) && (a < (x2 + 10)))
        if ((b > (y2 - 10)) && (b < (y2 + 10)))
          return true;
      return false;
    }
}
```

25.5.14 The TextFigure Class

This is also a subclass of Figure. It redefines some of the inherited behaviour. In particular, it redefines the contains method and the drawSelectedBoxes method:

```
package swingdraw;

import java.awt.*;

class TextFigure extends Figure {
  private String string = "";

  TextFigure(Point p, String s) {
    super(p, (s.length() * 6), 10);
    string = s;
  }

  public void paint (Graphics g) {
    super.paint(g);
    g.drawString(string, x, y);
  }

  public boolean contains (int a, int b) {
    boolean result = false;
    if ((a >= x) && (a <= (x + xsize)))
      if ((b >= (y - ysize)) && (b <= y))
        result = true;
    return result;
  }

  public void drawSelectedBoxes (Graphics g) {
    g.fillRect(x - 2, y - 2, 4, 4);
    g.fillRect(x - 2, (y - ysize), 4, 4);
    g.fillRect((x + xsize), y - 2, 4, 4);
    g.fillRect((x + xsize), (y - ysize), 4, 4);
  }
}
```

25.5.15 The TextDialog Class

When users wish to add a new TextFigure to the drawing, they are prompted for the text by a dialog box. This dialog box is implemented by the TextDialog class (a direct subclass of JDialog). It is a simple window which uses only a label and a text field. Notice how it passes information back to the application using the getString() method.

```java
package swingdraw;

import java.awt.*;
import javax.swing.*;

class TextDialog extends JDialog implements ActionListener {
  JTextField textField;
    Drawing drawing;
    TextDialog (JFrame parent, Drawing d, String label) {
    super(parent, "Text Dialog", true);
    drawing = d;

    Container pane = getContentPane();

    pane.add("North", new JLabel(label));

    textField = new JTextField(12);
    pane.add("Center", textField);
    textField.addActionListener(this);

    pack();
  }

  public void actionPerformed (ActionEvent e) {
    dispose();
  }

  public String getString () {
    return textField.getText();
  }
}
```

The getString method obtains the string from the dialog using the getText method of the textField.

25.6 Exercises

You could develop the SwingDraw application further by adding the following features:

- *A delete option* You can add a button labelled Delete to the window. It should set the mode to "delete". The drawingPanel must be altered so that the mouseReleased method sends a `delete` message to the drawing. The drawing must find and remove the appropriate graphic object and send the changed message to itself.

- *Save and load options* This involves saving the elements in the contents field of the drawing object in such a way that they can be restored at a later date. You can use serialization (see Chapter 17).
- *A resize option* This involves identifying which of the boxes surrounding the selected object is being dragged and altering the sizes appropriately.

25.7 Summary

This chapter introduced a larger application which includes mouse events and scrollable panes, as well as mixing Java's graphics facilities with its user interface facilities and Swing.

Chapter 26

Swing Data Model Case Study

26.1 Introduction

This chapter presents an example of a Swing component that uses a complex data model. In this case we will examine the JTree Swing component, which requires a data model that represents the tree being displayed. The JTree component renders the tree data model; thus if the data model changes, the tree rendered by JTree also changes. To illustrate these ideas we will construct a simple application which displays all the classes inherited by a specified class.

26.2 The JTree Swing Component

A JTree is a Swing component that can be used to display hierarchical data (in a similar manner to the way in which the Windows Explorer tool displays information about the directories and files on a PC). An example of the JTree displaying such data, taken from the SwingSet demonstration provided with Swing, is illustrated in Figure 26.1. Within a tree each row contains exactly one item of data, and every tree has a root (in this case labelled Music) from which other nodes *descend*. Nodes at the end of the tree which cannot possess children are called leaf nodes. Non-leaf nodes (which are also non-root nodes) can have any number of children (including zero). A node is made into a leaf node by calling setAllowsChildren(false) on the node.

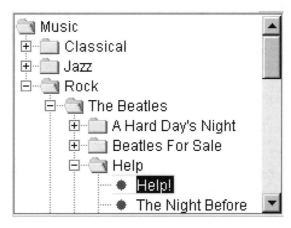

Fig. 26.1 A JTree component displaying hierarchical data.

Note that the JTree component does not contain the data being displayed; rather, it renders or displays a view onto that data (this is illustrated in Figure 26.2). This is due to the Model–View–Controller architecture underlying Swing components (as discussed in Chapter 22). Essentially, the JTree component is the View and Controller, while the data defining the hierarchical tree structure is the Model.

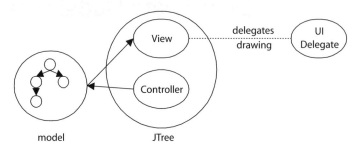

Fig. 26.2 The JTree architecture.

A node in the tree data model can either be visible (that is, currently displayed in the JTree component) or hidden (for example there may be more nodes under Jazz in Figure 26.1, but at present they are hidden. A node may also be expanded, such as the node labelled "Help" in the figure, or collapsed, such as the node labelled "A Hard Day's Night". Note that in Figure 26.1 expanded nodes are denoted by a box containing a minus sign and collapsed nodes are denoted by a box containing a plus sign. This is dependent upon the look and feel currently being used and is different in both the Metal and Motif look and feels.

You can programmatically add nodes to the tree, expand or collapse whole paths, and highlight individual nodes or whole paths. You can pick up whether a node has be clicked once or twice, you can catch events which cause the tree to expand or collapse, and you can interrogate the JTree component to find out what it is currently displaying. All in all, the JTree component is a very powerful and flexible GUI component.

You can also identify which node is selected, when this selection changes (using the TreeSelectionListener interface) and whether the user clicks once or twice on the node.

26.2.1 The JTree Constructors

The JTree Swing component defines the following JTree constructors:

- JTree() Returns a JTree with a sample model. Useful for testing (for example, to ensure that your TreeSelectionListener class is operating correctly).
- JTree(Hashtable) Constructs a JTree with each element of the Hashtable as the child of a root node.
- JTree(Object[]) Constructs a JTree with each element of the object array as the child of a root node.
- JTree(TreeModel) Constructs an instance of JTree using the JTreeModel as the data model to be displayed.

JTree(TreeNode) Returns a JTree with an instance of JTreeModel as its data model, rooted at the TreeNode passed to the constructor which is defined as a leaf node (i.e. it does not allow child nodes).

- `JTree(TreeNode, boolean)` Constructs a `JTree` with an instance of `JTreeModel` as its data model. The boolean parameter is passed into the constructor of `JTreeModel`, which will determine how `JTreeModel` tests for leafness. If the flag passed in is true, leafness is determined by messaging `getAllowsChildren`; otherwise `isLeaf` is messaged.
- `JTree(Vector)` Constructs a `JTree` with each element of the vector as the child of a root node.

The set of constructors described above allow a `JTree` component to be constructed from an existing data structure (e.g. a `Vector`, `Array` or `Hashtable`), building directly from a `TreeModel` and rooted on a single tree node.

26.2.2 The JTree API

The `JTree` Swing component has an extensive API which would run to too many pages to list here. Instead, the key methods of the `JTree` component are highlighted and the reader is pointed at the JDK documentation for more information.

Tree Expansion and Contraction

Setting the TreeExpansionListener
- `public void addTreeExpansionListener(TreeExpansionListener tel)` Adds tel as interested in receiving `TreeExpansion` events.
- `public void removeTreeExpansionListener(TreeExpansionListener tel)` Removes tel as being interested in receiving `TreeExpansion` events.

Expanding and Collapsing Trees
- `expandPath(TreePath path)` Ensures that the last item identified in path is expanded and visible.
- `public void expandRow(int row)` Ensures that the item identified by row is expanded.
- `public void collapsePath(TreePath path)` Ensures that the last item identified in path is collapsed and visible.
- `public void collapseRow(int row)` Ensures that the item identified by row is collapsed.

Testing for Expansion
- `public boolean isExpanded(TreePath path)` Returns `true` if the value identified by path is currently expanded; returns `false` if any of the values in path are currently not being displayed.
- `public boolean isExpanded(int row)` Returns `true` if the value identified by row is currently expanded.
- `public boolean isCollapsed(TreePath path)` Returns `true` if the value identified by path is currently collapsed; returns `false` if any of the values in path are currently not being displayed.
- `public boolean isCollapsed(int row)` Returns `true` if the value identified by row is currently collapsed.

Tree Selection

Setting the TreeSelectionListener
- `public void addTreeSelectionListener(TreeSelectionListener tsl)` Adds tsl as interested in receiving `TreeSelection` events.

- removeTreeSelectionListener public void removeTreeSelectionListener (TreeSelectionListener tsl) Removes tsl as being interested in receiving TreeSelection events.

Obtaining the Selection Path
- public TreePath getSelectionPath() Returns the path to the first selected value, or null if nothing is currently selected.
- public TreePath[] getSelectionPaths() Returns the path of the selected values, or null if nothing is current selected.
- public int[] getSelectionRows() Returns all of the currently selected rows.
- public int getSelectionCount() Returns the number of nodes selected.

Manipulating Tree Selection
- public void clearSelection() Clears the selection.
- public void addSelectionPath(TreePath path) Adds the path identified by path to the current selection. If any component of path is not visible, it will be made visible.
- public void addSelectionPaths(TreePath[] paths) Adds each path in paths to the current selection. If any component of any of the paths is not visible, it will be made visible.
- public void addSelectionRow(int rows) Adds the paths at each of the rows in rows to the current selection.
- public void addSelectionRows(int[] rows) Adds the paths at each of the rows in rows to the current selection.
- public void removeSelectionPath(TreePath path) Removes the path identified by path from the current selection.
- public void removeSelectionPaths(TreePath[] paths) Removes the paths identified by paths from the current selection.
- public void removeSelectionRow(int row) Removes the path at the index row from the current selection.
- public void removeSelectionRows(int[] rows) Removes the paths that are selected at each of the indices in rows.
- public void setSelectionPath(TreePath path) Sets the selection to the value identified by path. If any component of the path is not currently visible it will be made visible.
- public void setSelectionPaths(TreePath[] paths) Sets the selection to paths. If any component in any of the paths is not currently visible it will be made visible.
- public void setSelectionRow(int row) Sets the selection to the path at index row.
- public void setSelectionRows(int[] rows) The selection is set to the paths for the items at each of the rows in rows.

Testing
- public boolean isPathSelected(TreePath path) Returns true if item identified by path is currently selected.
- public boolean isSelectionEmpty() Returns true if the selection is currently empty.
- public boolean isRowSelected(int row) Returns true if the row identitifed by row is selected.

26.2.3 Changing the Model

These methods are used to changing the model currently being displayed by the JTree component:

- `public TreeModel getModel()` Returns the `TreeModel` that is providing the data.
- `public void setModel(TreeModel newModel)` Sets the `TreeModel` that will provide the data.

Note that in the Swing release 1.0.2 the `setModel(TreeModel)` method is missing and this is why the example presented later in this chapter does not use it. Instead it has to embark on a rather convoluted way of modifying the display.

26.3 The JTree Package

In addition to the `JTree` class there is also a tree package. This package is under Swing in a package called `tree` (thus it is `javax.swing.tree` or `javax.swing.tree.*` depending on your version of Swing). However, the Tree package provides a very useful set of interfaces and classes for building tree data structures (which also happen to work with the `JTree` Swing component. This is probably the best way to think about this package. The Tree package defines seven interfaces and four classes, described below.

26.3.1 Interfaces

These interfaces are used to specify the facilities required by nodes in a tree, by cell editors and renderers etc. Details of the interfaces are left as a reference to the `swing.tree` package API.

- `MutableTreeNode`
- `RowMapper`
- `TreeCellEditor` Adds to `CellEditor` the extensions necessary to configure an editor in a tree.
- `TreeCellRenderer`
- `TreeModel` The interface that defines a suitable data model for a `JTree`.
- `TreeNode`
- `TreeSelectionModel` This interface represents the current state of the selection for the tree component.

26.3.2 Classes

The classes in the `swing.tree` package provide the basics for tree creation and selection. In particular, the `DefaultMutableTreeNode` and `DefaultTreeModel` implement the basic facilities of a `MutableTreeNode` and a `TreeModel`.

- `DefaultMutableTreeNode` A `DefaultMutableTreeNode` is a general-purpose node in a tree data structure. It can be used to construct the tree data model used with the `JTree` Swing component. However, it can also be used to construct tree data structures in general.
- `DefaultTreeModel` A simple tree data model that uses `TreeNodes`. This class can also be used to construct the tree data model used with the `JTree` Swing component.
- `DefaultTreeSelectionModel` Implementation of `TreeSelectionModel`.
- `TreePath` Represents a path to a node.

26.3.3 The DefaultMutableTreeNode class

This class implements the MutableTreeNode interface to provide a basic implementation of a tree node for use in building tree data model for the Swing JTree component. A tree node may have at most one parent and zero or more children. DefaultMutableTreeNode provides operations for examining and modifying a node's parent and children and also operations for examining the tree that the node is a part of.

A node's tree is the set of all nodes that can be reached by starting at the node and following all the possible links to parents and children. A node with no parent is the root of its tree; a node with no children is a leaf. A tree may consist of many subtrees, each node acting as the root for its own subtree. DefaultMutableTreeNode also provides enumerations for efficiently traversing a tree or subtree in various orders or for following the path between two nodes.

This class provides the following constructors:

- DefaultMutableTreeNode() Creates a tree node that has no parent and no children, but which allows children.
- DefaultMutableTreeNode(java.lang.Object userObject) Creates a tree node with no parent and no children, but which allows children, and initializes it with the specified user object.
- DefaultMutableTreeNode(java.lang.Object userObject, boolean allowsChildren) Creates a tree node with no parent and no children, initialized with the specified user object, and which allows children only if specified.

While the full set of methods defined this class are not provided below, the key methods are listed (for further methods the reader is directed to the JDK API documentation).

Modifying the Tree
These methods are used to modify the contents of the tree associated with a given tree node.

- void add(MutableTreeNode newChild) Adds the MutableTreeNode as a child of the receiving node.
- void insert(MutableTreeNode newChild, int childIndex) Removes newChild from its present parent (if it has a parent), sets the child's parent to this node, and then adds the child to this node's child array at index childIndex.
- void remove(int childIndex) Removes the child at the specified index from this node's children and sets that node's parent to null.
- void remove(MutableTreeNode aChild) Removes aChild from this node's child array, giving it a null parent.
- void removeAllChildren() Removes all of this node's children, setting their parents to null.
- void removeFromParent() Removes the subtree rooted at this node from the tree, giving this node a null parent.

Enumerating Over the Tree
These methods allow the elements in a tree to be iterated over. Note that the enumeration interface is used rather than the newer Iterator interface defined in the JFC Collection classes:

- java.util.Enumeration breadthFirstEnumeration() Creates and returns an enumeration that traverses the subtree rooted at this node in breadth-first order.
- java.util.Enumeration depthFirstEnumeration() Creates and returns an enumeration that traverses the subtree rooted at this node in depth-first order.

- `java.util.Enumeration children()` Creates and returns a forward-order enumeration of this node's children.

Obtaining the Path
These methods allow the developer to obtain information about the path containing the current node.

- `TreeNode getParent()` Returns this node's parent or null if this node has no parent.
- `TreeNode[] getPath()` Returns the path from the root to get to this node.
- `TreeNode getRoot()` Returns the root of the tree that contains this node.

Testing the Tree
These methods allow the tree (or sub-tree) containing the current node to be tested:

- `boolean isLeaf()` Returns true if this node has no children.
- `boolean isNodeAncestor(TreeNode anotherNode)` Returns true if anotherNode is an ancestor of this node – i.e. if it is this node, this node's parent, or an ancestor of this node's parent.
- `boolean isNodeChild(TreeNode aNode)` Returns true if aNode is a child of this node.
- `boolean isRoot()` Returns true if this node is the root of the tree.

26.4 Building the Data Model

This section discusses the process by which the data model for the JTree component, used in the simple class hierarchy browser tool (described in detail later in the chapter), is constructed. In this example a class called `TreeGenerator` possesses a single static (class side) method called `createDataModel`. This method is used to build a tree of `DefaultMutableTreeNodes`, the root of which is returned. This is then used elsewhere in an application by a JTree Swing component or by anything else which requires a tree data structure. Branches in the tree are indicated by a vector inside the current level vector; nodes are indicated by strings.

```
package browser;

// As we are working with trees need to import
// the tree package. Note JTree is in the swing package.
import javax.swing.tree.*;
import java.util.*;

public class TreeGenerator {

    /**
     * This method converts a vector into a tree data model.
     * @param vector of contents of tree
     * @returns DefaultmutableTreeNode
     */
    public static DefaultMutableTreeNode createDataModel(Vector tree) {
        DefaultMutableTreeNode top, last, current = null;    // Root of tree

        // Get the node at the top of the tree
```

```
      top = new DefaultMutableTreeNode((String)tree.lastElement());
      tree.removeElement(tree.lastElement());
      last = top;

      // Process vector of strings in reverse order
      // adding each node to the tree
      for (int i = tree.size(); i > 0; i--) {
        Object element = tree.elementAt(i - 1);
        if (element instanceof String) {
          current = new DefaultMutableTreeNode(element);
        } else {
          current = createDataModel((Vector)element);
        }
        last.add(current);
        last = current;
      }
      return top;
  }

}
```

This method makes clear that a tree data model can be constructed without reference to the Swing component JTree. It also illustrates that the tree data model could now be used for any-one of a number of uses, as we have created a generic tree data structure which can be pro-cessed just like any other data structure. As we now have a tree data model we are ready to build an application around this class.

26.5 Building the GUI Application

The application we are going to consider is illustrated in Figure 26.3. It takes the fully qualified name of a class (that is, including its package specification) and constructs a tree of the classes it inherits from (using the reflection API described later in this book). A new class inheritance

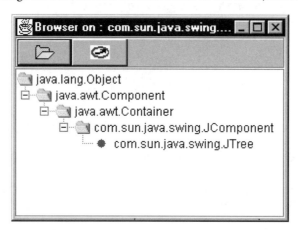

Fig. 26.3 The Browser application displaying JTree's hierarchy.

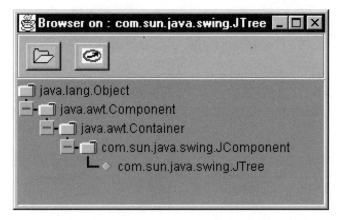

Fig. 26.4 The Browser using the Motif look and feel.

hierarchy can be displayed at any time by clicking on the open button (indicated by the open file button icon).

The buttons across the top of the browser application are actually held in a toolbar and are thus dockable. The first button indicates that a new tree is to be open for a new class, while the second button is used to exit the application.

As can be seen from the figure this browser is displaying the Windows look and feel. Figure 26.4 illustrates the same application run with the Motif look and feel. As you can see, the data is exactly the same: the only difference is that the way in which the tree is draw is different.

To create this application, all that is required is that the DefaultMutableTreeNode, returned by the static method of the TreeGenerator class, is passed to a suitable JTree constructor. To provide a scrollable view on the tree, so that scroll bars allow parts of the tree that are hidden to be viewed, the JTree component is placed inside a JScrollPane. This is then added to the JFrame's content pane. The JScrollPane is held in an instance variable treeView. This is all handled by the setClass(String) method. This means for a different class to be displayed, the setClass method can remove the current treeView and build a new data structure, JTree component and JScrollPane. This is only necessary because of the setModel() omission in Swing 1.0.2. If this had not been omitted, all that would have been required would be to set a new model for an existing JTree component.

The remainder of this application handles changing the tree being displayed, changing the look and feel, adding the toolbar and handling button events etc.

The Browser application code is presented below. As you have seen most of the features before we will not examine this class in detail.

```
package browser;

/*
 * Import both the AWT package and the swing package
 */
import java.awt.*;
import java.awt.event.*;
import javax.swing.*;
// As we are working with trees also need to import
// the tree package. Note JTree is in the swing package.
```

```java
import javax.swing.tree.*;
import java.util.*;

/**
 * This class provides a simple graphical browser for viewing
 * class inheritance hierarchies.
 * @author John Hunt
 * @version 1.0
 */
public class Browser extends JFrame {
  private DefaultMutableTreeNode root;
  private String classname;
  private Class classObject;
  private JTree tree;
  private JScrollPane treeView;

  /**
   * Used to initiate the execution of the application
   */
  public static void main (String args []) {
    if (args.length == 0)
      System.out.println("Usage: java Browser <fully qualified
        class name>");
    else
      new Browser(args[0]);
  }

  /**
   * Constructor used to create an instance of a Browser on a
   * particular class. For example:
   * <p>
   * new Browser("java.awt.Frame");
   * <p>
   * @param classname The class for which the inheritance hierarchy
   * is to be displayed.
   */
  public Browser(String classname) {
    super("Browser on : " + classname);

    // Create the class hierachy for classname
    setClass(classname);

    // Get the content pane
    Container pane = getContentPane();

    // Handle window events
    addWindowListener(new WindowHandler());

    //-------------------------------------
    // Create a toolbar
    //-------------------------------------
```

```
JToolBar toolBar = new JToolBar();

// Instantiate the handler for the toolbar buttons
ActionHandler handler = new ActionHandler(this);

// Define the new class button
ImageIcon buttonIcon = new ImageIcon("load.gif");
JButton button = new JButton(buttonIcon);
button.setToolTipText("New class hierarchy");
button.addActionListener(handler);
toolBar.add(button);

// Now create the exit button
buttonIcon = new ImageIcon("exit.gif");
button =new JButton(buttonIcon);
button.setToolTipText("Exit browser");
button.setActionCommand("Exit");
button.addActionListener(handler);
toolBar.add(button);

// Add the toolbar to the window
// using the content pane.
pane.add(toolBar, BorderLayout.NORTH);

// Set the look and feel to the Windows look and feel
if (!UIManager.getLookAndFeel().getName().equals("Windows")) {
  try {
    UIManager.setLookAndFeel
      ("com.sun.java.swing.plaf.windows.WindowsLookAndFeel");
    SwingUtilities.updateComponentTreeUI(this);
  } catch (Exception exc) {
    System.err.println("could not load Windows LookAndFeel");
  }
}

// Set the size of the window and make it visible
pack();
setVisible(true);

}

/**
 * Used to create the tree to be displayed by the
 * JTree GUI component.
 *
 * @return DefaultMutableNode root of tree
 */
private DefaultMutableTreeNode createTreeNodes() {
  Vector names = new Vector(10,10); // Holds list of classes in
                                    // reverse order
  DefaultMutableTreeNode root = null;   // Root of tree
```

```java
// Use reflection to obtain the class object for the
// specified classname. Using this object obtain the
// superclass. Repeat this process until the class Object
// has been found - all classes inherit from Object in Java.
try {
  classObject = Class.forName(classname);
  Class superClass = classObject.getSuperclass();
  String superclassname = superClass.getName();
  names.addElement(superclassname);

  while (!superclassname.equals("java.lang.Object")) {
    superClass = superClass.getSuperclass();
    superclassname = superClass.getName();
    names.addElement(superclassname);
  }

  names.insertElementAt(classname, 0);
  names.trimToSize();

  // the vector of class names will be converted into a tree data
  // structure - note single inheritance means a single branched tree
  root = TreeGenerator.createDataModel(names);

  } catch (ClassNotFoundException e)
    {System.out.println("Error: Class not found");}
  return root;
}

/**
 * Takes a string representing the class to generate the hierarchy
 * for and constructs a tree model which is placed in a JTree GUI
 * component which is added to the windows content pane.
 *
 * @param classname Name of class to display
 */
protected void setClass(String classname) {
  this.classname = classname;

  // Get the widnows content frame
  Container container = getContentPane();

  // If a tree is currently being displayed, remove it from the
  // window
  if (treeView != null)
    container.remove(treeView);
  // Create the nodes.
  root = createTreeNodes();
  tree = new JTree(root);
  tree.getSelectionModel().setSelectionMode
    (TreeSelectionModel.SINGLE_TREE_SELECTION);

  //Create the scroll pane and add the tree to it.
```

```java
      treeView = new JScrollPane(tree);

      // Add tree view to the content pane
      container.add(treeView);

      // Change title at top of window
      setTitle("Browser on : " + classname);
    }
  }

  /**
    * Helper class used to handle window events
    */
  class WindowHandler extends WindowAdapter {
    public void windowClosing(WindowEvent e) {System.exit(0);}
  }

  /**
    * Provides the listener for the tool bar in the Browser class
    */
  class ActionHandler implements ActionListener {
    Browser frame;

  /**
    * Constructor takes a reference to the Browser object so that it can
    * reference this object when a new class is to be displayed
    */
  public ActionHandler(Browser f) {
    frame = f;
  }
  public void actionPerformed(ActionEvent event) {
    String cmd = event.getActionCommand();
  // Select the action to perform depending on the button pressed
  if (cmd.equals("Exit")) {
    System.exit(0);
  } else {
    // Use a CLassRequestDialog to obtain the name of the
    // new class to display. Use the setClass method of Browser
    // to change the class being displayed and repack the window.
    ClassRequestDialog crd = new ClassRequestDialog(frame);
    crd.setVisible(true);
    String newclass = crd.getText();

    // Check to see if the cancel button was selected (returns null)
      if (!newclass.equals("")) {
        frame.setClass(newclass);
        frame.pack();
      }
    }
  }
}
```

To execute this application type java browser.Browser <fully qualified class name>. For example:

```
java browser.Browser javax.swing.Jtree
```

26.6 Online Resources

- The Swing Connection http://java.sun.com/products/jfc/tsc/index.html
- The Java Tutorial: How to Use Trees: http://java.sun.com/docs/books/tutorial/uiswing/components/tree.html
- The JFC Home Page: http://java.sun.com/products/jfc/index.html

Chapter *27*

Java: Speaking in Tongues

27.1 Introduction

Back in the days when I was in the second year of senior school, we were all encouraged to take at least one modern language, be it French, German or Spanish. The majority of people chose French, because that was what we had done in the first year. The idea was that we would be ready to work within a modern environment in which different languages would be needed. This situation of course has not changed, and is true not just of the working population, but also of software.

When software is to be used in different countries it is necessary for it to be able to use different languages, work with different business rules, apply different rates of taxation, use different currencies, and have different modes of operation provided and standard layouts modified. Even software that should be run in English-speaking countries is subject to such requirements. For example, consider the date 2.6.2002. What date does this represent? Is this the 2nd of June 2002 or the 6th of February 2002? Without knowing which country the writer was in (and what format that country uses) it is impossible to say for certain. If the author was British then the first interpretation is probably true; if American, then the second is correct. But what if the writer was Canadian? Which format do they use?

Obviously we don't want to have to implement different versions of the same software for each country, not least as this results in horrendous maintenance problems. Also, we don't really what to have to write huge "if-style" statements in our code to deal with all the options that may present themselves (as this is not only limiting but inefficient). What is required is some form of mechanism, built into a computer system, which allows the developer to specify that in the current environment the software system should be customized in a particular manner. This should be able to happen at run time, so that it is not necessary to determine all the various options at compile time (as new countries, options etc. may present themselves during the lifetime of the software system). This is particularly true of applets, as they may be downloaded anywhere in the world. This dynamic "localization" of software is directly supported by Java using `ResourceBundles`, text formatters and `Locales`.

Essentially, in Java a locale identifies where in the world the software is running, which allows an appropriate `ResourceBundle` to be loaded. This `ResourceBundle` can hold information that is used to customize an application for the current location. The text formatters can then deal with any locale-specific presentation issues (such as the ordering of dates or different types of currency symbols). We consider each of these in the remainder of this chapter.

27.2 Locale

A locale is a concept that is not new to Java, but which Java uses to identify a particular environment. That is, it can include information on the native language of the current environment (English, French, German, Greek etc.), the country (Great Britain, USA, Canada, France etc.) and sometimes the host platform (referred to as a Variant). ISO standards are used for the language (ISO-639) and country (ISO-3166) codes.

The class Locale can be found in the java.util package. It is not necessary to create your own locale as there is always one provided representing your current environment. This allows the locale to be used as a tool to allow the appropriate country-specific resource bundles and other country-specific preferences (such as dates) to be selected appropriately. However, you can find out which locale you are currently running in by using the class (static) method getDefault(). For example, the following program obtains a reference to the current default locale and obtains a reference to the current country, language and if available the variant:

```java
import java.util.Locale;

public class LocaleTest {
  public static void main(String args []) {
    Locale loc = Locale.getDefault();
    System.out.println(loc.getCountry() + "\t" + loc.getDisplayCountry());
    System.out.println(loc.getLanguage() + "\t" + loc.getDisplayLanguage());
    System.out.println(loc.getVariant() + "\t" + loc.getDisplayVariant());
  }
}
```

On my machine this produces the following output:

```
GB      United Kingdom
en      English
```

The Locale class provides a number of convenient constants that you can use to create Locale objects for commonly used locales. For example, the following creates a Locale object for the USA:

```java
Locale loc = Locale.US;
```

If we run the above program in the US locale the output changes to the following:

```
US      United States
en      English
```

It is also possible to change the default local setup for the current Java Virtual Machine (JVM) using the class-side (static) method setDefault(Locale newLocale). Thus if you wish to change the environment that your system believes it is running in from the UK to the US, you could set the default locale to be US; for example:

```java
Locale.setDefault(Locale.US);
```

27.3 Properties Objects

So far we have been able to identify the local environment in which our programs are currently executing. However, this is only part of the problem. Having identified where we are running, we now need to allow our programs to carry out whatever localization behaviour they need. We could of course do this by obtaining the current and language encodings manually and then using either if statements or possibly a Property object, obtain the necessary country-specific information (for example the text label for a button).

The class java.util.Property is a subclass of Hashtable that can be used to associate keys with values (although unlike Hashtable the values are limited to strings). There is already a property object provided with every JVM: the system property object. This object can be obtained from the System class using the class-side (static) method getProperties(). This is useful, as a number of the properties provide information which can be used to "localize" the current running program. For example, some of the keys available by default in the Java 2 SDK 1.3 are presented in Table 27.1.

Table 27.1 System properties.

Key	Typical value
java.vm.version	1.3beta-0
os.arch	x86
os.name	Windows 98
user.timezone	GMT
java.specification.version	1.3beta
user.language	en
java.version	1.3beta
user.region	GB
sun.cpu.isalist	pentium i486 i386

The following program will print out all the keys and their values in the system properties object:

```java
import java.util.*;

public class PropertyExample extends Object {
  public static void main (String args[]) {
    Properties prop = System.getProperties();
    Enumeration enum = prop.propertyNames();
    while (enum.hasMoreElements()) {
      String key = (String)enum.nextElement();
      System.out.println("Key : " + key + " | value : "
          + prop.getProperty(key));
    }
  }
}
```

If you wish you can add elements to the system properties from the command line using -D option (e.g. java -Dname=value Class). You can also define your own properties objects. These can be initialized programmatically or from a file (using the load method). The file loaded must contain a set of key–value pairs separated with either an equals sign ("=") or a colon (":"). For example, given the file labels.properties (note the file extension), the following program will load this properties file into a properties object and print out the results:

```
import java.util.*;
import java.io.*;

public class PropertiesLoader extends Object {
  public static void main(String [] args) throws IOException {
    Properties prop = new Properties();
    FileInputStream fis = new FileInputStream("labels.properties");
    prop.load(fis);
    Enumeration enum = prop.propertyNames();
    while (enum.hasMoreElements()) {
      String key = (String)enum.nextElement();
      System.out.println("Key : " + key + " | value : "
          + prop.getProperty(key));
    }
  }
}
```

The properties file might look like the following:

```
button1=Center
button2=Colour
currency=sterling
```

Using the local information we could now have a different properties file for each country or location within which we want our software to execute. Now, when the software runs, it can either check the locale for the country or system properties or use the command line-set information for location information and find and load the appropriate properties file. Indeed, this works well, but for the country-based option a great deal of the work has already been done for you via ResourceBundles. These are discussed below.

27.4 ResourceBundle Introduction

A ResourceBundle is similar to a properties object in that it holds associations between keys and values. It differs from properties objects in that two of the three types of ResourceBundle are classes in which you define the data (only the third can automatically be loaded from a file) and that the name of the resource bundle is directly related to the locale in which it is expected to be used. It also differs from properties objects in that there is an inheritance relationship between the information held in the various ResourceBundles, which we will look at later.

We will start by considering the three types of ResourceBundle in Java (see Figure 27.1). These are the abstract class ResourceBundle, and its subclasses ListResourceBundle (which is also abstract) and PropertyResourceBundle. Each of them has a specific purpose:

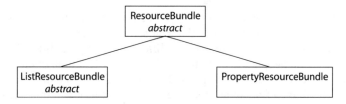

Fig. 27.1 The two abstract and one concrete class for dealing with resource bundles.

- ResourceBundle Root of the ResourceBundle hierarchy and can therefore be used as the basis of new, user-defined, resource bundles. It requires that the subclass implement the handleGetObjects and getKeys methods.
- ListResourceBundle This abstract subclass of ResourceBundle implements both the handleGetObjects and getKeys methods for you. However, it requires that you implement a method called getContents which returns an array of object arrays in which the inner array contains key–value pairs. This means that it is straight forward to create a ListResourceBundle subclass (e.g. JohnsListResourceBundle) which obtains this information from a instance variable, a file, a database or any other data source. As the array must be an array of objects any values can be provided, including instances of buttons, labels etc.
- PropertyResourceBundle This is a concrete class which provides the simplest approach to creating resource bundles. It reads data from appropriate properties files and uses this in response to requests for a key's value.

As the PropertyResourceBundle requires no new subclasses and little programming this is the approach we will look at in the remainder of this chapter.

27.4.1 Naming Properties Files

The naming of the properties files that the PropertyResourceBundle object will use is very significant. This is because the files should be named relative to a base name (such as EditorResource), but including the language and the country to which they are associated (using the ISO codes described earlier). Each file must then have a ".properties" extension. For example, consider the following properties files and their meaning:

```
EditorResource _en_GB .properties      UK English
EditorResource _en_US .properties      US English
EditorResource _fr_FR .properties      France French
EditorResource _fr_CA .properties      Canadian French
```

Thus we have one root name to these files, but different language and country additions. This allows the developer to specify that the EditorResource is required and the system examines the current locale to determine which version of the file is to be loaded. This is done using the ResourceBundle.getBundle() class-side method. This returns a PropertiesResourceBundle object related to the current locale.

In fact, getBundle is an overloaded method, allowing you to specify a locale as well as the resource bundle (e.g. ResourceBundle.getBundle("EditorResource", Locale.US);).

What happens if you specify a locale which does not currently have a properties file defined for it? This depends on the range of properties files defined as we will see below.

The first thing that happens is that the getBundle method attempts to load the most specific properties file it can find (e.g. "EditorResources_en_GB"). However, if that is not present, it then looks for a less specific version (e.g. "EditorResources_en") that matches the language of the current locale. The assumption is that the same language is likely to be similar in different countries; thus any language-specific differences are probably going to be understood. For example, most people will recognize Color in the UK, although they may not realise that this is actually the American spelling of colour rather than a spelling mistake!

If getBundle still fails to find an appropriate properties file, it will then look for the most generic option: a properties file named after the root name (in this case "EditorResources"). In fact, the search actually starts by considering the specific variant as well as the language and country. Thus the search pattern is actually:

1st	basename_language_country_variant
2nd	basename_language_country
3rd	basename_language
4th	basename

If a non-default locale is specified, then if the above search fails to find a properties file, it is repeated for the default locale.

27.4.2 Property Inheritance

As you have seen above, there can be a hierarchy of property files, each of which contains key–value pairs. As well as acting as alternatives for the search process, the more generic files can be used to supply default values which may or may not be overridden in more specific files.

For example, let us say that our basename English properties file will represent GB English. Many of the entries in this file will be the same whatever version of English is being used (American, Australian etc.). Rather than repeat each of them in each properties file, we can rely on the base properties files to supply them and only override those which are different, such as Color, Center and the like. The search algorithm will now look in the more generic properties files whenever it fails to find the key specified in the more specific properties files.

For example, consider the following properties files:

```
Labels_en            Labels_en_US
name=name            code=zip code
address=address      district=state
code=post code
district=county
```

The result would be that for a resource bundle object loaded via the US locale, the keys and values would be:

```
name=name
address=address
code=zip code
district=state
```

27.4.3 Accessing Property Values

All resource bundles provide a getObject(String key) method that allows the value associated with the given key to be obtained. Note that the return type for this method is Object; thus it is necessary to cast the returned object to the appropriate type (such as JButton or String).

For string values, there is also the option of using the getString(key) method, as this method returns objects of type String directly (thereby removing the need to cast the result to String). As PropertyResourceBundles can only hold Strings as their values, this method meets our needs and will be used in the following examples; however, generically resource bundles can hold any type of object, thus in many situations you must use the getObject method.

The following Java extract reads the Labels properties files, obtains the value for code and outputs the result:

```
ResourceBundle bundle = ResourceBundle.getBundle("Labels");
String codeLabel = bundle.getString("code");
System.out.println(codeLabel);
```

27.5 Formatting Output

We have now examined the concepts of locales and resource bundles; however, we have still to deal with the issues of formatting output. That is, we might well know that we are in the US locale and that we need to use the *_en_US properties files, but how do we deal with formatting items such as dates and currency as appropriate? The answer is a text formatter.

A text formatter is a template into which actual values are inserted at run time. This template is defined by a String (which can therefore be defined in a locale-specific properties file). This template string is provided as one of the parameters to a message formatter. The root class of all the formatters is the MessageFormat class of the java.text package.

The MessageFormat class has a class-side method format() that takes a template or format string and an object array. The array is used to supply the values for the template. For example:

```
String template = "{1, number, integer}/{0, number, integer}/00";
Object [] values = {new Integer(2), new Integer(6)};
String output = MessageFormat.format(template, values);
System.out.println(output);
```

This results in the following output:

6/2/00

Note that to change the position of the six and the two we only need to change the format string.

In the above example, not that substitution placeholders are indicated by curly braces ({ , }). Thus the template string states "first get the second element of the substitution array (index 1); this should be a number, and in particular it should be treated as an integer (other options are percent and currency); having got this number add a forward slash (/) and then get the first element in the substitution array (index 0). Obtain the integer value for that and then add the string /00 to the end". Notice that the placeholders in the template can reference arguments in any order and zero or more times.

The above example, is based on the idea of formatting a date as appropriate for the current locale. However, as this is such a common operation, Java provides the SimpleDataFormat class in the java.text package. This concrete class is able to convert a date object into a string, using a template to indicate the structure. This template is specific to the formatting of dates and times; thus it has its own set of symbols that are parsed by the SimpleDateFormat class. These symbols include:

Symbol		*Example*
y	year	1999
M	month in year	11
d	day in month	10
h	hour in am/pm (1–12)	12
H	hour in day (0–23)	20
m	minute in hour	15
s	second in minute	57

Thus the strings:

"yyyy.MM.dd", "dd.MM.yyyy" and "MM.dd.yyyy"

all represent different ways of specifying a date in days, months and years. These different formats can be added to properties files to indicate the way in which the date should be formatted for a particular locale. This string can then be used in the following manner:

```
SimpleDateFormat sdf = new SimpleDateFormat ("dd.MM.yyyy");
Date date = new Date();
String dateString = sdf.format(date);
System.out.println(dateString);
In this case the result is:
12.01.2000
```

27.6 Summary

Java provides extensive, although low-level, support that allows developers to internationalize their programs by specializing them for different world locations. These facilities are provided by the Locale class, the ResourceBundle classes and the text formatting facilities found in the java.text package.

27.7 Online References

You can find a full list of the ISO language codes at:

http://www.ics.uci.edu/pub/ietf/http/related/iso639.txt

You can find a full list of valid ISO country codes at:

http://www.chemie.fu-berlin.de/diverse/doc/ISO_3166.html

Chapter 28

The CUTting Edge

28.1 Introduction

Being able to cut and paste between different applications is a fundamental feature of today's desktop. Any applications that wish to be taken seriously should be able to support at least cut and paste style operations if not drag and drop style behaviour. For example, I expect to be able to cut or copy text to the system clipboard from one editor and paste it into another. For example, I often copy Java source from my programming editor and paste it into Word (and vice versa). Any Java text editor should allow me to do the same!

Being able to transfer data to and from the system clipboard requires the ability either to present the data in a standard format (or formats) or to be able to extract data in a standard format (or formats). For example, if I copy a diagram from my Visio application, I expect to be able to paste it into Word or AutoCad or any other appropriate application and for that application to carry out any conversion that is necessary. In the case of copying text between Word or a programming editor into an editor implemented in Java, not only must the Java editor be able to obtain the text in a format it can cope with, but also it may need to convert it into Unicode (essentially a superset of ASCII).

The ability to drag something and drop it where you want it to be used is not new. However, although it is related to the concept of cut (or copy) and paste it is somewhat more automatic. That is, the operation starts when the user starts to *drag* a component and terminates when the component is *dropped* onto some target component. This means that it is the action of the user that triggers off the drag operation and terminates it. The end result is that it is necessary to plug a draggable component into the Java drag and drop framework. In turn, the drop target for the dragged component also needs to be plugged into this framework.

In Java the end result is that we have two architectures which, although related, are different. The first, referred to as data transfer, handles transferring data to and from the system clipboard. The second, referred to as drag and drop, handles that type of operation. In the remainder of this column we will look at these two different architectures and develop a simple editor that incorporates cut and paste as well as drag and drop functionality.

28.2 The Simple Editor

The simple editor class provides a simple editor that can create new text and load and save text, html and RTF documents (as it uses the JEditorPane class to display text). The JEditorPane class is one of the Swing graphical components. It is useful as it can render plain text, text marked up using HTML or text formatted using RTF (Rich Text Format). The basic editor is presented in Figure 28.1. As we are not interested directly in how we implement the editor functions we will merely focus on the data transfer style operations.

28.3 Cutting and Copying Data

We shall first look at the way in which we copy or cut data and place it on the system clipboard. This is supported by a variety of classes and interfaces in the java.datatransfer package. We must first get hold of the data to be cut (or copied). In the case of our editor we shall implement a copy method which will copy the whole contents of the JEditorPane to the clipboard. This is done by using the getText() method of the JEditorPane, which returns a string representing the text currently being displayed. Having done this we need to obtain a reference to the underlying operating system's clipboard. This is done by obtaining a reference to the current toolkit object. This can be done from any java.awt.Component object (that is, any subclass of this class). As the copy method will be implemented inside the Editor class (which is a direct subclass of JFrame) we can obtain the Toolkit object from the Editor object itself.

The Toolkit (or in actual fact a subclass of the abstract java.awt.Toolkit class) is used, among other things, to provide a direct link to the native windowing system. As such it is able to obtain a reference to the native windowing systems clipboard. This reference is returned to a Java program wrapped up within a Clipboard object. A clipboard object acts as a local proxy and translates any operations between the Java program and the underlying native clipboard without the Java program needing to know which native windowing system is being used.

Having got hold of the toolkit we now need to package the string we obtained from the JEditorPane into a format which can be presented to the clipboard. Part of the issue here is that, depending on what is going to receive the data to be copied, we could present this data in different formats. For example, if the application that receives this data is a Java application, then we could provide it as a serialized Java object. However, we could also provide it as an array of UTF characters or even (if we know it is being passed to another JEditorPane) wrapped within a "document" object which maintains any formatting information. We cannot guarantee what the receiving application will be (it could be Word or it could be a text editor, such as UltraEdit); therefore we cannot assume anything. Instead, we should wrap our text up in different formats, so that the receiving application can select the most appropriate format for that data. These different formats can be ordered so that the format that maintains the most information is presented first, while that which is most generic (that is, maintains least information) is presented last. For example, in our case we might wrap our text up such that the formats it can be converted to are ordered as follows:

- Serialized Java string
- UTF-based character array

The different formats are referred to as DataFlavors (i.e. the data being presented has different flavours through which it can be accessed). The simpler the format the more like a vanilla flavour it is; the more richly featured, the more the flavour can contain (such as raspberry ripple).

Transferable objects are used to wrap an object up with the various flavours in which it can be represented. Transferable is actually an interface in the java.awt.datatransfer package. It defines three methods:

- Object getTransferData(DataFlavor flavor) Returns an object which represents the data to be transferred using the data flavour specified.
- DataFlavor[] getTransferDataFlavors() Returns an array of DataFlavor objects indicating the flavours the data can be provided in.
- Boolean isDataFlavorSupported(DataFlavor flavor) Used to indicate whether a particular data flavour is supported or not.

To transfer data within the cut and paste (or drag and drop) framework, you need to wrap it up within a Transferable object. To simplify this process for strings a class StringSelection is provided in the java.datatransfer package. This class implements the Transferable interface and therefore provides a transferable wrapper for strings that can be passed to and from the clipboard (or between components using drag and drop). As such it can support Java strings either as serialized objects or as UTF-based character arrays. In terms of precedence, the serialized Java string object has the higher priority.

Once we have this string selection object we can place it on the system clipboard. When we do this we need to specify a clipboard listener (which in this case will be the editor itself). The complete copy method is presented below:

```java
public void copy() {
    Clipboard clip = getToolkit().getSystemClipboard();
    StringSelection ss = new StringSelection(tx.getText());
    clip.setContents(ss, this);
}
```

A clipboard listener implements a method that acts as a callback method that is called when the data just placed on the clipboard is replaced by new data. The clipboard listener can then take some action if it requires, such as releasing its internal reference to this data. In our case we will merely print out a message to indicate that the editor has lost "control" of the clipboard. For simplicity's sake, we shall make our editor implement the ClipboardOwner interface; thus it will need to implement the lostOwnership method. The class definition for the editor will need to be modified such that the data transfer package is imported and the class implements the ClipboardOwner interface:

```java
import java.awt.datatransfer.*;

// Must implement ClipboardOwner for copy operation
public class Edit extends JFrame implements ClipboardOwner {
```

The Edit class must then implement the lostOwnership method of the ClipboardOwner interface. This is illustrated below:

```java
public void lostOwnership(Clipboard c, Transferable t) {
    System.out.println("Lost clipboard");
}
```

Once we have added a button to act as the trigger for the copy operation (using an ActionListener event handler) we will be able to copy text from the JEditorPane and place it on the system clipboard.

28.4 Pasting Data

Having implemented a copy method, the next thing we shall do is implement a paste method. This method is a little more complex than the copy method we have just looked at. It still needs to obtain a reference to the system clipboard in the same way as the copy method did. However, this time we then get hold of the contents of the clipboard. The contents of the clipboard will be any data that has been copied there from any application. It could therefore be a graphic element, it could be text from a word processor or it could be the text we copied using our own copy method. As we have no way of knowing where the data came from, it is presented to the paste method wrapped inside a `Transferable` object.

We can obtain information about the ways in which the data on the clipboard can be presented to our program by asking the `Transferable` object for the list of data flavours supported (note the spelling of flavours in the listing!). A `DataFlavor` is an object that represents a particular format in which data can be presented, an example of which is the `String` flavor.

Our `paste` method obtains the array of all data flavours and presents them to the user (this is really to illustrate that the data will be available in one or more formats). In our `paste` method, we choose the format that presents the data as a string. This is done by testing to see whether the object is really an instance of the class `String`. If it is, then the paste method places that string into the `JEditorPane`. Note that we could merely have asked for the string format of the transferable data object directly (as was mentioned earlier there are methods both to check that the transferable object supports a particular data flavour and to return the data using that data flavour).

Once we have implemented the `paste` method we can provide another method that will trigger the `paste` method using an appropriate `ActionListener` event handler. The final result is illustrated in Figure 28.1.

The `paste` method is presented below:

```java
public void paste() {
    Clipboard clip = getToolkit().getSystemClipboard();
    Transferable trans = clip.getContents(this);
    DataFlavor [] flavors = trans.getTransferDataFlavors();
    for (int i = 0; i < flavors.length; i++) {
        try {
            Object o = trans.getTransferData(flavors[i]);
            System.out.println("Flavor " + i +
                    " gives " + o.getClass().getName());
```

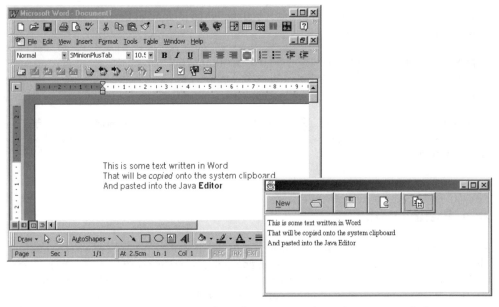

Fig. 28.1 The last two buttons on the toolbar are copy and paste buttons respectively.

```
      if (o instanceof String) {
        tx.setText((String)o);
      }
    } catch (Exception exp) {exp.printStackTrace(); }
  }
}
```

28.5 Drag and Drop

We will now consider how drag and drop functionality can be added to our simple editor. To do this we are going to need to define two new classes. One will act as the source of the drag action (i.e. the point at which the user starts to drag some graphical component). The second class will act as the target of the drag action (or the component over which the user will "drop" the dragged component). Our two classes will be DragLabel (which will be the draggable component) and DropTextArea (which will act as the drop target object). Within our editor we will modify the user interface such that the JEditorPane is replaced by the DropTextArea (this is actually a subclass of JEditorPane). We will also give our editor a palette from which the user will be able to drag various Java keywords onto the text area displayed, thus saving the user from repeatedly typing the same Java keywords (see Figure 28.2 for a diagram illustrating the overall structure of our application).

28.5.1 DragLabel

We will first consider the drag component. This component, the DragLabel, is a direct subclass of the swing JLabel class. It thus has all the same functionality as a label, plus the ability to be involved in a drag event. To do this it needs to follow these steps:

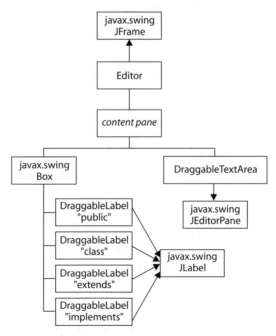

Fig. 28.2 The structure of the drag and drop editor.

1. A DragGestureListener must be implemented.
2. A DragSource object must be created.
3. A link between the object to be copied and the type of drag action must be specified and a link to the DragGestureListener must be created,
4. The listener method must initiate the actual copy.

These steps are considered in more detail below.

The DragGestureListener interface specifies a single method dragGestureRecognized-(DragGestureEvent e). This method is called when a drag event is to be started. It is this method which will start the drag operation and result in some visual feedback to the user (for example, the icon used by the cursor can be set to an appropriate platform-specific copy or icon). In our example, this is done in the following Java statement:

```
dragSource.startDrag(e, DragSource.DefaultCopyDrop, text, null);
```

The startDrag method takes the initiating event as the first parameter. The type of cursor to be used to indicate that the drag action has been started is the second parameter. The Transferable object to be passed to the drop target (in our case we are using a StringSelection object, as described earlier) is presented as the third parameter and optionally a DragSourceListener (which in our case we do not implement) is the fourth parameter (i.e. null).

The DragLabel, in order to be draggable, must register itself with a drag source object. A drag source object is responsible for initiating a drag action (referred to as a gesture within the terminology of Java's drag and drop). As this is used in a number of places we store it in an instance variable.

To register the object we need to specify that this component is the component to be dragged, what type of action is to be performed (we will assume a move action; others include copy and link – see the java.awt.dnd.DndConstants class) and the object to be used as the DragGestureListener. This is done in the constructor, so that whenever a DragLabel is created it will be available for drag and drop.

The complete listing for the DragLabel is presented below:

```
import javax.swing.*;
import java.awt.*;
import java.awt.datatransfer.*;
import java.awt.dnd.*;

public class DragLabel extends JLabel implements DragGestureListener {

    DragSource dragSource new DragSource();;

    public DragLabel(String s) {
        super(s);
            dragSource = dragSource.createDefaultDragGestureRecognizer(
                    this,  // component to be dragged
                    DnDConstants.ACTION_MOVE,
                    this); // dragGestureListener
    }

    public void dragGestureRecognized(DragGestureEvent e) {
        StringSelection text = new StringSelection(getText());
```

```
            System.out.println("Starting drag element for " + getText());
            dragSource.startDrag(e, DragSource.DefaultCopyDrop, text, null);
        }
    }
```

28.5.2 DropTextArea

The DropTextArea is a class that will act as the drop target of a drag and drop action. In this case, this means that it will receive a DragLabel when a user releases the mouse, during a drag operation, when over the DropTextArea instance. To act as a drop target the DropTextArea must follow these steps:

1. Implement the DropTargetListener interface.
2. Register with an instance of the DropTarget class.
3. Ensure that the drop method (of the DropTaggetListener accepts or rejects the drop).

These steps are considered in more detail below.

The DropTargetListener interface (of the java.awt.dnd package) specifies five methods that are listed below (along with a description of when they are called):

- void dragEnter(DropTargetDragEvent event) A drag operation has encountered the DropTarget. This method must check to see that the operation specified when the drag action started is supported by this drop target. In our case this means ensuring that the action is a move action (as defined by the DnDConstants class). Otherwise the drag is rejected. As this test needs to be performed a number of times in different situations we will wrap it up into a private method called checkAction.
- void dragExit(DropTargetEvent event) The drag operation has departed the DropTarget without dropping. As we don't care what users do if they don't drop the component on this text area, we implement this method using a null body.
- void dragOver(DropTargetDragEvent event) A drag operation is ongoing on the DropTarget. As this method needs to check the same condition as the dragEnter operation (in our case) we will use the checkAction method defined earlier.
- void dropActionChanged(DropTargetDragEvent event) The user has modified the current drop gesture, possibly by pressing a modifying key such as Shift. Again we check the resulting action using the checkAction method.
- void drop(DropTargetDropEvent event) The drag operation has terminated with a drop on this DropTarget. We will consider this method in more detail below.

The drop method is where all the work is done in our case. It is the point at which the draggable object is presented to the drop target (i.e. the information provided by the DragLabel is presented to the DropTextArea). As such it is this method which will receive the transferable data that it must interpret and display as appropriate. To do this it must check that the action being attempted is supported by the component and that the transferable object can present its data in a format that the drop target can understand. In our case this means checking to see that the action is a move action, and that the data can be presented as a String. If both these conditions are met then the drop target accepts the drop event (otherwise the drop is rejected). It must then obtain the string from the transferable object and display it within the text area. Once it has done this, it needs to indicate that the drop event had been completed (using e.dropComplete(true)).

The source code for the DropTextArea is presented below:

```java
import javax.swing.*;
import java.awt.*;
import java.awt.datatransfer.*;
import java.awt.dnd.*;
public class DropTextPane extends JTextPane implements DropTargetListener {

    public DropTextPane() {
        // Set up this as a drop target
        // This is both the target component and the listener
        new DropTarget(this, this);
    }

    // Validation method to be used below
    private void checkAction(DropTargetDragEvent e) {
        int action = e.getDropAction();
        if (action == DnDConstants.ACTION_MOVE) {
            e.acceptDrag(action);
        } else {
            e.rejectDrag();
        }
    }

    public void dragEnter(DropTargetDragEvent e) { checkAction (e);   }
    public void dragOver(DropTargetDragEvent e) { checkAction (e);   }
    public void dragExit(DropTargetEvent e) { }
    public void dropActionChanged(DropTargetDragEvent e) { checkAction (e);  }

    public void drop(DropTargetDropEvent e) {
        int action = e.getDropAction();
        Transferable tr = e.getTransferable();
        if ((action == DnDConstants.ACTION_MOVE) ||
                tr.isDataFlavorSupported(DataFlavor.stringFlavor)) {
            e.acceptDrop(action);
            try {
                String s = (String)tr.getTransferData(DataFlavor.stringFlavor);
                setText(getText() + s);
                e.dropComplete(true);
            } catch (Exception exp) {  e.rejectDrop(); }
        } else {
            e.rejectDrop();
        }
    }
}
```

The result of adding a Box container to the left-hand side of the editor containing a set of DragLabels is illustrated in Figure 28.3. Note that a Box is very similar to a Panel with a FlowLayout, except that the box can display components in either the *x* or the *y*-axis.

In Figure 28.3 the original JEditorPane has been replaced by a DropTextArea. The user now drags the syntax keywords they are interested in onto the text area and they are automatically added.

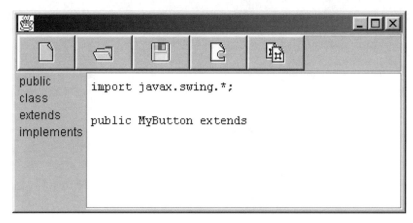

Fig. 28.3 The drag and drop editor. The draggable labels can be used to add syntax words directly into the text area without the need for extensive typing.

28.6 Summary

The cut and paste and drag and drop features of Java 2 are very easy to use and work well with the host platforms (although note that the cut and paste operations do not work with OpenWindows!). They allow users to integrate their Java applications with other applications as well as providing sophisticated user interaction. As Java is platform-independent the same behaviour can be provided on multiple platforms without the need to learn different APIs.

Part **6**

Internet Working

Chapter 29

Sockets in Java

29.1 Introduction

A "socket" is an end point in a communication link between separate processes. In Java, sockets are objects which provide a way of exchanging information between two processes in a straightforward and platform-independent manner (see the classes in the java.net package).

29.2 Socket to socket communication

When two processes wish to communicate they can do so via sockets. Each process has a socket which is connected to the other's socket. One process can then write information out to the socket, while the second process can read information back in from their socket. To achieve this the streams model, already used for file access, is exploited. Associated with each socket are two streams: one for input and one for output. Thus to pass information from one process to another, you write that information out to the output stream of one socket and read it from the input stream of another socket (assuming the two sockets are connected). This is illustrated in Figure 29.1. This has the great advantage that once the network connection has been made, passing information between processes is not significantly different from reading and writing information with any other stream.

29.3 Setting Up a Connection

To set up the connection, one process must be running a program that is waiting for a connection while the other must try to reach the first. The first is referred to as a server socket while the second is known just as a socket.

For the second process to connect to the first (the server socket) it must know what machine the first is running on and which port it is connected to. A port number is a logical point of communication on a computer. Port numbers in the TCP/IP system are 16 bit numbers in the range 0–65535 (a description of TCP/IP is beyond the scope of this book; see Parker (1994) for further information). Generally, port numbers below 1024 are reserved for pre-defined services (which means that you should avoid using them unless you wish to communicate with one of those, services such as telnet, SMTP mail or ftp).

For example, in Figure 29.1 the server socket connects to port 5432. In turn, the client socket connects to the machine on which the server is executing and then to port number 5432 on that machine. Nothing happens until the server socket accepts the connection. At that point the sockets are connected and the socket streams are bound to each other.

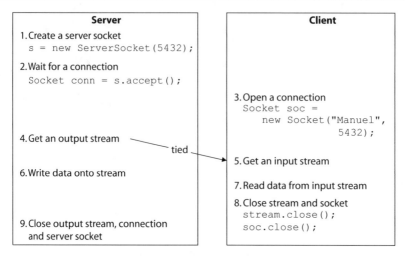

Fig. 29.1 Socket to socket communication.

29.4 An Example Client–Server Application

29.4.1 The System Structure

Figure 29.2 illustrates the basic structure of the system we are trying to build. There will be a server object running on one machine and a client object running on another. The client will connect up to the server using sockets in order to obtain information.

The actual application being implemented is an address book. The addresses of employees of a company are held in a hash table. This hash table is set up in the Server's constructor, but could equally be held in a database etc.

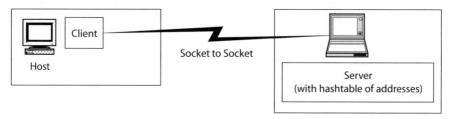

Figure 29.2 The simple client–server application.

29.4.2 Implementing the Server Application

We shall describe the server application first. This is the Java application program that will service requests from client applets for information. To do this it must provide a server socket for clients to connect to. Listing 29.1 presents the annotated source code for the Server class.

Listing 29.1 The server application.

```
import java.net.*;
import java.io.*;
```

```java
import java.util.*;

public class Server {
  // Instance variable to hold names and addresses
  private Hashtable addressTable;

  // Main method to start the erver application
  public static void main (String args []) {
    Server s = new Server();
    s.start();
  }

  public Server() {
    // Set up names and addresses
    addressTable = new Hashtable(10);
    addressTable.put("John", "C45");
    addressTable.put("Denise", "C44");
    addressTable.put("Phoebe", "B52");
    addressTable.put("Isobel", "E23");
  }

  public void start() {
    // Set up the server socket
    ServerSocket serverSocket = null;
    Socket socket;
    InputStream socketIn;
    OutputStream socketOut;
    DataInputStream dataInputStream;
    DataOutputStream dataOutputStream;
    ObjectInputStream objectInputStream;
    ObjectOutputStream objectOutputStream;

    // Register service on port 1234
    try {
      serverSocket = new ServerSocket(1234);
    } catch (IOException e) {System.out.println("Server socket
      registration failed");}

    // Wait for a connection from a client
    while (true) {
      try {
        // Wait here and listen for a connection
        socket = serverSocket.accept();
        socketIn = socket.getInputStream();
        dataInputStream = new DataInputStream(socketIn);
        objectInputStream = new ObjectInputStream(dataInputStream);
        String queryString = (String)objectInputStream.readObject();

        // Now obtain information from addressTable
        // need to cast the result ot a string as Object is returned
        // by default.
```

```
                String result = (String)addressTable.get(queryString);

                // Return information to client
                // Get a communications stream from the socket
                socketOut = socket.getOutputStream();
                dataOutputStream = new DataOutputStream(socketOut);
                objectOutputStream = new ObjectOutputStream(dataOutputStream);
                objectOutputStream.writeObject(result);

                // Now close the connections, but not the server socket
                dataInputStream.close();
                dataOutputStream.close();
                socketIn.close();
                socketOut.close();
                socket.close();
            } catch (IOException e) {
                System.out.println("Error during socket communications: " +
                    e.getMessage());
                  e.printStackTrace();
            } catch (ClassNotFoundException e) {
                System.out.println("Error reading object in from socket: " +
                    e.getMessage());
                  e.printStackTrace();
            }
        }
      }
    }
```

Essentially the Server in Listing 29.1 sets up the addressTable to contain a Hashtable of the names and addresses available. It then waits for a client to connect to it. This is done by creating a serverSocket (in this case on port 1234). It then enters a loop where it continually waits for connections, processes requests and waits for the next connection. When the connection is made, it uses the input stream of its socket to obtain the information provided by the client. Note that although this is a socket to socket communication, as streams are used the way to pass an object is exactly the same as writing that object out to a file. Thus serialization is used to pass the string between the two processes (remember that a Java string is an object). It then queries the addressTable and returns the result (again using serialization to write the string to the output stream). Having done all this it closes its connection to the socket. It is now ready for the next query. As you can see from this, the program is actually very straightforward. This is thanks primarily to the Java ServerSocket and Stream classes which hide a great deal of the implementation details often associated with socket communications.

29.4.3 Implementing the Client Application

The client application is essentially a very simple program that creates a link to the server application. To do this it creates a socket that connects to the server's host machine, and in our case this socket is connected to port 1234. It then uses an object output stream to pass a string to the server. Having done that, it waits for the server to provide a response. The response is the result of query the database for the address associated with the supplied name. This is then printed out with an appropriate message.

The annotated source code for the Client applet is presented in Listing 29.2.

Listing 29.2 The Client applet.

```java
import java.net.*;
import java.io.*;

public class Client {

  public static void main (String args []) {
    String query = null;
    if (args.length == 0) {
      System.out.println("Usage: java Client <name>");
    } else {
      query = args[0];
    }

    try {
      // First get a socket connection to the Server object
      Socket socket = new Socket("jhunthome", 1234);
      OutputStream outputStream = socket.getOutputStream();
      DataOutputStream dataOutputStream = new
          DataOutputStream(outputStream);
      ObjectOutputStream objectOutputStream = new
          ObjectOutputStream(dataOutputStream);
      // Now send a query requesting the required information
      objectOutputStream.writeObject(query);

      // New get the response
      InputStream inputStream = socket.getInputStream();
      DataInputStream dataInputStream = new DataInputStream(inputStream);
      ObjectInputStream objectInputStream = new
          ObjectInputStream(dataInputStream);

      String results = (String)objectInputStream.readObject();

      // Once we get the result - print it out
      if (results == null) {
        System.out.println("No address is held for " + query);
      } else {
        System.out.println("Address for " + query + " is : ");
        System.out.println(results);
      }

      dataOutputStream.close();
      dataInputStream.close();
      outputStream.close();
      inputStream.close();
      socket.close();

    } catch (IOException e) {
```

```
        System.out.println("Error during socket communications: " +
            e.getMessage());
        e.printStackTrace();
    } catch (ClassNotFoundException e) {
        System.out.println("Error reading object in from socket: " +
            e.getMessage());
        e.printStackTrace();
    }
  }
}
```

An example of using the client to query the server is presented below:

```
C:\jjh\JAVA\chap30>java chap30.Client James
No address is held for James
C:\jjh\JAVA\chap30>java chap30.Client Phoebe
Address for Phoebe is :
B52
```

Chapter 30

Applets and the Internet

30.1 Introduction

Java burst on to the computer scene back in 1995. At this time, it looked unlikely that any new programming language could become as influential as Java has within a few years. However, Java had an ace up its sleeve. This ace was not that it was a pure object-oriented language, nor was it that it compiled to an intermediate form which could run, without recompilation, on different platforms. Rather, it was that it could be used with the rapidly growing Internet to produce programs which could run within a Web browser (such as Netscape Navigator or Internet Explorer). The first Web browser to show this was HotJava, which was also written in Java. The fact that it could run Web pages caught people's imagination and the rest, as they say, is history.

A Java applet is a program which can run within a Web browser (or the JDK appletviewer) as illustrated in Figure 30.1. That is all that it is. That "all" hides a lot, as anyone who has attempted to build Web systems in C, CGI scripts, TCP/IP etc. can tell you. From the point of view of constructing applications, Java applets hide issues such as communications protocols and

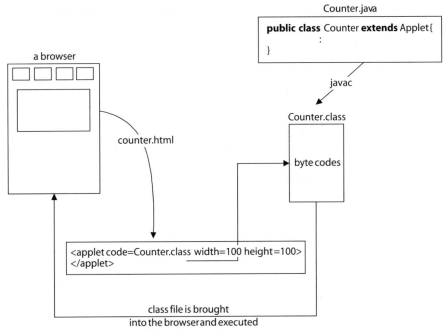

Fig. 30.1 Loading an applet into a browser.

hardware platforms from you. You are concerned only with constructing useful, reliable, maintainable applications (which just happen to run within a Web browser).

The name "applet" originally signified a small program which should be run within a larger program (such as a Web browser), in much the way that a piglet indicates a small pig. However, there is no reason why an applet should be particularly small, just as there is no reason why an application should be particularly large. Indeed, numerous applets are now being implemented which are large applications in their own right. They are merely applets because their users access them via a Web browser (either locally or remotely).

The primary class which makes applets possible is the Applet class, which is a subclass of Panel. This in itself tells you something about the way in which an applet operates (but we come back to that later).

The Applet class must be the superclass of any class which acts as the root for an application which is to be accessed by a Web browser or the JDK appletviewer. This is because it provides a standard interface between the application and its operating environment which allows the parent application to provide information to and obtain information from the applet (and vice versa).

30.2 Applet Security

Applets differ from applications in another important respect. Applets have far less access to the host environment than applications. This is to provide some degree of protection against rogue applets (you may be welcoming programs written by someone else onto your machine – you don't want them tampering with your environment).

There have been a number of security scares over applets and Web browsers; however, these tend to be due to limitations in the Web browsers' implementations of the Java security model. The security model is quite straightforward: *applets are not allowed to do anything which may harm your host environment.* This means that applets cannot access your local file store, run local programs, access information about the host machine or communicate with other machines (other than the server from which they were downloaded).

In some cases, applets have slightly more access. If an applet is loaded into a browser using the load local file option, rather than over the Internet, it can connect to other hosts, load Java libraries and find out information about the user.

The JDK appletviewer can also execute applets. The appletviewer mimics the behaviour of a Web browser when running an applet. However, it allows significantly greater permission to the applets. In fact, the only difference between an application and an applet running in the appletviewer is that the applet cannot delete a file (see Table 30.1).

Applets may be signed, which means that the supplier of the applet is registered along with the applet. If you trust the supplier, you can give the applet greater freedom. Signed applets have proved invaluable to organizations wishing to make use of Java for distributed solutions to applications as diverse as MIS and Computer-Aided Engineering (within an organizational intranet).

30.3 The Applet Class

Figure 30.2 illustrates the inheritance hierarchy from Object. Applets can contain graphic components and containers, redraw themselves, and operate inside a containing object.

The fact that applets are a subclass of Panel provides the key to the way in which they are used. In essence, the encapsulating application (e.g. Netscape) acts as the frame within which

Table 30.1 Applet and application permissions.

Operation	Remote	Local	Appletviewer	Application
Read local file	No	No	Yes	Yes
Write local file	No	No	Yes	Yes
Obtain file information	No	No	Yes	Yes
Delete file	No	No	No	Yes
Run local executable	No	No	Yes	Yes
Load Java library	No	Yes	Yes	Yes
Call exit	No	No	Yes	Yes
Connect to other host	No	Yes	Yes	Yes

Fig. 30.2 The Applet inheritance hierarchy.

the applet displays. If you think of the Web browser as providing the subclass of Frame within which your applet displays, you begin to understand how they operate.

A consequence of this is that applets do not need to define a main method (indeed if they do, then it is ignored when running under a Web browser). Instead, a series of messages are sent by the encapsulating application to the applet (the browser – applet protocol illustrated in Figure 30.3). These messages trigger various methods, the most important of which is the init method. Others include the start, stop and destroy methods (the sequence of messages between the browser and the applet is illustrated in Figure 30.3).

- void init()
  The browser sends the init message to the applet once it has constructed the applet and completed the background work. The init method should carry out all initialization, because an applet cannot link to other objects or generate graphic displays until it has been created, for security reasons.

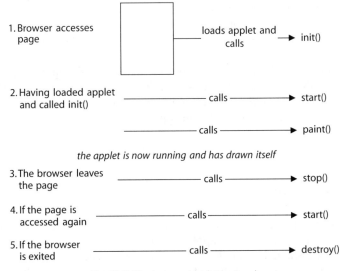

Fig. 30.3 The browser/applet protocol.

- void start()
  After sending the init message to the applet, the browser then sends it the start message. The start message is sent every time the user returns to the Web page containing the applet. Thus the start method may execute more than once. You should, therefore, place code which should only be run once in the init method, and code which should be run every time the applet is started in the start method.
- void stop()
  The stop message is automatically sent to the applet whenever the user leaves the Web page containing the applet. Leaving a Web page does not terminate the applet; it merely suspends it. Anything which must be tidied up before the applet is suspended should be placed in the stop method.
- void destroy()
  The destroy message is sent to an applet when the browser terminates normally. You do not need to close the window (panel) in which the applet is running, as the browser does that. However, you can use the destroy method to tidy up any system resources your applet uses. If the applet is running when the user quits the browser, the stop method executes before the destroy method.

30.4 Working With Applets

The actual process of constructing a system to be run as an applet is not complex. I use the term "program" to refer to the Java code in order to avoid confusion between applets and applications.

1. The root class of the program must inherit from the Applet class.
2. It must then define the init method, which should define all elements of the program which need to be initialized once. This is the code which would have been placed in a constructor within a normal application.
3. You may need to select a layout manager. As Applet is a subclass of Panel, it uses the flow layout manager. If you wish to use a different layout (such as BorderLayout), you must set it. You can do this in the init method.
4. You may define the start, stop and destroy methods.
5. You must define a Web page to hold the applet using HTML (see Figure 30.1).

Once you have done these things you have done enough to run the applet. Of course, you still need to define what the applet does, but those definitions are the same as for any Java program. As Applet is a subclass of Panel, all the graphic and GUI classes and methods which you can use with a Panel are also available within an applet.

30.5 The Account Applet

You can develop an applet as an application first and then port it to an applet later. This can make the debugging and testing of the applet easier. It is certainly a useful way to illustrate the differences between a standalone application and an applet. Therefore we amend the Account application presented earlier in this book to make it an applet, following these steps:

1. Make the root class inherit from `Applet` rather than `Frame`.
2. Remove the `WindowListener` interface and method definitions (applets cannot close themselves, so there is no reason to handle window-closing events).
3. Delete the `main` method.
4. Define an `init` method and move the contents of the constructor into it.
5. Set the layout manager to the border layout manager.
6. Delete the constructor.
7. Remove window resizing, visibility and title methods. An applet does not define its window title or its size. These operations are performed by the Web browser using parameters passed to it by the HTML on the initiating Web page.
8. Define an HTML file for the applet.

30.5.1 Change the Root Class Definition

We must change the parent class and remove the `WindowListener`.

```
import Java.applet.*;
import Java.awt.*;
import Java.util.Observable;
import Java.util.Observer;
public class AccountApplet extends Applet implements Observer {
  protected TextPanel textPanel;
  protected Account account = new Account(0.0);
  ... remainder of class definition ...
}
```

Compare this class definition with that presented in Chapter 23, and notice that we have also deleted the links to the Exit button and the Exit button controller. They have no meaning for the applet. We have also changed the name of the root class from `AccountInterface` to `AccountApplet`, just to avoid confusion. Finally, in order to inherit from the `Applet` class, we have imported the `java.applet` package.

30.5.2 Define the `init` Method

We must move the contents of the constructor into this method. We have removed the references to the Exit button and its controller. We have also removed the `setTitle`, `addWindowListener(this)`, `setSize(180, 140)` and `setVisible(true)` calls. Thus, the `init` method is quite a bit smaller than the original constructor:

```
public void init () {
  /* Add the interface as an observer of the account */

  account.addObserver(this);
  /* Specify layout manager as flow is the default */

  setLayout( new BorderLayout());

  /* Create the Button panel object and
     its controller */
  ButtonPanel buttonPanel = new ButtonPanel(this);
```

```
    add("North", buttonPanel);
    /* Next set up the text panel */

    textPanel = new TextPanel();
    add("Center", textPanel);
}
```

In the above method, we have set the layout manager as suggested earlier. We can delete the empty constructor and the methods implementing the WindowListener interface (such as WindowClosed and windowClosing). We have now done enough to run this program as an applet. You must execute the appletviewer on the HTML file:

```
C: >appletviewer account.HTML
```

Figure 30.4 shows the result in the JDK appletviewer.

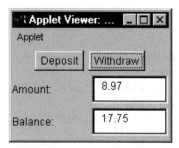

Fig. 30.4 Running the Account applet.

30.6 A Brief Introduction to HTML

One area which was ignored above is the definition of a Web page within which to run the applet. You do this using the HyperText Markup Language (HTML), which tells a Web browser how to lay out a Web page. The basics of the language are quite straightforward, although the language as a whole is quite large. Essentially, an HTML page is made up of the following parts:

- A title, indicated by <title> some text </title>.
- A body, indicated by <body> some text </body>.

Notice that the keywords used in HTML have a starting element and an ending element. Thus whatever is being laid out is surrounded by two keywords (or tags). Some tags merely indicate a particular feature, for example:

- <p> tells the browser to start a new paragraph.
- <hr> tells the browser to insert a horizontal line.

A complete description of HTML is beyond the scope of this book. However, there are many books on HTML available and you should read one of them for further information.

30.7 The `<applet>` HTML Tag

The `<applet>` tag is an extension to the original HTML. However, almost all browsers available today support it. Browsers created before the advent of Java are programmed to ignore tags they do not understand.

The `<applet>` tag allows you to specify which class to run, the size and position of the applet, the data to pass into the applet, and some text to display if the browser does not understand the tag. The applet tag has the following basic format:

```
<applet code=classfile width=pixels height=pixels
    ... optional applet information>
</applet>
```

Table 30.2 Mandatory `<applet>` tag fields.

Field	Description
code	Specifies the name of the file containing the root applet class, which should be in the same directory as the HTML file. As an alternative, you can specify an object field.
object	Specifies the name of the file that contains a serialized representation of an applet. The applet is deserialized. The init method is not invoked, but the start method is. This is because before the applet could be serialized, it must have been initialized, started and then stopped. As an alternative, you can specify a code field.
width	Specifies the width, in pixels, of the applet.
height	Specifies the height, in pixels, of the applet.

The field names can be in upper case or lower case; thus WIDTH is equivalent to width.

We now know enough to look at the HTML file that defines the Web page containing the Account applet (in a file called Account.HTML):

```
<HTML>
<title>Account Applet</title>
<body>
<applet code="AccountApplet.class"
        width=180 height=100>
</applet>
</body>
</HTML>
```

This specifies that the Web browser (or appletviewer) should run the applet defined in the AccountApplet.class file. Notice that we specify the byte-encoded compiled version, rather than the .java file. This means that any language which can be compiled into Java byte codes can be accessed in this way. The applet is displayed in a window 180 pixels wide by 100 pixels high.

The HTML `<applet>` tag provides a range of optional fields which provide additional information for the applet or the Web browser. In the following full syntax description, required elements are in bold, optional elements are in regular typeface, and elements you specify are in italics:

```
<APPLET
   CODEBASE = codebaseURL
   ARCHIVE = archiveList
   CODE = appletFile    or   OBJECT = serializedApplet
   ALT = alternateText
```

```
    NAME = appletInstanceName
    WIDTH = pixels  HEIGHT = pixels
    ALIGN = alignment
    VSPACE = pixels  HSPACE = pixels
 >
 <PARAM NAME = appletAttribute1 VALUE = value>
 <PARAM NAME = appletAttribute2 VALUE = value>
    ...
 alternateHTML
 </APPLET>
```

These fields are described in Table 30.3.

Table 30.3 Optional applet tag fields.

Field	Description
CODEBASE	Specifies the base URL, i.e. the directory that contains the applet's code. If it is not specified, then the document's URL is used.
ARCHIVE	Describes one or more archives, containing classes and other resources, that are "preloaded".
ALT	Specifies any text that should be displayed if the browser understands the applet tag but cannot run Java applets.
NAME	Specifies a name for the applet instance, which makes it possible for applets on the same page to find (and communicate with) each other.
ALIGN	Specifies the alignment of the applet (left, right, top, middle, baseline and bottom).
VSPACE	Specifies the number of pixels above and below the applet.
HSPACE	Specifies the number of pixels on each side of the applet.
<PARAM NAME ...>	Specifies an applet-specific attribute.
alternateHTML	Specifies text which is used instead of the applet, if the Web browser does not understand the applet tag. This text can use other HTML tags.

Applets access their attributes with the getParameter method. Parameters always return their values as strings. For example, if the HTML file includes the following tag:

```
<PARAM NAME=pictureSize VALUE="100">
```

the applet can access this information in the following manner:

```
int size = Integer.parseInt(getParameter("pictureSize"));
```

We have to use the class-side parseInt method to convert the string "100" to the integer 100. If the parameter name, pictureSize, had been omitted, the value null would have been returned. Also note that parameter names are case-sensitive; you must use exactly the same case to get the value.

30.8 Accessing HTML Files

Although it is outside the scope of this book, and many of you are already familiar with Web browsers, this section introduces the concept of a Uniform Resource Locator (URL) . A URL

Table 30.4 The structure of a URL.

Section	Example
Scheme	`http:`
Separator	`//`
Computer name	`www`
Domain name	`jaydeetee.co.uk`
Path to the file	`/JavaBook/chap30/Account.HTML`

consists of the address of a file on the Internet and a scheme for interpreting that file (Table 30.4). The particular scheme of interest for HTML files is the HyperText Transfer Protocol (HTTP). For example, to access the HTML file described above, you might provide a URL such as the following:

```
http://www.jaydeetee.co.uk/JavaBook/chap30/Account.HTML
```

You can access HTML files locally, by replacing the `http:` scheme with the `file:` scheme and omitting the Internet address. For example, if the file is on the C drive of your PC you might access it by specifying the following URL:

```
file:///c:/users/jjh/JavaBook/chap30/Account.HTML
```

30.9 Swing and Applets

The Swing set of components provides a Swing version of an applet called a `JApplet`. It is very similar to the `Applet` class except that it has a `BorderLayout` by default rather than a `FlowLayout`. It also has a `ContentPane` in a similar way to the `JFrame`.

30.10 Exercise: Tic-Tac-Toe Applet

The aim of this exercise is to write a very simple Tic-Tac-Toe (or Noughts and Crosses) applet.

30.10.1 What to Do

The applet should place an X or an O in a square depending on which turn should be made. To keep things simple it is assumed that this is a two-player game in which the applet merely displays the result of each move. It is up to the players to identify a win situation. (Note that if you use the `JButton` class from the Swing components then you could use icons for the Xs and Os). An example of what the display should look like is presented in Figure 30.5.

The HTML used to run the applet is:

```
<applet code=TicTacToe.class width=160 height=120>
</applet>
```

You should not try to do anything complicated.

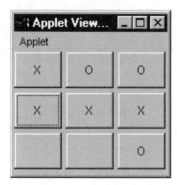

Fig. 30.5 The Tic-Tac-Toe applet.

You need to respond to a mouse click and then to place an X or an O in the appropriate location. You could this using a MouseListener and the paint() method. However, the above example actually makes use of the Button class and the GridLayout manager to do the work.

30.10.2 Notes

If you use the approach I used then the following may be useful for you to know:

1.   Use an ActionListener
2.   You can change the label on a button using the setLabel(<string>) method.
3.   The GridLayout manager has a constructor which takes four arguments: the first two are the size of the grid and the second two are the horizontal and vertical gap.

30.11 Summary

This chapter has illustrated how applets can be defined within Java. It has also shown how they can be accessed via a Web browser or the appletviewer. It also considered how Java applets can access resources on the Internet via URLs.

Applets open up a huge potential for applications which would have been too difficult to contemplate only a short time ago (except by the dedicated and knowledgeable few).

30.12 Further Reading

You may wish to delve further into HTML and TCP/IP as well as Java applets. There are many books on HTML available, including Scharf (1995).

TCP/IP stands for Transmission Control Protocol/Internet Protocol. TCP uses IP as its underlying protocol for routing and delivering information to the correct address. TCP takes care of creating, managing and closing the end-to-end connection which exists during the transfer of information. FTP (File Transfer Protocol) uses TCP, which in turn supports HTTP. A good book to start with on TCP/IP is Parker (1994).

There is a wide range of books which consider applets in great detail. Indeed, the majority of books on Java concentrate on applets. Cornell and Horstmann (1997) provide some excellent examples without becoming applet-obsessed.

Chapter *31*

Servlets: Serving Java up on the Web

31.1 Introduction

Java has primarily been a language used to implement browser-side programs, also known as applets, when it comes to the Web. However, with the Java Servlet API, the power of Java can be applied to server-side software as well as to the client-side (browser) software. This chapter tells you how servlets are written, what they are used for and how they interact with browser requests.

Just as applets are (at least conceptually) small applications, in the same way as a piglet is a little pig, Servlets are programs that run on the Web server. Of course, just as with applets, the size of a servlet is not restricted and it may be anything from a few lines of code to many thousands (or more) lines of code.

The key is that a servlet runs on the server and will respond to requests from a client either from HTML pages or indeed from applets. Thus a servlet is used in situations where CGI (Common Gateway Interface) scripts might be used. These scripts are more often than not implemented in Perl (a scripting language) and sometimes in C. So why should you write a servlet in Java rather than write a Perl script? The primary reasons are that:

- Java is a high-level language with very many good software engineering features. In contrast, Perl is a difficult language to write, can be hard to comprehend and is certainly difficult to maintain. Ask anyone who has written a particularly difficult bit of Perl what that code does just a few days later. Many will find it hard to give you a detailed answer.
- Java code is platform-independent. Thus a servlet is platform-independent. In contrast, a Perl script (or indeed a C program) may well be platform-dependent.

Table 31.1 summarizes the contrast between servlets and CGI scripts. Essentially, servlets offer a great deal to the developer over Perl CGI scripts. For example, the Web server loads

Table 31.1 Comparison of CGI and servlets.

	CGI scripts	Servlets
Persistence	No	Yes
Speed	Lower	Higher
Platform	Specific	Independent
Extensible	Hard	Hey – it's just Java
Invocation	Possible	Only through server
Maintainability	Poor	Good
Comprehensibility	Poor	Good
Accessibility	Limited	Good

servlets only once. They can therefore maintain state and resources between multiple information requests. In contrast, CGI scripts are run each time they are called. They are thus transient
and cannot hold the system state.

31.2 How Servlets Work

The servlet life cycle is illustrated in Figure 31.1.

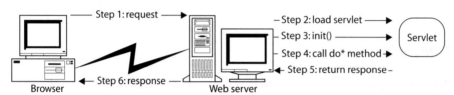

Fig. 31.1 Browser–server–servlet interaction.

- *Step 1*: A user using a Web browser requests some information from the Web server via an
  http request.
- *Step 2*: The Web server receives the request. If the request is for a straightforward HTML
  page then the appropriate HTML file will be loaded. If the request is to a servlet, then the
  servlet invoker will load and initiate the servlet (unless it was already running). This is
  done by running the servlet on a Java Virtual Machine (JVM).
- *Step 3*: The servlet's init() method is then executed. This method is the equivalent of the
  init() method defined for applets; that is, it is executed only once, when the servlet is
  first created. It should be used in the same way as the init() method for applets; that is, as
  the servlet's initialisation method (rather than defining a constructor). The init()
  method must complete before any requests are handled.
- *Step 4*: The servlet will receive the HTTP request and perform some type of process. Each
  request is handled by its own thread (lightweight Java process). Depending upon the request, one of the following methods will be called to handle the request:
  - doGet – handles GET, conditional GET and HEAD requests.
  - doPost – handles POST requests.
  - doPut – handles PUT requests.
  - doDelete – handles DELETE requests.
- *Step 5*: The servlet will return a response back to the Web server from one of the above
  methods.
- *Step 6*: The Web server will forward the response to the client.
- *Step 7*: When requested, the Web server will terminate the servlet. This may be done by the
  Web server administrator. At this time the destroy() method is called. This method runs
  only once and is used to "tidy" up any system resources used by the servlet etc. For the
  servlet to be run again, it must be reloaded by the Web server.

There are some things to note to note about servlets as opposed to applets.

Firstly, the servlet and its environment are completely under the control of those deploying
the servlet. That is, you have control of which JVM is used and that this is independent of the
browser used by the user. This is important, as it removes concerns associated with the so-
called "browser wars".

Secondly, a servlet is not constrained by the applet sandbox. This means that a servlet can reside behind a firewall and can communicate with any and all systems that it needs to. For example, JavaIDL can be used to connected to a CORBA-compliant Object Request Broker (ORB) or sockets to connect to legacy systems (for example implemented in C).

Thirdly, the client Web browser does not communicate directly with the servlet. Rather, the browser communicates with the Web server, which in turn communicates with the servlet. Thus if the Web server is secure behind a firewall, then the servlet is also secure.

31.3 The Structure of the Servlet API

The servlet API is made up of a number of packages, including the `javax.servlet` and `javax.servlet.http` packages. Note that these package names do not start with `java` but with `javax`. This indicates that they are a Java standard extension to the basic Java platform (a standard introduced with JDK 1.2). This means that a Java vendor does not have to support this API (although many vendors are already supporting it). You can obtain the Java Servlet Development Kit 2.0 (the JSDK 2.0) from Sun's Java Web site (see `http://java.sun.com/products/`). This development kit can be used to develop and test server extensions based on the servlet API. Included in the development kit is the servlet source code, reference documentation and tutorial, as well as a standalone server (called servletrunner) that can be used to test servlets before running them in a servlet-enabled Web server.

The JSDK 2.0 serves as the reference implementation for the Java Servlet API and can be used with the JDK 1.1.*. If you are interested in developing servlets with JDK 1.2, there is no need to use this JSDK, as the servlet API is bundled with JDK 1.2.

The key classes and interfaces in the Servlet API are presented below and are illustrated in Figure 31.2, along with associated classes and interfaces:

- `Servlet` This interface defines all the methods that a servlet must respond to (including `init()` and `destroy()`). Classes that implement this interface can be used as servlets.
- `HttpServlet` This is an abstract class that is intended to simplify writing HTTP servlets. It extends the `GenericServlet` base class and provides a framework for handling the http protocol. The methods that are overridden by subclasses are `doGet`, `doPost`, `doPut`, `doDelete` and `getServletInfo`. The four do* methods have already been mentioned. The `getServletInfo` method provides information through a service's administrative interfaces. Note that a developer need only override one of these methods and not all of them.
- `HttpServletRequest` This is actually an interface specification which extends the `ServletRequest` interface. It provides a definition for an object which provides data from the client to the servlet for use in the `HttpServlet`'s methods.
- `HttpServletResponse` This is actually an interface specification which extends the `ServletResponse` interface. It defines the protocol for an object that manipulates http-protocol specified header information and returns data to its client.

These are the main interfaces and classes used by a servlet. Of course, these are not the only ones available; however, they are the key ones.

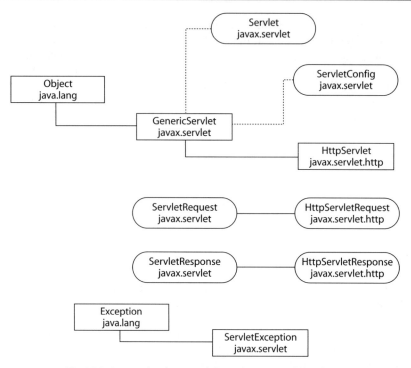

Fig. 31.2 Java servlet classes and their inheritance relationships.

31.4 An Example Servlet

As we have now considered how servlets work as well as what the structure of a servlet is, we will look at a simple implementation. Listing 31.1 presents the SampleServer class. This is a fully functional (if somewhat limited) servlet. It responds to POST requests for information. Essentially, a user inputs a name on a Web page and "submits" the information on that page to the Web server. The Web server in turn loads and runs this servlet. The servlet responds by generating an HTML page which includes the name of the wife of the specified man.

Note that the init() method, although it is used to set up the hash table of names, first classes the super.init() method. This illustrates how the init() method should be over-ridden. That is, the super version of the method should be called first (super causes the method search to start in the parent class rather than the current class).

The doPost() method responds to requests generated by a Web client via the post option on the method parameter of the form tag (see later). There are actually two ways in which a Web client can send information to a server: POST and GET. We will only look at the approach used with posted information.

This method is overridden in a subclass of the GenericServlet class (or as in this case one of its subclasses). It takes two parameters: one a request object and one a response object. The request object is used to access the information provided when the client "posted" the request. In this case it will be used to access the name text field on an HTML page. In turn, the response object is used to return the result (which is probably going to be in the form of HTML). To use the response object the developer of the servlet must set entity headers in the response, access the output stream of the response and use this output stream to write any response data. The headers that are set should include content type and encoding. If a writer is to be used to write response data, the content type must be set before the writer is accessed. In general, the servlet implementer must write the headers before the response data because the headers can be flushed at any time after the data starts to be written.

To set the content type of the response, the setContentType() method is used. This method may only be invoked once for each execution of the doPost() method.

Notice that the doPost() method throws two types of exception: the IOException and the ServletException. The IOException may be thrown during the process of reading from the request object or writing to the response object. In turn, the ServletException may be thrown if the request could not be handled.

The source of the simple servlet used in this article is presented in Listing 31.1. The servlet is called SampleServer.

Listing 31.1 The SamplerServer.java file.

```
import java.util.*;
import javax.servlet.*; import javax.servlet.http.*;

public class SampleServer extends HttpServlet {
  Hashtable table = new Hashtable();
  public void init(ServletConfig sc)
    throws ServletException {
    super.init(sc);

  // Set up info for servlet example
  table.put("John", "Denise");
  table.put("Paul", "Fiona");
  table.put("Peter", "Karen");
}

public void doPost(HttpServletRequest req, HttpServletResponse res)
  throws ServletException, IOException {

  // Set the content type header of the response
  res.setContentType("text/html");

  // Get the output stream to write the html out to
  PrintWriter output. res.getWriter();

  // Get value passed to servlet from the html page
  String name = req.getParameter("Name");

  // Generate response in HTML
  String result = table.get(name);
  output.println("<html>\n<head><body>");
  output.println("<title>Example</title></head>");
  output.println("<p>");
  output.println("The wife of " + name + " is " + result);
  output.println("</p></body></html>");
  output.flush();
}
```

```
public void destroy() {
  super.destroy();
  // Anything specific to this application
  }
}
```

Note that to generate the HTML which is output back to the Web server and subsequently to the Web browser we actually use a `PrintWriter` and the `println` method. This is exactly the same as if we were writing to a stream for any other purpose (such as writing to a file or a socket).

Also note that in this case, although the `init()` method is actually used to set up the hash table to be used by the `doPost()` method, the `destroy()` method does not need to be included. It is presented here to illustrate how it should be overridden. That is, the super version of the method should be called first.

Having defined the servlet we now need to define an HTML page which will request services on that servlet. Listing 31.2 provides just such an HTML page (Figure 31.3). This HTML page is very simple. It uses a form to allow a user to enter a name. This name is passed to the servlet when the Submit button is pressed. Notice that the form header tag specifies the action to perform when the Submit button is pressed. Thus in this case it specifies the `SimpleServer` servlet. It does this by specifying the Web server from which the servlet should be downloaded and then the directory on that server containing the servlet (plus the name of the servlet). Note that in this case the method associated with the action is POST – thus the `doPost()` method will be called on the servlet.

Listing 31.2 The HTML page.

```
<html>
<head>
<title> HTML to Servlet Example</title>
</head>
<body>
<form action="http://www.ttc.demon.co.uk/servlet/SimpleServer">
Input a name:
<input type=text name=name size=10>
<input type=submit value="Submit">
</form>
</body>
</html>
```

A form rather than an applet was used in this example as the client is significantly simpler, particularly for this very simple system. However, it is important to realise that rather than a form, the request could have come from an applet.

HTML forms provide a way of interacting with a Web page that requires no scripting or applet writing. In addition, almost every type of browser, from whichever vendor, supports HTML forms. This makes the form a very sensible choice for Web developers. As forms are just HTML, they follow the familiar tag structure seen with other HTML constructs. They possess a start tag and an end tag. Between these tags you can use standard HTML to lay out your form, as well as special form tags to provide for interactivity. These form tags include buttons, text fields and text areas, selection boxes etc.

Fig. 31.3 The HTML page used to access the servlet.

One button used with a form is of particular interest: the Submit button. This button (illustrated in Listing 31.2 and Figure 31.3) invokes a Web server-side action by requesting some service. This service could be provided by a CGI script, or as in this case by a servlet. The effect of the user selecting the submit button is that all the input information (in Listing 31.1 the information entered into the text field) is collected together and sent to the to the server along with the service requested. In our case this results in the server loading and initializing the servlet and then invoking the doPost() method. The information collected from the form is provided to the servlet via the HttpServletRequest object.

Once the SampleServer processes the request it returns a response in terms of HTML as described earlier. The resulting Web page is illustrated in Figure 31.4.

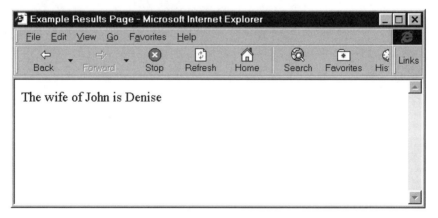

Fig. 31.4 The result of querying the servlet.

31.5 Why Use Servlets?

There are a wide range of situations in which you might wish to use Servlets. The example given here is for processing data POSTed over HTTPS using an HTML form. This example could be extended further and could be used as the basis of an e-commerce system. For example, an order entry and processing system could be implemented in this way. The servlet could receive and process the information provided. It could then generate a transaction which could be passed to the enterprise's main sales system and on to the deployment and payment systems (remember that a servlet is not restricted in what it can connect to in the way that an applet would be).

Other situations in which you might want to use a Servlet include providing real-time updates to a Web page. Rather than gaining a static Web page generated, say, the night before, the Web page viewed by the user could present the latest data. This could be used to view the current state of stocks and shares etc.

A servlet can also be used to help balance the load on a server. If a server receives a request for a service, but decides that the current server is too heavily loaded, it could forward that request to other servers and servlets, thus allowing a single logical service to be presented to the user that actually exploits multiple servers.

31.6 Summary

Java servlets are an enormously useful extension to the standard Java platform. They can be used instead of CGI scripts and offer greater portability, maintainability and reliability than such scripts. In addition they are not constrained by the "sandbox" in the way that Java applets are constrained. It is likely that they will be used in many client–server Web-based applications using XML and HTML rather than applets.

31.7 Further Reading

For further information about servlets, read Moss (1998).

The Java Servlet Development Kit can be downloaded from `http://java.sun.com/prod-ucts/`.

Chapter 32

Java Server Pages

32.1 Introduction

First there were servlets, then there were Java Server Pages (also known as JSPs). Both can serve up data on request, and, in the case of HTTP servlets, both can serve up Web pages on demand. So why have two approaches? The primary problem with servlets is that if you don't already know Java, it is very difficult to write a servlet!

Servlets mix presentation with processing – that is, an HTTP servlet both generates the HTML to be rendered by the client browser and contains the logic that generates that HTML. The end result of this is that the servlet developer must know both Java and HTML (and possibly scripting languages such as JScript, the use of DHTML etc.).

In general, Web designers and Java developers are not the same people, yet the servlet approaches assumes that they are (or at least that they can work closely together to produce the necessary results). The core issue here is that the presentation (the HTML) and the processing (what should be done to generate that HTML) are mixed into one single entity – the servlet.

JSPs are a direct extension to servlets that attempt to separate out the presentational aspects from the logical aspects. That is, a JSP focuses on the presentation (i.e. the HTML tags) while the Java code called from the JSP deals with the business logic.

A JSP is essentially an HTML file that uses a .jsp extension and provides some additional JSP tags. These tags are defined by a tag library that can be extended for custom applications.

32.2 What Is a JSP?

The main aim of the JSP framework is the separation of presentation from application logic. That is, it aims to allow non-Java developers to design the JSP pages using:

- HTML markup
- XML-like tags known as JSP tags

These JSP tags can then access server-side Java code that adheres to the JavaBeans naming conventions. In addition, JSPs can also access Enterprise JavaBeans. Thus the separation of concerns is achieved by allowing Java developers to focus on standard JavaBeans and Enterprise JavaBeans and Web designers to concentrate on HTML, DHTML and the JSP tags.

The JSP tags are very powerful. They allow the developer to:

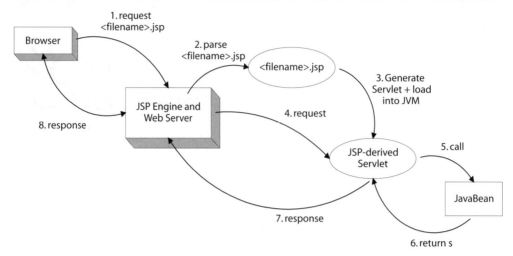

Fig. 32.1 Translating a JSP into a servlet.

- instantiate JavaBeans
- access Java code
- request services of Enterprise JavaBeans
- cause applets to be downloaded
- include the output of additional JSPs
- cause servlets to be executed

In turn, servlets can trigger JSPs.

It is useful to consider what happens to a JSP when a client requests a JSP and its relationship to servlets (remember above we noted that JSPs were a direct extension to servlets).

Figure 32.1 illustrates the steps that occur the first time a user requests a JSP. These steps are described in more detail below (but note that the end result is that the JSP is translated into a servlet that is then compiled and loaded into the Web server):

1. Request `<filename>.jsp`. The first step is that the client browser must request the JSP file from the JSP-enabled Web server. This may be done directly or via some form of mapping. For example, `www.jaydeetechnology.co.uk/welcome` may map to `www.jaydeetechnology.co.uk/home/sayhello.jsp`.
2. The Web server than passes the request onto the JSP engine (which is running within a JVM). This causes the JSP to be parsed and a servlet file to be generated. This servlet provides a direct mapping from the JSP into a servlet that supplies the HTML page defined by the JSP.
3. The generated servlet is then compiled and loaded into the JVM of the JSP engine (with is therefore also a servlet engine).
4. The Web server then passes the request on to the servlet implementation of the JSP.
5. This servlet can then call out to other Java code as required.
6. Any information provided by the Java code is appended to the HTML from the JSP as required.
7. The HTML generated is returned to the Web server.
8. The Web server returns the HTML page back to the client browser.
9. The client browser renders the response without ever seeing any Java.

There are some things to note from this description. Firstly, as a JSP is compiled into a servlet all the features available for a servlet are available to any Java code embedded in the JSP. Thus the request and response objects are available as well as the session object etc. Secondly, a JSP and a servlet end up being the same thing. Thus servlets can call JSPs and vice versa because they are essentially exactly the same type of object. Thirdly, just as with a normal servlet, once a JSP has been translated into a servlet, compiled and loaded into the JVM on the Web server, it remains in memory. Thus the second time a servlet is called the JSP file is not parsed nor is it translated and compiled. Instead, the request is passed immediately on to the servlet available within the JVM.

32.3 A Very Simple JSP

To illustrate the ideas discussed above we will look at a very simple JSP. The JSP we will define is the JSP version of Hello World. We will create a JSP that presents "Hello" followed by a `String` supplied from a Java class called `BasicHello` in a package `hello`. The JSP, saved in a file called `hello1.jsp`, is presented in Listing 32.1 and the JavaBean is presented in Listing 32.2 (note that the only thing that makes `BasicHello` a JavaBean is that we have followed the JavaBeans naming conventions for the get method).

Listing 32.1 A very simple JSP: `hello1.jsp`.

```
<html>
<body>
<%@ page import="hello.BasicHello" %><jsp:useBean id="hello" scope="page"
class="hello.BasicHello"/><h1>Basic Hello World</h1>
This is a simple test
<p> <hr> <p>
Hello <jsp:getProperty name="hello" property="name"/><p> <hr>
</body></html>
```

We will work through this simple JSP.

- The first two lines in the JSP are standard HTML tags.
- `<%@ page import="hello.BasicHello" %>` provides information for the whole page. In particular, it tells the JSP that the class `BasicHello` in the package `hello` will be used (note that this will be converted into a Java import statement when the JSP is translated into a servlet).
- `<jsp:useBean>` This locates and creates the specified JavaBean. Essentially it states that a new instance of the class `hello.BasicHello` will be created and made available via the "variable" `hello` that exists only for the current page (i.e. it does not persist over multiple calls to the JSP).
- The next three lines are standard HTML that provide a heading (Basic Hello World) and some simple formatting.
- `<jsp:getProperty>` This gets a property value of the JavaBean `BasicHello`. It assumes that there is a method `get<PropertyName>` available (in this case `getName()`).
- The output of `getName()` is then concatenated with HTML strings.
- The final lines are all HTML and deal with completing the HTML page.

Form this we know some things about the Java class that must implement `BasicHello`. These are that:

- It must be in a package called hello.
- It must provide a method getName() that returns a name to be added to the HTML page

However, it need not do anything else. Indeed, at present, if it does do more then those features will not be used by the JSP file. Listing 32.2 presents the simple BasicHello class.

Listing 32.2 The BasicHello class.

```
package hello;
public class BasicHello {
  public String getName() {
    return "John";
  }
}
```

As this is only an example, Listing 32.2 is very basic. The string returned by the class is hard coded to be "John". However, this string could be provided by some other Java code, read from a database or accessed from some legacy code etc.

The BasicHello class must be compiled using javac in the normal manner. However, rather than run the class directly the .class file must be installed in the appropriate place on the Web server (exactly where this is will depend on the JSP engine being used).

The end result of installing the JSP file and BasicHello class file correctly on your Web server is illustrated in Figure 32.2.

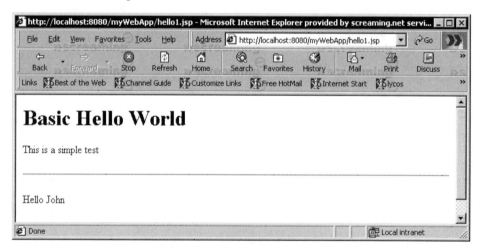

Fig. 32.2 The result of running the simple JSP.

Although the example presented in Listing 32.1 is a very simple example, it does show a JSP that obtains some of its data from a Java class – this is the essence of all JSPs!

32.4 The Components of a JSP

A JSP file is make up of text, HTML tags and a number of additional components: directives, actions, implicit objects and scripts. Each of these is considered briefly below.

32.4.1 Directives

Directives are the JSP components that provide global processing instructions for a whole JSP file. the syntax of a directive is:

```
<%@ directive {attribute="value"} %>
```

For example:

```
<%@ page import="shop.BookList" %>
```

This states that the JSP should import the class BookList in the package shop. This means that the class generated from the JSP will have a normal Java import statement for this class added to it.

There are several commonly used directives:

- The page directive. This defines information for the current JSP page. It provides information on the scripting language to be used, the parent class for the servlet generated from the JSP, whether sessional data will be available etc. Defaults are available for these attributes and thus only those that do not use the default value need to be provided.
- The include directive. This is used to include text and code into a JSP at translation time.
- The taglib directive. This directive allows a particular tag library to be used with the current JSP.

32.4.2 Actions

Actions provide standard tasks such as creating or accessing Java objects (normally those that conform to the JavaBeans naming conventions). The JSP framework provides the following commonly used actions:

- <jsp:useBean> This action links an instance of a Java class (the JavaBean) with a given ID and a scope. The scope can be page, request, session or application. For example:

  ```
  <jsp:useBean id="total" scope="session"
    class="com.jaydeetee.Totalizer" />
  ```

  - page scope – implies that the object only exists for the current page
  - request scope – indicates that the object is only available to pages processing the same request
  - session scope – indicates that the object exists for the current session
  - application scope – states that the object is available with the current Web application context; if the user requests go outside of the current Web application, the object is not available
- <jsp:setProperty> sets the value of a bean's property
- <jsp:getProperty> obtains the value of a bean's property and converts it to a String. This string is then concatenated with the current output stream.
- <jsp:forward> allows the JSP engine to forward the current request to another JSP or servlet at run time. The current JSP terminates.

32.4.3 Implicit Objects

Within a JSP there are a number of "implicit" objects that are available to the developer. In general these are available through the Servlet that the JSP will be translated into. For example, the request and response objects are available. There is also a session object and the `ServletContext` (available via a variable called `application`). There is also a variable `out` that the `JspWriter` object linked to the response object is maintained in. This provides methods such as `print` and `println`.

32.4.4 JSP Scripting

JSP scripting allows code fragments to be directly embedded in the JSP page. There are three elements that make up JSP scripting: declarations, expressions and scriptlets. We shall assume that Java is being used as the scripting language within the JSP – remember that this is server side and that the JSP will be converted into a Java servlet).

Declarations

These are used to declare variables and methods in the scripting language. The syntax of a declaration is:

```
<%! declaration %>
```

For example:

```
<%! String name = "John"; %>
<%! public String getName() { return name; } %>
```

Expressions

These allow fragments of code to be written whose result will be added to the output of the JSP. The syntax of an expression is:

```
<%= expression %>
```

For example:

```
Hello <%= getName() %>
```

Scriptlets

Scriptlets can contain any code that is valid in the scripting language. They can use the variables and methods defined in declarations, implicit objects, JavaBeans etc. The syntax for a scriptlet is:

```
<% scriplet %>
```

For example:

```
<% out.println("Hello " + hello.getName()); %>
```

32.5 Making JSPs Interactive

Data can be obtained from request attributes in the same way that it can be obtain from the request object in servlets. However, it is not necessary for the developer to code this; instead, by using the correct actions and directives in the JSP the necessary code can be automatically generated. This leaves the JSP designer to concentrate on the presentation issues and not the code of the Java servlet.

For example, a common scenario is for a JSP to generate a form that actions the same JSP. The first time the JSP is called it generates the HTML form; however, the second time it is called it retrieves the information entered into the form and triggers some behaviour (within the related Java code). As a simple example, consider the JSP file presented in Listing 32.3.

Listing 32.3 Interactive servlet: hello2.jsp.

```
<html><body>
<%@ page import="hello.Hello" %>
<jsp:useBean id="hello" scope="session" class="hello.Hello" />
<jsp:setProperty name="hello" property="*"/>
<h1>Hello World</h1>
   <p>Bean has been accessed <jsp:getProperty name="hello"
      property="count"/> times.
   <p><hr><p>
<% if (!hello.hasName()) { %>
      This is a simple form:   <p>
      <form method="get" action="hello2.jsp">
      What's your name? <input type="text" name="name">
      <input type="submit" value="Submit">
      </form>
<% } else { %>
      Hello <jsp:getProperty name="hello" property="name"/> <p><hr>
<% } %> </body></html>
```

The servlet in Listing 32.3 has a number of features worth noting. Firstly, `<jsp@setProperty name = "hello" property="*"/>` action specifies that we want the hello bean (that is, the Java object referenced by the id "hello") and to automatically set the properties on this bean within the form. That is, we tell the set property action to search the request object for parameter names that match the properties of the hello bean. If there are any matches, then the action will set the bean properties to those values.

The next thing to note from this JSP is that we have embedded some Java within the JSP. This is indicated by:

```
<% if (!hello.hasName()) { %>
```

This is an example of a scriptlet described earlier. This code will be extracted and incorporated into the underlying servlet. Thus this is a piece of Java that will be used by the servlet to determine what should happen when the servlet executes. Note that the scriptlet contains part of a Java if statement, the else part is further down in the listing and the final closing bracket is at the start of the final line of the listing. Thus you can embed any Java into your JSP as required. This of course muddies the separation of presentation from content, but does provide a great deal of flexibility and power. For example, it is possible to embed into the JSP a section of Java code that will use JDBC to access a database and retrieve information that can be directly incorporated into the JSP itself. However, in doing this you end up with the same issues as exist for servlets – presentation and logic being mixed!

The Java class (hello.Hello) is presented in Listing 32.4.

Listing 32.4 The Hello Java class.

```
package hello;
public class Hello {
  private String username;
  private boolean flag = false;
  private int count = 0;

  public String getName() {  return username;  }
  public void setName(String name) {
    username = name;
    flag = true;
  }
  public boolean hasName() {  return flag;  }
  public int getCount() {  return ++count;  }
}
```

The result of running this "Web application" (i.e. the combination of the JSP and the Java class) is illustrated in Figure 32.3. The Web page on the left illustrates the result of running the JSP the first time. The Web page on the right is the result of selecting Submit on the first Web page – i.e. the result of running the JSP a second time.

32.6 Why Use JSPs?

A question that is worth considering is why use JSPs at all – we already have servlets and for those who are Java developers there is less to learn! The main answer relates to the motivation behind JSPs that was mentioned at the start of this chapter - JSP designers don't need to know Java (as much). That is, the JSP is oriented around HTML and XML-like (and thus HTML-like) JSP tags. It is thus easy for a HTML Web site designer to get familiar with the JSP concepts and structures etc. It is also possible for developers to extend the JSP tag library with project-specific tags that will provide easy access to project-specific resources (again hiding the non-HTML parts from the JSP designer). Certainly it's a lot easier to produce sophisticated HTML-based pages using JSP than straight servlets.

32.7 Problems With JSPs

The main problem with JSPs is that although the aim in JSPs is to separate presentation from the application logic, they don't completely succeed. Indeed, if the developer wishes to the presentational aspect of JSPs can be heavily mixed with embedded scripts that contain extensive Java code. As an example consider the following JSP page that might form part of an online book store:

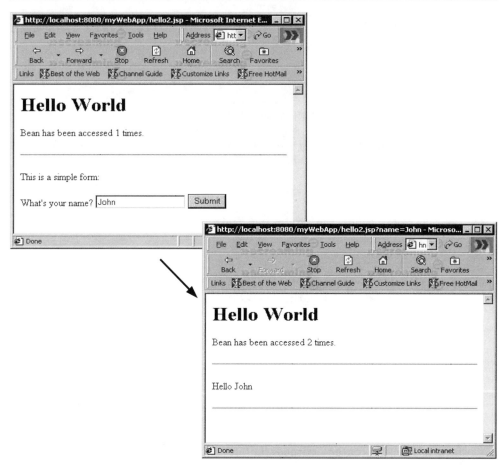

Fig. 32.3 The effect of running the Web application.

```html
<html>
<body>

<%@ page import="com.jaydeetee.shop.Basket" %>

<jsp:useBean id="basket" scope="session"
class="com.jaydeetee.shop.Basket" />

<h1>Welcome to the online shop</h1>

<%
  if (basket.isEmpty())
    String user = request.getParamter("user");
    String passwd = request.getParamter("password");
    if (user != null) {
      if (passwd != null) {
        if (basket.checkUser(user, passwd)) {
          String book = request.getParamter("title");
          String author = request.getParamter("author");
```

```
            double price = Double.parseDouble(request.getParamter("price"));
            basket.addBook(book, author, price);
        }
    }
}
} else {
    String book = request.getParamter("title");
    String author = request.getParamter("author");
    double price = Double.parseDouble(request.getParamter("price"));
    basket.addBook(book, author, price);
}
%>
```

So far you have bought the following books:

```
<%

  String [] books = basket.getAllBooks();
  for (int i=0; i<books.length; i++) {
    oup.println(books[i] + " <br> ");
  }

%>
```

If you wish to purchase another book then enter the detail in the following form:

```
<hr>
  <form action='welcome2' method='GET'>"
    Input a book to buy<p>"
      Title:
        <input type=text name=title size=10>"
      <br>Author:
        <input type=text name=author size=10>"
      <br>Price:
        <input type=text name=price size=10>"
      <br>
        <input type=submit value='Submit'>
  </form>
<p>
<hr>

</body>
</html>
```

As this page illustrates, the scriptlet is doing a great deal of Java processing. This could be repeated many times in the JSP.

Care needs to be taken to try to refrain from this sort of mixing. One approach is to use JSPs where the majority of the result is HTML and servlets where you need to initiate a great amount of Java processing/business logic.

Chapter *33*
Java Database Connectivity

33.1 Introduction

Officially, JDBC is not an acronym; however, to all intents and purposes it stands for Java Data-Base Connectivity. This is the mechanism by which relational databases are access in Java. Java is an (almost) pure object-oriented language; however, although there are some object-oriented databases available, many database systems presently in commercial use are currently relational. It is therefore necessary for any object-oriented language which is to be used for commercial development to provide an interface to such databases. However, each database vendor provides its own proprietary (and different) API. In many cases they are little more than variations on a theme; however, they tend to be incompatible. This means that if you were to write a program that was designed to interface with one database system, it is unlikely that it would automatically work with another.

Of course one of the philosophies of Java is *"write once, run anywhere"*. This means we do not want to have to rewrite our Java code just because it is using a different database on different platforms (or even the same platform). JDBC is Sun's attempt to provide a vendor-independent interface to any relational database system. This is possible, as most vendors implement most (if not all) of the standard SQL, thus allowing a common denominator. SQL stands for Structured Query Language, which is used for obtaining information from relational databases. SQL is a large topic in its own right and is beyond the scope of this chapter. Reference is therefore made to appropriate books at the end of the article.

One potential problem with such an approach is that although the developers' interface is the same, different implementations of an application would be needed to link to different databases. In the JDBC this is overcome by providing different back-end drivers. Developers are now insulated from the details of the various relational database systems that they may be using and have a greater chance of producing portable code.

In the remainder of this chapter we consider JDBC and these database drivers in more detail. We then look at some examples of typical database operations and consider the implications for applets.

33.2 What Is JDBC?

The JDBC allows a Java developer to connect to a database, to interact with that database via SQL, and of course to use those results within a Java application or applet. The combination of Java and JDBC allows information held in databases to be easily and quickly published on the Web (via an applet). It also provides a bridge that supports the Open Database Connectivity

(ODBC) standard. The first version of the JDBC was released in the summer of 1996. It is an important addition to Java's armoury, as the JDBC provides programmers with a language and environment that is platform- and database vendor-independent. This is (almost) unique. Most developers who use the ODBC C API are database vendor-independent, but find it non-trivial to port their C application to a different platform due to windowing differences, hardware-dependent language features etc.

ODBC is a database access standard developed by Microsoft. This standard has been widely adopted not only by the vendors of Windows-based databases but by others as well. For example, a number of databases more normally associated with Unix-based systems or IBM mainframes now offer an ODBC interface. Essentially, ODBC is a basic SQL interface to a database system that assumes only "standard" SQL features. Thus specialist facilities provided by different database vendors cannot be accessed. In many ways JDBC has similar aims to ODBC. However, one major different is that JDBC allows different database drivers (interfaces) to be used, one of which is the ODBC driver.

At present, the JDBC only allows connection to, and interaction with, a database via SQL. Features such as those found in tools like Delphi and Visual Basic are not available. For example, there are no database controls, form designers, query builders etc. Of course, it is likely that such tools will become available either from Sun or third-party vendors. This situation will change in the future as many JFC components (or Java Foundation Classes) are data-aware. The JFC provides an enhanced set of tools, including GUI components, in Sun's JDK 1.2.

The JDBC is able to connect to any database by using different (back-end) drivers. These act as the interfaces between the JDBC and databases such as Oracle, Sybase, Microsoft Access and shareware systems such as MiniSQL. The idea is that the front end presented to the developer is the same whatever the database system, while the appropriate back end is loaded as required. The JDBC then passes the programmer's SQL to the database via the back end. Java is not the first system to adopt this approach; however, a novel feature of the JDBC is that more than one driver can be loaded at a time. The system will then try each driver until one is found that is compatible with the database system being used. Thus multiple drivers can be provided, and at run time the appropriate one is identified and used. This is illustrated in Figure 33.1.

Figure 33.1 illustrates some of the most commonly used methods provided by the JDBC along with two database drivers (namely the Mini SQL driver – see Section 33.9 – and the ODBC driver; note that any number could have been provided). Such a setup would allow a Java program to connect to an mSQL database via the mSQL driver and to any database that supports the ODBC standard through the ODBC driver. The getConnection(), executeQuery() and executeUpdate() methods will be looked at in more detail later in this chapter.

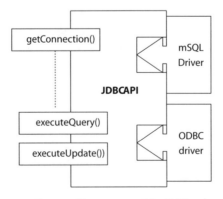

Fig. 33.1 The structure of the JDBC.

There are an increasing number of database drivers becoming available for JDBC. At present databases such as Oracle, Sybase and Ingres all have their own drivers. This allows features of those databases to be exploited. However, even databases that are not directly supported can be accessed via the ODBC driver, thus making a huge range of databases available to the Java developer.

There is a very definite series of steps that must be performed by any JDBC program. These involve loading an appropriate driver, connecting to a database, executing SQL statements and closing the connection made. These are discussed in more detail later in this article.

33.3 What the Driver Provides

What actually is a driver? In practice it provides the concrete implementation for a number of interfaces defined in the SQL package. In particular, it defines implementations for the interfaces and classes (such as `Driver`, `Connection`, `Statement` and `ResultSet`) which form a major part of the SQL API. Each of these will be considered in more detail later. However, essentially they comprise the way to connect to a database, to pass SQL statements to be executed to that database, and to examine the results returned. Note that, unlike some object-to-relational database interfaces, JDBC does not try to objectify the results of querying a relational database. Instead, the results are returned in a table-like format within a results set. It is then up to the developer to decide how to handle the information retrieved.

33.4 Registering Drivers

As part of the JDBC API a JDBC driver manager is provided. This is the part of the JDBC that handles the drivers currently available to a JDBC application. It is therefore necessary to "register" a driver with the driver manager. There are three ways of doing this:

1. Passing a command line option to a Java application using the -Dproperty=value parameter. For example:

   ```
   java -Djdbc.drivers=jdbc.odbc.JdbcOdbcDriver queryDB
   ```

2. For applets it is possible to set the `jdbc.drivers` system property. In HotJava this can be done in the properties file of the `.hotjava` directory. For example:

   ```
   jdbc.drivers=jdbc.odbc.JdbcOdbcDriver:imaginary.sql.iMsqlDriver
   ```

3. Programmatically by requesting the class of the driver to be loaded using the static method `forName()` in the class `Class`. For example:

   ```
   Class.forName("sun.jdbc.odbc.JdbcOdbcDriver");
   Class.forName("COM.imaginary.sql.msql.MsqlDriver");
   ```

   This will cause the associated class (in this case the driver) to be loaded into the running application.

As was mentioned earlier, you can install more than one driver in your JDBC program. When a request is made to make a connection to a database each one will be tried in turn until one accepts that request. However, using more than one driver will slow down both system start-up (as each must be loaded) as well as your run-time (as each may need to be tried in turn). For this reason, it may be best to select the most appropriate driver and stick with that one.

The JDBC ODBC driver is provided as part of Sun's JDK 1.1. However, other drivers can be obtained and used with the JDBC. For example, the mSQL driver mentioned above was downloaded from the Web and installed in an appropriate directory. In this way database vendors can supply their own proprietary database drivers, which developers can then utilize in their own applications.

33.5 Opening a Connection

Listing 33.1 presents a simple class that uses the ODBC driver to connect to a Microsoft Access database. We must first make the JDBC API available; this is done by importing the SQL package. Next the application loads the JDBC ODBC driver and then requests that the DriverManager makes a connection with the database testDB. Note that to make this connection a string (called url) is passed to the driver manager along with the user id and the password.

Listing 33.1 `TestConnect.java`.

```java
import java.sql.*;
public class TestConnect {

    public static void main (String args []) {
        String url = "jdbc:odbc:testDB";

        if (args.length < 2) {
            System.out.println("Usage: java TestConnect userid password");
            System.exit(1);
        }

        String userid = args[0];
        String password = args[1];

        try {
            Class.forName("sun.jdbc.odbc.JdbcOdbcDriver");
            Connection con =DriverManager.getConnection(url, userid, password);
            con.close();
            System.out.println("All okay");
        } catch (Exception e) {
            System.out.println(e.getMessage());
            e.printStackTrace();
        }

    }
}
```

The string specifying the database to connect to is formed from a JDBC URL. This is a URL comprising three parts:

1. The JDBC protocol indicator (`jdbc:`)
2. The appropriate sub-protocol such as `odbc:`
3. The driver specific components (in this case `JdbcOdbcDriver`)

URLs are used as the Java program accessing the database may be running as a standalone application or may be an applet needing to connect to the database via the Web. Note that different database drivers will require different driver-specific components. In particular, the mSQL driver requires a URL of the following format:

```
jdbc:msql://hal.aber.ac.uk:1112/testDB
```

In this case it is necessary to provide the host name, the port on that host to connect to and the database to be used.

Once a connection has successfully been made to the database, the program then does nothing other than to close that connection. This is important, as some database drivers require the program to close the connection while others leave it as optional. If you are using multiple drivers it is best to close the connection.

Note that we placed the attempt to load the driver and make the connection within a `try {}` `catch{}` block. This is because both operations can raise exceptions and these must be caught and handled (as they are not run-time exceptions). The `forName()` method raises the `ClassNotFoundException` of it can't find the class which represents the specified driver. In turn, the `getConnection()` static method raises the `SQLException` if the specified database cannot be found.

The `try {} catch {}` block works by trapping any exceptions raised in the `try` part within the `catch` part (assuming that the exception raised is an instance of the specified class of exception or one of its subclasses).

An example of using this application is presented below:

```
java TestConnect jeh popeye
```

Here I am passing in the user id `jeh` and the password `popeye`.

33.6 Obtaining Data From a Database

Having made a connection with a database we are now in a position to obtain information from it. Listing 33.2 builds on the application in Listing 33.1 by querying the database for some information. This is done by obtaining a `Statement` object from the `Connection` object. SQL statements without parameters are normally executed using `Statement` objects. However, if the same SQL statement is executed many times, it is more efficient to use a `PreparedStatement`. In this example we will stick with the `Statement` object.

Listing 33.2 `TestQuery.java`.

```
import java.sql.*;
public class TestQuery {
```

```
public static void main (String args []) {
  String url = "jdbc:odbc:testdb";

  if (args.length < 2) {
    System.out.println("Usage: java TestQuery userid password");
    System.exit(1);
  }

  String userid = args[0];
  String password = args[1];

  try {
    Class.forName("sun.jdbc.odbc.JdbcOdbcDriver");
    Connection con = DriverManager.getConnection(url, userid, password);
    Statement statement = con.createStatement();
    ResultSet results =
        statement.executeQuery("SELECT address FROM addresses
             WHERE name = 'John' ");
    System.out.println("Addresses for John:");
    while (results.next()) {
      System.out.println(results.getString("address"));
    }
    statement.close();

    con.close();
  } catch (Exception e) {
    System.out.println(e.getMessage());
    e.printStackTrace();
  }
}
```

Having obtained the statement object we are now ready to pass it some SQL. This is done as a string within which the actual SQL statements are specified. In this case the SQL statement is:

```
SELECT address
  FROM addresses
  WHERE name = 'John'
```

This is pure SQL. The SELECT statement allows data to be obtained from the tables in the database. In this case the SQL states that the address field (column) of the table addresses should be retrieved where the name field of that row equals 'John'.

This string is passed to the statement object via the executeQuery() method. This method also generates an SQLException if a problem occurs. The method passes the SQL to the driver previously selected by the driver manager. The driver in turn passes the SQL on to the database system. The result is then returned to the driver, which in turn returns it to the user's program as an instance of ResultsSet. A results set is a table of data within which each row contains the data which matched the SQL statement. Within the row, the columns contain the fields specified by the SQL. A ResultSet maintains a cursor pointing to its current row of data. Initially the cursor is positioned before the first row. The next() method moves the cursor to the next row.

The ResultsSet class defines a variety of get methods for obtain information out of the ResultsSet table: for example, getBoolean(), getByte(), getString(), getDate() etc. These methods are provided by the JDBC driver and attempt to convert the underlying data to the specified Java type and return a suitable Java value. In Listing 33.2 we merely print out each address in turn using the next() method to move the table cursor on.

Finally, the statement and the connection are closed. In many cases it is desirable to immediately release a statement's database and JDBC resources instead of waiting for this to happen when it is automatically closed; the close method provides this immediate release.

33.7 Creating a Table

So far we have examined how to connect to a database and how to query that database for information. However, we have not considered how that database is created. Obviously the database may not be created by a Java application; for example, it could be generated by a legacy system. However, in many situations it is necessary for the tables in the database to be updated (if not created) by a JDBC program. Listing 33.3 presents a modified version of Listing 33.2. This listing shows how a statement object can be used to create a table and how information can be inserted into that table. Again the strings passed to the statement are pure SQL; however, this time we have used the executeUpdate() method of the Statement class.

Listing 33.3 TestCreate.java.

```java
import java.sql.*;
public class TestCreate {

    public static void main (String args []) {
        String url = "jdbc:odbc:testdb";

        if (args.length < 2) {
            System.out.println("Usage java TestCreate userid password");
            System.exit(1);
        }
        String userid = args[0];
        String password = args[1];

        try {
            Class.forName("sun.jdbc.odbc.JdbcOdbcDriver");
            Connection con = DriverManager.getConnection(url, userid, password);
            Statement statement = con.createStatement();

            statement.executeUpdate(
                "CREATE TABLE addresses (name char(15), address char(3))");
            statement.executeUpdate(
                "INSERT INTO addresses (name, address) VALUES('John', 'C46')");
            statement.executeUpdate(
                "INSERT INTO addresses (name, address) VALUES('Myra', 'C40')");

            statement.close();
            con.close();
```

```
    } catch (Exception e) {
      System.out.println(e.getMessage());
      e.printStackTrace();
    }
  }
}
```

The executeUpdate() is intended for SQL statements which will change the state of the data-base, such as INSERT, DELETE and CREATE. It does not return a result set; rather, it returns an integer indicating the row count of the executed SQL. You can either use this value or ignore it (as in Listing 33.3).

33.8 Applets and Databases

By default, applets are not allowed to load libraries or read and write files. In addition, applets are not allowed to open sockets to machines other than those they originated from. These restrictions cause a number of problems for those wishing to develop applets that work with databases. For example, many drivers rely on the ability to load native code libraries that actu-ally generate the connection to the specified database. One way around these restrictions is to turn them off in the browser being used. This is acceptable for an intranet being used within a single organization; however, it is not acceptable as a general solution.

Another possibility is to use drivers that are 100% pure Java, such as the mSQL driver. However, even using an mSQL driver, the applet is still restricted to connecting to a database on the originating host. Thus the developers must ensure that the Web server that serves the applets is running on the same host as the mSQL daemon. This may or may not be a problem.

Another option is to use a separate database server application (note application and not applet) which runs on the same host as the Web server. Applets can then connect to the data-base server application requesting that it connect to databases, execute updates, perform queries etc. The database server application is then the program that connects to and interacts with the database. In such a setup the applet does not directly communicate with the database system and is thus not hindered by the restrictions imposed on applets. This is illustrated in Figure 33.2. In this figure a user's browser has connected to the Web server and downloaded the

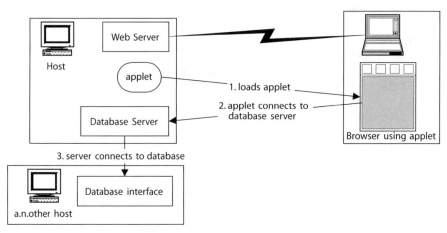

Fig. 33.2 Using JDBC within an applet.

applet. The applet then connects to the database server application. The server application then connects to the database management system on another host.

With the advent of signed applets, some of the above problems go away; however, signed applets are far from universal. In addition, some organizations are still using browsers that do not support them.

33.9 Mini SQL

Mini SQL or mSQL is a lightweight database server originally developed as part of the Minerva Network Management Environment. Its creator, David Hughes, has continued its development and makes mSQL available as a shareware product for a very small fee. MSQL provides fast access to stored data with low memory requirements through a subset of ANSI SQL (i.e. it does not support views or sub-queries etc.). It is available for Unix-compatible operating systems as well as for Windows 9x/NT/2000/XP and OS/2. However, it is worth noting that the Unix version tends to be ahead of the PC-oriented versions. The mSQL package includes the database engine, a terminal "monitor" program, a database administration program, a schema viewer, and C and Java language APIs. A Java JDBC driver for mSQL is also available.

mSQL is a very popular choice amongst Java developers because it is available on a wide variety of platforms, the mSQL driver is 100% Pure Java (and thus there is no problem about loading a native library when writing applets), and of course it is shareware. The downside is that the performance of mSQL is not as good as that of commercial database systems. With regard to applets it is worth noting that an applet (by default) is not allowed to make a network connection to any other computer other than the machine from which it was loaded. Thus the Web server and the mSQL demon must be running on the same machine.

For more information on mSQL see Jepson (1998).

33.10 Further Reading

The following books provide detailed information about Java database programming: Jepson (1997), Reese (1997), Hamilton et al. (1997), Microsoft (1997) and Stephens (1997).

33.11 Online References

- Sun's JDBC home page can be found at `http://java.sun.com/products/jdbc`.
- Information on available JDBC drivers can be obtained from `http://industry.java.sun.com/products/jdbc/drivers`
- mSQL is available for anonymous ftp from `ftp://bond.edu.au/pub/Minerva/msql`

Part **7**
Java Development

Chapter **34**

Java Style Guidelines

34.1 Introduction

Good programming style in any language helps promote the readability, clarity and comprehensibility of your code. In many languages, there are established standards to which many people adhere (sometimes without realizing it). For example, the way in which a C or Pascal program is indented is a standard. However, style guidelines which have evolved for these procedural languages do not cover many of the issues which are important in Java. As languages that are not object-oriented do not have the concepts of classes, instances and methods, they do not have standards for dealing with them.

Of course you should not forget all the pearls of wisdom and programming practices that you have learned using other languages. There are a number of acknowledged bad practices which are not specific to Java – for example, the use of goto-style constructs. In this chapter, we assume that you do not need an explanation of the basic concepts; instead, we try to concentrate on style issues specific to Java.

34.2 Code Layout

Java has inherited much of its language style from C, and many programmers have adopted a C style for program layout. Indeed, if you examine the system-provided classes (the source code of which is available within the JDK; for example, on a PC, look in the directories within JDK1.4\src\java\ or similar), this style has been used throughout. Thus an if-then statement is laid out in the same way as in a C program:

```
if (size == 20) {
   total = total * size;
}
```

For more information on the style of C programming see Kernighan and Ritchie (1988).

34.3 Variables

34.3.1 Naming Variables

In Java, variable names such as t1, i, j or temp should rarely be used. Variable names should be descriptive (semantic variables) or should indicate the type of object which the variable holds (typed variables). The approach that you choose depends on personal style and the situation in which the variables are used.

Semantic Variable Names

Instance and class variables tend to have semantic names. The semantic approach has the advantage that you need to assume less about what the variable is used for. Since subclasses can inherit instance and class variables, the point at which they are defined and the point at which they are used may be very distant. Thus, any contextual meaning and commentary provided with their definition is lost. Examples of semantic variable names include:

```
score
currentWorkingMemory
TotalPopulationSize
```

Typed Variable Names

The typed approach is often adopted for parameter names to indicate the class of object that is required by the method. For example:

```
add(Object anObject)
push(Object object)
```

Some methods use both the semantic and typed approaches:

```
put(Object key, Object object)
```

Temporary Variables

Temporary variables, which are local to a method, often have a mixture of semantic and typed names. They may also have temp or tmp as part of their name to indicate their temporary nature. Larger methods often have semantic local variable names due to the additional complexity of such methods.

If you must use very short variable names (which are acceptable, for example, as counters in loops), stick to the traditional names. For example, using variables such as i, j, k for counters is a shorthand (inherited from Fortran) with which most people are familiar. Similarly, a temporary generic exception is often named e in Java; you can adopt the same convention.

Multiple Part Variable Names

If the variable name is made up of more than one word, the words should not be separated by "-" or "_", but by giving the first letter of all but the first word an initial capital:

```
theDateToday     employeeRecord     objectInList
```

This approach is often referred to as title case (or modified title case for names starting with a lower-case letter). Whether the first word in the variable is capitalized or not depends on the type of variable. Table 34.1 summarizes the conventions.

In the system-provided classes, the parts of a class variable name are separated by underscores:

Table 34.1 Variable naming conventions.

Variable type	Convention
Class variable	Upper case
Class names	Initial capital
Temporary variables	Lower case
Instance variables	Lower case
Method parameters	Lower case

```
Double.MAX_VALUE
StreamTokenizer.TT_EOF
```

You should follow this convention, but the Java system classes do not adhere rigidly to it. Some classes, such as `File`, use a title case approach and others, such as `Color`, ignore the convention completely:

```
File.pathSeparator
Color.red
```

34.3.2 Using Variables

- *Instance variables* should be used to hold local data or references to other objects. The other objects should be involved in some form of collaboration with the object (otherwise it does not need a reference to them).
- *Class variables* should be used as "constant" values which are referenced by all instances of a class. They should never be used as a form of global variable (such a use is frequently an indication that a solution has not been designed with the proper amount of care and attention). Occasionally, a class may use its class variables to hold information about the instances, such as the number of instances created. However, this information should be private to the class.

Defining and Initializing Instance and Class Variables

You can declare class and instance variables anywhere within the body of a class. However, it is good style to declare them at the beginning. It is easier to follow the class structure if all the class variables (statically defined variables) are declared first, followed by the instance variables. If another programmer can find all such declarations in the same place, the code is easier to understand and maintain.

You should initialize variables when you declare them. If you cannot initialize them with the actual value to be used, then you should use a default value and set the actual value as soon as possible. For class variables you may do this within a static initialization block; for instance variables, you may do it within a constructor or an init method (depending on whether it is a standalone application or an applet).

One reason that you should initialize a variable is that it provides an indication to others of the information to be held by the variable. For example, stating that a variable can hold a string does not say very much. However, if you initialize the variable with the string "Mr. Joe Bloggs", it says much more. The other reason that you should initialize a variable is that the Java compiler does not warn you about uninitialized class and instance variables (they are set to null). Your code may attempt to use a variable which has not been initialized, thus raising an exception.

Defining Temporary Variables

Temporary variables can be defined anywhere within a method body. However, it is good style to declare them at the start of the method, as, once again, this is easier to read. It also implies that the programmer has given some thought to the variables that are required.

As a variable can be declared where and when it is used, it is common to find a variable declared within a loop. This means that it is declared every time the loop is executed:

```
for (i = 0; i < 10; ++i) {
    Integer count = new Integer(i);
}
```

This is very bad style, but is an easy mistake to fall into if variables are declared anywhere.

Accessing Instance and Class Variables

In general it is always better to access instance and class variables via intermediate methods, referred to as *accessor* (or *getter* and *setter*) methods, rather than accessing or setting them directly. This is called variable-free programming and it promotes the modularity of your methods. It insulates the methods against changes in the way the object (or class) holds instance (or class) information. This is a very important concept, as direct access to instance variables can limit the power of subclassing.

You can also protect variables from undesired changes. For example, you can put preconditions on an access method, or return a copy of the contents of the variable so that it cannot be directly affected. To implement this, you should make judicious use of the Java visibility modifiers described earlier in the book.

34.4 Classes

34.4.1 Naming Classes

The naming of a class is extremely important. The class is the core element in any object-oriented program and its name has huge semantic meaning which can greatly affect the clarity of the program. Examples of Java system classes include:

```
HashTable
FileInputStream
SecurityManager
```

The above names are good examples of how a name can describe a class. The name of a class is used by most developers to indicate its purpose or intent. This is partly due to the fact that it is the class name which is used when searching for appropriate classes (for example, by using the documentation generated by javadoc).

You should, therefore, use descriptive class names; classes with names such as MyClass or ProjectClass1 are of little use. However, class names should not be so specific that they make it appear that the class is unlikely to be of use except in one specific situation (unless, of course, this is the case). For example, in an application that records details about university lecturers, a class with a name such as ComputerScienceDepartmentLecturer is probably not appropriate, unless it really does relate only to lecturers in the Computer Science department. If this is the case, you need to ask yourself in what way computer science lecturers are different from other lecturers.

34.4.2 The Role of a Class

A subclass or class should accomplish one specific purpose; that is, it should capture only one idea. If more than one idea is encapsulated in a class, you should break the class down into its constituent parts. This guideline leads to small classes (in terms of methods, instance variables and code). Breaking a class down costs little but may produce major gains in reusability and flexibility.

A subclass should only be used to modify the behaviour of its parent class. This modification should be a refinement of the class and should therefore extend the behaviour of the class in some way. For example, a subclass may redefine one or more of the methods, add methods which use the inherited behaviour, or add class or instance variables. A subclass which does not do at least one of these is inappropriate.

34.4.3 Creating New Data Structure Classes

When working with data structures, there is always the question of whether to create a new data structure class to hold your data or whether to define a class which holds the data within one of its instance variables and then provide methods which access that variable.

For example, let us assume that we wish to define a new class, called `Account`, which holds information on deposits and withdrawals. We believe that we should use a hash table to hold the actual data, but should `Account` be a subclass of `HashTable` or of something else (for example, `Object`, with an instance variable holding an instance of `HashTable`)? Of course, it depends on what you are going to do with the `Account` class. If it provides a new data structure class (in some way), even if it is only for your application, then you should consider making it a subclass of `HashTable`. However, if you need to provide a functionally complex class which just happens to contain a hash table, then it is almost certainly better to make it a subclass of `Object`.

There is another point to consider: if `Account` is a subclass of `HashTable`, then any instance of `Account` responds to the whole of the `HashTable` protocol. You should ask yourself whether this is what you want, or whether a more limited protocol (one appropriate to an account object) is more suitable.

34.4.4 Class Comments

Every class, whether abstract or concrete, should have a class comment. This comment is the basic documentation for the class. It should, therefore, tell a developer creating a subclass from the class, or a user of the class, what they need to know. The comment may also contain:

- information about the author
- a history of modifications to the class
- the purpose, type and status of the class
- information about instance and class variables (including the class of object they hold and their use)
- information about collaborations between this class and others
- example usage
- copyright information

- class specific information, such as the things that a subclass of an abstract class is expected to redefine

You should place the class comment just before the class, using the /** */ form of syntax which allows javadoc to pick up the comment and generate HTML documentation. A common trick is to use /** followed by **/:

```
/**
   This is a javadoc comment
**/
```

This makes it easy to find the start and end of javadoc comments by searching for the two asterisks. You can use tags such as @author, @see and @version to ensure that these items are highlighted. For methods, you can use @return, @param and @exception to document the return value, any parameter values and any exceptions raised.

Finally, to help with the layout of the comment once it is converted into HTML, you can embed HTML tags within the comment. For example, <p> forces a new paragraph.

34.4.5 Using a Class or an Instance

In situations where only a single instance of a class is required, it is better style to define a class which is instantiated once than to provide the required behaviour in class-side methods.

Using a class instead of an instance is very poor style, breaks the rules of object orientation and may have implications for the future maintenance of the system.

34.5 Interfaces

An interface is a way of specifying the protocol which should be implemented by a set of objects which are members of different class hierarchies. You should use an interface in the following situations:

- as a specification mechanism, where one or more classes are intended to provide the same functionality
- where one or more (as yet undefined) user classes are anticipated and you must ensure that they provide the correct protocol
- where you must specify the type of a variable for a set of (as yet undefined) user classes

The above points assume that the classes come from different parts of the class hierarchy. If all classes have the same superclass, then you can use an abstract superclass instead of an interface.

34.6 Enumerated Types

Java does not provide explicitly for enumerated types. However, an interface can mimic part of the functionality of an enumerated type. In such an interface, only public static variables are defined. These variables are assigned numeric values which can indicate their ordering. For example, the following interface defines the equivalent of a Week enumerated type:

```java
public interface Week {
  public static final Monday = 1;
  public static final Tuesday = 2;
  public static final Wednesday = 3;
  public static final Thursday = 4;
  public static final Friday = 5;
}
```

Any class which implements this interface can then reference the variables Monday, Tuesday etc., directly and can compare them:

```java
if (Monday < Tuesday) ...
```

Of course, a class does not need to implement this interface; it could reference Monday via the interface:

```java
Week.Monday
```

34.7 Methods

34.7.1 Naming Methods

A method name should always start with a lower-case letter. If the method name is made up of more than one element then each element after the first should start with a capital letter (modified title case):

```java
account deposit(100);
account printStatement();
```

The naming of methods is as important as the naming of classes. An appropriate method name not only makes the code easier to read, it also aids in reuse. You should select a method's name to illustrate the method's purpose. In addition, many programmers try to select a name which makes it possible to read an expression containing the method in a similar manner to reading a sentence.

In many situations, you define multiple methods with the same name but different parameters. This is possible because Java identifies a method by both its name and its parameter classes. Thus, different methods can be supplied to deal with different situations, resulting in less complex code and more flexibility. For example:

```java
statement deposit(100);
statement deposit(date, 100);
statement deposit(100, date);
```

Methods which return true and false as the result of a test follow a common naming format throughout the Java system. These methods use a verb such as "is" or "equals" concatenated with whatever is being tested. In some cases, the method name expresses the test itself:

```
equals(Object)
startsWith(String)
isAlive()
isInterrupted()
```

In the first case, the method tests to see whether the receiver is the same as the parameter. This method name is used in many different classes (for example, Integer and String).

In the second example, the method only tests part of the receiver, and its name reflects that. In the next two cases, some aspect of the receiver is tested. The third method tests whether a process is active, and the value being tested for is used as part of the method name.

34.7.2 Using Methods

In general, you should put a method as high up in the inheritance hierarchy as possible (as long as it makes sense to do so). The higher the method, the more visible it is to classes in other branches of the hierarchy, and the more method level reuse you can achieve.

Think carefully about the purpose and placement of methods within a class. Just as a class should have a specific purpose, a method should also have a single purpose. If a method performs more than one function, then you should divide it into separate methods. In general terms, a method should be no longer than one A4 page.

Deciding how to break up the desired functionality into elements can be difficult in a procedural programming language. In Java, it is made more difficult by considerations of object encapsulation and reuse. However, you can bear the following questions in mind when determining whether your code is correctly placed within the methods:

- If the method does not refer to any aspect of the object (i.e. it does not use super, this, instance variables etc.), what does it do? Should it be there?
- How many objects does the method reference? A method should only send messages to a limited set of objects. This promotes maintainability, comprehensibility and modularity.
- Have you used accessor methods to access instance variables? Variable-free programming can greatly insulate the method from changes within the object.
- Is the behaviour encapsulated by the method intended for public or private (to the object) use? If it is a mixture of the two, then the method should be decomposed into two or more methods. The private code should be placed in a method which is defined to be private. This indicates to a developer (and enforces) that the method is not intended for external use.
- Does the method rely more on the behaviour of other objects than on its own object (that is, a series of messages is being sent to some object other than this)? If so, the method may be better placed in another object (or objects).

This last point is worth considering in slightly more detail. The series of messages in such a method may be better placed in a method in the class of the receiver object. This is because it really describes behaviour associated with that object. By placing it with the receiver object's class, all modifications to the behaviour of the receiver are encapsulated in that object. In addition, this behaviour may be useful to other objects; if you encode it within the receiver's class, other objects can gain access to that behaviour (rather than duplicating it in a number of places).

It is not easy to achieve good reuse of method level code when code is poorly placed. Most messages should be sent to this. Structuring the code appropriately is probably one of the hardest things to do well in object-oriented programming; however, if you do it correctly, it can pay very high dividends.

34.7.3 Class Methods and Instance Methods

The distinction between class and instance methods was discussed in more detail in Chapter 7. The main points are presented again here, as they are relevant to considerations of style in Java.

You should use the `main` method to create instances and invoke the initial behaviour. You should use other class methods for only the following purposes:

- information about the class
- instance management and information
- documentation and examples
- testing facilities (regression-style)
- support for one of the above

Any other purposes should be performed by an instance method.

34.7.4 Static Initialization Blocks

You should only use a static initialization block to initialize class variables which cannot be initialized by a simple initialization clause. It is easy to produce cyclic static initialization blocks, and the result of such initialization is likely to be incorrect. A static initialization block should immediately follow the class variable declarations and precede any method definitions (e.g. the `main` method).

34.7.5 Constructors

You should only use a constructor to initialize an instance of a class in an appropriate manner. Do not place instance-style functionality within the constructor. Instead, provide a separate method and call it from the constructor, so that you can reinitialize the object later, if necessary.

34.7.6 The `finalize` Method

This method is executed when the garbage collector picks up an object. You should only use it to perform housekeeping operations which can be left until the object is destroyed. Do not place operations which should be performed as soon as all references to the object are removed (for example, closing a file) in the `finalize` method because you cannot guarantee exactly when the garbage collector will deal with the object.

34.7.7 Programming in Terms of Objects

It is all too easy, when you first start with Java, to write procedure-oriented code within methods. Indeed, many publicly available Java classes contain code which has clearly been written by a C or C++ programmer, rather than by someone writing in an object-oriented manner. In Java, you should try to think in terms of objects.

34.7.8 Positioning of Methods

Just as with variables, you should present class methods first, followed by instance methods. How you arrange the class methods is a matter of personal style – there is no real standard (as yet). However, you should at least follow these guidelines:

- Place the static initialization block immediately after the variable declarations.
- Group all constructors together.
- Place the main method before general-purpose class methods.
- Group related class methods together.

Figure 34.1 shows a recommended order of methods.

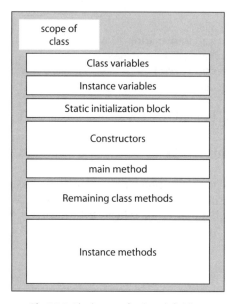

Fig. 34.1 The layout of a class definition.

34.8 Scoping

Scope modifiers can be applied to classes, class and instance variables, and methods. In general, you should attempt to hide as much as possible from other objects; you should only make public items that must be public.

- When you decide that you must make a class public, limit access to it as much as possible.
- If a class or instance variable cannot be private, limit access to it. That is, use the default modifier in preference to protected (by default, the variable is only visible in the current package; protected means that it is visible in the package and in subclasses in other packages).
- If you do not want to allow something to be changed, make it final. You can make classes, instance or class variables, and methods final.
- Make a method private unless it is needed outside the class. If it is needed, limit access to it as much as possible.

If you are unclear about the modifiers and their meaning, refer to back to their definitions.

34.9 Statement Labels

One part of the Java language which has not been discussed in this book is the use of statement labels. You can use labels in conjunction with the break and continue statements.

You label a statement by preceding it with a word followed by a colon:

```
label: statement
```

Although we have only considered the break statement within the context of a switch statement, you can use a break statement to terminate any loop or block of code (for loops, if statements etc.). If the break statement is unlabelled then it terminates the innermost loop or block. However, if you label a statement, you can break out to the level of the label through any number of loops or blocks:

```
if (x == 3)
   outer: for (i = 0; i < 10; ++i) {
          for (j = 0; j < 10; ++j) {
            if ((i + j) == 19)
               break outer;
          }
   }
```

You can also use the continue statement within a loop. It jumps to the end of the loop and causes the condition to be evaluated. If the condition allows the loop to continue, then the next iteration of the loop is executed. You can use a label with the continue statement to jump to an outer loop rather than just an inner loop.

It can be argued that the use of a labelled break or continue is not a form of goto, as they are more controlled. That is, they can only be used to jump from one part of the code to another within a loop (or a block). However, it is as easy to produce obfuscating code with breaks, continues and labels as it is with gotos. Good programming style should remove the need to use these parts of the Java language. If you find you need to use them, then you are probably producing a poorly thought-out implementation.

Chapter 35

Exception Handling

35.1 Introduction

This chapter considers exception handling and how it is implemented in Java. You are introduced to the object model of exception handling, to the throwing and catching of exceptions, and to defining new exceptions and exception-specific constructs.

35.2 What Is an Exception?

In Java, almost everything is an object, including exceptions. All exceptions must extend the class `Throwable` or one of its subclasses, which allows an exception to be thrown or raised. Figure 35.1 presents the `Exception` class hierarchy.

The `Throwable` class has two subclasses: `Error` and `Exception`. Errors are unchecked exceptions generated at run time. These are errors from which it is unlikely that a program can

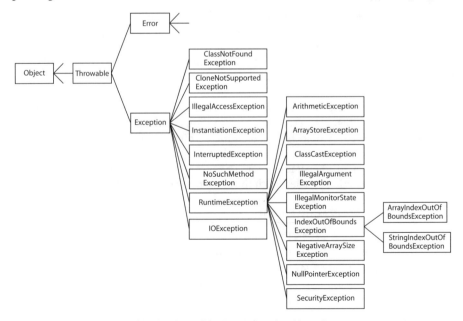

Fig. 35.1 Part of the `Exception` class hierarchy.

recover (such as out of memory errors). Your methods are not expected to deal with them and the compiler does not check that the methods deal with them.

There are two types of Exception subclass. One set, the checked exceptions, ensure that problems such as a file not being available are explicitly dealt with. The other set, unchecked exceptions, deal with problems which may occur at run time but which are not due to the environment.

Your methods must deal with checked exceptions. The compiler checks to see that methods only throw exceptions that they can deal with (or which are passed up to other methods to handle).

An exception can be thrown explicitly by your code or implicitly by the operations you perform. In either case, an exception is an object, and you must instantiate it before you do anything with it. You do this by sending the throw message to an instance of the appropriate exception. For example, to raise an ArithmeticException for a divide by zero error, we write:

```
throw new ArithmeticException("Division By Zero");
```

The exception is caught by the first handler (try block) which is defined on the ArithmeticException (or one of its parent signals).

35.3 What Is Exception Handling?

An exception moves the flow of control from one place to another. In most situations, this is because a problem occurs which cannot be handled locally, but which can be handled in another part of the system. The problem is usually some sort of error (such as dividing by zero), although it can be any problem (for example, identifying that the postcode specified with an address does not match). The purpose of an exception, therefore, is to handle an error condition when it happens at run time.

The terminology used in excpetion handling is listed in Table 35.1.

It is worth considering why you should wish to handle an exception; after all, the system does not allow an error to go unnoticed. For example, if we try to divide by zero, then the system generates an error. This may mean that the user has entered an incorrect value, and we do not want users to be presented with a dialog suggesting that they enter the system debugger. We can use exceptions to force the user to correct the mistake and rerun the calculation.

Different types of error produce different types of exception. For example, if the error is caused by dividing an integer by zero, then the exception is a *divide by zero* exception. The type of exception is identified by objects called signals, which possess exception handlers. Each handler can deal with exceptions associated with its class of signal (and its subclasses).

An exception is initiated when it is thrown. The system searches back up the execution stack until it finds a handler which can deal with the exception (i.e. it searches for a try block of the

Table 35.1 Terms used in exception handling.

Exception	An error which is generated at run time
Raising an exception	Generating a new exception
Throwing an exception	Triggering a generated exception
Handling an exception	Processing code that deals with the error
Handler	The code that deals with the error (referred to as the catch block)
Signal	A particular type of exception (such as *out of bounds* or *divide by zero*)

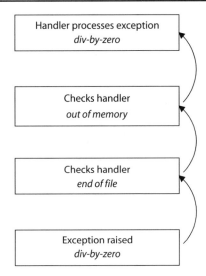

Fig. 35.2 Searching through the execution stack.

appropriate type). The associated handler then processes the exception. This may involve performing some remedial action or terminating the current execution in a controlled manner. In some cases, it may be possible to restart executing the code.

As a handler can only deal with an exception of a specified class (or subclass), an exception may pass through a number of other blocks before it finds one that can process it.

Figure 35.2 illustrates a situation in which a *divide by zero* exception is raised. This exception is passed up the execution stack, where it encounters an exception handler defined for an *End of File* exception. This handler cannot handle the *divide by zero* exception and so it is passed further up the execution stack. It then encounters a handler for an *out of memory* exception. Again, it cannot deal with a *divide by zero* exception and the exception is passed further up the execution stack until it finds a handler defined for the *divide by zero* exception. This handler then processes the exception.

In Java, exceptions are objects and you create and throw an exception by sending messages.

35.4 Throwing an Exception

Chapter 17 says that you need to handle the IOException (or one of its subclasses) when performing IO using files. It also says that you do this by delegating responsibility for the exception back up the execution chain. You do this using the throws clause after the method name declaration (but before the method body):

```
public void handleInput () throws IOException {
    ...
}
```

However, this approach is too simplistic and relies on someone else doing something sensible with the IOException. There are three choices with exceptions:

- Declare the exception in the throws clause and let the exception pass back up the call stack.
- Catch the exception and handle it within the method.
- Catch the exception and map it onto your own exceptions by throwing a new exception.

Passing the exception back up the execution stack is acceptable as long as you know that it is dealt with sensibly. Java forces you either to handle the exception locally or to pass it back up the execution stack explicitly in order to ensure that you think about what should happen if the exception occurs. You must consider carefully whether to throw or handle the exception.

The general syntax for passing the exception out of a method is:

```
access-modifier return-type method-name(parameters)
        throws exception-class {
    ... method body ...
}
```

where *exception-class* indicates the class of exception handled. Subclasses of the named exception class are also handled in this way.

35.5 Catching an Exception

You can catch an exception by implementing the try-catch-finally construct. This construct is broken into three parts:

- try block
  The try block indicates the code which is to be monitored for the exceptions listed in the catch expressions.
- catch expressions
  You can use an optional catch expression to indicate what to do when certain classes of exception occur (e.g. resolve the problem or generate a warning message). If no catch expression is included, the defining methods must use the throws clause.
- finally block
  The optional finally block runs after the try block exits (whether or not this is due to an exception being raised). You can use it to clean up any resources, close files etc.

This construct may seem confusing at first; however, once you have worked with it for a while you will find it less daunting. Typically, you use the same incantation of the construct; concentrate on the details of the code within the try block and do not worry about the exception handling mechanism.

The following example uses the construct to read data from a file and process it. The try block incorporates the file access code, and the code in the catch block states what should happen if an IOException is raised. In this case, it prints a message. The message in the finally block is always printed. It brings together many of the aspects of the Java language. It includes a vector, a switch statement, and while and for loops.

```
import java.io.*;
import java.util.*;

public class Grades {
```

```java
public static void main (String argv []){
  Grades grades = new Grades();
  grades.calculateGrades();
}

// Instance variables
Vector names = new Vector();
Vector marks = new Vector();

public void calculateGrades () {
  int i;

  loadData("input.data");

  for (i = 0; i < names.size(); i++) {
    System.out.print(names.elementAt(i));
    System.out.println("\t " + marks.elementAt(i));
  }
}

public void loadData (String filename) {
  // Define local variables
  FileInputStream inputFile;
  Reader reader;
  StreamTokenizer st;
  String aString;
  int aNumber, next;

  try {
    // Set up link to file and token reader
    inputFile = new FileReader("input.data");
    reader = new BufferedReader(inputFile);
    st = new StreamTokenizer(reader);
    System.out.println("--------------------------");

    // Read contents of file
    while ((next = st.nextToken()) != st.TT_EOF) {
      switch (next) {
        case st.TT_NUMBER: {
          aNumber = (int) st.nval;
          System.out.println("--------------------");
          marks.addElement(new Integer(aNumber));
          break;
        }
        default : {
          aString = st.sval;
          System.out.println(aString);
          names.addElement(aString);
        }
      }
    } // End of while
```

```
      // Now close the file
      inputFile.close();
    }
    catch (IOException e) {
      System.out.println("Whoops we have a problem");
    }
    finally {
      System.out.println("All's well that ends well!");
    }
  }
}
```

The Grades application reads data from a file called input.data which has the following format:

```
"Bob" 45 "Paul" 32 "Peter" 76 "Mike" 29 "John" 56
```

The loadData method uses the FileInputStream, BufferedReader and Stream-Tokenizer classes (see Chapter 17) to read the file. The data is placed in one of two vectors depending on the type of data (either string or integer). This code is wrapped up in a try block. If this code raises an IOException, the message "Whoops we have a problem" is printed. Once the try block is processed, the finally block prints out "All's well that ends well!". The calculateGrades method loads in the data file and prints out the data in the two vectors as a table. Figure 35.3 shows the result of executing the Grades application.

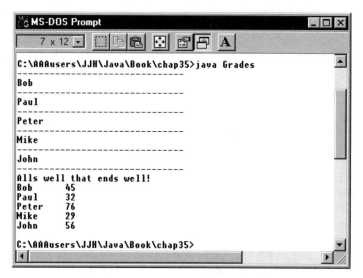

Fig. 35.3 Running the Grades application.

35.6 Defining an Exception

You can define your own exceptions, which can give you more control over what happens in particular circumstances. To define an exception, you create a subclass of the Exception class or one of its subclasses. For example, to define a DivideByZeroException, we can extend the Exception class and generate an appropriate message:

```
public class DivideByZeroException extends Exception {
  public Object offender;

  public DivideByZeroException (Object anObject) {
    super("Divide by zero in " + anObject);
  offender = anObject;
  }
}
```

This class explicitly handles divide by zero exceptions. We could have made it a subclass of ArithmeticException; however, it is an unchecked exception and we wish to force the programmer to handle this exception if it is raised. The following code is an example of how we might use DivideByZeroException:

```
public class Example {
  int x, y;

  public static void main (String args []) {
    Example temp = new Example(5, 0);
    try {
      temp.test();
    }
    catch (DivideByZeroException exception) {
      System.out.println("Oops");
    }
  }

  public Example(int a, int b) {
    x = a;
    y = b;
  }

  public void test() throws DivideByZeroException {
    if (y == 0)
      throw new DivideByZeroException(this);
    else
      System.out.println(x / y);
  }
}
```

In this example, we check to see whether the divisor is zero. If it is, we create a new instance of the DivideByZeroException class and throw it. The test method delegates responsibility for this exception to the calling method (in this case, the main method). The main method catches the exception and prints a message.

Chapter 36

Concurrency

36.1 Introduction

This chapter presents and explains a short example of how concurrency can be accomplished within Java.

36.2 Concurrent Processes

The concepts behind object-oriented programming lend themselves particularly well to the concepts associated with concurrency. For example, a system can be described as a set of discrete objects communicating with one another when necessary. In most Java implementations, only one object may execute at any one moment in time. However, conceptually at least, there is no reason why this restriction should be enforced. The basic concepts behind object orientation still hold, even if each object executes within a separate independent process.

Traditionally, a message send is treated like a procedural call, in which the calling object's execution is blocked until a response is returned. However, we can extend this model quite simply to view each object as a concurrently executable program module, with activity starting when the object is created and continuing even when a message is sent to another object (unless the response is required for further processing). In this model, there may be very many (concurrent) objects executing at the same time. Of course, this introduces issues associated with resource allocation etc., but no more so than in any concurrent system.

One implication of the concurrent object model is that objects are larger than in the traditional single execution thread approach, because of the overhead of having each object as a process. A process scheduler for handling these processes and resource allocation mechanisms means that it is not feasible to have integers, characters etc. as separate processes.

Java has limited built-in support for concurrency. It does support processes and synchronization of methods; however, the processor scheduler (part of the Java Virtual Machine) implements a naïve non-preemptive scheduling policy, with limited support for rescheduling within a particular priority level. Further, once a high-priority process is running, no lower priority process runs until the high-priority process suspends or terminates. For these reasons, the basic Java system contains only a few processes and typical applications using concurrency do not create more than a few tens of processes.

36.3 Threads

A Java process is a preemptive lightweight process termed a *thread*. Every thread (process) has an associated priority and a Java thread runs to completion unless a higher priority process attempts to gain control. Java does not share the processor time among processes of the same priority. Threads with a higher priority are executed before threads with a lower priority. A thread with a higher priority may interrupt a thread with a lower priority. By default, a process inherits the same priority as the process which spawned it. You can change the priority of a process using the setPriority message.

A thread is a "lightweight" process because it does not possess its own address space and it is not treated as a separate entity by the host operating system. Instead, it exists within a single machine process using the same address space.

It is useful to get a clear idea of the difference between a thread (running within a single machine process) and a multiprocess system.

36.3.1 Thread States

The thread which is currently executing is termed the active thread. A thread can also be suspended (i.e. waiting to use the processor) or stopped (waiting for some resource). Figure 36.1 illustrates the thread states and the messages or actions that cause the state to change.

Notice that a thread is considered to be alive unless its run method terminates (or the deprecated stop method has been called) after which it can be considered dead. A live thread can be running, sleeping, interrupted, waiting etc. The runnable state indicates that the thread can be executed by the processor, but it is not currently executing. This is because an equal or higher priority process is already executing and the thread must wait until the processor becomes free. Thus the diagram shows that the scheduler can move a thread between the running and runnable states. In fact, this could happen many times as the thread executes for a while and is then removed from the processor by the scheduler and added to the waiting queue, before being returned to the processor again at a later date. Note that stop, suspend and resume have been deprecated as of Java 2.

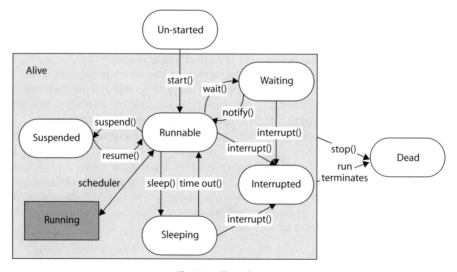

Fig. 36.1 Thread states.

36.3.2 Creating a Thread

There are two ways in which to initiate a new thread of execution (this chapter considers only the first way):

- Create a subclass of the Thread class and redefine the run method to perform the set of actions that the thread is intended to do.
- Define a new class that implements the Runnable interface. It must define the run method and can be started by passing an instance of the class to a new Thread instance.

In both cases, we define a class that specifies the operations or actions that the new thread (of execution) performs. Thus a thread is an independent object running on the processor (in this case, the JVM). As a thread is an object, it can be treated just like any other object: it can be sent messages, it can have instance variables and it can provide methods. Thus, the multi-threaded aspects of Java all conform to the object-oriented model. This greatly simplifies the creation of multi-threaded systems as well as the maintainability and clarity of the resulting software.

Once a new instance of a thread is created, it must be started. Before it is started it cannot run, although it exists (see Figure 36.1).

36.3.3 Thread Groups

You can group threads into a ThreadGroup. Indeed, by default every thread is part of the group of the thread that created it. The thread group defines a set of threads that can be treated as a whole. For example, they can all be suspended, resumed or stopped. A thread group can be made up of other thread groups (referred to as sub-thread groups) as well as individual threads. The primary use of thread groups is as a way to enforce security policies by dynamically restricting thread operation access to members of the same group.

36.4 The Thread Class

The Thread class defines all the facilities required to create a class that can execute within its own lightweight process (within the JVM) (Tables 36.1 and 36.2).

There are a number of methods that obtain information about the status of the process:

- isAlive() tests to see whether the thread has started execution and has not yet terminated.
- isInterrupted() tests to see whether the thread has been interrupted.

The run method specifies what the thread does. This method must be overwritten in any subclasses of Thread (the method defined in Thread does nothing unless it has a class implementing the Runnable interface available to it). The specification of the run method is:

Table 36.1 Thread class variables.

MIN_PRIORITY	An integer which defines the minimum priority of a thread
NORM_PRIORITY	An integer which defines the default priority of a thread
MAX_PRIORITY	An integer which defines the maximum priority of a thread

Table 36.2 Methods that change the state of a thread (see Figure 36.1).

`start()`	Schedules the thread (makes it runnable)
`resume()`	Reschedules a thread that has been suspended. Deprecated in Java 2 and above
`suspend()`	Unschedules the thread temporarily. It must wait until it receives a `resume(0)` message before it can claim the processor. Deprecated in Java 2 and above
`stop()`	Unschedules the thread permanently. That is, it changes the process state to "dead". Deprecated in Java 2 and above
`sleep(long milliseconds)`	Suspends the thread for the specified number of milliseconds
`yield()`	Forces the thread to relinquish the processor momentarily, thus allowing other threads to execute

```
public void run() {...}
```

There are messages associated with a thread's priority, including:

- `setPriority(int priority)`, which sets the priority of the thread
- `getPriority()`, which returns the priority of the thread

Every thread has a unique name. If you do not provide one, then a name is automatically generated by the system. There are two methods that access and set a thread's name:

- `getName()` obtains the name of the thread
- `setName(String string)` sets the name of the thread to the `string` parameter

36.4.1 Implementing a Thread

To create a class which can be executed as a separate thread, you must define either a new subclass of Thread or a class which implements the Runnable interface.
    To create a subclass of Thread, you must follow these steps:

1. Define a new subclass of Thread.
2. Define the run method.

```
class SampleThread extends Thread {
  String string;
  public SampleThread (String aString) {
    string = aString;
  }
  public void run () {
    while (isAlive()) {
      System.out.print(string);
    }
  }
}
```

3. Create an instance of the class.

4. Send the start message to the thread instance. This schedules the new thread and causes the run method to execute.

```
SampleThread thread = new SampleThread("SampleThread");
thread.start();
```

To implement the Runnable interface, you must follow these steps:

1. Define a class which implements the Runnable interface.
2. Define the run method in this class.
3. Create an instance of this class.
4. Create an instance of the Thread class using the Thread(Runnable target) constructor.
5. Send the message start to the thread instance (not the instance which implements the Runnable interface). This schedules the new thread, which in turn initiates the run method on the Runnable object.

36.4.2 Synchronization

Semaphores provide a simple means of synchronization between multiple threads. If two processes are executing and one must not pass a certain point until the other has completed some operation, then a semaphore between the two threads can indicate to the first process that the operation has been completed.

The Thread class provides facilities for simple synchronization on methods within the same class. The synchronized keyword specifies that the associated methods cannot run at the same time as other synchronized methods defined by the class. Each instance has a single semaphore. If one method is executing, others must wait for it to finish.

You can use the synchronized keyword in two ways. The first version allows control over exactly which parts of a method are protected by the synchronized keyword:

```
public void nextSlice() {
  synchronized (this) {
    ...
  }
}
```

The second approach is simpler (but it synchronizes the whole method). If the whole method is synchronized, the javadoc tool includes this fact in the resultant documentation files.

```
public synchronized void nextSlice() {
  ...
}
```

The advantage of the synchronized flag approach is simplicity and efficiency. The disadvantage is that it does not directly support more complex synchronization.

In some situations, you want one thread to wait for another thread to complete before it continues past a certain point. You can specify this using the join method. This method waits for the receiving thread to die before allowing the sending thread to continue:

```
...
anotherThread.join();
... code executes after another thread terminates
```

Other versions of join specify a certain amount of time to wait before continuing; for example, join(long milliseconds). If the receiving thread has not terminated after the time specified in milliseconds, the sending thread resumes.

36.5 A Time Slicing Example

This example shows how to achieve time slicing using Java. The basic idea behind the effective control of multiple processes within Java is the introduction of a high-priority process. This process wakes up every few milliseconds and regroups the processes in a waiting queue of lower processes. It then goes back to "sleep". It thus slices time between the various processes at the lower priority.

36.5.1 Using Schedulers

If it is necessary to develop a preemptive scheduler (that is, one that shares processor time between a given number of processes), then you can do it by using the facilities provided by the standard scheduler. This results in two schedulers: the system scheduler and a user-defined scheduler.

The system scheduler still enables a process to execute. For example, it is still this scheduler which suspends or interrupts a process. The user-defined scheduler manages the queue of user processes waiting to be handed to the system scheduler whenever it "wakes up". Of course, in order to gain control of the processor, the user-defined scheduler must have a higher priority than all other user processes. It can then interrupt the user processes and select which process to initiate.

The key to the user-defined scheduler is that it "wakes up" every few milliseconds. You can use the sleep(milliseconds) message to suspend the scheduler process until the associated timer sends the process a resume message. The resume message causes it to take control of the processor again.

When the process is awake, it can determine which of the processes currently waiting to use the processor to resume. One way to do this is with an index indicating the currently executing process. This index can be incremented to indicate the next process to resume; this ensures that a different process is resumed every time the scheduler process "goes back to sleep".

36.5.2 The Time Slicing Source Code

This example is based on a new subclass of Thread called TimeSlice. It is a high-priority thread which cycles between a sleep state and a running state. When it runs, it selects a new process for execution using the nextSlice method. You can achieve this sleeping and slicing cycle by spawning a new process (with the highest allowable priority).

The TimeSlice class sets up the processes to be sliced in initializeTimeSlicing() and initiates the time slicing operation within the run method. The sleep message can throw an instance of the InterruptedException class. You must therefore handle this exception (for example, within a try–catch block, as discussed in the previous chapter).

The initializeTimeSlicing method sets the priority of the TimeSlice thread to the highest priority available. It creates three new processes, and gives each of them the normal priority. It then starts and suspends each of these processes. Notice that the instances are held in an instance variable, threads. Having set up the threads, the start message is sent to the object, which schedules the TimeSlice thread object and sends it the message run.

```java
import java.util.*;

public class TimeSlice extends Thread {
  private Vector threads = new Vector(3);
  private SampleThread currentThread;
  private int index = 0;

  public static void main (String args []) {
    TimeSlice timeSlicer = new TimeSlice();
    timeSlicer.initializeTimeSlicing();
  }

  public void initializeTimeSlicing() {
    int i;
    SampleThread aThread;
    System.out.println("Initializing Time Slicing");
    setPriority(Thread.MAX_PRIORITY);
    threads.addElement(new SampleThread("a"));
    threads.addElement(new SampleThread("b"));
    threads.addElement(new SampleThread("c"));
    for (i = 0; i < threads.size(); i++) {
      aThread = (SampleThread)threads.elementAt(i);
      aThread.setPriority(Thread.NORM_PRIORITY);
      aThread.start();
      aThread.suspend();
    }
    start();
  }

  public void run () {
    System.out.println("Starting time slicing");
    while (isAlive()) {
      nextSlice();
      try {
        sleep(100);
        System.out.println("\n-----");
      }
      catch (InterruptedException e) {
        System.out.println("Interrupted stopping..");
        stop();
      }
    }
  }

  public void nextSlice () {
```

```
      if (currentThread != null) {
        currentThread.suspend();
      }
      index++;
      if (index == threads.size()) {
        index = 0;
      }
      currentThread =
        (SampleThread)threads.elementAt(index);
      currentThread.resume();
    }
  }
```

The run method defined for TimeSlice continuously loops while the thread is active. This
is common behaviour for a run method and is better style than looping while true (for
threads). The run method first calls the nextSlice method, which selects the next thread
to execute and then sends itself to sleep for 100 milliseconds. The selected thread can then
execute until the 100 milliseconds are up. Then the lower priority process suspends and the
TimeSlice thread resumes. The call to sleep is wrapped in a try–catch block so that if an
InterruptedException is raised it is handled locally.

The nextSlice method first suspends the current (lower priority) thread and then selects
the next thread to execute. This is where the real business of the time slicing operation occurs.
The algorithm describing this method's operation is:

1.   Find the current executing lower priority thread.
2.   Suspend it.
3.   Select a new thread to resume.
4.   Send the selected thread the resume message.

This is a very simple algorithm, but it works! The implementation uses an index to record the
position of the current thread within the vector of threads. This index is incremented each time
nextSlice is called. When the index is greater than the number of threads, it is reset to zero
(vectors are indexed from zero). The current thread object is held in the currentThread instance variable.

To test out the effects of this approach to time slicing, the main method creates a new
TimeSlice instance and sends it the initializeTimeSlicing message.

The SampleThread class is a very simple process which extends Thread. It merely prints a
string, passed to it by its constructor, on the console while it is active:

```
class SampleThread extends Thread {
  String string;
  public SampleThread (String aString) {
    string = aString;
  }
  public void run () {
    while (isAlive()) {
      System.out.print(string);
    }
  }
}
```

Figure 36.2 shows the result of running the TimeSlice application.

Fig. 36.2 Running the time slicing example.

Part **8**

Object-Oriented Design

Chapter 37

Object-Oriented Analysis and Design

37.1 Introduction

This chapter surveys the most significant object-oriented design and analysis methods to emerge since the late 1980s. It concentrates primarily on OOA (Coad and Yourdon, 1991) and Booch (Booch, 1991, 1994), Object Modeling Technique (Rumbaugh *et al.*, 1991), Objectory (Jacobson, 1992) and Fusion (Coleman *et al.*, 1994). It also introduces the Unified Modeling Language (Rational, 2001; Jacobson *et al.*, 1998).

This chapter does not aim to deal comprehensively with either the range of methods available or the fine details of each approach. Rather, it provides an overview of the design process, and the strengths and weaknesses of some important and reasonably representative methods.

37.2 Object-Oriented Design Methods

The object-oriented design methods that we consider are all architecture-driven, incremental and iterative. They do not adopt the more traditional waterfall software development model; instead, they adopt an approach which is more akin to the spiral model of Boehm (1988). This reflects developers' experiences when creating object-oriented systems – the object-oriented development process is more incremental than that for procedural systems, with less distinct barriers between analysis, design and implementation. Some organizations take this process to the extreme and adopt an evolutionary development approach. This approach delivers system functions to users in very small steps and revises project plans in the light of experience and user feedback. This philosophy has proved very successful for organizations which have fully embraced it and has led to earlier business benefits and successful end products from large development projects.

37.3 Object-Oriented Analysis

We first consider the Object-Oriented Analysis approach (OOA) of Coad and Yourdon (1991). The identification of objects and classes is a crucial task in object-oriented analysis and design, but many techniques ignore this issue. For example, both the Booch method and OMT do not deal with it at all. They indicate that it is a highly creative process which can be based on the identification of nouns and verbs in an informal verbal description of the problem domain. A different approach is to use a method such as OOA as the first part of the design process and then to use another object-oriented design method for the later parts of the process.

OOA helps designers identify the detailed requirements of their software, rather than how the software should be structured or implemented. It aims to describe the existing system and how it operates, and how the software system should interact with it. One of the claims of OOA is that it helps the designer to package the requirements of the system in an appropriate manner (for object-oriented systems?) and to reduce the risk of the software failing to meet the customer's requirements. In effect, OOA helps to build the Object Model, which we look at in more detail when we look at OMT.

There are five activities within OOA which direct the analyst during the analysis process:

- Finding classes and objects in the domain.
- Identifying structures (amongst those classes and objects). Structures are relationships such as *is a* and *part of*.
- Identifying subjects (related objects).
- Defining attributes (the data elements of the objects).
- Defining services (the active parts of objects that indicate what the object does).

These are not sequential steps: as information becomes available, the analyst performs the appropriate activity. The intention is that the analyst can work in whatever way the domain expert finds it easiest to express their knowledge. Thus the analyst may go deeper into one activity than the others as the domain expert provides greater information in that area. Equally, the analyst may jump around between activities identifying classes one minute and services the next.

37.4 The Booch Method

The Booch method (also known as Booch and Object-Oriented Development, or OOD) is one of the earliest recognizable object-oriented design methods. It was first described in a paper published in 1986 and has become widely adopted since the publication of a book describing the method (Booch, 1991; Booch, 1994).

The Booch method provides a step-by-step guide to the design of an object-oriented system. Although Booch's books discuss the analysis phase, they do so in too little detail compared with the design phase.

37.4.1 The Steps in the Booch Method

Identification of classes and objects involves analyzing the problem domain and the system requirements to identify the set of classes required. This is not trivial and relies on a suitable requirements analysis.

Identification of the semantics of classes and objects involves identifying the services offered by an object and required by an object. A service is a function performed by an object and, during this step, the overall system functionality is devolved among the objects. This is another non-trivial step and it may result in modifications to the classes and objects identified in the last step.

Identification of the relationships between classes and objects involves identifying links between objects as well as inheritance between classes. This step may identify new services required of objects.

Implementation of classes and objects attempts to consider how to implement the classes and objects and how to define the attributes and provide services. This involves considering algorithms. This process may lead to modifications in the deliverables of all of the above steps and may force the designer to return to some or all of the above steps.

During these steps, the designer produces

- Class diagrams which illustrate the classes in the system and their relationships.
- Object diagrams which illustrate the actual objects in the system and their relationships.
- Module diagrams which package the classes and objects into modules. These modules illustrate the influence that Ada had on the development of the Booch method (Booch, 1987).
- Process diagrams which package processes and processors.
- State transition diagrams and timing diagrams which describe the dynamic behaviour of the system (the other diagrams describe the static structure of the system).

Booch recommends an incremental and iterative development of a system through the refinement of different yet consistent logical and physical views of that system.

37.4.2 Strengths and Weaknesses

The biggest problem for a designer approaching the Booch method for the first time is that the plethora of different notations is supported by a poorly defined and loose process (although the revision to the method described in Booch (1994) addresses this to some extent). It does not give step-by-step guidance and possesses very few mechanisms for determining the system's requirements. Its main strengths are its (mainly graphical) notations, which cover most aspects of the design of an object-oriented system, and its greatest weakness is the lack of sufficient guidance in the generation of these diagrams.

37.5 The Object Modeling Technique

The Object Modeling Technique (OMT) is an object-oriented design method which aims to construct a series of models which refine the system design until the final model is suitable for implementation. The design process is divided into three phases:

- The Analysis Phase attempts to model the problem domain.
- The Design Phase structures the results of the analysis phase in an appropriate manner.
- The Implementation Phase takes into account target language constructs.

37.5.1 The Analysis Phase

Three types of model are produced by the analysis phase:

- *The object model* represents the static structure of the domain. It describes the objects, their classes and the relationships between the objects. For example, the object model might represent the fact that a department object possesses a single manager (object) but many employees (objects). The notation is based on an extension of the basic entity–relationship notation.

- *The dynamic model* represents the behaviour of the system. It expresses what happens in the domain, when it occurs and what effect it has. It does not represent how the behaviour is achieved. The formalism used to express the dynamic model is based on a variation of finite state machines called statecharts. These were developed by Harel and others (1987, 1988) to represent dynamic behaviour in real-time avionic control systems. Statecharts indicate the states of the system, the transitions between states, their sequence and the events which cause the state change.
- *The functional model* describes how system functions are performed. It uses data flow diagrams which illustrate the sources and sinks of data as well as the data being exchanged. They contain no sequencing information or control structures.

The relationship between these three models is important, as each model adds to the designer's understanding of the domain:

- The object model defines the objects which hold the state variables referenced in the dynamic model and are the sources and sinks referenced in the functional model.
- The dynamic model indicates when the behaviour in the functional model occurs and what triggers it.
- The functional model explains why an event transition leads from one state to another in the dynamic model.

You do not build these models sequentially; changes to any one of the models may have a knock-on effect in the other models. Typically, the designer starts with the object model, then considers the dynamic model and finally the functional model, but the process is iterative.

The analysis process is described in considerable detail and provides by step-by-step guidance. This ensures that the developer knows what to do at any time to advance the three models.

37.5.2 The Design Phase

The design phase of OMT builds upon the models produced during the analysis phase:

- *The system design step* breaks the system down into subsystems and determines the overall architecture to be used.
- *The object design step* decides on the algorithms to be used for the methods. The methods are identified by examining the three analysis models for each class etc.

Each of the steps gives some guidelines for their respective tasks; however, far less support is provided for the designer than in the analysis phase. For example, there is no systematic guidance for the identification of subsystems, although the issues involved are discussed (resource management, batch versus interactive modes etc.). This means that it can be difficult to identify where to start, how to proceed and what to do next.

37.5.3 The Implementation Phase

The implementation phase codifies the system and object designs into the target language. This phase provides some very useful information on how to implement features used in the model-based design process used, but it lacks the step-by-step guidance which would be useful for those new to object orientation.

37.5.4 Strengths and Weaknesses

OMT's greatest strength is the level of step-by-step support that it provides during the analysis phase. However, it is much weaker in its guidance during the design and implementation phases, where it provides general guidelines (and some heuristics).

37.6 The Objectory Method

The driving force behind the Objectory method (Jacobson, 1991) is the concept of a *use case*. A use case is a particular interaction between the system and a user of that system (an actor) for a particular purpose (or function). The users of the system may be human or machine. A complete set of use cases therefore describes a system's functionality based around what actors should be able to do with the system. The Objectory method has three phases which produce a set of models.

37.6.1 The Requirements Phase

The requirements phase uses a natural language description of what the system should do to build three models.

- *The use case model* describes the interactions between actors and the system. Each use case specifies the actions which are performed and their sequence. Any alternatives are also documented. This can be done in natural language or using state transition diagrams.
- *The domain model* describes the objects, classes and associations between objects in the domain. It uses a modified entity–relationship model.
- *The user interface descriptions* contain mock-ups of the various interfaces between actors and the system. User interfaces are represented as pictures of windows while other interfaces are described by protocols.

37.6.2 The Analysis Phase

The analysis phase produces the analysis model and a set of subsystem descriptions. The analysis model is a refinement of the domain object model produced in the requirements phase. It contains behavioural information as well as control objects which are linked to use cases. The analysis model also possesses entity objects (which exist beyond a single use case) and interface objects (which handle system–actor interaction). The subsystem descriptions partition the system around objects which are involved in similar activities and which are closely coupled. This organization structures the rest of the design process.

37.6.3 The Construction Phase

The construction phase refines the models produced in the analysis phase. For example, interobject communication is refined and facilities provided by the target language are considered. This phase produces three models:

- Block models represent the functional modules of the system.
- Block interfaces specify the public operations performed by blocks.

- Block specifications are optional descriptions of block behaviour in the form of finite
  state machines.

The final stage is to implement the blocks in the target language.

37.6.4 Strengths and Weaknesses

The most significant aspect of Objectory is its use of use cases, which join the building blocks of
the method. Objectory is unique among the methods considered here, as it provides a unifying
framework for the design process. However, it still lacks the step-by-step support which would
simplify the whole design process.

37.7 The Fusion Method

The majority of object-oriented design methods currently available, including those described
in this chapter, take a systematic approach to the design process. However, in almost all cases
this process is rather weak, providing insufficient direction or support to the developer. In
addition, methods such as OMT rely on a "bottom up" approach. This means that the developer
must focus on the identification of appropriate classes and their interfaces without necessarily
having the information to enable them to do this in an appropriate manner for the overall
system. Little reference is made to the system's overall functionality when determining class
functionality etc. Indeed, some methods provide little more than some vague guidelines and
anecdotal heuristics.

In contrast, Fusion explicitly attempts to provide a systematic approach to object-oriented
software development. In many ways, the Fusion method is a mixture of a range of other
approaches (indeed, the authors of the method acknowledge that there is little new in the
approach, other than that they have put it all together in a single method; see Figure 37.1).

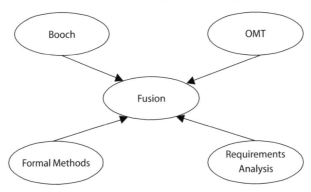

Fig. 37.1 Some of the influences on Fusion.

As with other object-oriented design methods, Fusion is based around the construction of
appropriate models that capture different elements of the system and different knowledge.
These models are built up during three distinct phases:

- *The analysis phase* produces models that describe the high-level constraints from which
  the design models are developed.

- *The design phase* produces a set of models that describe how the system behaves in terms of a collection of interacting objects.
- *The implementation phase* describes how to map the design models onto implementation language constructs.

Within each phase a set of detailed steps attempts to guide the developer through the Fusion process. These steps include checks to ensure the consistency and completeness of the emerging design. In addition, the output of one step acts as the input for the next.

Fusion's greatest weakness is its complexity – it really requires a sophisticated CASE tool. Without such a tool, it is almost impossible to produce a consistent and complete design.

37.8 The Unified Modeling Language

The Unified Modeling Language (UML) is an attempt by Grady Booch, Ivar Jacobson and James Rumbaugh to build on the experiences of the Booch, Object Modeling Technique (OMT) and Objectory methods. Their aim is to produce a single, common, and widely useable modelling language for these methods and, working with other methodologists, for other methods. This means that UML focuses on a standard language and not a standard process, which reflects what happens in reality: a particular notation is adopted as the means of communication on a specific project and between projects. However, between projects (and sometimes within projects), different design methods are adopted as appropriate. For example, a design method intended for the domain of real-time avionics systems may not be suitable for designing a small payroll system. The UML is an attempt to develop a common meta-model which unifies semantics and from which a common notation can be built.

37.9 Summary

In this chapter, we have reviewed a number of object-oriented analysis and design methods and the Unified Modeling Language. We have briefly considered the features, strengths and weaknesses of each method.

In all these systems, during the design process it is often difficult to identify commonalities between classes at the implementation level. This means that during the implementation phase, experienced object-oriented technicians should look for situations in which they can move implementation-level components up the class hierarchy. This can greatly increase the amount of reuse within a software system and may lead to the introduction of abstract classes which contain the common code.

The problem with this is that the implemented class hierarchy no longer reflects the design class hierarchy. It is therefore necessary to have a free flow of information between the implementation and design phases in an object-oriented project.

Chapter 38

The Unified Modeling Language

38.1 Introduction

The Unified Modeling Language (UML) is part of a development to merge (unify) the concepts in the Booch, Objectory and OMT methods (Jacobson *et al.*, 1998; Rational, 2001). The method is still under development (and has taken a low profile recently); however, the notation underlying this method is nearing completion. This notation is now the focus of the current work of Booch, Rumbaugh and Jacobson and is receiving a great deal of interest. Microsoft, Hewlett-Packard, Oracle and Texas Instruments have all endorsed the UML.

The UML is a third generation object-oriented modeling language (Rational, 2001) which adapts and extends the published notations used in the works of Booch, Rumbaugh and Jacobson (Booch, 1994; Rumbaugh *et al.*, 1991; Jacobson, 1992) and is influenced by many others such as Fusion (Coleman *et al.*, 1994), Harel's statecharts (Harel *et al.*, 1987; Harel, 1988) and CORBA (Ben-Natan, 1995), as illustrated in Figure 38.1.

The UML is intended to form a single, common, widely useable modelling language for a range of object-oriented design methods (including Booch, Objectory and OMT). It is also intended that it should be applicable in a wide range of applications and domains. It should be equally applicable to client–server applications and to real-time control applications.

The justification for UML is that different organizations, applications and domains require (and use) different design methods. An organization may develop its own methods or modify other methods through experience. Different parts of the same organization may use different methods. The notation that they use acts as a language to communicate the ideas represented in part (or all) of the design.

For example, the production of shrink-wrapped, off-the-shelf software, is different from the creation of one-off bespoke software. However, both activities may be carried out by a software

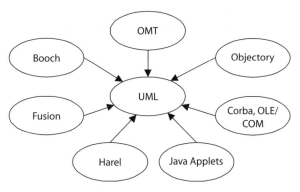

Fig. 38.1 The influences on the UML notation.

company. Such an organization may well wish to exchange ideas, designs or parts of a design among its departments or operational units. This kind of exchange relies on the availability of a common language; UML provides such a language.

At present, the UML is in draft form (Booch *et al.*, 1996); however, it is being presented to the Object Management Group (OMG), in the hope that it will be accepted as a standard (this is an ongoing process and is part of the OMG's call for information on object-oriented methods). For the latest information on the UML (and other developments on the unification front) see the Rational Software Corporation's Web site (http://www.rational.com/).

This chapter provides a brief introduction to the UML. It considers how the UML represents the classes, objects, relationships and attributes in an object-oriented system. It also considers sequence and collaboration diagrams, state diagrams and deployment diagrams.

For further information, see version 1.0 of the UML documentation set. There is also a series of books on the UML, including a Reference Manual and a User Guide (Booch *et al.*, 1997). Other books are becoming available, for example a Process Book (which, at the time of writing, is still in the pipeline) and Fowler and Scott (1997).

38.2 The Meta-Model

The UML is built upon a common meta-model which defines the semantics of the language. On top of this, there is a common notation which interprets these semantics in an easily (human) comprehensible manner.

A meta-model describes the constituents of a model and its relationships. It is a model which documents how another model can be defined. Such models are important because they provide a single, common and unambiguous statement of the syntax and semantics of a model. A meta-model allows CASE tool builders to do more than provide diagramming tools. The meta-model serves several purposes:

- defining the syntax and describing the semantics of the UML's concepts
- providing a (reasonably) formal basis for the UML
- providing a description of the elements of the UML
- providing the basis for the interchange of models between vendors' tools

In the normal course of events, a user of the UML (or indeed of a tool which supports the UML) need not know about the meta-model. However, for the developers of the UML and for tool vendors in general the meta-model is a valuable, indeed essential, feature.

At present, the UML meta-model is defined in terms of the UML and textual annotations (although this may appear infinitely recursive, it is possible). Work on the meta-model is still progressing; the authors of the UML are attempting to make it more formal and simpler.

38.3 The Models

The UML defines a number of models and their notations:

- *Use case diagrams* organize the use cases that encompass a system's behaviour (they are based on the use case diagrams of Objectory).

- *Class diagrams* express the static structure of the system (they derive from the Booch and OMT methods), for example the *part-of* and *is-a* relationships between classes and objects. The class diagrams also encompass the object diagrams. Therefore, in this book, we refer to them as the Object Model (as in OMT).
- *Sequence diagrams* (known as message-trace diagrams in version 0.8 of the Unified Method draft) deal with the time ordered sequence of transactions between objects.
- *Collaboration diagrams* (previously known as object-message diagrams) indicate the order of messages between specified objects. They complement sequence diagrams as they illustrate the same information. Sequence diagrams highlight the actual sequence, while collaboration diagrams highlight the structure required to support the message sequence.
- *State machine diagrams* are based on statecharts, like those in OMT. They capture the dynamic behaviour of the system.
- *Component diagrams* (known as module diagrams in version 0.8 of the Unified Method draft) represent the development view of the system; that is, how the system should be developed into software modules. You can also use them to represent concepts such as dynamic libraries.
- *Deployment diagrams* (previously known as platform diagrams) attempt to capture the topology of the system once it is deployed. They reflect the physical topology upon which the software system is to execute.

38.4 Use Case Diagrams

Use case diagrams explain how a system (or subsystem) is used. The elements which interact with the system can be humans, other computers or dumb devices which process or produce data. The diagrams thus present a collection of use cases which illustrate what the system is expected to do in terms of its external services or interfaces. Such diagrams are very important for illustrating the overall system functionality (to both technical and non-technical personnel). They can act as the context within which the rest of the system is defined.

The large rectangle in Figure 38.2 indicates the boundaries of the system (a telephone help desk adviser). The rectangles on either side of the system indicate external actors (in this case, a Service Engineer and a Telephonist) which interact with the system. The ovals inside the system box indicate the actual use cases themselves. For example, both the actors need to be able to "load a casebase".

The notation for actors is based on "stereotypes" (which are discussed in more detail later). An actor is a class with a stereotype: <<actor>> indicates the actor stereotype and the stick figure is the actor stereotype icon. Although we have used the class icon (a box) as well as the stereotype icon (the stick man), we could have used only one of them if we had so wished.

Each individual use case can have a name, a description explaining what it does, and a list of its responsibilities, attributes and operations. It may also describe its behaviour in the form of a statechart. The most appropriate form of description for a use case differs from one domain to another and thus the format should be chosen as appropriate. This illustrates the flexibility of the UML; it does not prescribe the actual format of a use case.

You can use sequence diagrams and collaboration diagrams with use case diagrams to illustrate the sequence of interactions between the system and the actors. You should also annotate use cases with a statement of purpose to place the use case in context.

Finally, the relationship between use case diagrams and class diagrams is that use cases are peers of classes. Depending on the size of the system, they can be grouped with the object model in a package or remain totally independent.

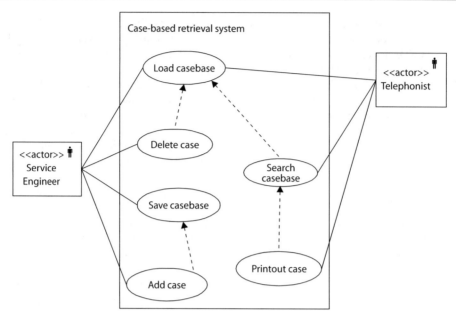

Fig. 38.2 Use case diagram.

38.5 The Object Model

The object model is the key element of the UML. The constituent diagrams illustrate the static structure of a system via the important classes and objects in the system and how they relate to each other. The UML documentation currently talks about class diagrams (and within this about object diagrams) stating that "class diagrams show generic descriptions of possible systems and object diagrams show particular instantiations of systems and their behaviour". It goes on to state that class diagrams contain classes, while object diagrams contain objects, but that it is possible to mix the two. However, it discusses both under the title *class diagrams*. To avoid confusion, we adopt the term Object Model to cover both sets of diagrams (following the approach adopted in both the Booch and OMT methods).

38.5.1 Representing Classes

A class is drawn as a solid-outline rectangle with three components. The class name (in bold type) is in the top part, a list of attributes is in the middle part and a list of operations is in the bottom part. Figure 38.3 illustrates two classes: `Car` and `File`. The `Car` class possesses three attributes (`name`, `age` and `fuel` are `string`, `integer` and `string` types, respectively) and four operations (`start`, `lock` and `brake` take no parameters, while `accelerate` takes a single parameter, `to`, which is an integer that represents the new speed).

An attribute has a name and a type specified in the following format:

name: type = initialValue

The name and type are strings that are ultimately language-dependent. The initial value is a string representing an expression in the target language.

Car
name: string age: integer fuel: string
start() lock() accelerate(to:integer) brake()

File
fileName: string size: integer lastUpdate: string
print()

Fig. 38.3 Classes with attributes and operations.

An operation has a name and may take one or more parameters and return a value. It is specified in the following format:

name (parameter : type = defaultValue, ...): resultType

The constituent parts are language-dependent strings.

You can hide the attribute and operation compartments from view to reduce the detail shown in a diagram. If you omit a compartment, it says nothing about that part of the class definition. However, if you leave the compartment blank, there are no definitions for that part of the class. Additional language-dependent and user-defined information can also be included in each compartment in a textual format. The intention of such additions is to clarify any element of the design in a similar manner to a comment in source code.

A class *stereotype* tells the reader what "kind" of class it is (for example, exceptions, controllers, interfaces, etc.). You show the stereotype as a normal font text string between << >> centred above the class name (see Figure 38.4).

However, UML makes no assumptions about the range of stereotypes which exist and designers are free to develop their own. Other (language-specific) class properties can also be indicated in the class name compartment. For example, in Figure 38.4 the Window class is an abstract class.

You can also indicate the intended scope of attributes and operations in the class definition. This can be useful even for languages, such as Smalltalk, which do not support concepts such as public, private and protected attributes and operations. The absence of any symbol in front of an attribute or operation indicates that the element is public for that class. The significance of this depends on the language. The symbols currently supported are shown in Figure 38.4. You

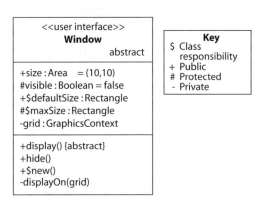

Fig. 38.4 Class with additional annotations.

can combine symbols to indicate, for example, that an operation is a class-side public method (such as +$new()).

38.5.2 Representing Objects

An object is drawn as a hexagon with straight sides and a slight peak at the top and bottom (see Figure 38.5). If you are familiar with Booch clouds, you can think of it as a structured cloud.[1]

repMobile1 : Car

name = XK8
age = 1
fuel = petrol

Fig. 38.5 An object.

The object symbol is divided into two sections. The top section indicates the name of the object and its class in the format *objectName : className*. In Figure 38.5, the object is repMobile1 and the class is Car (see Figure 38.3 for the definition of the Car class). The object name is optional, but the class name is compulsory. You can also indicate how many objects of a particular class are anticipated by entering the maximum value, range etc. in the top compartment. The lack of any number indicates that a single object is intended. The lower compartment contains a list of attributes and their values in the format *name type = value* (although the type is usually omitted). You can suppress the bottom compartment for clarity.

38.5.3 Representing Relationships

A relationship between classes or objects is represented by an association drawn as a solid line (see Figure 38.6). An association between classes may have a name and an optional direction arrowhead that shows which way it is to be read. For example, in Figure 38.6 the relationship called hasEngine is read from the Car class to the Engine class. In addition, each end of an association is a *role*. A role may have a name that illustrates how its class is viewed by the other class. In Figure 38.6, the engine sees the car as a name and the car sees the engine as a specified type (e.g. Petrol, Diesel, Electric).

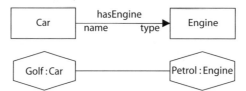

Fig. 38.6 Association between classes and links between objects.

---

1   From September 1996, the 0.91 addendum to the UML states that an object is now drawn as a rectangle, with the objectName:className underlined. This is a major notational change which the UML authors made so that they do not have to invent a different symbol every time they have a type–instance relationship. However, it means that the distinction between objects and classes in diagrams is minimal and can easily lead to confusion. In an attempt to make objects clearly distinguishable, we continue to use the structured cloud symbol.

Each role (i.e. each end of the association) indicates the multiplicity of its class; that is, how many instances of the class can be associated with one instance of the other class. This is indicated by a text expression on the role: * (indicating zero or more), a number or a range (e.g. 0..3). If there is no expression, there is exactly one association (see Figure 38.7). You can specify that the multiple objects should be ordered using the text {Ordered}. You can also annotate the association with additional text (such as {Sorted}), but this is primarily for the reader's benefit and has no meaning in UML.

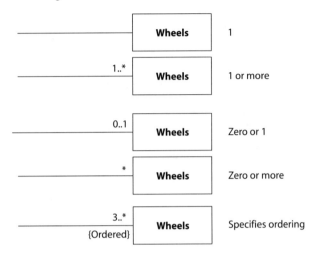

Fig. 38.7 Annotated associations.

In some situations, an association needs attributes. This means that you need to treat the association as a class (see Figure 38.8). These associations have a dashed line from the association line to the association class. This class is just like any other class and can have a name, attributes and operations. In Figure 38.8, the associations show an access permissions attribute which indicates the type of access allowed for each user for each file.

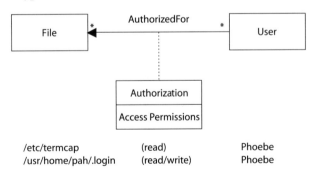

Fig. 38.8 Associations with attributes.

Aggregation indicates that one or more objects are dependent on another object for their existence (*part–whole* relationships). For example, in Figure 38.9, the Microcomputer is formed from the Monitor, the System box, the Mouse and the Keyboard. They are all needed for the fully functioning Microcomputer. Aggregation is shown by an empty diamond on the role attached to the whole object.

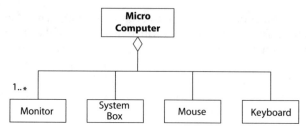

Fig. 38.9 Aggregation tree notation.

It is sometimes useful to differentiate between by-value and by-reference references (see Figure 38.10). If the aggregation symbol is not filled, it indicates a by-reference implementation (i.e. a pointer or other reference); if the aggregation symbol is filled, it indicates a by-value implementation (i.e. a class that is embedded within another class).

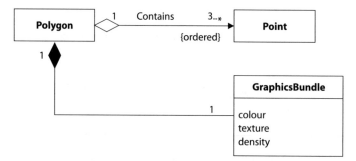

Fig. 38.10 Reference implementation.

A qualified association is an association which requires both the object and the qualifier to identify uniquely the other object involved in the association. It is shown as a box between the association and the class. For example, in Figure 38.11, you need the catalogue and the part number to identify a unique part. Notice that the qualifier is part of the association, not the class.

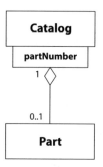

Fig. 38.11 Qualified associations.

A ternary (or higher order) association is drawn as a diamond with one line path to each of the participating classes (see Figure 38.12). This is the traditional entity–relationship model symbol for an association (the diamond is omitted from the binary association to save space).

Ternary associations are very rare and higher order associations are almost non-existent. However, you can model them if necessary.

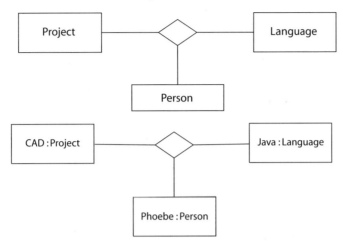

Fig. 38.12 Ternary associations.

Inheritance of one class by a subclass is indicated by a solid line drawn from the subclass to the superclass with a large (unfilled) triangular arrowhead at the superclass end (see Figure 38.13). For compactness, you can use a tree structure to show multiple subclasses inheriting from a single superclass.

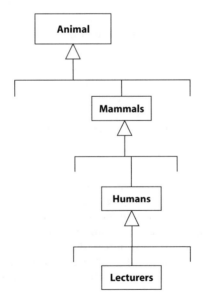

Fig. 38.13 Inheritance hierarchy.

You can also model multiple inheritance, as languages such as the Common Lisp Object System (CLOS) and C++ support it. Multiple inheritance is represented by inheritance lines from a single subclass to two or more superclasses as in Figure 38.14. In this figure, the class *Motor powered water vehicle* inherits from both *Motor powered* and *Water vehicle*.

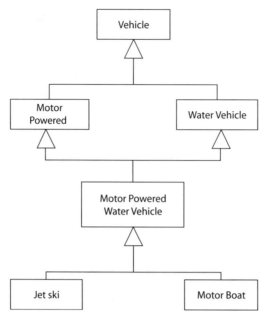

Fig. 38.14 Multiple inheritance.

A derived value can be represented by a slash ("/") before the name of the derived attribute (see Figure 38.15). Such an attribute requires an additional textual constraint defining how it is generated; you indicate this by a textual annotation below the class between curly brackets ({}).

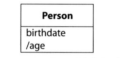

{age = currentDate - birthdate}

Fig. 38.15 Derived values.

A class may define a pattern of objects and links that exist whenever it is instantiated. Such a class is called a composite, and its class diagram contains an object diagram. You may think of it as an extended form of aggregation where the relationships among the parts are valid only within the composite. A composite is a kind of *pattern* or *template* that represents a conceptual clustering for a given purpose. Composition is shown by drawing a class box around the embedded components (see Figure 38.16) which are prototypical objects and links. That is, a composite defines a context in which references to classes and associations, defined elsewhere, can be used.

38.6 Packages

Packages group associated modelling elements such as classes in the object model (or subsystems in component diagrams). They are drawn as tabbed folders.

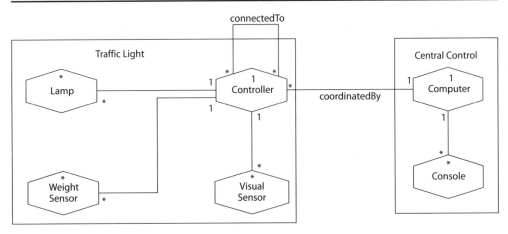

Fig. 38.16 Composite classes.

Figure 38.17 illustrates five packages called Clients, Business Model, Persistent Store, Bank and Network. In this diagram, the contents of Clients, Persistent Store, Bank and Network have been suppressed (by convention, the package names are in the body) and only Business Model is shown in detail (with its name in the top tab). Business Model possesses two classes, Customer and Account, and a nested package, Bank. The broken lines illustrate dependencies between the packages. For example, the package Clients directly depends on the packages Business Model and Network (i.e. at least one element in the Clients package relies on at least one element in the other two packages).

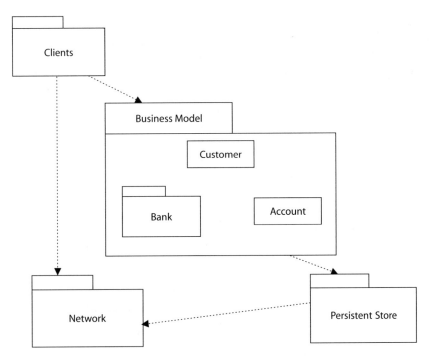

Fig. 38.17 Packages with dependencies.

A class may belong to exactly one package but make reference to classes in other packages. Such references have the following format:

```
packageName :: className
Business Model :: Customer
```

Packages allow you to structure models hierarchically; they organize the model and control its overall complexity. Indeed, you may use a package to enable top-down design of a system (rather than the bottom-up design typical of many object-oriented design methods) by allowing designers to specify high-level system functionality in terms of packages which are "filled out" as and when appropriate.

38.7 Sequence Diagrams

A *scenario* shows a particular series of interactions among objects in a single execution of a system. That is, it is a history of how the system behaves between one start state and a single termination state. This differs from an *envisionment*, which describes all system behaviours from all start states to all end states. Envisionments thus contain all possible histories (although they may also contain paths which the system is never intended to take).

Scenarios can be presented in two different ways: *sequence diagrams* and *collaboration diagrams*. Both these diagrams present the same information although they stress different aspects of this information. For example, sequence diagrams stress the timing aspects of the interactions between the objects, whereas collaboration diagrams stress the structure between these objects (which helps in understanding the requirements of the underlying software structure).

Figure 38.18 illustrates the basic structure of a sequence diagram. The objects involved in the exchange of messages are represented as vertical lines (which are labelled with the object's name). Caller, Phone Line and Callee are all objects involved in the scenario of dialling the Emergency services. The horizontal arrows indicate an event or message sent from one object to another. The arrow indicates the direction in which the event or message is sent. That is, the

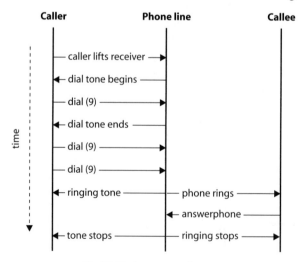

Fig. 38.18 A sequence diagram.

receiver is indicated by the head of the arrow. Normally return values are not shown on these diagrams. However, if they are significant, you can illustrate them by annotated return events.

Time proceeds vertically down the diagram, as indicated by the broken line arrow, and can be made more explicit by additional timing marks. These timing marks indicate how long the gap between messages should be or how long a message or event should take to get from the sender to the receiver.

A variation of the basic sequence diagram (called a focus-of-control diagram) illustrates which object has the thread of control at any one time. This is shown by a fatter line during the period when the object has control (see Figure 38.19). Notice that the bar representing the object C only starts when it is created and terminates when it is destroyed.

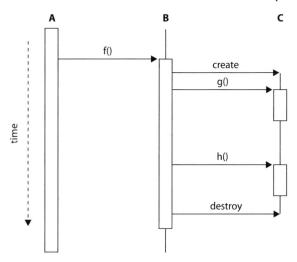

Fig. 38.19 Sequence diagram with focus-of-control regions.

38.8 Collaboration Diagrams

As stated above, collaboration diagrams illustrate the sequence of messages between objects based around the object structure (rather than the temporal aspects of sequence diagrams). A collaboration diagram is formed from the objects involved in the collaboration, the links (permanent or temporary) between the objects and the messages (numbered in sequence) that are exchanged between the objects. An example collaboration diagram is presented in Figure 38.20.

Objects which are created during the collaboration are indicated by the label *new* before the object name (e.g. the Line object in Figure 38.20). Links between objects are annotated to indicate their type, permanent or temporary, existing for this particular collaboration. These annotations are placed in boxes on the ends of the links and can have the following values:

A   Association (or permanent) link
F   Object field (the target object is part of the source object)
G   Global variable
L   Local variable
P   Procedure parameter
S   Self reference

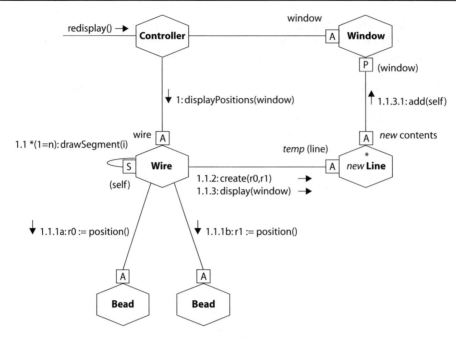

Fig. 38.20 An example collaboration diagram.

You can add role names to distinguish links (e.g. self, wire and window in Figure 38.20). Role names in brackets indicate a temporary link, i.e. one that is not an association.

The messages which are sent along links are indicated by labels next to the links. One or more messages can be sent along a link in either or both directions. The format of the messages is defined by the following (some of which are optional):

1. A comma-separated list of sequence numbers in brackets, e.g. [seqno, seqno] which indicate messages from other threads of control that must occur before the current message. This element is only needed with concurrency.
2. A list of sequence elements separated by full stops, "." which represent the nested procedural calling sequence of the message in the overall transaction. Each element has the following parts:
    – A letter (or name) indicating a concurrent thread. All letters at the same level of nesting represent threads that execute concurrently i.e. 1.2a and 1.2b are concurrent. If there is no letter, it usually indicates the main sequence.
    – An integer showing the sequential position of the current message within its thread. For example, message 2.1.4 is part of the procedure invoked by message 2.1 and follows message 2.1.3 within that procedure.
    – An iteration indicator (*), optionally followed by an iteration expression in parentheses, which indicates that several messages of the same form are sent either sequentially (to a single target) or concurrently (to the elements of a set). If there is an iteration expression, it shows the values that the iterator assumes, such as (i=1..n); otherwise, the details of the iteration must be specified in text or simply deferred to the code.
    – A conditional indicator (?), optionally followed by a Boolean expression in parentheses. The iteration and conditional indicators are mutually exclusive.

3. *A return value name followed by an assignment sign* (:=) which indicates that the proce-
    dure returns a value designated by the given name. The use of the same name elsewhere in
    the diagram designates the same value. If no return value is specified, then the procedure
    operates by side-effects.
4. *The name of the message* which is an event or operation name. It is unnecessary to specify
    the class of an operation since this is implicit in the target object.
5. *The argument list of the message* which is made up of expressions defined in terms of input
    values of the nesting procedure, local return values of other procedures and attribute val-
    ues of the object sending the message.

You may show argument values and return values for messages graphically using small data
flow tokens near a message. Each token is a small circle, with an arrow showing the direction of
the data flow, labelled with the name of the argument or result.

38.9 State Machine Diagrams

Scenarios are used to help understand how the objects within the system collaborate, whereas
state diagrams illustrate how these objects behave internally. State diagrams relate events to
state transitions and states. The transitions change the state of the system and are triggered by
events. The notation used to document state diagrams is based on *statecharts*, developed by
Harel (Harel *et al.*, 1987; Harel, 1988).

Statecharts are a variant of the finite state machine formalism, which reduces the apparent
complexity of a graphical representation of a finite state machine. This is accomplished
through the addition of a simple graphical representation of certain common patterns of finite
state machine usage. As a result, a complex sub-graph in a "basic" finite state machine is
replaced by a single graphical construct.

Statecharts are referred to as state diagrams in UML. Each state diagram has a start point at
which the state is entered and may have an exit point at which the state is terminated. The state
may also contain concurrency and synchronization of concurrent activities.

Figure 38.21 illustrates a typical state diagram. This state diagram describes a simplified
remote control locking system. The chart indicates that the system first checks the identification code of the handheld transmitter. If it is the same as that held in the memory, it allows the
car to be locked or unlocked. When the car is locked, the windows are also closed and the car is
alarmed.

A state diagram consists of a start point, events, a set of transitions, a set of variables, a set of
states and a set of exit points.

38.9.1 Start Points

A start point is the point at which the state diagram is initialized. In Figure 38.21, there are four
start points indicated (Start, lock, close and unlock). The Start start point is the initial
entry point for the whole diagram, while the other start points are for substate diagrams.

Any preconditions required by the state diagram can be specified on the transition from the
start point (for example, the transmittedID must be the same as the memoryID). It is the initial
transition from which all other transitions emanate. This transition is automatically taken
when the state diagram is executed. Notice that the initial Start point is not equivalent to a
state.

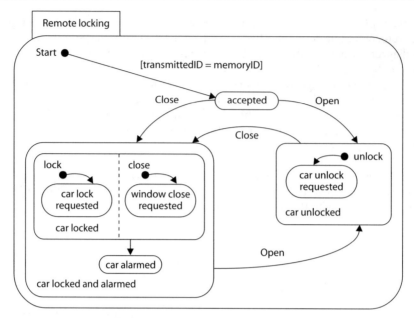

Fig. 38.21 An example state diagram.

38.9.2 Events

Events are one-way asynchronous transmissions of information from one object to another. The general format of an event is as follows:

```
eventName (parameter:type, ...)
```

Of course, many events do not have any associated parameters.

38.9.3 A Set of Transitions

These are the statements which move the system from one state to another. In a state diagram, each transition is formed of four (optional) parts:

1. An event (e.g. lock).
2. A condition (e.g. transmittedID = memoryID)
3. The initiated event (e.g. ^EngineManagementUnit.locked)
4. An operation (e.g. /setDoorToLock)

The event is what triggers the transition; however, the transition only occurs if the condition is met. If the event occurs and the conditions are met, then the associated operation is performed. An operation is a segment of code (equivalent to a statement or program or method) which causes the system state to be altered. Some transitions can also trigger an event which should be sent to a specified object. The above example sends an event locked to the EngineManagementUnit. The process of sending a global event is a special case of sending an event to a specified object. The syntax of an event is as follows:

```
event(arguments) [condition] ^target.sendEvent(arguments) /
operation(arguments)
```

38.9.4 A Set of State Variables

These are variables referred to in a state diagram, for example, memoryID. They have the follow-ing format:

    name: type = value

38.9.5 A Set of States

A state represents a period of time during which an object is waiting for an event to occur. It is an abstraction of the attribute values and links of an object. A state is drawn as a rounded box containing the (optional) name of the state. A state may often be composed of other states (the combination of which represents the higher level state). A state has duration; that is, it occupies an interval of time.

A state box can contain two additional sections: a list of state variables and a list of triggered operations (see Figure 38.22).

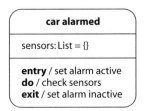

Fig. 38.22 State box with state variables and triggered operations.

An operation can be of the following types:

- *entry* operations are executed when the state is entered. They are the same as specifying an operation on a transition. They are useful if all transitions into a state perform the same operation (rather than specifying the same operation on each transition). Such op-erations are considered to be instantaneous.
- *exit* operations are executed when the state is exited. They are less common than entry ac-tions and indicate an operation performed before any transition from the state.
- *do* operations are executed while the state is active. They start on entry to the state and ter-minate when the state is exited.
- *events* can trigger operations while within a particular state. For example, the event *help* could trigger the *help* operation while in the state *active*.

Each operation is separated from its type by a forward slash (/). The ordering of operations is:

1. Operations on incoming transitions
2. Entry operations
3. Do operations
4. Exit operations
5. Operations on outgoing transitions

State diagrams allow a state to be a single state variable, or a set of substates. This allows for complex hierarchical models to be developed gradually as a series of nested behaviour patterns. This means that a state can be a state diagram in its own right. For example, *car alarmed* is a single state and *car locked* is another state diagram. Notice that the transition from *car alarmed* to *accepted* jumps from an inner state to an outer state.

The broken line down the middle of the *car locked* state indicates that the two halves of that state run concurrently. That is, the car is locked as the windows are closed.

A special type of state, called a history state, represents a state which must be remembered and used the next time the (outer) state is entered. The symbol for a history state is an H in a circle.

38.9.6 A Set of Exit Points

Exit points specify the result of the state diagram. They also terminate the execution of the state diagram.

38.10 Deployment Diagrams

The elements in Figure 38.23 are called nodes. They represent processors (PCs and Server) and devices (Printer and Fax). A node is thus a resource in the real world upon which we can distribute and execute elements of the (logical) design model. A node is drawn as a three-dimensional rectangular solid with no shadows. The <<device>> stereotype designation of the Fax and Printer indicates that these nodes are not processors. That is, they do not have any processing ability (from the point of view of the model being constructed). You can also show how many nodes are likely to be involved in the system. Thus the Order Entry PC is of order * (0 or more), but there is exactly one server, printer, fax etc. Finally, the diagram also shows the roles of the associations between nodes and their stereotype. For example, the *Receiving* association on one PC uses a type of ISDN connection (which has yet to be specified).

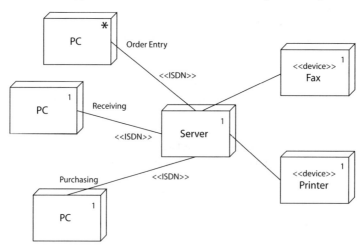

Fig. 38.23 Nodes in a deployment diagram.

38.11 Summary

This chapter has presented an overview of the Unified Modeling Language. The UML is an attempt to develop a third generation object-oriented modelling language for use with a variety of object-oriented design methods. It can be used for documenting the design of client–server, real-time, distributed and batch applications. It captures the best elements of the notations used by a number of existing design methods, including Booch, OMT and Objectory while attempting to remain extensible, simple, clear and (relatively) concise. Many CASE tool vendors are already committed to supporting the UML and it is being presented to the OMG by a consortium of organizations as the basis of a standard notation for object-oriented systems development.

Chapter 39

The Unified Process

39.1 Introduction

This chapter provides an overview of the Unified Process (for more details on this design process see Hunt (2000) and Jacobson *et al.* (1998)).

39.2 The Unified Process

The Unified Process is a design framework that guides the tasks, people and products of the design process. It is a framework because it provides the inputs and outputs of each activity, but does not restrict how each activity must be performed. Different activities can be used in different situations, some being left out, others being replaced or augmented. The Unified Process comprises a number of different hierarchical elements (see Figure 39.1).

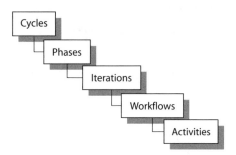

Fig. 39.1 Key building blocks of the Unified Process.

   The Unified Process actually comprises low-level activities (such as finding classes), which are combined together into workflows (which describe how one activity feeds into another). These workflows are organized into iterations. Each iteration identifies some aspect of the system to be considered. How this is done is considered in more detail later. Iterations themselves are organized into phases. Phases focus on different aspects of the design process, for example requirements, analysis, design and implementation. In turn phases can be grouped into cycles. Cycles focus on the generation of successive releases of a system (for example, version 1.0, version 1.1 etc.).

39.2.1 Overview of the Unified Process

There are four key elements to the philosophy behind the Unified Process. These four elements are:

- iterative and incremental
- use case-driven
- architecture-centric
- acknowledges risk

Iterative and Incremental

The Unified Process is iterative and incremental as it does not try to complete the whole design task in one go. In contrast to the waterfall model, the Unified Process has an iterative and incremental model. That is, the design process is based on iterations which either address different aspects of the design process or move the design forward in some way (this is the incremental aspect of the model). The end result is that you incrementally produce the system being designed.

Use Case-Driven

The Unified Process is also use case-driven. This is because use cases help identify the primary requirements of the system. Use cases are then used to ensure that the evolving design is always relevant to what the user required. Indeed, the uses cases act as the one consistent thread through out the whole of the development process, as is illustrated in Figure 39.2. For example, at the beginning of the design phase one of the two primary inputs to this phase is the use case model. Then, explicitly within the design model, are use case realisations which illustrate how each use case is supported by the design. Any use case which does not have a use case realisation is not currently supported by the design.

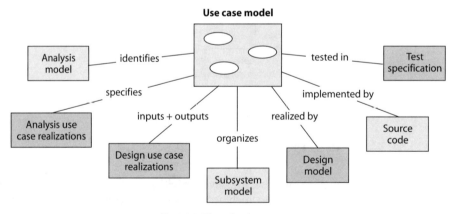

Fig. 39.2 The role of use cases.

Architecture-Centric

One problem with having an iterative and incremental approach is that while one group may be working on part of the implementation another group may be working on part of the design. To ensure that all the various parts fit together there needs to be something. That something is an

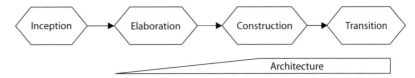

Fig. 39.3 The development of the architecture.

architecture. An architecture is the skeleton on which the muscles (functionality) and skin (the user interface) of the system will be hung. A good architecture will be resilient to change and to the evolving design. The Unified Process explicitly acknowledges the need for this architecture by being architecture centric. It describes how you identify what should be part of the architecture and how you go about designing and implementing the architecture. The remainder of the Unified Process then refers back to that architecture.

Obviously the generation of this architecture is both critical and very hard. Therefore the Unified Process prescribes the successive refinement of the executable architecture, thereby attempting to ensure that the architecture remains relevant.

Acknowledges Risk

Finally, the Unified Process explicitly acknowledges the risk inherent in software design and development. It does this by highlighting unknown aspects in the system being designed and other areas of concern. These areas are then targeted as either being critical to the system and therefore part of the architecture, or areas of risk that need to be addressed early on in the design process (when there is more time) rather than later on (when time tends to be short).

39.2.2 Life Cycle Phases

The Unified Process comprises four distinct phases. These four phases focus on different aspects of the design process. The four phases are Inception, Elaboration, Construction and Transition. The four phases and their roles are outlined below.

- *Inception* This phase define the scope of the project and develops the business case for the system. It also establishes the feasibility of the system to be built. Various prototypes may be developed during this phase to ensure the feasibility of the proposal.
- *Elaboration* This phase captures the functional requirements of the system. It should also specify any non-functional requirements to ensure that they are taken into account. The other primary task for this phase is the creation of the architecture to be used throughout the remainder of the Unified Process.
- *Construction* This phase concentrates on completing the analysis of the system, performing the majority of the design and the implementation of the system. That is, it essentially builds the product.
- *Transition* The transition phase moves the system into the users' environment. This involves activities such as deploying the system and maintaining it.

Each phase has a set of major milestones that are used to judge the progress of the overall Unified Process (of course with each phase there are numerous minor milestones to be achieved). The primary milestones (or products) of the four phases are illustrated in Figure 39.4.

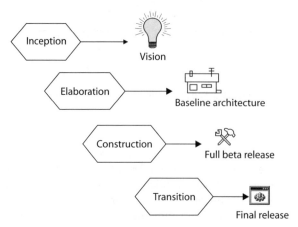

Fig. 39.4 Major deliverables of each phase.

A milestone is the culmination of a phase and is comprised of a set of artefacts (such as specific models) which are the product of the workflows (and thus activities) in that phase. The primary milestones for each phase are:

- *Inception* The output of this phase is the vision for the system. This includes a very simplified use case model (to identify that the primary functionality of the system is), a very tentative architecture and the most important or significant risks are identified and the elaboration phase is planned.
- *Elaboration* The primary output of this phase is the architecture along with a detailed use case model and a set of plans for the construction phase.
- *Construction* The end result of this phase is the implemented product which includes the software as well as the design and associated models. The product may not be without defects, as some further work has yet to be completed in the transition phase.
- *Transition* The transition phase is the last phase of a cycle. The major milestone meet by this phase is the final production quality release of the system.

39.2.3 Phases, Iterations and Workflows

There can be confusion over the relationship between phases and workflows. Not least because a single workflow can cross (or be involved in) more than one phase (see Figure 39.5). One way to view the relationships is that the workflows are the steps you actually follow. However, at different times we can identify different major milestones that should be met.

For the majority of this chapter we will focus on the various workflows (not least because this is the emphasis which the designer typically sees).

The five workflows in the Unified Process are Requirements, Analysis, Design, Implementation and Test (as indicated in Figure 39.5). Note that the Design, Implementation and Test workflows are broken Unified Processes. This is to indicate that elements of each workflow may take place earlier than the core parts of the workflow. In particular the design, implementation and testing of the architecture will happen early on (in the Elaboration phase). Thus part of each of the Design, Implementation and Test workflows must occur at this time.

The focus of each workflow is described below (their primary products are illustrated in Figure 39.6):

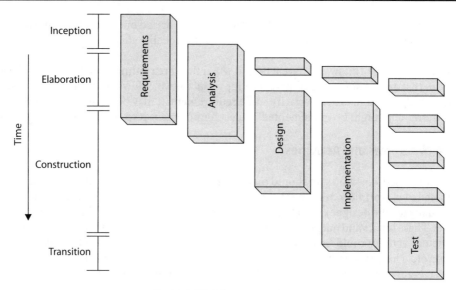

Fig. 39.5 Workflows versus phases.

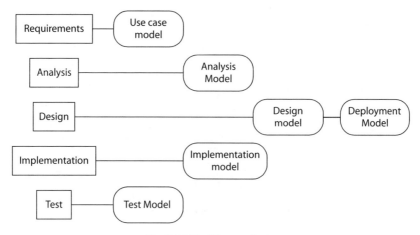

Fig. 39.6 Workflow products.

- *Requirements* This workflow focuses on the activities which allow the functional and non-functional requirements of the system to be identified. The primary product of this workflow is the use case model.
- *Analysis* the aim of this workflow is to restructure the requirements identified in the requirements workflow in terms of the software to be built rather than in the users' less precise terms. It can be seen as a first cut at a design; however, that is to miss the point of what this workflow aims to achieve.
- *Design* The design workflow produces the detailed design which will be implemented in the next workflow.
- *Implementation* This workflow represents the coding of the design in an appropriate programming language (for this book that is Java) and the compilation, packaging, deployment and documenting of the software.

- *Test* The test workflow describes the activities to be carried out to test the software to ensure that it meets the users requirements, that it is reliable etc.

Notice that the workflows all have a period when they are running concurrently. This does not mean that one person is necessarily working on all the workflows at the same time. Instead, it acknowledges that in order to clarify some requirement, it may be necessary to design how that requirement might be implemented and even implement it to confirm that it is feasible.

39.2.4 Workflows and Activities

Having discussed workflows we should make mention of what workflows do and what they are comprised of. A workflow describes how a set of activities are related. Activities are the things that actually tell the designer what they should be doing. An activity takes inputs and produces outputs. These inputs and outputs are referred to as artefacts. An artefact that acts as an input to a particular activity could be a use case, while the output from that activity could be a class diagram etc. The actual activities that comprise each of the workflows will be discussed below; however, Figure 39.7 lists the primary activities for each of the workflows.

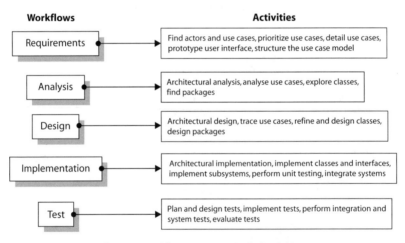

Fig. 39.7 Workflows are comprised of activities.

39.3 Requirements Workflow

This section provides an introduction to requirements workflow of the Unified Process. The intention of the use case analysis is to identify how the system is to be used and what it is expected to do in response to this use. To help in identifying the use cases, you can ask the following questions (Jacobson, 1992):

- What are the main tasks of each actor?
- Will the actor have to read/write/change any of the system information?
- Will the actor have to inform the system about outside changes?
- Does the actor wish to be informed about unexpected changes?

Having identified the use cases, we can identify the steps performed within each use case.

39.3.1 Interface Descriptions

Having defined the actors in the system and the uses they make of the system, the next step is often to specify the interfaces between the actors and the system. For human users of the system, these interfaces may well be graphical user interfaces (GUIs). You can draw them with a drawing tool or develop a mock-up using some form of interface simulation software. For non-human interfaces any proposed communications protocols can be defined and checked (for example, that the interacting system is capable of sending and receiving the appropriate information).

39.4 Analysis Workflow

The aim of the analysis workflow is to analyse the requirements identified in the use case analysis (the requirements workflow) and to structure them in terms of the internals of the system. That is, the requirements are converted from the external user's view into "what the system needs to do to support the user's requirements". This does not mean how the system will do it, merely what it must do. For example, the user may be unaware that they have an internal *profile* which specifies what they can and cannot do, however an *internal* requirement on the system might be to check the users' actions against their profile.

Four primary activities comprise the analysis workflow. These activities are:

- generation of analysis classes
- generation of analysis packages
- analysis of use cases for the generation of use case realizations

Once again this process is not as sequential as this list might suggest, rather it is iterative. In addition each activity may effectively be carried out in parallel. Thus the results of one activity may impact on another.

The analysis model is the key element of the analysis workflow. It is the first step in the understanding of how the system should be formed. The analysis model is essentially comprised of the analysis class diagrams. These diagrams illustrate the static structure of a system via the important analysis classes in the system and how they relate to each other.

The information for the analysis model comes from:

- the problem statement (possibly written in natural language)
- a requirements analysis process
- the domain experts
- general knowledge of the real world
- and, in particular, the use case model

The analysis model should be viewed as elucidating the requirements as described in the use case model.

39.4.1 Analysis Model Classes

Analysis model classes represent an abstraction of one or more classes or subsystem (in the final design model). This is because the level of detail expected in the design model is explicitly not required nor appropriate for the analysis model. The focus here is on handling functional requirements at a high level of abstraction. Thus analysis classes are distinguished from design classes, as they:

- *Have responsibilities not operations.* These responsibilities should be documented in textual form. In addition a textual description of the purpose of the class should also be provided.
- *Have high-level attributes described in domain terms.* That is, an attribute in the analysis model may represent a complex concept which will need to be expanded in the design model. For example, an invoice can be treated as a simple attribute in the analysis but not in the design. Another example, would be that an amount in a bank account can be treated as currency without worrying about how currency should be represented.
- *Have relationships,* but these relationships are concept-oriented rather than implementation-oriented. They thus express the abstract relationship between two classes rather than how two classes should be linked in order to be implemented.
- All analysis classes should be *directly involved in one or more use case realizations.* No analysis classes should exist which are not directly used to explain how a use case could be implemented (in terms of the analysis model).
- *Are all of one of three types of class.* These classes are entity, boundary or control classes.

As analysis classes are quite distinct from design classes they have been given their own stereotype with a stereotype icon to illustrate them. These stereotypes are illustrated in Figure 39.8. The three types of analysis class are described below:

- *Entity classes.* Such classes represent data that tends to exist over a period of time (such as a customer's bank account), important concepts in the system, major components or significant elements in the system (such as a fundamental subsystem). If an entity class represents some data, then in many cases this information is persistent and may be stored in some form of long-term storage (such as a database). Entity classes most often model information, concepts or real-life objects or events. In many cases, entity classes are an abstraction of some more complex concept that will need to be expanded on and explored in the design model. These are the real nuggets of gold which the analysis model is attempting to mine. It is these classes we need to identify in order to have a chance in creating a robust, reusable, stable architecture.
- *Boundary classes.* These are classes that are used to model the interaction with the actors (i.e. the users of the system). This interaction involves sending, receiving (or both) information. Thus boundary classes often represent abstractions of graphical user interfaces or external APIs or indeed protocols such as http or ftp.

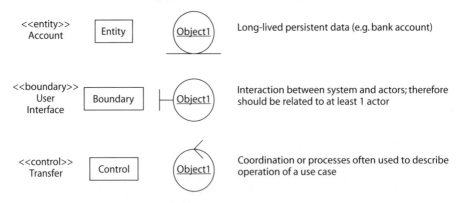

Fig. 39.8 Types of analysis class.

- *Control classes.* A control class represents the functionality required to manage the inter-action between the user via the boundary class and the data in the entity class (i.e. it is the set of events in the user case re-stated in the terminology of the system). That is, control classes encapsulate the coordination and sequencing of the interactions between other classes. Note that a single user-oriented event in a use case might map into a number of actions within the control class. Thus it is not necessarily a one-to-one mapping between the events in the use case and the actions described by the control class.

39.4.2 Constructing the Analysis Model

The analysis model may be constructed by following these steps:

- Identify objects and classes.
- Generate use case realizations.
- Prepare a data dictionary.
- Identify associations (including aggregations) between objects.
- Identify attributes of objects at an abstract (probably textual) level.
- Organise and simplify object classes using inheritance.
- Iterate and refine the model.
- Group classes into modules.

You should not take the sequence of these steps too strictly; analysis and design are rarely completed in a truly linear manner.

Identifying Objects and Classes

The first step in constructing the object model is to identify the objects in the domain and their classes. Such objects may include:

- physical entities such as petrol pumps, engines and locks
- logical entities such as employee records, purchases and speed
- soft entities such as tokens, expressions or data streams
- conceptual entities such as needs, requirements or constraints

As long as an item makes sense for the application and the domain, then it is a candidate object or class. The only things you should avoid are objects which relate to the proposed computer implementation.

Once you have a comprehensive list of candidate classes, you can discard any unnecessary or incorrect ones by using the following criteria:

- Are any of the classes redundant?
- Are any of the classes irrelevant?
- Are any of the classes vague?
- Are any of the classes really attributes of other classes?
- Are any of the classes really operations?
- Does the name of the class represent its intrinsic nature and not its role in the application? For example, the class Person might represent an object in a restaurant booking system, but the class Customer is a better representation of its role in the system.
- Is a class really an implementation construct?

Generate Use Case Realizations

In order to generate the analysis use case realizations it is necessary to examine each of the use cases in turn. For each use case you need to:

- Start by considering the event generated by the actor which triggers the use case realization. This should be sent to a boundary class and is the starting point for finding classes.
- Move through the flow of events identifying the classes involved in the flow of events and the messages and links between the classes.
- Identify all the analysis classes involved in the use case sequence of events.
  - Each time you need to find a class examine those already in the data dictionary to see if there is one which matches your requirement.
  - If new classes are found then they need to be added to the use case realization and to the data dictionary. Note that it is often very useful to appoint a librarian who will be responsible for the data dictionary, for maintaining it, for updating it and for managing the identification and acceptance of new classes.
- Distribute the use cases behaviour among the classes.
  - Record the responsibilities of the classes in the data dictionary (and with the class itself).
  - Classes can have more then one responsibility (as they are abstractions of what will be in the design model). However, the responsibilities should be related to keep the class consistent.
- Note any special requirements from the use cases or identified during the analysis workflow with the use case realization.
- Record interactions between classes.
- The basic path associated with all use cases should produce one collaboration diagram.
- Alternative paths may produce one or more collaboration diagrams. A useful rule of thumb is to break the alternative paths into multiple collaboration diagram if they become too complex to explain in one sentence.

Note that you are not expected to find all the classes first time, nor just by considering the use cases. Generating the use case realizations and the process of generating the analysis classes themselves is really a very iterative process in which many different techniques come into play.

Preparing a Data Dictionary

A data dictionary provides a definition for each of the terms or words used in the evolving analysis models. Each entry precisely describes each object class, its scope, any assumptions or restrictions on its use and its attributes and operations (once they are known).

Identifying Associations Between Objects

The next step is to identify any (and all) associations between two or more classes. In particular, look for the following types of relationships:

- physical location (next to, part of, contained in)
- directed actions (drives)
- communication (talks to)
- ownership (has, part of)
- satisfaction of some condition (works for, married to, manages)

You should consider which classes are likely to need to work with which other classes (e.g. the accounts clerk may need to work with the salaries clerk).

Once you have a set of candidate associations, you can refine them using the following criteria:

- Is the association between eliminated classes?
- Are any of the associations irrelevant or implementation associations?
- Are any associations transient?
- Are any of the associations ternary? It is a good idea to keep things simple and only have binary relationships.
- Are any of the associations derivable?
- Are any of the associations misnamed?
- Add role names where appropriate.
- Are there any qualified associations?
- Specify multiplicity on the associations.
- Are there any missing associations?

Identifying Attributes of Objects

An important point to note is that you should only be trying to identify application domain attributes. This means that attributes which are needed during the implementation of the system should not be included at this stage. Next you should refine the attributes:

- Should the attribute be an object?
- Is an attribute really a name?
- Is an attribute an identifier?
- Is an attribute really a link attribute?
- Does the attribute represent an internal state of the object which is not visible outside the object?
- Does the attribute represent fine detail?
- Are any of the attributes unlike the others in their class?

Using Inheritance

You can refine your classes using inheritance in both directions. That is, you can group common aspects of existing classes into a superclass, or you can specialize an existing class into a number of subclasses that serve specific purposes.

Testing Access Paths

This step involves checking that paths in the model make sense, are sufficient and are necessary.

Iterating and Refining the Model

To refine your model you can ask yourself the following questions:

- Are there any missing objects?
- Are there any unnecessary classes?
- Are there any missing associations (such as a missing access path for some operation)?
- Are there any unnecessary associations?

- Are all attributes in the correct class?
- Are all associations in the correct place?

Grouping Classes into Packages

The final step associated directly with the object model is to group classes into packages.

39.5 Design Workflow

The primary inputs to the design workflow come from the use case analysis and the analysis workflow. The design workflow differs from the analysis workflow as it is aimed at implementation abstraction, i.e. how the system should be built, rather than trying to rephrase the system requirements (at a high level of abstraction). There are four primary activities in the design workflow, these are:

- *Generation of design classes.* We are now interested in all the details required to design the system. Thus there will be many more classes required to support the use case realizations than was the case in the analysis workflow.
- *Identification of design interfaces.* To reduce the dependency between classes, we will also identify the key interfaces in the system.
- *Generation of design use case realizations.* We now need to consider how the design implements the use cases identified during the requirements workflow.
- *Generation of subsystems.* We are also interested in producing actual subsystems, rather than subsystems that help us understand the system.

Note that the design class notation does not use the three stereotype classes presented in the analysis workflow. This is because we are now interested in the classes which will actually form part of the system, rather than an abstraction of what the system needs to do. Thus we use the standard box notation with the attribute and operation compartments fully documented.

39.5.1 Identifying Classes

First look at the analysis classes in the analysis model:

- For *Boundary* classes you should "implement" then with appropriate interface classes. Or you may need to specify a design class that provides a particular protocol etc.
- For *Entity* classes you will need to determine what classes, files, database etc. will "implement" these classes. It is often the case that one entity class will result in multiple design elements, even to the extent of representing a design subsystem, and care needs to be taken with this analysis. Remember that the entity classes describe the key concepts in the system; thus whatever they evolve into in the design will be key elements in the design!
- *Control* classes. Essentially the behaviour encapsulated in the analysis control classes needs to be divided between the various design classes that will implement that behaviour.

It is also likely that you will need to consider additional support classes, above and beyond what might have been identified straight from the use cases and the analysis classes.

39.5.2 Refining the Set of Classes

Once you have an initial set of classes you will need to start refining them (just as you did in the analysis workflow). The issues you will need are essentially the same as in the analysis phase, with the addition of:

- Do any subsystem interfaces imply classes?
- Do any other interfaces need classes?
- Are any of the classes vague?
- Are any of the classes really operations?
- Do any of the classes map directly to Java classes?
- Is it too big – would it benefit from being broken down into a number of different classes?
- Instead of using inheritance, can you identify any component-based reuse which will allow you to modifying the class's behaviour by "plugging in" another class to provide that behaviour?

39.5.3 Identifying and Refining Attributes

As you are identifying your classes, you should also be thinking about the attributes they possess. This is important, as it will not only help you to identify other classes (when an attribute is a composite of a grouping of information) but also help you to identify classes that are really the same – just with different names.

Once you have an initial set of attributes for a class you are ready to refine them (this is really an iterative process of discovery and refinement). To refine the attributes you have identified for a design class you can apply essentially the same questions as were used in the analysis phase.

39.5.4 Identifying and Refining Operations

When searching for the operations that an object should perform, you should look for:

- Operations implied by the responsibilities documented on analysis classes.
- Operations implied by the steps performed by the analysis workflow control classes (and where they should be located).
- Operations implied by events and particularly interactions with actors.
- Operations implied by interaction diagrams such as collaboration or sequence diagrams. The messages in these diagrams usually map onto operations.
- Transitions implied by statecharts.
- Interfaces implemented by a class.
- Operations implied by state actions and activities.
- Application or domain operations.

Special requirements on analysis classes.

Once you have identified an initial set of operations you can begin to refine them. Once again the process of discovering operations and refining them is an iterative and incremental one. The things to consider when refining the operations include:

- Look for simplifying operations. For example, view the description associated with the operation. Does the operation attempt to fulfil more than one role? If so, can it be broken down?

- Visibility of operations.
- Every operation should be traceable to a use case realization.
- Ensure all roles played by the class are supported by the operations.
- All operations should be documented with functionality performed, pre- and post-conditions, meaning of inputs, return value etc.
- Dependencies implied by parameters or return types.

39.5.5 Design Use Case Realizations

You should now consider the design equivalents of the use case realizations you produced for the analysis workflow. These are necessary so that you can be sure that all use cases are supported by your design. Of course, the classes in your design model are influenced by the use cases and the use case realizations, so these processes are likely to be iterative and incremental and tightly coupled. Design use case realizations are made up of:

- textual flow of events description
- class diagrams
- interaction diagrams
- subsystems and system interfaces involved in use cases

You may also wish to document any non-functional requirements that are either annotated on the use cases or analysis realizations or that are identified during the generation of the design use case realizations. It is also useful to include a list of implementation issues that should be dealt with during the implementation workflow.

39.5.6 Generating a Sequence Diagram

There are a variety of ways in which you could generate a sequence diagram. The following presents a series of steps which can act as a guideline relating to how to do this:

- Identify all the classes involves in a particular sequence. You may notice that this statement assumes that all the classes are already defined; however, as with much of the design process, this is really an iterative process in which, as the classes become clearer, so the sequence diagrams may evolve.
- Determine the life line of the objects; that is, when they are created and when they are destroyed. If the sequence diagram creates or destroys the object then you will need to make this clear.
- Identifying the initiating event (you should look to the use cases for this).
- Determine the subsequent message(s), i.e. what does the "boundary" object do when the actor initiates the event? Then consider the behaviour of the receiving object and what messages it might send etc.
- Identify the focus of control for the object.
- Identify any returned messages (returned values)
- Identify any deviations (either annotate them on the sequence diagram or generate separate sequence diagrams for each deviation).

39.5.7 Building a Statechart Diagram

You should construct a state diagram for each object class with nontrivial dynamic behaviour. Every sequence diagram (and thus collaboration diagram) corresponds to a path through a state diagram. Each branch in control flow is represented by a state with more than one exit transition. The procedure for producing state diagrams is summarized by the following algorithm:

1. Pick a class.
2. Pick one sequence diagram involving that class.
3. Follow the events for the class; the gaps between the events are states. Give each state a name (if it is meaningful to do so).
4. Draw a set of states and the events that link them based on the sequence diagrams.
5. Find loops – repeated sequences of states – within the diagram.
6. Choose another sequence diagram for the class and produce the states and events for that diagram. Merge these states and events into the first diagram.
7. Repeat Step 6 for all sequence diagrams involving this class.
8. Repeat from Step 1 for all classes.

After considering all normal events, add boundary cases and special cases. You should now consider any conditions on the transitions between states and any events that are triggered off by these transitions.

39.5.8 Identifying and Refining Associations

To identify design associations between design classes:

- Look at the analysis entity class associations.
- Look at messages in interaction diagrams. Every time an event of operation is sent between two objects in an interaction diagram, there needs to be an association place.
- Look at use of interfaces. If one class implements an interface and another class uses that same interface, then there is an implied association between the two.
- Look at access paths. Make sure that any collaborations which are required to support all use cases are supported by appropriate associations.
- Consider association multiplicity, role names, association classes, ordering etc.
- Consider whether association is aggregation (i.e is an inner class required)?

Having identified an initial set of associations, it is still necessary to refine them. The questions you ask to refine associations are the same as those asked in the analysis phase.

39.5.9 Identifying Interfaces and Inheritance

As with the analysis phase you should now attempt to identify any inheritance and system (as well as core entity) interfaces. As noted although this chapter, this is more incremental than is implied here. The places to look for interfaces include:

- Interfaces between subsystems, as these are considered architecturally significant
- Dependencies between classes, classes and subsystems, subsystems and subsystems
- Dependencies between layers

Places to look for inheritance include:

- Common operations and attributes between classes (Generalization)
- Special cases of classes (Specialization)
- Functionality provided by Java classes
- Common associations and dependencies – may imply a package

Move functionality and attributes up the hierarchy as high as possible.

39.5.10 Remaining Steps

The remaining steps that you should consider in this phase are:

- Optimize the design by looking for redundant associations that will simplify the implementation or rearranging the computation for greater efficiency etc.
- Test all access paths.
- Design the form of control to be used in the application (for example determine how and where events will be triggered).
- Adjust the class structure in light of the evolving design.
- Determine how associations will be implemented.

39.6 Implementation Workflow

This section considers the implementation workflow of the Unified Process. This workflow is concerned with implementing the design produced by the design workflow (that is, in Java terms it concentrates on implementing classes and interfaces, creating packages and producing class files). It also deals with the remaining non-functional requirements and the deployment of the "executable" modules (in our case Java class files) onto nodes (such as specific processors etc.). It must therefore deal with any implementation issues that have been left as too specific during the design workflow.

You should treat the implementation of an object-oriented system in just the same way as you would treat the implementation of any software system. This means that it should be subject to, and controlled by, the same processes as any other implementation.

39.7 Testing Workflow

The aim of the test workflow is to ensure that the system provides the required functionality. As the required functionality was originally captured in the form of the use cases in the use case model, there is obviously some form of relationship between the two. Therefore the system as implemented should be tested against the use cases as originally identified. You should therefore start to build you test plan based on your use cases. However, you should not be blind to other sources of test information, as use cases are just one source of test information (albeit a very important one).

39.8 Summary

To conclude, the Unified Process is a design process framework that is hierarchical, as it is made from a Unified Process of cycles, comprised of phases, which are themselves made from a Unified Process from workflows that describe how activities are linked.

Part **9**
The Future

Chapter 40

Areas of Java and Object Technology not Covered

40.1 Introduction

This chapter discusses a number of Java-related topics which are not covered in this book. In general, these are more advanced concepts or new concepts in the latest version of Java. It is useful for you to know what you do not know, not least so that, when you are talking to others about Java, you know what they mean when they say, for example, "Oh yes, well we use Enterprise JavaBeans".

40.2 Language Areas

40.2.1 Native Code

There are some situations in which it is necessary or desirable to use a language other than Java. For example, you may need to integrate a Java application with an existing (legacy) system or use specific facilities provided by a particular language (such as numerical packages in Fortran). Part of the overall system may be time-critical or require low-level access to hardware (in which case, you may use C).

In any of these situations, linking Java to the associated system is referred to as linking it to native code. This can be done either from Java to the relevant language or vice versa.

Java provides a number of features that enable this, in particular, a new keyword, native, and a new tool, javah. The native keyword indicates that a particular method is implemented using native code (e.g. another language):

```
public class NativeExample {
    public native static void accessExample();
}
```

This example declares that the method accessExample is provided by a separate implementation. Notice that it is defined as a static method because it is simpler to do this for static class-side methods. You can also declare instance methods as native; however, you would need to consider parameter passing (for further details see Cornell and Horstmann (1997)).

If we were going to build this application using Java and, for example, C, we would now write the corresponding C function.

40.3 Java Virtual Machine

This book has not attempted to discuss any issues associated with the Java Virtual Machine (also known as the JVM or the Java run-time). The JVM is the run-time environment within which the Java byte codes execute. A detailed discussion of the JVM is beyond the scope of this book and interested readers should see Lindholm and Yellin (1996). However, there are a number of points that you should note.

Although the byte codes are platform-independent, the virtual machine must be ported to each individual platform. Each of these virtual machines must be developed, tested, verified etc. This means that some platforms receive preferential treatment over others. For example, the Mac OS version of the JDK always follows some months after the Solaris and Windows versions. It also means that your applications may behave differently depending on the particular platform (due to underlying problems in the virtual machine or the host platform).

Not only is any virtual machine, even a Just in Time (JIT) based system, less efficient than some form of machine executable, but the instruction set architecture is not particularly efficient. For example, good instruction sets should facilitate fast implementations using instruction set parallelism (such as pipelining and superscalar). However, the JVM does not make the task of producing fast implementations particularly easy. It uses variable-length instructions, which make parallel instruction fetching and decoding harder.

Native code compilers are available for Java. These will, of course, produce faster executables; however, they will lose the portability provided by the JVM. This may not be a problem for software houses, as they have the source code that merely requires recompilation on different platforms. However, few organizations will wish to make their source code generally available for downloading over the Web so that you can compile it locally for performance (this ignores public domain and shareware software, particularly from the academic arena).

40.4 JavaBeans

JavaBeans is an architecture for defining and reusing software components. The Beans Development Kit 1.0 (BDK), which was first released in February 1997, contains the JavaBeans API sources (the class files were already part of JDK 1.1), the Bean Box test container, some examples, and tutorial documentation (see also Englander (1997)). You can maintain contact with the JavaBeans project via http://java.sun.com/products/javabeans/.

The primary aim of the JavaBeans architecture is to allow developers and third-party software vendors to supply reusable components in a simple to use and unified manner. For example, you may wish to incorporate a simple word processor into your application. If this word processor is available as a bean, you can add it to your application without needing to refine the bean. Sun intends that most beans should be reusable software components that can be manipulated visually in some sort of builder tool. Thus we may select the word processor bean from a menu, drop it onto an application, and position its visual representation (i.e. the text writing area) as required.

Of course, the facilities provided by a builder tool depend both on the types of component being used and on the intended use of the builder. Examples of such builders, cited in the Java Beans 1.0 API Specification, include visual application builders, GUI layout builders, Web page builders or even server application builders. Indeed, sometimes the "builder tool" may be an editor that includes some beans as part of a larger application.

Java Beans may vary in size and complexity. Simple ones may be buttons or sliders; more complex examples may be database viewers, word processors or spreadsheets. In practice, it is expected that bean components will be small to medium-sized controls.

It is intended that JavaBeans will be architecture-neutral, except where they interface to the underlying platform. Thus, beans which handle buttons will be independent of the platform on which they are run. A bridge between JavaBeans and Microsoft's ActiveX was released in March 1997, which allows a bean to use the ActiveX facilities. Other bridges are being actively developed to Live Connect (for Netscape Navigator) and Live Object (previously OpenDoc). A given bean should use the appropriate platform features but present a common face to the Java environment. This has been one of the largest constraints on the development of JavaBeans and it has taken a lot of work to ensure that the various bean APIs can be cleanly converted to these component models.

Beans differ from class libraries in that they are intended for visual manipulation and customization via their properties, while class libraries are intended for programmatic use and for customization either through instantiation or subclasses. Thus the Java Database Connectivity API is not a bean, although a database access bean for Sybase, for example, would make sense. Such a bean would be built on top of the JDBC.

The JavaBean architecture relies extensively on events as the basic means of communication. For example, if one bean wishes to inform other beans that something interesting has happened, it raises an event. Those components that have registered an interest in this event are then informed that the event has occurred.

It is probable that the JavaBean architecture will become very influential and that many software vendors will package their products as beans. Thus the future of Java and that of JavaBeans will be tied inextricably to each other.

40.5 Enterprise JavaBeans

Do not be fooled by the name: Enterprise JavaBeans have very little to do with JavaBeans. JavaBeans are client-side components primarily used for constructing graphical clients. Enterprise JavaBeans, on the other hand, are server side components focussed on managing, handling, processing and representing business logic and data.

They provide a great deal of the infrastructure necessary for building server-side components within *n*-tier clients. As such, they form part of a middle framework – that is, they are the components developers build to represent the logic or data required in the middle tier of an *n*-tier architecture. They thus hide much of the network, security and transaction issues typically associated with such architectures from the EJB developers. This does not mean that those issues are ignored, but they are handled by the infrastructure surrounding the EJBS (as implemented by the EJB containers and servers).

There are two fundamental types of EJB: session beans and entity beans. Session beans typically represent non-persistent data and business logic, whereas entity beans represent persistent data (often in some form of database or legacy system).

There are various elements that make up the EJB and its environment (as illustrated in Figure 40.1). These are:

- The EJB Server that holds a container and provides server-based services.
- The EJB Container that holds one or more EJB components. It provides transaction control and resources, and handles container-managed persistence of entity beans. It is also responsible for registering the EJB Home object via the JNDI with the naming service being used.
- The EJB Home object provides a bootstrapping mechanism for obtaining access to the EJB via the EJB Object.

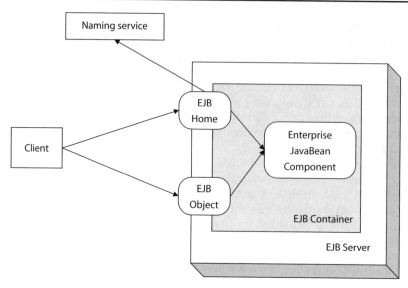

Fig. 40.1 The structure of the EJB framework.

- The EJB Object provides an interface that specifies what services the EJB provides to clients.
- The EJB component then implements these services. In doing so it may define additional methods that are not available to clients over the network. It may also use any classes available to it to enable it to complete its task (i.e. it is essentially just a Java class).

A client can communicate with an EJB over a network using RMI, CORBA or potentially any other networking protocol (for RMI and CORBA see later in this chapter).

To use an EJB a client must first obtain a reference to the EJB Home remote object via a naming service. Once it has done this it can then obtain a reference to the EJB Object via the EJB Home. At this point it is then ready to request services of the EJB.

Note that it is the combination of the component, the home and the EJB object that together comprise the EJB itself.

This may seem a bit long-winded, but it abstracts the actual component from the client. Thus the client does not know anything about the actual component; nor does the component actually have direct communication with the client. This benefits security and flexibility. For example, one EJB component may be shared transparently with many clients.

40.6 Remote Method Invocation

The primary aim of the Remote Method Invocation (RMI) API is to allow remote objects (i.e. objects running in separate address spaces, possibly on different machines) to communicate. The RMI assumes that the objects communicating are all written in Java. If the remote objects are implemented in other languages (such as C++ and Smalltalk), then the Java IDL allows communication via an object request broker.

Using RMI, a Java object on one machine can request information from, or services provided by, an object on a separate machine. The mechanism by which this occurs is hidden from the programmer, thus greatly simplifying the development task. For example, the way in which a message is sent to a remote object is exactly the same as if it was a local object. One minor difference is that variables, which are used to reference the remote object, are specified as holding an object which implements a given interface (as opposed to the actual class).

Programs that use RMI require more setup than ones which do not. For example, if two applications are to communicate then they should both be running before a remote object is referenced. The programmer must also define an appropriate set of interfaces even if they are only implemented by one class. Of course, the underlying communications mechanism must also be in place (TCP/IP must be available) You must also define server classes, which inherit from RemoteServer (or one of its subclasses).

In addition, the RMI mechanism must be invoked. The Java Remote Object Registry initiates a remote object registry that acts as a bootstrap naming service used by RMI servers to bind remote objects to names. Clients can then look up remote objects and make remote method invocations. The Java RMI stub compiler (rmic) takes compiled Java classes that contain remote object implementations and generates stub and skeleton classes for use with clients and servers.

40.7 Java and C++

Java is an object-oriented language that possesses a very similar syntax to C++ but without many of the more problematic feature of that language and with a number of good features from languages such as LISP and Smalltalk. The language tends to be compiled into an intermediate byte code form, which is then run on a virtual machine. This promotes portability of applications and is often described as allowing Java programs to be architecture-neutral. The language itself is rather compact, unlike languages such as Ada, which are very large.

However, the Java environment includes very many system-provided classes. Unlike many languages (including C++), Java has associated with it a large (and fairly standard) set of classes. These classes make Java very powerful and promote a standard development style. It also means that, while the Java language is relatively small, the Java environment is much larger.

However, there is a range of C++ facilities or syntax which Java does not provide. These are listed below:

- No pointers (or at least no pointer arithmetic)
- No structs or unions
- No functions
- No typedefs
- No multiple inheritance
- No gotos (although it does have a *continue from label* construct)
- No operator overloading
- No automatic coercion
- No pre-processor (#define)
- No memory allocation or deallocation

One of the aims of the Java developers was to produce a safe language (using C/C++ style syntax). This means that an attempt has been made to ensure that all violations of language semantics must be detected and reported. For example, Java has full run-time checking (such as checking array bounds and raising an out-of-bounds exception if necessary) as well as extensive compile-time checks (such as checking adherence to type rules). From this you can see that Java is far more than just a cut-down C++.

40.8 CORBA

The Common Object Request Broker Architecture (CORBA) is a standard produced by the Object Management Group (OMG) in collaboration with many organizations (which are members of the OMG). The OMG adopts and publishes interfaces; it publishes "standards", but never gets involved in the creation, selling or re-selling of software. This is accomplished via a competitive selection process based on proposals generated outside the OMG. Interface documents published by the OMG give the standard interface; implementations of those specifications are available from other companies, such as Hewlett-Packard and Sun, which develop software systems that they can then sell as matching one of these specifications.

CORBA specifies the architecture of CORBA-compliant Object Request Brokers (ORBs). An ORB is a mechanism that allows objects to communicate between processes, processors, hardware, operating systems, etc. Calls in an ORB are treated as client–server calls. That is, the calling object is halted until a reply is received. The structure of a request from one object on one machine to another object on another machine is illustrated in Figure 40.2.

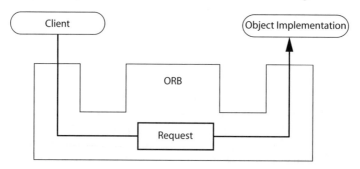

Fig. 40.2 CORBA: what actually happens.

However, although the process is as illustrated in Figure 40.2, to the programmer, the call appears as illustrated in Figure 40.3. That is, it appears to the programmer that the server object is held locally and that the message is sent from the client to a local object. This greatly simplifies the programming task.

Fig. 40.3 CORBA: how the system appears to the programmer.

The way in which this process works is that, when a client requests information from, or a service provided by, a remote object, the client stub and the ORB cooperate to pass the request to the implementation skeleton. The skeleton then passes the request to the actual object. Once the object has processed the request (returning the required data etc.), the skeleton takes any results produced and uses the ORB to pass those results back to the client stub. The stub then passes the results to the client object.

In order to facilitate this process, the ORB needs to do a number of things. In particular, it needs to keep track of where the objects are and handle any conversions or translations required when crossing platform boundaries (both machine and operating system boundaries). It may also need to handle the creation and deletion of objects as well as activating objects before passing requests to them. In particular, it must handle object references persistently.

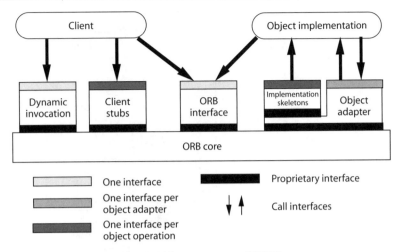

One interface

One interface per object adapter

One interface per object operation

Proprietary interface

Call interfaces

Fig. 40.4 The components of CORBA.

To facilitate the integration of different languages into the ORB framework, Interface Definition Languages (IDLs) are provided. A number of IDLs have now been provided for Java (for example, ORBIX provide a CORBA-compliant ORB and a Java IDL). An IDL defines the interfaces provided by an object. This information is used to produce client stubs and implementation skeletons (Figure 40.4).

40.9 Java Naming and Directory Interface

Naming and directory services provide access to mappings between keys and values. For example, a naming service may provide mappings between names and resources. Thus, www.jaydeetechnology.co.uk may map to 198.122.142.22. A naming service such as DNS maintains this mapping and allows other applications to obtain this mapping on request. A directory service, on the other hand, provides the ability to search for resources by attributes. For example, a directory service might be used to search for all two-sided colour printers currently on the network etc. Examples of these services include the Domain Name System (DNS), the Lightweight Directory Access Protocol (LDAP), NISS and NISS+, as well as the rmiregistry provided with Java's Remote Method Invocation system.

JNDI (the Java Naming and Directory Interface) provides a common interface to different naming and directory services. The aim of the JNDI is to provide a common API that allows Java programs to access these different services in the same way. Thus developers need only learn the JNDI API once and then they should have access to any naming or directory service. This is illustrated in Figure 40.5. Note that different services can be registered with the JNDI, but all are accessed by a common front end (API).

This works to some extent; however, you need to learn how to specify the initial context for each service in order to use JNDI (the initial context essentially tells JNDI how to find and connect to the service you require).

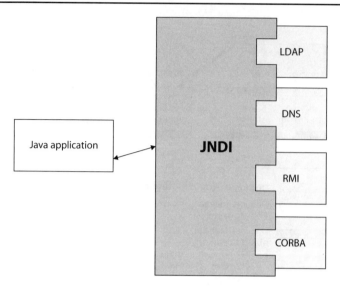

Fig. 40.5 The architecture of JNDI.

40.10 Java and XML

XML has been one of the most hyped technologies of the late 1990's and early years of this century. Java has not been slow to exploit this and, to be fair, was one of the first languages used to process XML. There are now several Java to XML libraries available, including Sun's own JAXP library. JAXP stands for Java API for XML Parsing (there is also an API for XML messaging).

The JAXP library provides a SAX and DOM parser as well as an XSL Translator. SAX stands for Simple API for XML parsing. This is a simple parser that notifies a handler class when different XML tags are encountered (and the information they contain). It is very fast and light-weight, and is very useful for extracting data from XML documents.

The DOM stands for the Document Object Model API. A DOM parser loads the XML document into memory and provides a tree-like structure (see Figure 40.6). This allows a Java program to process the tree: manipulating it, extracting information, adding and modifying information in the tree. In the case of the JAXP it also allows a new XML document to be saved to file via the DOM.

XSL stands for XML Style Language. XSL is a way of specifying how an XML file should be processed either for presentation (via formatting objects) or for translation into something else (such as HTML). This later version of XSL is often referred to as XSLT and is essentially rule based.

The JAXP XSLT transformer package (also known as Xalan) takes an XML document and an XSL file and creates a class that can convert the XML file into (for example) HTML. This allows an XML file to be viewed in a Web browser etc.

40.11 Java 2D and Java 3D

The Java 2D and 3D APIs provide sophisticated 2D and 3D facilities within Java. Java 2D and Java 3D are a set of libraries that offer many features for developing Java applications that require either 2D or 3D graphical processing, manipulation and generation.

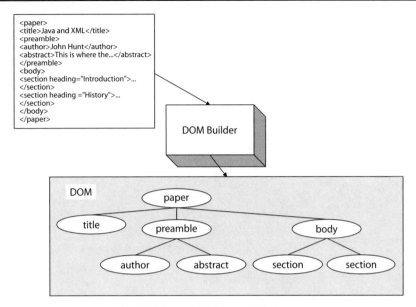

```
<paper>
<title>Java and XML</title>
<preamble>
<author>John Hunt</author>
<abstract>This is where the...</abstract>
</preamble>
<body>
<section heading="Introduction">...
</section>
<section heading ="History">...
</section>
</body>
</paper>
```

Fig. 40.6 Building a DOM from an XML document.

40.12 Object-Oriented Databases

An object-oriented database system relies on an object-oriented view of the world. That is, it uses classes and objects as the basic storage mechanism rather than forms and tables. In general, these databases are flexible about the types of data they hold, including text, programs, graphics, video and sound. However, object-oriented databases have been fairly thin on the ground until recently. The main players in this field have tended to concentrate on Smalltalk-based systems, either providing Smalltalk binding or implementing the system in Smalltalk and treating Smalltalk as the database scripting and query language. Recently however, a great deal of interest has been shown in using object-oriented databases with the Web. A number of object-oriented databases (such as O2) now provide Java interfaces.

Appendix

Appendix **A**

The Java API Packages

The Java 2 SDK provides many packages (for example, even JDK 1.1 had 26 packages) and others are being developed (such as the 2D, 3D and Media packages). You must prefix the names of the packages in Table A.1 with "java.".

Table A.1 The Java API packages.

Package name	Contents
applet	Applet related classes
awt	Platform-independent windowing classes
awt.datatransfer	Support for cut and paste style operations
awt.event	Delegation event model classes
awt.image	Image manipulation classes
awt.peer	Native windowing facilities classes
beans	Beans facilities for developers
io	Input and output classes
lang	Basic Java classes
lang.reflect	Java reflection classes
math	BigDecimal and BigInteger classes
net	Java networking facilities
rmi	Remote method invocation classes
rmi.dgc	Distributed garbage collection
rmi.registry	Facilities for mapping names to remote objects
rmi.server	Facilities for the server side of RMI
security	Java Security for signed applets
security.acl	Access control list
security.interfaces	Digital Signature Algorithm interface specifications
sql	JDBC SQL interface classes
text	Internationalization facilities
util	General utility classes
util.zip	Java Archive (JAR) support classes

For further information on these packages, see books such as Chan *et al.* (1997, 1998, 1999) and Gosling and Yellin (2000).

Java Keywords

B.1 Keywords

There are 45 keywords and three literals (`true`, `false` and `null`) in Java:

abstract	boolean	break	byte
case	catch	char	class
continue	default	do	double
else	extends	false	final
finally	float	for	if
implements	import	instanceof	int
interface	long	native	new
null	package	private	protected
public	return	short	static
super	switch	synchronized	this
throw	throws	transient	true
try	void	volatile	while

Notice that `goto` and `const` are also reserved, but they currently have no meaning.

B.2 Java Comments

There are three types of comment in Java:

`//`	Single line comments.
`/* */`	'C' style comments (rarely used in Java).
`/** */`	javadoc style comments (used to document classes, instance and class variables, and methods).

References

Alexander, C., Ishikawa, S. and Silverstein, M. (with Jacobson, M., Fiksdahl-King, I. and Angel, S.) (1977). *A Pattern Language: Towns, Buildings, Construction*. New York: Oxford University Press.

Alexander, C. (1979). *The Timeless Way of Building*. New York: Oxford University Press.

Arnold, K. and Gosling, J. (2000). *The Java Programming Language*. Reading, MA: Addison Wesley.

Beck, K. and Johnson, R. (1994) Patterns generate architectures. *Proceedings of ECOOP'94*, pp. 139–149.

Ben-Natan, R. (1995). *CORBA: A Guide to Common Object Request Broker Architecture*. New York: McGraw-Hill.

Binder, Robert V. (ed.) (1994). Special Issue of *Communications of the ACM: Object-Oriented Software Testing* 37(9). ACM Press.

Binder, Robert V. (1994). Design for testability in object-oriented systems. *Special Issue of Communications of the ACM: Object-Oriented Software Testing*, 37(9), 87–101.

Birrer, A. and Eggenschmiler, T. (1993). Frameworks in the financial engineering domain: an experience report. *Proceedings of ECOOP'93*, pp. 21–35.

Boehm, B. W. (1988) A spiral model of software development and enhancement. *IEEE Computer*, May, 61–72.

Booch, G. (1986). Object-oriented Development. *IEEE Transactions on Software Engineering*, February, **12**(2), 211–221.

Booch, G. (1987). *Software Components with Ada*. Menlo Park, CA: Benjamin Cummings.

Booch, G. (1991). *Object-Oriented Design with Applications*. Menlo Park, CA: Benjamin Cummings.

Booch, G. (1994). *Object-Oriented Analysis and Design with Applications*, 2nd edn. Redwood City, CA: Benjamin Cummings.

Booch, G. (1996). *Object Solutions: Managing the Object-Oriented Project*. Menlo Park, CA: Addison–Wesley.

Booch, G., Jacobson, I. and Rumbaugh, J. (1997). *The Unified Modeling Language User Guide*. Reading, MA: Addison–Wesley.

Brooks, F. (1987). No silver bullet: essence and accidents of software engineering, *IEEE Computer*, April.

Brown, A. L. (1989). *Persistent Object Stores*. Ph.D. Thesis, University of St Andrews, Scotland.

Budd, T. (1991). *An Introduction to Object-Oriented Programming*. Reading, MA: Addison–Wesley.

Budinsky, F. J. *et al.* (1996). Automatic code generation from design patterns. *IBM Systems Journal*, **35**(2).

Buschmann, F. *et al.* (1996). *Pattern-Oriented Software Architecture – A System of Patterns*. Chichester: Wiley.

Chan, P., Lee, R. and Kramer, D. (1997). *The Java Class Libraries*, Vol. 2. Reading, MA: Addison-Wesley.

Chan, P., Lee, R. and Kramer, D. (1998). *The Java Class Libraries*, Vol. 1. Reading, MA: Addison-Wesley.

Chan, P., Lee, R. and Kramer, D. (1999). *The Java Class Libraries*, 2nd edn, Vol. 1. Supplement for the Java 2 Platform, Standard Edition, v1.2. Reading, MA: Addison Wesley; ISBN: 0201485524

Coad, P. and Yourdon, E. (1991). *Object-Oriented Analysis*. Englewood Cliffs, NJ: Yourdon Press.

Coleman, D., Arnold P. *et al.* (1994). *Object-Oriented Development: The Fusion Method*. Englewood Cliffs, NJ: Prentice Hall.

Cook, S. and Daniels, J. (1994). *Designing Object-Oriented Systems: Object-Oriented modelling with Syntropy*. New York: Prentice Hall.

Coplien, J. O. and Schmidt, D. C. (eds.) (1995). *Pattern Languages of Program Design*. Reading, MA: Addison–Wesley.

Cornell, G. and Horstmann, C. S. (1997). *Core JAVA*, 2nd edn. Upper Saddle River, NJ: Prentice Hall.

Cox, B. J. (1990). There *is* a silver bullet. *BYTE*, October, pp. 209–218.

Cox, B. J. and Novobilski, A. (1991). *Object-Oriented Programming: An Evolutionary Approach*, 2nd edn. Reading, MA: Addison–Wesley.

Derr, K. W. (1995). *Applying OMT: A Practical Step-by-Step Guide to Using the Object Modeling Technique*. Upper Saddle River, NJ: Prentice Hall.

ECOOP'89, *Third European Conference on Object-Oriented Programming* (S. Cook ed.). The British Computer Society Workshop series. Cambridge: Cambridge University Press.

ECOOP'92, *European Conference on Object-Oriented Programming* (O. Lehrmann Madsen ed.). Lecture Notes in Computer Science series. Berlin: Springer-Verlag.

ECOOP'93, *European Conference on Object-Oriented Programming*. Lecture Notes in Computer Science 707. Berlin: Springer-Verlag.

ECOOP'94, *European Conference on Object-Oriented Programming*. Lecture Notes in Computer Science 821. Berlin: Springer-Verlag.

ECOOP'95, *Ninth European Conference on Object-Oriented Programming*. Lecture Notes in Computer Science 952. Berlin: Springer-Verlag.

Englander, R. (1997). *Developing JavaBeans*. Sebastopol, CA: O'Reilly.

Flanagan, D. (1996). *Java in a Nutshell*. Sebastopol, CA: O'Reilly.

Fowler, M. (1997). *Analysis Patterns: Reusable Object Models*. Reading, MA: Addison–Wesley.

Fowler, M. and Scott, K. (1997). *UML Distilled*. Reading, MA: Addison–Wesley.

Freedman, R. S. (1991). Testability of software components. *IEEE Trans. Softw. Eng.*, **17**(6), 553–564.

Gamma, E., Helm, R., Johnson, R. and Vlissides, J. (1993). Design patterns: abstraction and reuse of object-oriented design, *ECOOP'93* (Lecture Notes in Computer Science 707), pp. 406–431. Berlin: Springer-Verlag.

Gamma, E., Helm, R., Johnson, R. and Vlissides, J. (1995). *Design Patterns: Elements of Reusable Object-Oriented Software*. Reading, MA: Addison–Wesley.

Geary, D. M. and McClellan, A. L. (1997). *Graphic Java*. SunSoft Press.

Goldberg, A. (1984). *Smalltalk-80: The Interactive Programming Environment*. Reading, MA: Addison–Wesley.

Goldberg, A. and Robson, D. (1983). *Smalltalk-80: The Language and its Implementation*. Reading, MA: Addison–Wesley.

Goldberg, A. and Robson, D. (1989). *Smalltalk-80: The Language*. Reading, MA: Addison–Wesley.

Gosling, J. and Yellin, F. (1996). *The Java Application Programming Interface, Vol. 1: Core Packages*. Reading, MA: Addison–Wesley.

Gosling, J. and Yellin, F. (1996). *The Java Application Programming Interface, Vol. 2: Window Toolkit and Applets*. Reading, MA: Addison–Wesley.

Gosling, J., Joy, B. and Steele, G. (1996). *The Java Language Specification*. Reading, MA: Addison–Wesley.

Hamilton, G., Cattell, R. and Fisher, M. (1997). *JDBC Database Access With Java: A Tutorial and Annotated Reference*. Reading, MA: Addison-Wesley,.

Harel, D. (1988). On visual formalisms. *Communications of the ACM*, **31**(5), 514–530.

Harel, D., Pnueli, A., Schmidt, J. and Sherman, R. (1987). On the formal semantics of statecharts, *Proceedings of the 2nd IEEE Symposium on Logic in Computer Science*, Ithaca, NY, pp. 54–64.

Harmon, P. and Taylor, D. (1993). *Objects in Action: Commercial Applications of Object-Oriented Technologies*. Reading, MA: Addison–Wesley.

Hoffman, D. and Strooper, P. (1995). The testgraph methodology: automated testing of collection classes. *Journal of Object-Oriented Programming*, **8**(7), 35–41.

Hopkins, T. and Horan, B. (1995). *Smalltalk: An Introduction to Application Development Using VisualWorks*. Upper Saddle River, NJ: Prentice Hall.

Hunt, J. E. (1997). Constructing modular user interfaces in Java. *Java Report*, **2**(8), 25–32.

Hunt J. E. (2000). *The Unified Process for Practitioners*. London: Springer-Verlag.

ISO (1993). *Information Technology, Software Packages, Quality Requirements and Testing*. ISO Draft International Standard, ISO/IEC DIS 12119.

Jacobson, I. (1992). *Object-Oriented Software Engineering: A Use Case Driven Approach*. Reading, MA: Addison–Wesley.

Jacobson, I., Booch, G. and Rumbaugh, J. (1998). *The Unified Software Development Process*. Reading, MA: Addison-Wesley.

Jepson, B. (1997). *Java Database Programming*. Chichester: John Wiley.

Jepson, B. (1998). *Official Guide to Mini SQL 2.0* Chichester: John Wiley.

Johnson, R. E. (1992). Documenting Frameworks with Patterns. *Proceedings of OOPSLA'92, SIGPLAN Notices*, **27**(10), 63–76.

Kemerer, C. F. (1987). An Empirical validation of software cost estimation models. *Communications of the ACM*, **30**(5), 416–429.

Kernighan, B. W. and Ritchie, D. M. (1988). *The C Programming Language*, 2nd edn. Englewood Cliffs, NJ: Prentice Hall.

Krasner, G. E. and Pope, S. T. (1988). A cookbook for using the Model-View Controller user interface paradigm in Smalltalk-80. *Journal of Object-Oriented Programming*, **1**(3), 26–49.

Kuhn, T. (1962). *The Structure of Scientific Revolutions*. Chicago, IL: University of Chicago Press.

Lalonde, W. and Pugh, J. (1991). Subclassing /= subtyping /= Is-a. *Journal of Object-Oriented Programming*, January, 57–62.

Lindholm, T. and Yellin, F. (1996). *The Java Virtual Machine Specification*. Reading, MA: Addison–Wesley.

Love, T. (1993). *Object Lessons: Lessons Learned in Object-Oriented Development Projects*. New York: SIGS Books.

Meyer, B. and Nerson, J. (1993). *Object-Oriented Applications*. Englewood Cliffs, NJ: Prentice Hall.

Meyer, B. (1988). *Object-Oriented Software Construction*. Englewood Cliffs, NJ: Prentice Hall International.

Microsoft (1997). *Microsoft ODBC 3.0 Software Development Kit and Programmers Reference*. Redmond, WA: Microsoft Press.

Moser, S. and Nierstrasz, O. (1996). The effect of object-oriented frameworks on developer productivity. *IEEE Computer*, September, 45–51.

Moss, K. (1998). *Java Servlets*. New York: McGraw-Hill.

Myers, G. J. (1979). *The Art of Software Testing*. Chichester: John Wiley.

OOPSLA/ECOOP'90, *Joint Conference on Object-Oriented Programming: Systems, Languages and Applications* (N. Meyrowitz ed.). Reading, MA: Addison–Wesley.

OOPSLA'91, *Conference on Object-Oriented Programming Systems, Languages and Applications*; also as *ACM SIGPLAN Notices*, **26**(11) (A. Paepcke ed.). Reading, MA: Addison–Wesley.

OOPSLA'92, *Seventh Annual Conference on Object-Oriented Programming Systems, Languages and Applications*; also as *ACM SIGPLAN Notices*, **27**(10) (A. Paepcke ed.). Reading, MA: Addison–Wesley.

OOPSLA'93, *Conference on Object-Oriented Programming Systems, Languages and Applications*. Reading, MA: Addison–Wesley.

Orfali, R., Harkey, D. and Edwards, J. (1995). *The Essential Distributed Objects Survival Guide.* Chichester: John Wiley.

Ousterhout, J. K. (1994). *TCL and the TK Toolkit.* Reading, MA: Addison–Wesley.

Palmer, I. (2001) *Essential Java3D Fast.* London: Springer-Verlag.

Parker, T. (1994). *Teach yourself TCP/IP in 14 Days.* Indianapolis, IN: Sams Publishing.

Perry, D. E. and Kaiser, G. E. (1990). Adequate testing and object-oriented programming. *Journal of Object-Oriented Programming*, **2**(5), 13–19.

Rational (2001). *UML Resource Center.* Rational Software Corporation (http://www.rational.com/uml/).

Reese, G. (1997). *Database Programming with JDBC and Java.* Sebastopol, CA: O'Reilly.

Rumbaugh, J., Blaha, M., Premerlani, W., Eddy, F. and Lorensen, W. (1991). *Object-Oriented Modeling and Design.* Englewood Cliffs, NJ: Prentice Hall.

Scharf, D. (1995). *HTML Visual Quick Reference.* Indianapolis, IN: Que.

Sevareid, J. (1997). The JDK 1.1's new delegation event model. *Java Report*, **2**(4), 59–79.

Smith, D. N. (1994). *IBM Smalltalk: The Language.* New York: Benjamin Cummings.

Sparks, S., Benner, K. and Faris, C. (1996). Managing object-oriented framework reuse. *IEEE Computer*, September, 52–61.

Stephens, R. K. (1997). *Teach Yourself SQL in 21 Days*, 2nd edn. Indianapolis, IN: Sams.

Taylor, D. A. (1992). *Object-Oriented Information Systems: Planning and Implementation.* New York: John Wiley.

van der Linden, P. (2001). *Just Java 2.* SunSoft Press.

Vlissides, J. M., Coplien, J. O. and Kerth, N. L. (1996). *Pattern Languages of Program Design 2.* Reading, MA: Addison–Wesley.

Winston, P. H. and Narasimhan, S. (2001). *On to Java*, 3rd edn. Reading, MA: Addison–Wesley.

Wirfs-Brock, R., Wilkerson, B. and Wiener, L. (1990). *Designing Object-Oriented Software.* Englewood Cliffs, NJ: Prentice Hall.

Yourdon, E. (1994). *Object-Oriented Systems Design.* Upper Saddle River, NJ: Prentice Hall.

Index